MARVELOUS Transforming Toys

With Complete Instructions and Plans

MARVELOUS Transforming Toys

With Complete Instructions and Plans

Jim Makowicki

Edited by John Lehmann-Haupt

Publisher: Jim Childs

Associate Publisher: Helen Albert

Associate Editor: Strother Purdy

Editor: John Lehmann-Haupt

Copy Editor: Daphne Hougham

Cover and Interior Designer: Mary Skudlarek

Layout Artist: Mary Skudlarek

Photographer: Judi Rutz

Illustrator: Jim Makowicki and Mario Ferro

Illustration Text: Gerhard Richter

for fellow enthusiasts

Printed in the United States of America
10 9 8 7 6 5 4 3 2 1

The Taunton Press, Inc., 63 South Main Street,
P.O. Box 5506, Newtown, CT 06470-5506
e-mail: tp@taunton.com

Distributed by Publishers Group West

Library of Congress Cataloging-in-Publication Data
Makowicki, Jim.
Marvelous transforming toys : with complete instructions and plans / Jim Makowicki; edited by John Lehmann-Haupt.
p. cm.
ISBN 1-56158-381-2
1. Wooden toy making. 2. Vehicles. I. Title: Transforming toys. II. Lehmann-Haupt, John. III. Title.
TT174.5.W6 M33 2000
745.592—dc21 00-044116

Safety Note
Working with wood is inherently dangerous. Using hand or power tools improperly or ignoring safety practices can lead to permanent injury or even death. Don't try to perform operations you learn about here (or elsewhere) unless you're certain they are safe for you. If something about an operation doesn't feel right, don't do it. Look for another way. We want you to enjoy the craft, so please keep safety foremost in your mind whenever you're in the shop.

To my kids, Stephen, Sandee, and Wayne, for being so special.

ACKNOWLEDGMENTS

I am indebted to my editor, John Lehmann-Haupt, for accepting the challenge of working on this book. His work helped to clarify and communicate the construction of these often complex toys. I thank him for his professional and personal contribution.

I also am grateful to Helen Albert for making my second book a reality, and to Strother Purdy for his contribution in coordinating such a fine team to develop this book and in its final editing.

For the outstanding layout and production work, I thank art director Paula Schlosser and the whole art department. I thank photographer Judi Rutz for putting up with me for several days (a true test) in my shop to get the photos of the toys and building processes. Finally, special thanks to Sara Elizabeth Hetzer, Duncan and Kevin Engel, Emily Weber, India Alexandra Butler, and Jimmy Spencer—all wonderful kids who played with the toys for the camera.

CONTENTS

INTRODUCTION

I've been a lifelong woodworker, and as a father of three (and now a grandfather of three, too), I've been making wooden toys for more than a few years. As my skills and designs evolved, what had begun as a family-oriented hobby began to attract outside attention, and three of my toys were eventually chosen by a manufacturer for a limited production run. One of the three, an earlier version of the Houses system detailed in this book, won a Parents' Choice Award, given by *Parents' Choice*, a magazine dedicated to the promotion of toys with high educational value.

Around the same time, some friends at a Connecticut library who had seen my work suggested that I start teaching toy making to children. The classes were a great success with the kids and ultimately caught the notice of the folks at nearby Taunton Press. The result was *Making Heirloom Toys* (published in 1996), which featured 22 of my individual toys—various trains, trucks, animal pull toys, and others, most with a traditional accent.

Making Heirloom Toys was a great success, and I've received many appreciative letters that I'll keep always. I've certainly felt encouraged to do a second book. At the same time, this book is a real departure for me, focusing as it does on the system-based toys that have fascinated me in recent years. Although system toys like Tinker Toys, Lincoln Logs, and Lego have been around for years, mine are different in that each system part is an identifiable component of the finished item. A child recognizes what he's assembling right away, without having to go through a long process. And he can easily change the image by just moving a couple of pieces.

Each of the six systems—Boats, Trucks, Houses, Planes, Vehicles, and Ships—focuses on a specific theme, with components that are assembled in a variety of ways. Friction-fittings, nut-and-bolt assemblies, stacking dowels, locking rods, and lugged nesting parts are all used, sometimes in combination with each other.

It's also been my goal in writing this book to engage the creativity of both the child who plays with the toys and the craftsman who makes them. I've watched a lot of children (and adults, too!) encounter these toys for the first time, and the process is always the same: Initial curiosity leads quickly to complete absorption in the multiple possibilities of each system. For the younger children, there's also the benefit of developing hand-eye coordination through assembling the parts. But it's also my hope that craftsmen will share my experience—that in the course of building the various systems, new variations will begin to suggest themselves with growing speed and clarity.

My toys are made with select hardwoods and finished with top-grade materials that enhance the wood's natural beauty while providing a protective surface not usually found on commercial toys. There's nothing precious about them—they're built to be played with for years.

These toys are small, but that doesn't mean they're simple. The projects in this book, which are presented roughly in order of complexity, can take as long to build as a major piece of furniture. Patience and precision are essential. Cutting and drilling small parts can also pose serious safety hazards, and I've detailed several jigs, fixtures, and techniques throughout that will both facilitate awkward maneuvers and minimize the risk of injury.

Building Safe Toys

The craftsman's safety is only half of the story; the safety of the child playing with the toy is equally important and should be a prime consideration in toy design and construction. I avoid the use of potentially hazardous hardware such as hooks, and I round over all edges and corners. And since younger children are in the habit of putting playthings in their mouths, it's essential that you use the nontoxic finishes I recommend. They'll also be easier on your lungs—and on the environment, too.

It's a good idea to inspect the toys periodically; parts like the lugs glued to the cabin of the Ships system may loosen in time. Safety regulations and guidelines can help us in the design and construction of toys for young children, but ultimately nothing can replace parental watchfulness and common sense.

chapter 1
TECHNIQUES AND MATERIALS

Woodworking on a toy-size scale poses a particular challenge. You'll often cut and shape parts that are well under 6 in. long to close tolerances, and to ensure both accuracy and your own safety, you'll need some special approaches. I've developed several jigs, fixtures, and techniques that I strongly recommend.

I also value my eyesight and my time too much to look at those little 1⁄32-in. marks on my rule any more than I absolutely have to, so I've developed procedures that allow me to execute repeat operations reliably without having to measure each time. Additionally, I've acquired some tools and come up with some processes that eliminate tearout and promote safety at the same time.

GENERAL GUIDELINES

Each project includes all the pattern drawings you'll need and a complete parts list. The sequence of procedures is important, so I'll be emphasizing that throughout. I'll also be telling you about some specialty tools that are invaluable in toy making.

Layouts and patterns

Accurate work requires accurate layouts, but the layout is only as good as the surface it is on. Before beginning a project, I always check to make sure that the stock I'm using is straight, square, and flat.

I also suggest investing in a set of basic drafting instruments (see photo A) to draw precise layouts for reference purposes on your workpieces. You should have a compass, a protractor, a divider, calipers, a machinist's try square, a radius gauge set, and a good ruler, preferably 18 in. or longer. I've found the Starrett 18-in. ruler no. 604R to be a good one.

I've provided many pattern drawings for the project parts. Where the book's dimensions prohibit full-sized drawings, they are at scale, with percentage indications to facilitate their enlargement to size on a copier.

Transferring patterns

There are a number of ways to transfer patterns to the surface of your stock. Some craftsmen use carbon paper, but it's too messy for my taste.

A neater, easier way is to photocopy the pattern from the book, lay the copy facedown on the stock, and run a hot iron over the backside, transferring the heat-set toner neatly to the stock's surface. This leaves you with a sharp, clean image. The only problem with this method is that since it produces a mirror image of the original, it won't work for parts that aren't symmetrical.

For nonsymmetrical patterns, I trace the image onto tracing paper with a soft black pencil. I then turn the paper over and redraw the pattern on the backside, following the lines showing through the paper. I place the paper, facedown, onto the stock, and go over the lines on the front once again; the pencil pressure transfers the lines on the back to the surface just as carbon paper does, but minus the mess.

Working from the center out

Once I have the pattern laid out, I work from the center of the stock out whenever possible: That is, I make any internal cuts and drill any internal holes before bringing the piece to its final overall shape. This leaves me with reliably square edge surfaces to measure from and to place against fences, stops, and tables.

Since I usually start with stock a little thicker than the finished thickness, the final shaping of the perimeter will clean up tearout or splintering that may have occurred during the internal operations.

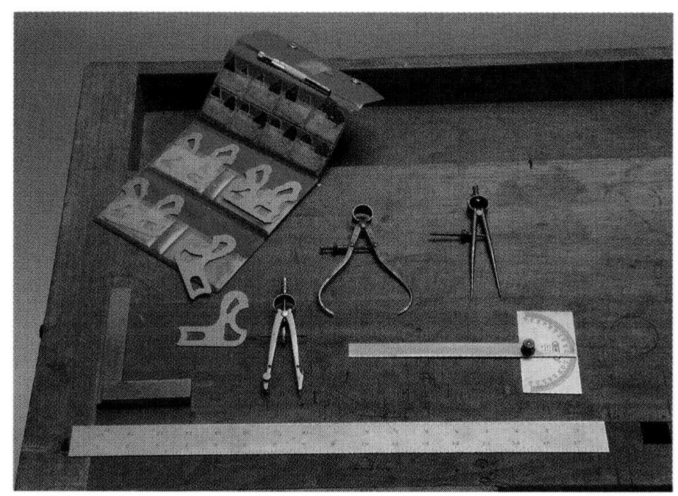

Photo A • *For accurate layouts, precision drafting instruments are essential.*

It's also a good idea to make final crosscuts first, so the final ripcuts will eliminate any corner tearout.

Using the parts list

Each parts list consists of a description of every part, the quantity needed, dimensions, and suggested material. All dimensions are in inches and indicate the overall finished size, with the third dimension as the preferred grain direction (length), except as noted (an example is "Main deck cabin, 1½ x 13⁄16 x 4, 1, Maple"). As explained above, in some cases you'll need to cut the blank oversize and then trim to final size after completing internal cutting and drilling operations.

Using commercial parts

Some parts, such as wheels, the threaded rods and nuts in the Trucks and Planes systems, and human figures, are easier to buy ready-made than to handcraft (see Resources on p. 217). Just make sure to buy these parts before beginning a project, because their exact fit may require some adjustment of other dimensions.

Tools

To build the toys in this book, you'll need the usual complement of hand tools and machines—table saw, bandsaw, drill press, high-speed router, lathe, and scrollsaw. There are also a few specialty tools that I've found to be invaluable aids to accurate work (see photo B on p. 8). These include a center finder, a set of metal-cutting countersinks, a full set of drill bits, and a thin-bladed metal letter opener. Their specific applications will be described in the project chapters.

The center finder I use is called a Wiggler, is made by General Hardware (item # S-389-4), and is available from most industrial-supply stores. It consists of a needle pointer connected to an arbor with a ball-and-socket joint. To use the Wiggler, chuck it into your drill press and turn on the machine. Press gently against the side of the needle until it appears not to be turning; this aligns it with the chuck's exact center. Then turn off the drill press, align the workpiece to be drilled with the needle point (see photo C on p. 8), clamp it in place, and replace the Wiggler with the desired drill bit.

Metal-cutting countersinks don't leave chatter marks around the hole, so I prefer them over countersinks sold for wood. Radius gauges are ideal for drawing rounded corners on small parts, and a pro-

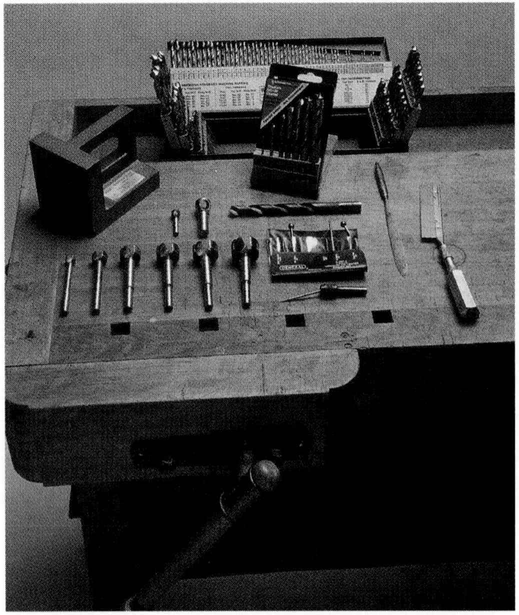

Photo B • *Tools that come in handy in making these toys include a complete set of metal drill bits from 1/16 in. to 1/2 in., with number bits from 1 to 60 and letter bits from A to Z; a set of brad-point bits from 1/8 in. to 3/8 in.; selected Forstner bits; a 33/64-in. high-speed steel drill bit; a set of metal-cutting countersinks; a center finder; a right-angle steel block; an X-Acto razor saw; and a letter opener.*

Photo C • *A center finder is useful to position the workpiece accurately under the drill-press chuck. This one is called the Wiggler.*

tractor head is very handy for laying out precise angles on workpieces.

I've also found it useful to have a full set of drill bits (American made are best), to drill accurate holes for dowels, which tend not to be true to size. I'd recommend a set that includes all the letter sizes, number sizes, and fractional sizes from 1/16 in. to 1/2 in. in 1/64-in. increments.

I have recently heard of a number of mail-order outfits that provide accurate-sized dowels, which are particularly desirable for the Trucks system. Buying them is preferable to making them, but consistency in sizing is important. You'll find more information in Resources on p. 217.

I keep a pair of two-flute center-cut end mills (normally used to cut aluminum) for routing out cavities with flat bottoms, as found in the Ships system and in the base of the Houses system. (If you haven't used center-cut end mills before, I suggest getting in some practice first, since they have a feel of their own and the workpiece must be securely clamped.)

A letter opener with a metal blade is ideal for scratch-free separation of a workpiece and an auxiliary block that have been joined by double-sided tape.

Choice of woods

My concerns in choosing woods for my toys are both structural and aesthetic. My first choice is usually poplar, a dependable hardwood at a reasonable price. I also use a lot of birch, and I've found Baltic birch plywood to be ideal for wings, thin walls, and other long, flat surfaces. For contrast and for accents, I like maple, cherry, and walnut.

When making toy parts, I always cut extra pieces, so I can experiment with different designs. And I always have scrap stock on hand to check my machine setups; I never commit good wood to a process until I know the setup is right.

• DESIGNING TOYS

A wooden toy is not a replica, and keeping this in mind is the key to designing toys that are both compelling and functional. It's easy to get sidetracked by details that involve components too fussy and delicate to be suitable for small children to handle.

The challenge, then, is to come up with something that's sturdy and invitingly manageable, but that also evokes its model—be it a boat, a plane, or anything else—effectively enough to engage a child's sense of fantasy. So one of the first things I do is determine how much detail I can incorporate without sacrificing the toy's "playability," a process that usually follows the perusal of a lot of books, magazines, and old catalogs.

In developing my designs, I give a lot of thought not only to the blocks of wood that make up a toy but also to the space that surrounds and, in many cases, penetrates it. This "negative" space adds character and visual interest to any toy. My favorite example of this is the windows in the sides of the Ferryboat (see photo D), which contribute greatly to this toy's charm.

Combining these design principles and my research, I create some preliminary drawings, modifying them until I come up with what I think is just the right balance of detail and utility. Then the fun begins. Although I've gotten better at not designing parts that are too fragile or nearly impossible to make, it's only when I get into the shop that I really find out where the shortcomings are. Many of my toys have been designed and built a half-dozen times before I'm satisfied. At this point I'll develop my final drawings. But it doesn't end there; each time I make a particular toy, I'm likely to try yet another variation.

The process is, if anything, more involved when I'm designing the system toys that are this book's theme. My first efforts in this direction were a response to a request from a Maine-based wooden-product manufacturer to come up with some new toys that could be put together in different conformations. The result was the first three systems in this book.

But something new happened when I began designing these toys. As I turned my attention to them, I felt that the ideas actually fed me and that new variations seemed to emerge with no effort on my part.

I do hope that my designs spark this inspiration in others. Toy design consists of a series of choices guided by the craftsman's interests, his sensibilities, and his level of skill. Much of this can't be taught, but it can certainly be motivated. This book is, as much as anything, an invitation to the craftsman to create his own extension of the existing projects, not just to accept them as presented.

A toy's safety must be a basic aspect of its design. I always consider the age of the child who will be playing with the toy, although the same toy can be made appropriate for children of different ages. For example, the Houses system as presented here involves a lot of loose dowels for stacking the components onto the base; these can be a choking hazard for a small child. But the system can also be built without the base, and the necessary dowels glued into the components, as they are in the Ships system. Safety also dictates that you use only nontoxic finishes (see Resources on p. 217).

Toy designing is a dynamic process that usually achieves success through evolution. The more you experiment, the more you'll learn. But remember always that you're making a toy—something to be handled and played with, a touchstone for a child's imagination.

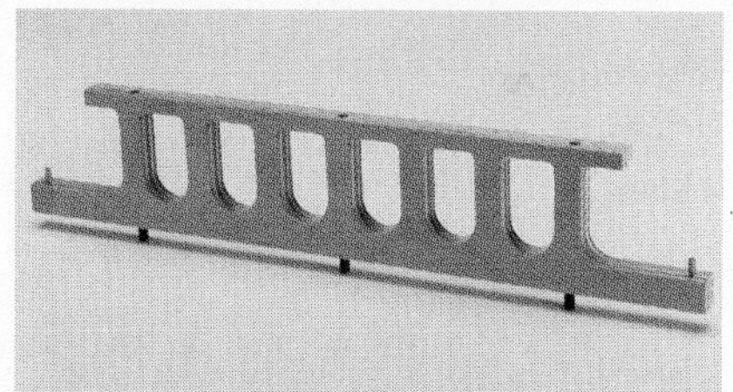

Photo D • *The "negative" space of the Ferryboat's cutout windows do much to define its overall appearance. Windows drawn on the wood would not be as nice.*

■ SAFE WORK HABITS

Toy making involves shaping and cutting a lot of small parts, which can be dangerous if you hold them by hand. For safety always use a jig, a fixture, or a clamp to hold the workpiece, keeping your fingers away from sawblades and other high-speed cutters.

Of course, all the usual woodworking precautions also apply to toy making: Wear safety glasses, ear protection, and a dust mask or respirator when appropriate, and never wear loose clothing or long sleeves when working with power tools. *And consider your own skills. If you feel uncomfortable performing any of the operations in this book, use an alternate method.*

WORKING SMARTER

How much double-sided tape is enough? There's more to this than you might think. A thin workpiece that's been fastened too effectively to an auxiliary block may split when you detach it. And if the tape runs right up to the part's edge, you may have trouble working in the letter opener to pry it loose. Different tapes have different levels of adhesion. Experimentation on scrap pieces is the key.

Push sticks

I always use a push stick when ripping small parts on the table saw. For particularly narrow ripcuts, I use a 10-in.-long flat metal bar, 1⁄16 in. thick by 7⁄8 in. wide, that's been cut to a point to push stock through the saw, as shown in photo E. This bar is so thin it can ride between the fence and the blade on all but the thinnest of cuts without danger of hitting the blade. And the flexibility of the thin bar helps hold the workpiece against the fence. The pointed tip gives a good grip, but on finished pieces I tape a small piece of scrap pine to the workpiece to keep from marring the surface (see photo F).

Double-sided tape

One "tool" that I've come to rely on heavily is double-sided carpet tape. I use it so often for so many different operations that I don't know how I ever got along without it. A small toy part can be fastened to a larger piece of stock with double-sided tape and safely sawed, drilled, or routed without your fingers ever getting close to the cutters. Double-sided tape is also handy for holding parts in jigs or for keeping them in place while trial-fitting an assembly. As I mentioned earlier, the ideal tool for separating a workpiece and an auxiliary block that have been taped together is a letter opener.

USING SPACER BLOCKS

Many of the components in this book call for incrementally stepped operations, such as drilling rows of equally spaced holes or making a series of repeat cuts (see, for example, the many portholes in the Boats and Ships systems). One technique that I've found to be both handy and accurate is to use a stop block and a set of spacer blocks, as shown in photo G. The spacer-block technique requires a relatively simple setup and can be used with a variety of tools. To illustrate the procedure, I'll first

Photo E • *Always use a push stick when ripping small parts on the table saw. For added safety, fasten the workpiece to an auxiliary block with double-sided tape and set the fence farther from the blade.*

Photo F • *An auxiliary block fastened to the top of a workpiece protects the surface from being marred by the tip of the push stick. Use a softwood block to give the stick something to bite into.*

describe the steps necessary to drill a set of evenly spaced holes on the drill press, and then I'll explain how to make repeat cuts on the table saw.

Drill-press setup

To use the spacer-block technique on the drill press, you'll need an auxiliary fence and a stop block. You can simply use a board clamped to the drill-press table for the fence and a small block clamped to the fence for the stop block. But a fence and stop block are so handy on a drill press that I've added them and an auxiliary table to mine permanently, as shown in the drawing on p. 12.

To make the spacer blocks, rip a strip of wood to the desired width (the on-center distance between the holes) on the table saw, and then cut the strip into the number of pieces required. You'll need one fewer spacer blocks than the number of holes to be drilled.

Start by using a center finder to position the first hole on the right end of the stock under the chuck. With the stock clamped in place against the fence, butt the stop block against the left end of the stock.

Clamp the stop block to the fence (my auxiliary fence has an adjustable stop block with a built-in locking mechanism). Remove the center finder, replace it with the appropriate drill bit, and drill the first hole.

Now slide the stock to the right and insert the appropriate-sized spacer block between the stop block and the stock. Drill the second hole. Repeat this procedure to complete the series of holes.

You can also work the spacer block technique in the opposite direction, removing blocks instead of adding them. Start with all the spacer blocks in place, drill the first hole, remove a spacer, drill the second hole, and so on. The approach is different, but the result's the same.

If the series of holes needs to be centered on the stock, lay out the holes and make the setup as above with the center finder, but before changing to the drill bit, measure from the needle point to the right end of the stock.

Then slide the stock to the right, insert all the spacers you'll be using to drill the series of holes between the stop block and the stock, and then measure the distance from the needle point to the left end of the stock. It should be the same as the distance at the right end. If not, make the required adjustment on the stop block and recheck.

Photo G • *Using the spacer-block technique ensures evenly spaced holes.*

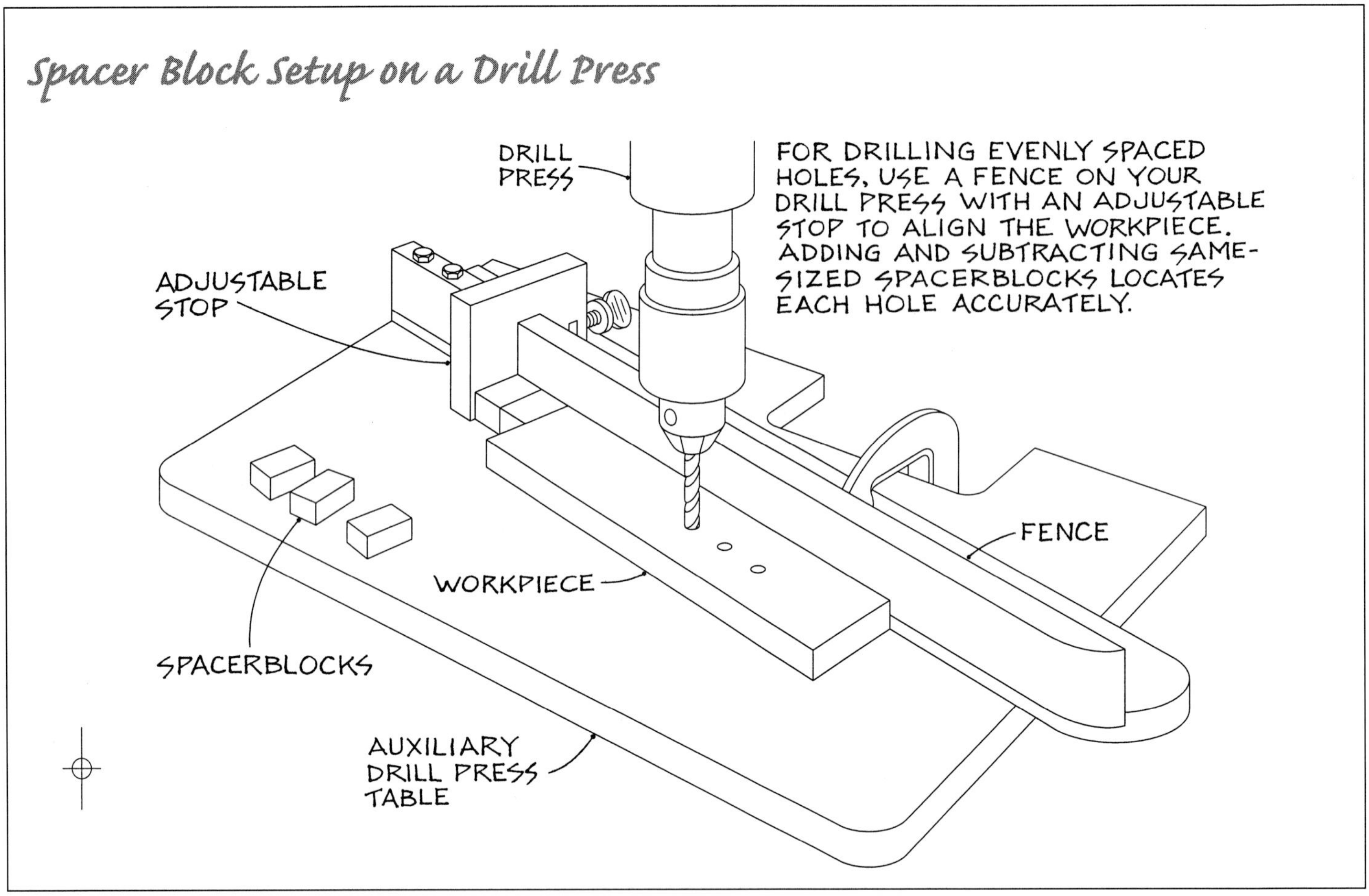

Spacer Block Setup on a Drill Press

DRILL PRESS

FOR DRILLING EVENLY SPACED HOLES, USE A FENCE ON YOUR DRILL PRESS WITH AN ADJUSTABLE STOP TO ALIGN THE WORKPIECE. ADDING AND SUBTRACTING SAME-SIZED SPACERBLOCKS LOCATES EACH HOLE ACCURATELY.

ADJUSTABLE STOP

FENCE

WORKPIECE

SPACERBLOCKS

AUXILIARY DRILL PRESS TABLE

Table-saw setup

The spacer-block technique can be used on the table saw with either the miter gauge, for crosscuts, or the rip fence, for ripcuts. The ripcut technique is used only in the Vehicles system, so it's covered in that chapter.

For crosscuts, attach an auxiliary fence to the miter gauge (see photo H and the drawing on p. 13), and then clamp a stop block to the auxiliary fence. Place stock that is longer than the distance from the stop block to the blade path against the stop block, and make a preliminary cut to square off the workpiece flush with the sawblade. Then insert spacer blocks one at a time between the stop block and the workpiece for subsequent cuts. The number of blocks will be equal to the number of cuts required.

Photo H • *To make repeat crosscuts on the table saw, place the stock against the stop block and make an initial cut to square it off flush with the sawblade. Add a spacer block for each subsequent cut.*

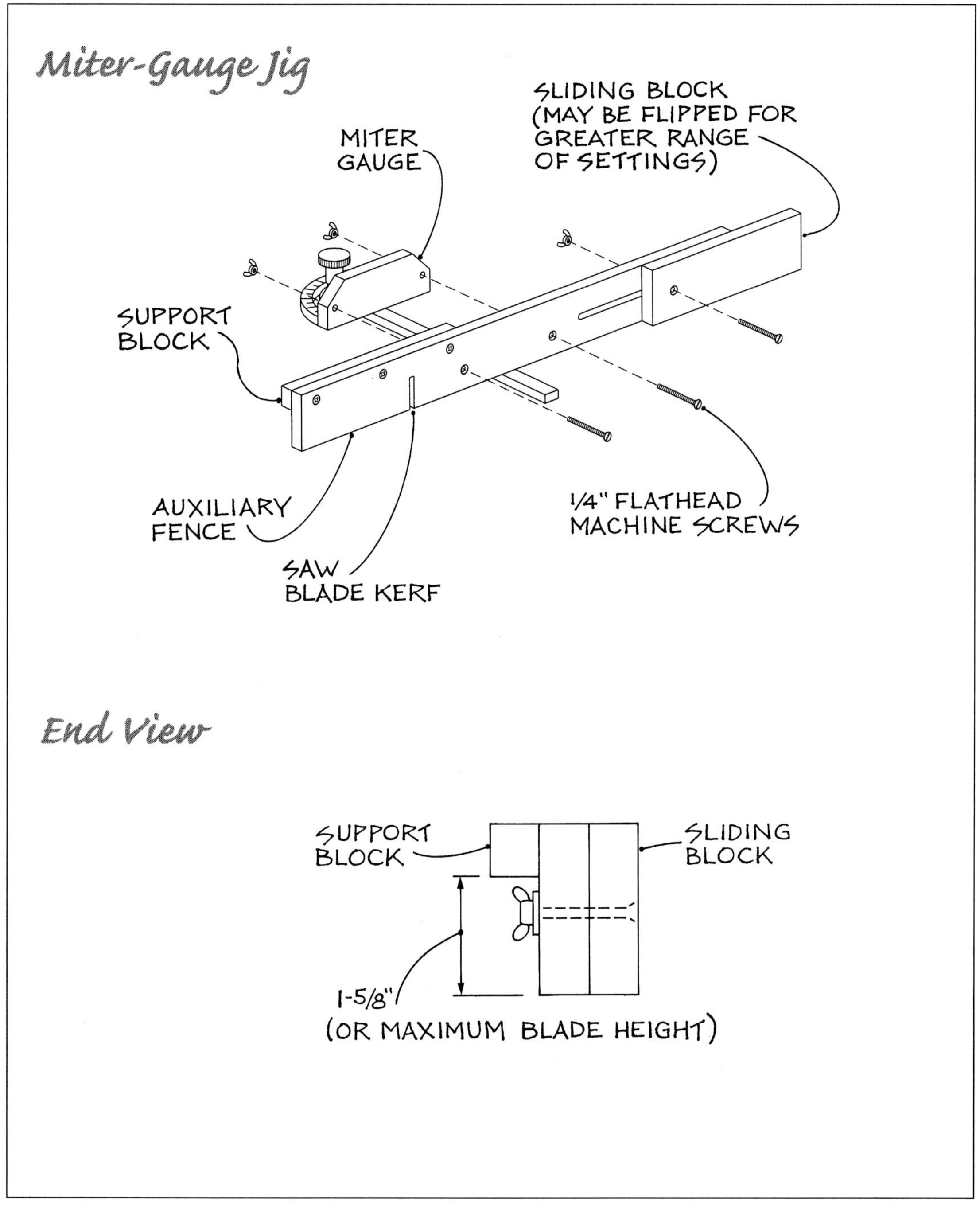

ANGLE-CUTTING STRATEGIES

One feature that helps distinguish my toys from the usual chunky blocks scroll-sawed from low-grade lumber is the variety of angles that each system incorporates. Unless these angles are accurately cut, however, you're not going to get the quality you're after. To obtain most of these angles and tapers, I use a simple jig (see photo I on p. 14).

The jig consists of a baseplate of squared-off scrap plywood (the thickness isn't critical), with two strips of straight

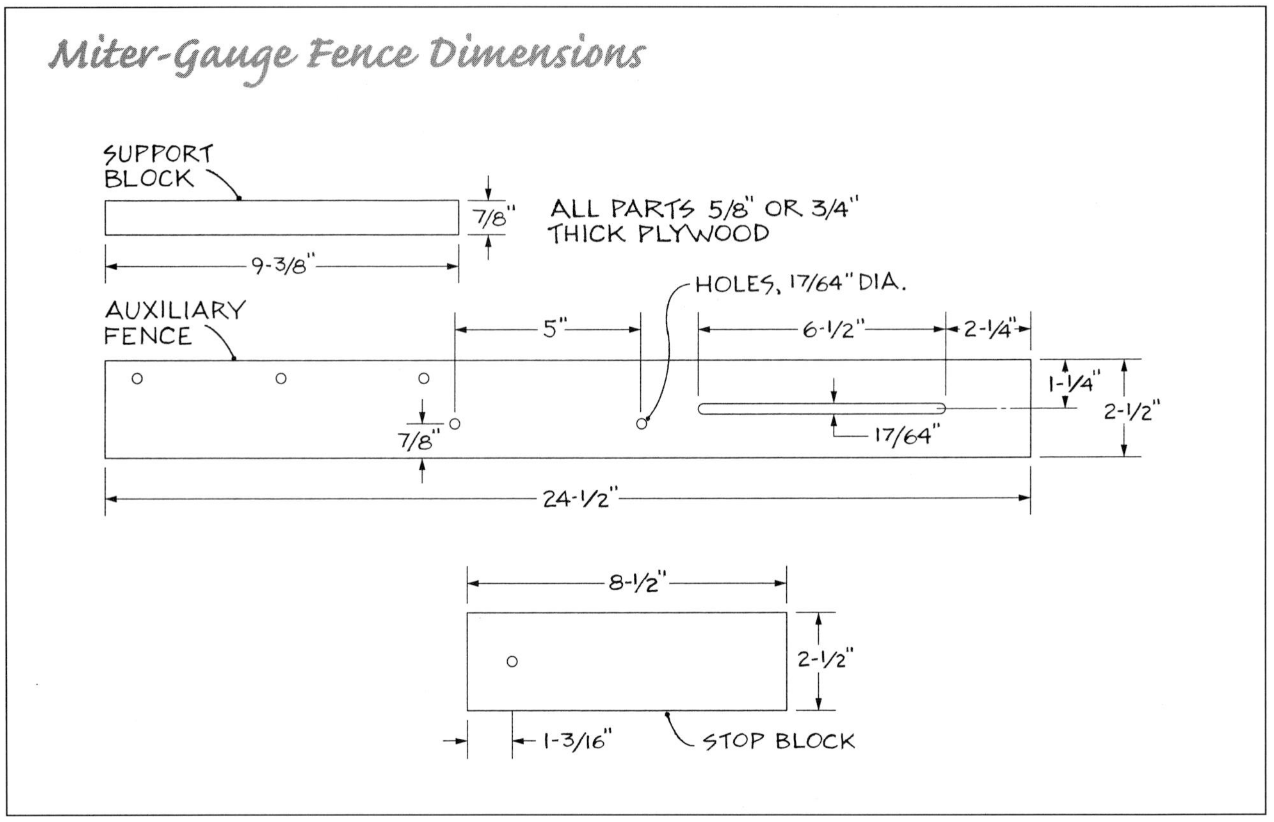

scrap about ½ in. thick glued onto it square to each other, forming a reverse letter L from the user's point of view. The longer strip is positioned at the desired angle relative to the baseplate's sides. The right side of the baseplate rides along the fence, and the strips hold the blank.

Note that the sawblade may actually pass through the baseplate, depending on its width, which is not critical. Double-sided tape affixed to the underside of the blank will help keep it securely in place; be sure no tape lies in the blade path.

Photo I • *This simple jig made of plywood and scrap strips makes accurate angle-cutting easy. The jig's baseplate also provides a surface for double-sided tape to hold the workpiece securely.*

DRILLING TECHNIQUES

A drilling operation of one sort or another is common to every one of the projects in this book from drilling simple axle holes to making a complex series of holes for a major design element. Although drilling a hole may seem like a simple enough task, poor drilling technique can lead to splintered holes, torn wood fibers, or poorly fitting parts. The jigs, fixtures, and tips featured in this section will make drilling operations easy.

• JIGS, PLAIN AND FANCY

It's easy to forget that jigs are a means to an end, not an end in themselves. Although you'll see photos in this book of jigs I've spent some time developing, building, and finishing, there are also plenty that I cut from scrap, use for an operation, and then throw away.

Not every jig has to be a shining jewel; in fact, it's best to build a rough version first that you can try out and modify until it's just right. Only build a fancy version (which should be finished with sanding sealer to help control wood movement) if it's one you'll be using often. You'll be saving valuable time, and you'll be more likely to take a few minutes to make the jig that just might save some fingers on a dangerous procedure.

And don't forget, just fastening a smaller piece to a larger board with double-sided tape is a quick and easy way to keep your fingers away from the blade.

Start by mounting a dowel that's been cut to the correct length into the lathe's headstock, which should be fitted with a three-jaw universal chuck. A piece of flexible plastic wrapped around the workpiece will protect it from being marred. To ensure proper alignment, be sure the plastic doesn't overlap itself. The plastic they sell in craft stores for stencils is ideal for this, but you can also cut yourself a strip from the lid of a large yogurt or deli container.

The tailstock should be fitted with a ½-in. Jacobs chuck, to receive a bit of the desired diameter. Bring the tip of the bit up just short of the workpiece, and select the appropriate speed—lower for larger bits, higher for smaller. Advance the bit into the stock with the crank at the tailstock end. The precise depth of the hole is usually not critical.

Eliminating tearout on closely spaced holes

The biggest problem with drilling a series of closely spaced holes is that when the drill bit emerges from the back side of the stock, it invariably tears out chunks of wood between the holes. I solve this problem by using stock about ¼ in. thicker or wider than I actually need, then drilling just until the point of the drill breaks through the backside of the piece. Then I saw the extra ¼ in. off the backside to expose holes as clean as those on the front.

Boring out dowels

Several of the projects in this book involve smokestacks, which are made from lengths of dowel bored out to enable stacking on smaller dowels or plastic lugs. I've found the wood lathe to be a much handier tool for this than the drill press (see photo J).

Photo J • *Boring out dowels is easily done on a lathe. A piece of flexible plastic wrapped around the dowel protects its surface from chuck marks.*

WHEELS AND AXLES

Many of the toys in this book require one or more pairs of wheels. Although you can purchase them ready-made (see Resources on p. 217), they're not always available in the right size or wood species, so you'll sometimes need to make your own. Here, too, the right approach will save you time and give you the best possible results.

Cutting and truing wheels

When I'm making my own wheels, I always cut the blanks with a hole saw and then touch them up on the lathe to get just the right size and detail, as in photo K. To facilitate removing the blanks from the hole saw, I first cut about 80 percent of the way through the stock, with the pilot bit penetrating the backside of the stock. Then I flip the workpiece over, align the pilot drill with the center hole, and finish up the cut.

When cutting several wheels, I align the outer perimeter of the hole saw with the kerf of the wheel that's just been cut, as shown in photo L. Working this way allows sawdust to escape, speeds up the cutting process, and helps reduce heat buildup. Be careful, however, not to create little islands of waste stock between the wheels that could break loose and become an airborne eye hazard.

Cutting axles to length

Although commercially made wheels come with their own mounting pegs, you'll need to fit axles to ones that you make yourself. To get the length of axles just right, I first cut them long and dry-assemble them onto the vehicle with the wheels and spacer washers in place. I then mark the axles, disassemble the unit, and trim them to length.

If the wheels are to be glued on (as in the Vehicles system), I crimp glue grooves into the axles' ends with a pair of Channelock pliers, which have sharp, well-defined teeth. For pressure-fit wheels like those in the Trucks system, the axles' ends will be slotted.

Drilling wheel wells

Some of the projects, such as the van and the pickup truck in the Vehicles system, require cutting wheel wells with a Forstner-type bit. However, the wheel well is only a partial hole, and the actual center

Photo K • *Separate wheel blanks you're turning on the lathe with a couple of washers so that you can round the edges without cutting into another wheel.*

Photo L • *When cutting a series of wheels, align the perimeter of the hole saw with the kerf of the previous wheel.*

of the bit may fall below the bottom of the chassis. To give the bit's center some stock to drill into and to prevent tearout along the bottom edge of the vehicle, I clamp a scrap block to the bottom of the chassis, as shown in photo M.

Finishing

The difference between a toy that's valued and kept for years and one that gets banged around and thrown away is very often the finish. A toy with a nice finish commands respect, whether it's at a craft-market sales booth, on the shelf of a collector, or in the hands of a happy child. By sealing the pores, a quality finish helps protect the wood from the normal dust and dirt encountered in use and in storage. It also creates a harder, more durable surface that helps deflect the abuse that children will inevitably inflict on any toy that's designed to be played with, as all of mine are. Hard play may eventually wear away the finish, but the finishes I use are easily renewed.

Safe finishes

Safety is the most important consideration in selecting a finish for a toy. I use any durable oil-based polyurethane that the manufacturer claims is nontoxic when fully cured. Check the label for curing time. A finish that's nontoxic when dry may not be nontoxic in the can, so in application be sure to follow any safety precautions on the label. Always apply finishes in a well-ventilated area, and keep young children and pregnant women away from the finishing area.

Finishing parts before assembly

I like to finish as many of the parts of a toy before final assembly as possible. Many of them are so small that sanding and finishing them first allows me to reach spots that will be awkward or impossible to get to when the toy is completed. It also enables me to use long, sweeping brush strokes and avoids building up finish in the corners. Just be sure to avoid finishing areas that are to be glued.

Sanding

To prepare parts for sanding, I first sand them to 120 or 150 grit, apply a coat of sanding sealer for a smoother surface, and then lightly sand again with 220-grit paper. After each sanding, I vacuum the pieces and wipe them with a tack cloth. To avoid sucking the smaller pieces into the vacuum, I tape a piece of window screening over the vacuum nozzle. Cloth-type screening

Photo M • *When cutting wheel wells, clamp a scrap block to the bottom of the workpiece to give the bit's center some stock to drill into and to prevent tearout along the bottom edge of the vehicle.*

works better than wire because it's easier to wrap around the nozzle and also won't scratch the workpiece.

For sanding small flat pieces, I've designed some sanding blocks that really come in handy (see the drawing below). I size the blocks to accept quarter, half, and whole sheets of sandpaper. One side of the block is padded with cork or foam rubber, and the other is hard, to suit a variety of sanding needs. Changing paper is simple. You just pull out the wedge in the side of the block, discard the old paper, wrap a new piece around the block, and reinsert the wedge to hold the paper firmly in place. The blocks are so simple to make that I have several in each size. I'm always ready to go with whatever grit is needed.

A common problem when sanding dowels is that the sandpaper can slip around in your hand. I've found it helps to roll a couple of strips of masking tape into tubes (adhesive side out) and apply them diagonally across the back of the sandpaper, as shown in photo N. (You can also use double-sided tape, but it's more expensive.) The tape sticks to the palm of your hand and won't shift around when you wrap it around the dowel and start sanding.

Applying the finish

Woodworkers with large shops may have the luxury of a separate finishing room, but most of us have to cut, sand, and finish in the same space. After sanding and wiping off all the parts, I clean up the shop, dusting and vacuuming everything within the area designated for finishing. Then I go do something else for a couple of hours to let all the dust I've stirred up settle out of the air.

When I return to the shop, I wipe the pieces with a tack cloth one last time and begin brushing on the finish. I leave finish-

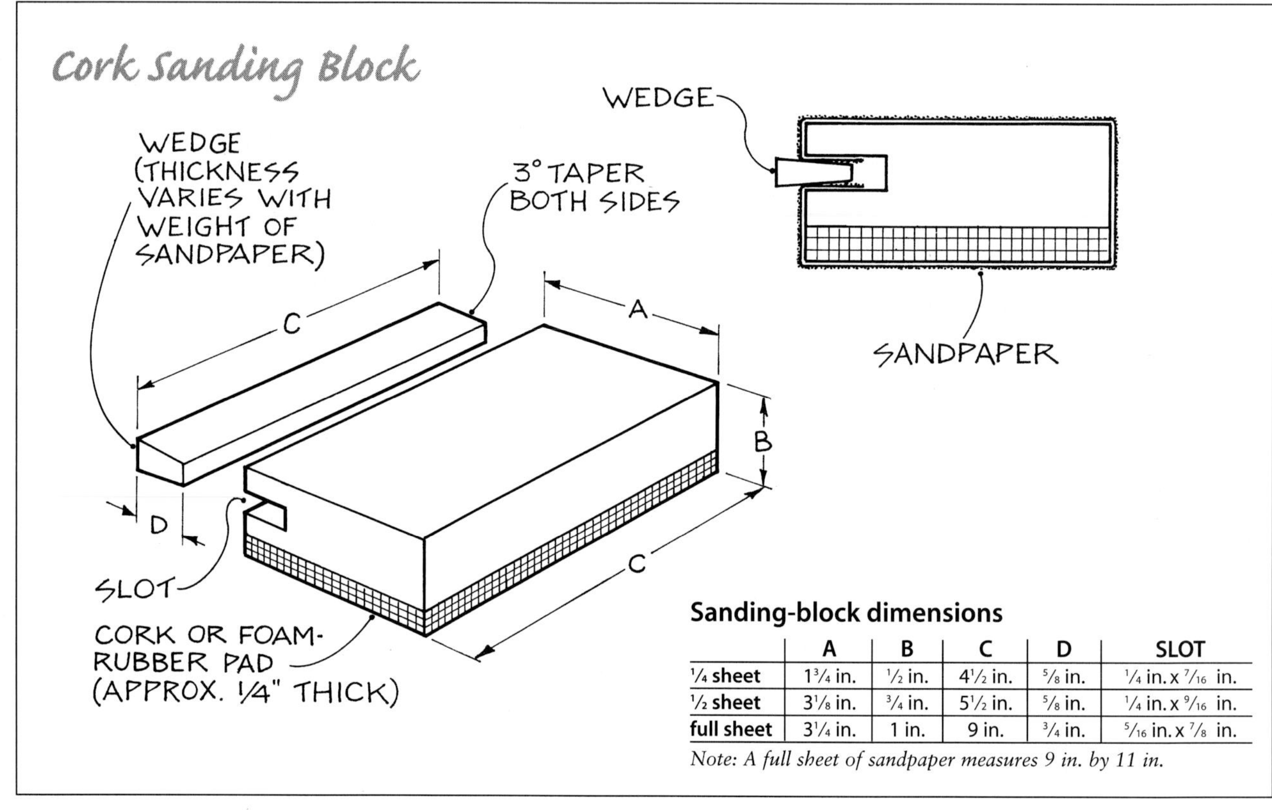

Sanding-block dimensions

	A	B	C	D	SLOT
1/4 sheet	1 3/4 in.	1/2 in.	4 1/2 in.	5/8 in.	1/4 in. x 7/16 in.
1/2 sheet	3 1/8 in.	3/4 in.	5 1/2 in.	5/8 in.	1/4 in. x 9/16 in.
full sheet	3 1/4 in.	1 in.	9 in.	3/4 in.	5/16 in. x 7/8 in.

Note: A full sheet of sandpaper measures 9 in. by 11 in.

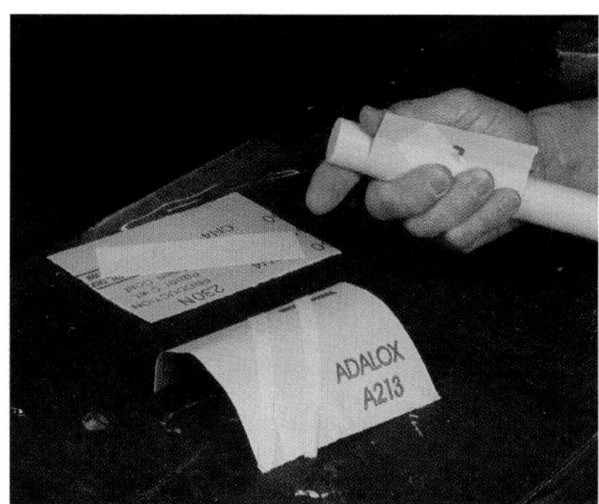

Photo N • *For a firm grip when sanding dowels, apply rolled strips of masking tape (sticky side out) or double-sided tape to the back of the sandpaper.*

ing for the last task of the day. That way, the wet pieces can dry overnight before I stir up any more dust.

For toys that will be played with, I prefer to use a high-gloss polyurethane because it dries harder and is more durable than a satin (semigloss) or flat finish. I've had good luck with both Zip-Guard high-gloss urethane wood finish and Minwax high-gloss polyurethane. For display toys or showpieces, I use a semigloss urethane because it's easier on the eyes than the high-gloss sheen, and still does offer plenty of protection from the handling that these toys naturally invite.

I apply the finish with an artist's brush made of red sable or camel hair. Because most of the pieces are small, a 1-in.-wide brush is plenty big enough. You can expect to pay $10 to $20 for a good artist's brush, but as long as it's taken care of properly it should last a lifetime.

I brush the finish on in long sweeping strokes to minimize brush marks. If the piece is large enough, I hold it in my hand, grasping it top and bottom, and apply finish to the sides and top around my finger, leaving the bottom for later. Then I place the piece on a rain-gutter screen to dry, as shown in photo O. The screen suspends the piece above the work surface, preventing it from sticking as it dries. For smaller pieces, and to finish off the top of each of the larger pieces, I lightly hold the piece right on the screen with the point of a divider while applying the final brush strokes. After the finish has dried, I flip the pieces over and finish the bottoms.

For hardwoods like maple, I usually find one coat to be sufficient. For poplar and pine (poplar's technically a hardwood, but it's significantly softer than maple), once the first coat has dried, I sand the entire surface with 220-grit production-grade sandpaper, making sure to sand off any drips or runs that might have worked their way to the bottom surface. After vacuuming and wiping the piece with a tack cloth, I'll apply a second coat.

WORKING SMARTER

I always try to do my finishing on a dry day; the finish seems to come out a little duller when it's humid.

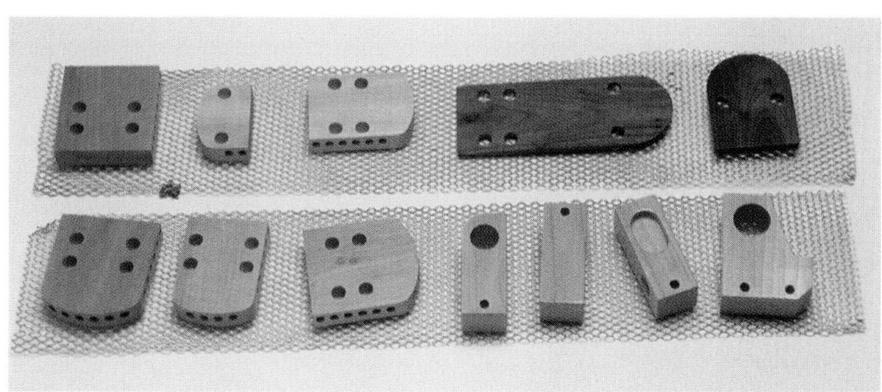

Photo O • *Small pieces dry well on a piece of rain-gutter screen.*

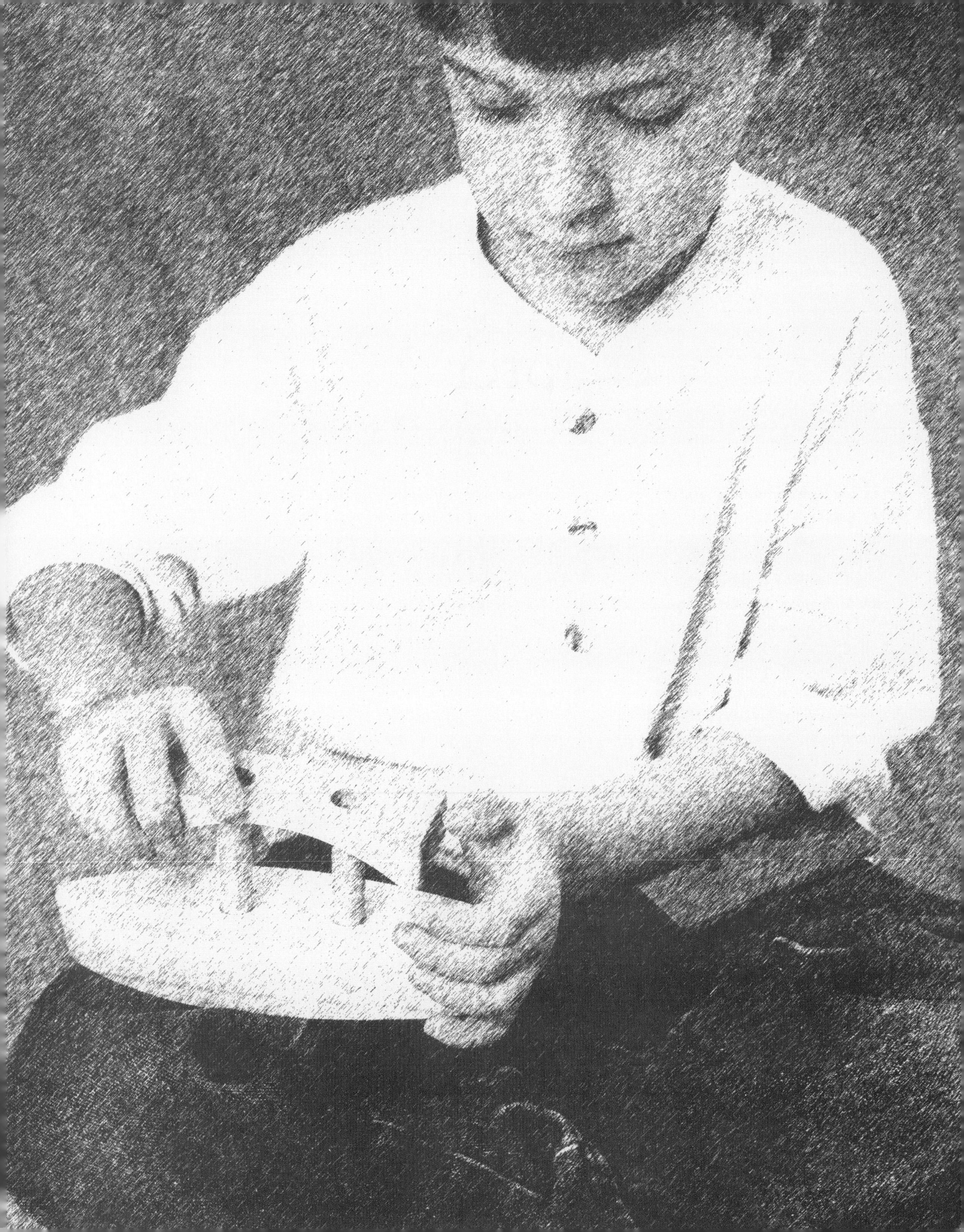

chapter 2
BOATS

This was the first system toy I developed, and, not surprisingly, it's the simplest in design and assembly procedure. It employs the principle of stacking various interchangeable components onto two dowels inserted into a generic hull to create several types of boat.

I've chosen maple and walnut for the elements of this system, to give a nice visual contrast.

There are parts to make variations on five basic boats: a tugboat (my favorite!), a cabin cruiser, a motorboat (the cabin cruiser without the bridge), Noah's ark, and a houseboat.

As I said in Chapter 1, I almost always work from blanks that are oversize in some or all of the dimensions, saving the final overall shaping of a piece for last. I'll be reminding you of this as we go along.

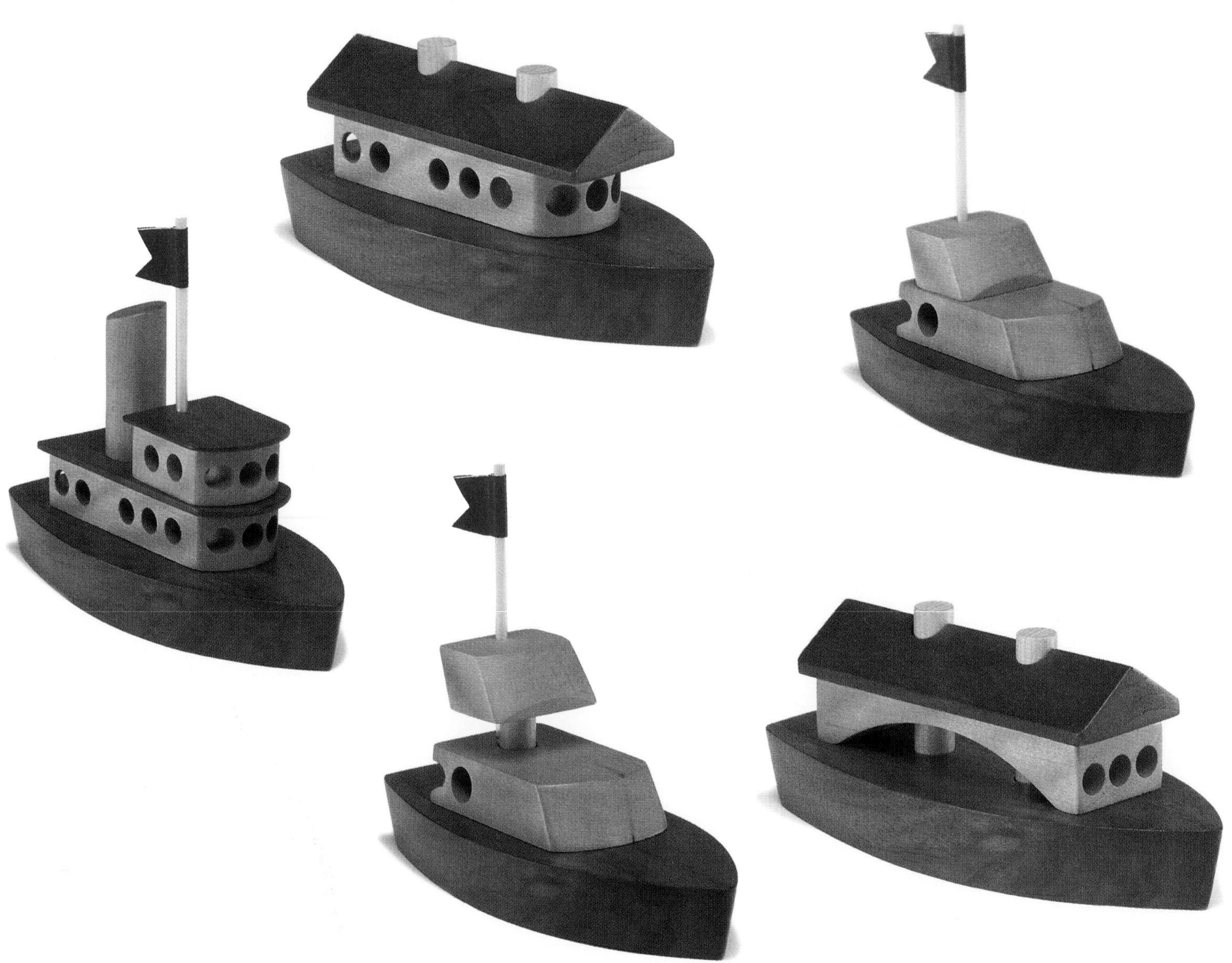

Hull

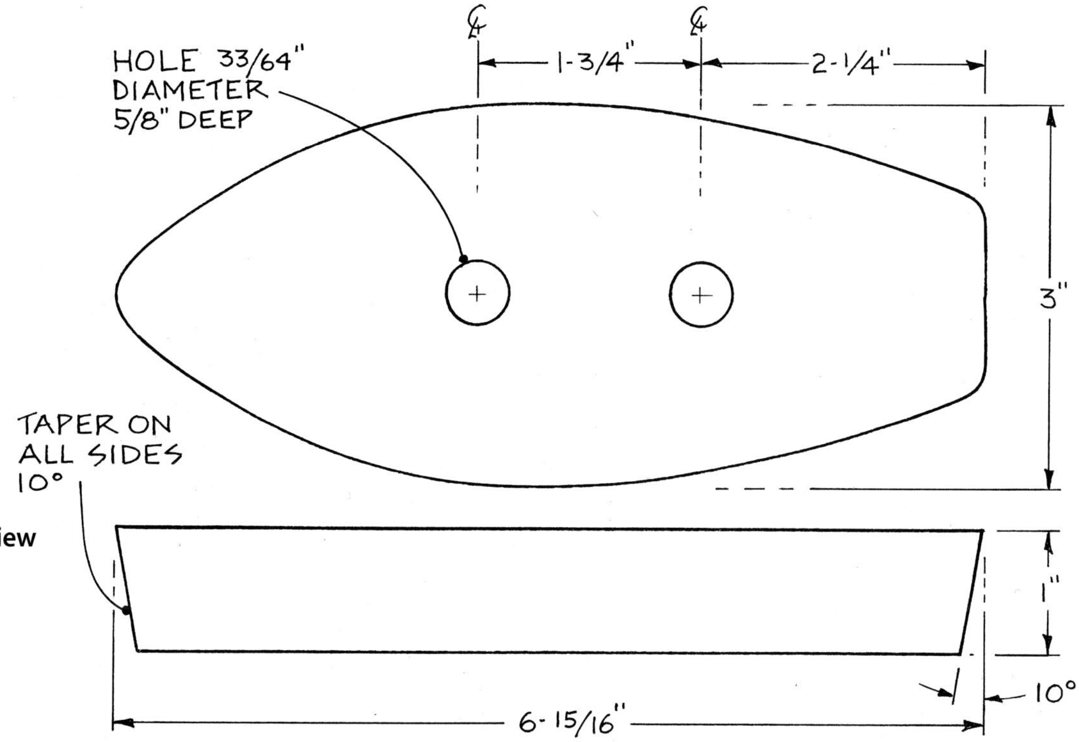

HOLE 33/64"
DIAMETER
5/8" DEEP
1-3/4"
2-1/4"
3"
TAPER ON
ALL SIDES
10°
Side View
1"
10°
6-15/16"

Flagstaff and Dowels

CON-TACT
PAPER
PLASTIC STRAW
3/16" DIAMETER
X 4-5/8"
3-1/2"
2-3/8"
1-3/4"
1"
1/2"

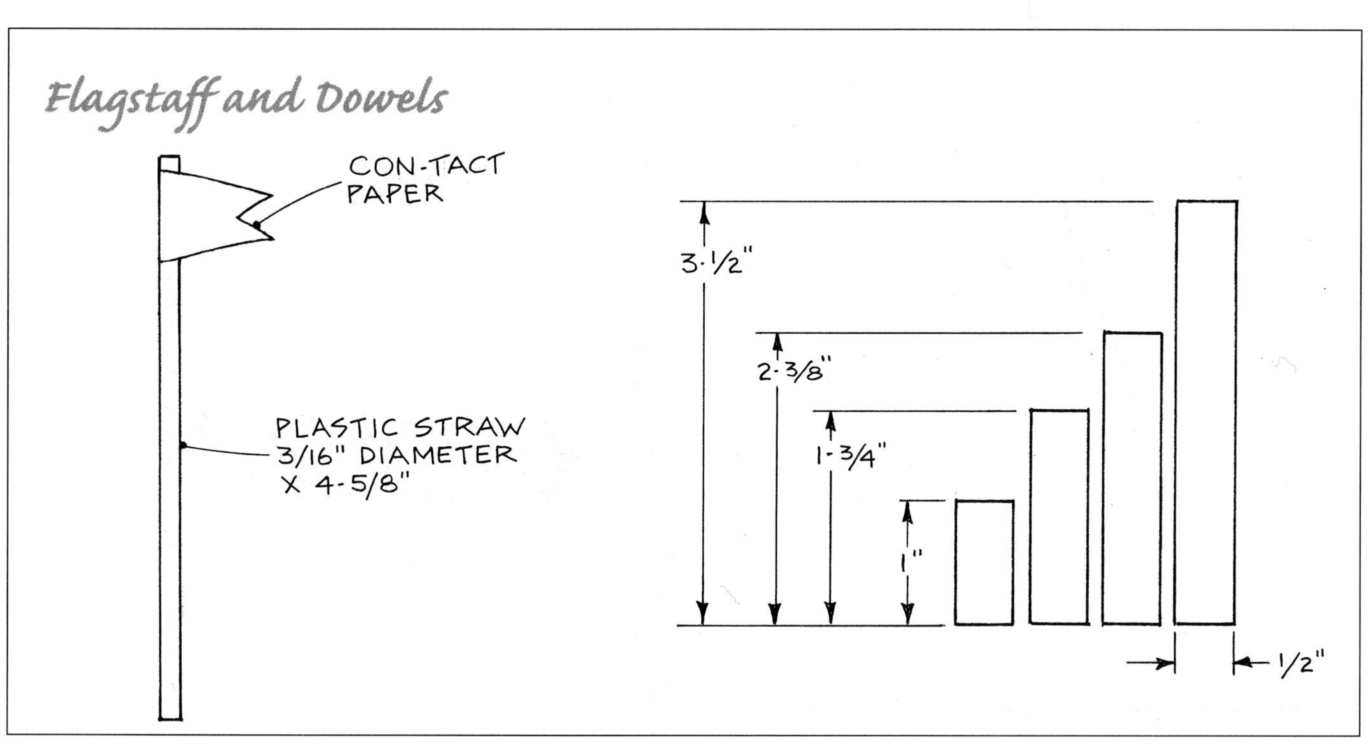

FABRICATION OF COMPONENTS

■ BASIC BOAT PARTS

Note that all dimensions indicate a part's final size. As a rule, blanks should start oversize, as indicated in text.

PART	SIZE (IN.)	QUANTITY	MATERIAL
Generic hull	3 x 1 x $6\frac{15}{16}$	1	Walnut
$\frac{1}{2}$-in.-dia. dowel	$1\frac{3}{4}$, $2\frac{3}{8}$, $3\frac{1}{2}$ long	2 each	Dowel
$\frac{1}{2}$-in.-dia. dowel	1 long	1	Dowel
Flagstaff	Approx. $\frac{3}{16}$ dia. x $4\frac{5}{8}$	1 long	Plastic straw
Flag	As desired	1	Con-Tact paper

Generic hull

1. Cut a slightly oversize blank for the hull.
2. Using the drill-press fence and the stop block (see "Using Spacer Blocks" on p. 10), position the workpiece and drill the first hole. Insert the $1\frac{3}{4}$-in. spacer block between the workpiece and the stop block and drill the second hole (see photo A). You'll use this method on all components that have dual stacking holes.

***Photo A** • Use the spacer-block technique on the drill press for all stacking holes. This ensures they all line up.*

3. Lay out the hull shape from the pattern on the plan drawing on p. 23. Cut the straight end on the table saw at a 10-degree angle. Then cut the curved sides on the bandsaw, with the table tilted to the same angle (see photo B).

***Photo B** • The bandsaw's tilting table provides the 10-degree angle of the hull's curved perimeter.*

Stacking dowels and flagstaff

I buy accurately sized ½-in. dowels (see Resources on p. 217) and cut them to the various lengths indicated. For the flagstaff, any thin plastic drinking straw will do. The flag is cut to shape from colored Con-Tact paper and then affixed to the staff.

■ TUGBOAT COMPONENTS

I've always thought there was something toylike about real-life tugboats at work alongside huge barges and liners, which must be why they strike me as perfect toy subjects.

■ TUGBOAT

Note that all dimensions indicate a part's final size. As a rule, blanks should start oversize, as indicated in text.

PART	SIZE (IN.)	QUANTITY	MATERIAL
Smokestacks	7/8 dia. x 1 7/8 long	2	Dowel
Main deck cabin	1 1/2 x 13/16 x 4	1	Maple
Cabin deck cap	1 3/4 x 1/8 x 4 5/16	1	Walnut
Bridge cabin	1 1/2 x 13/16 x 1 15/16	1	Maple
Bridge roof cap	1 3/4 x 1/8 x 2 1/4	1	Walnut

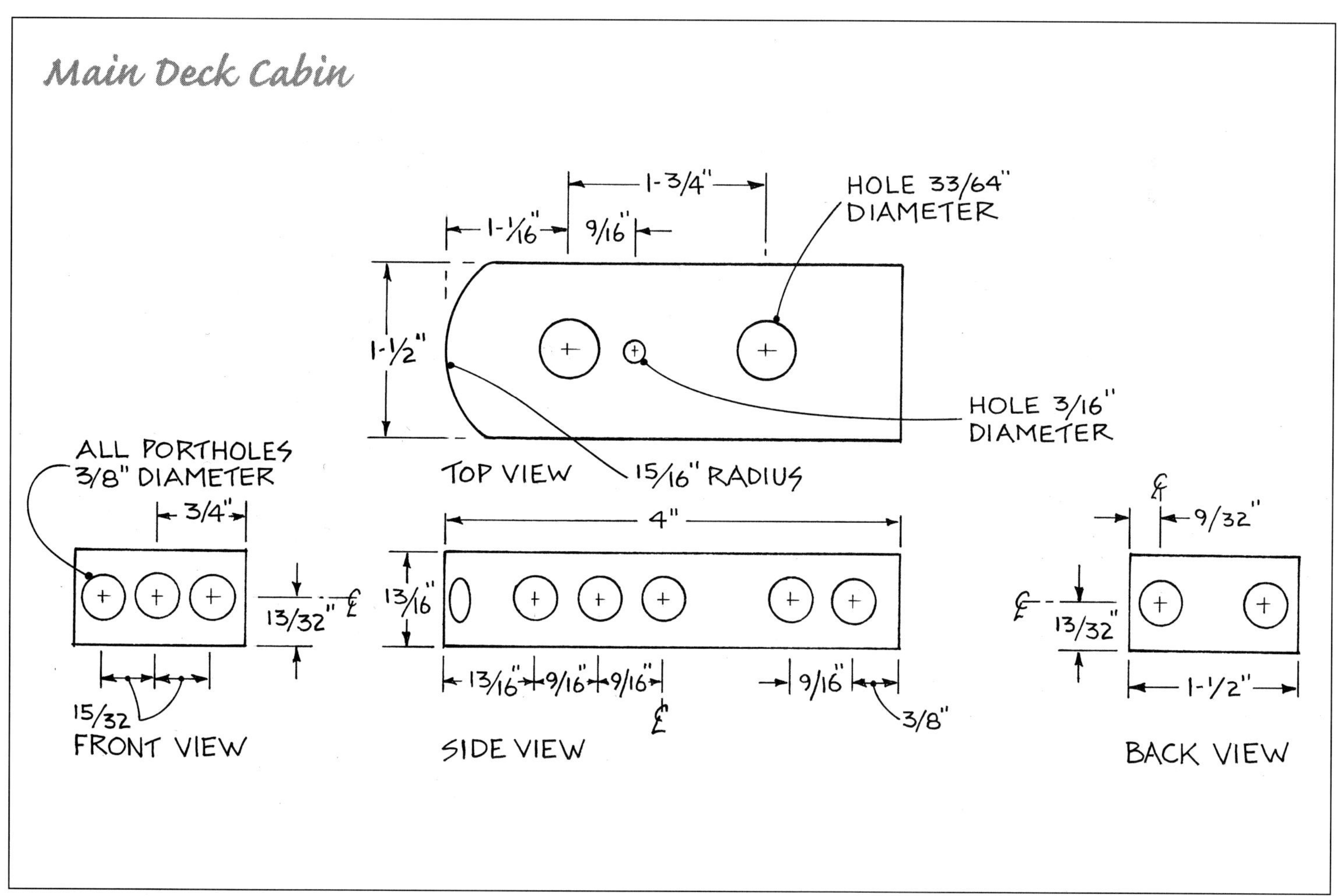

Photo C • *Tugboat components.*

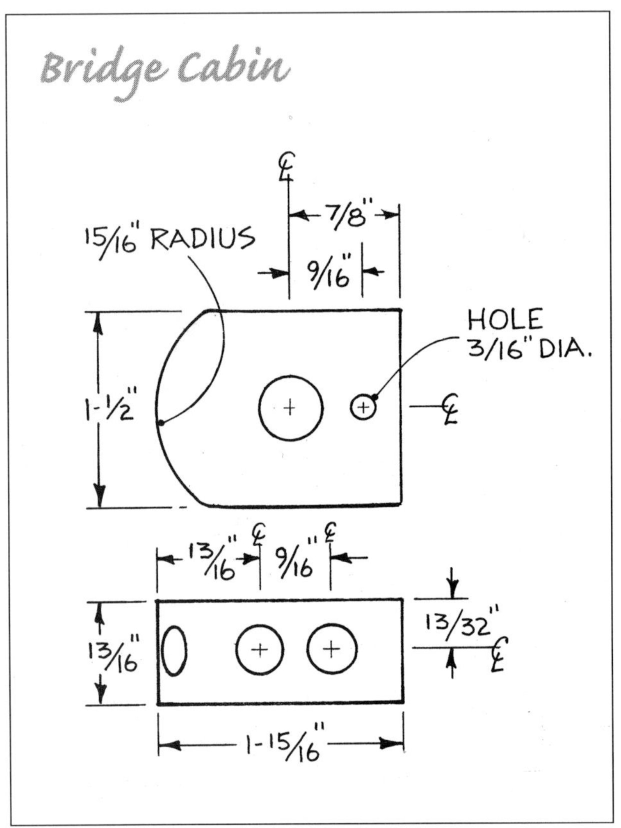

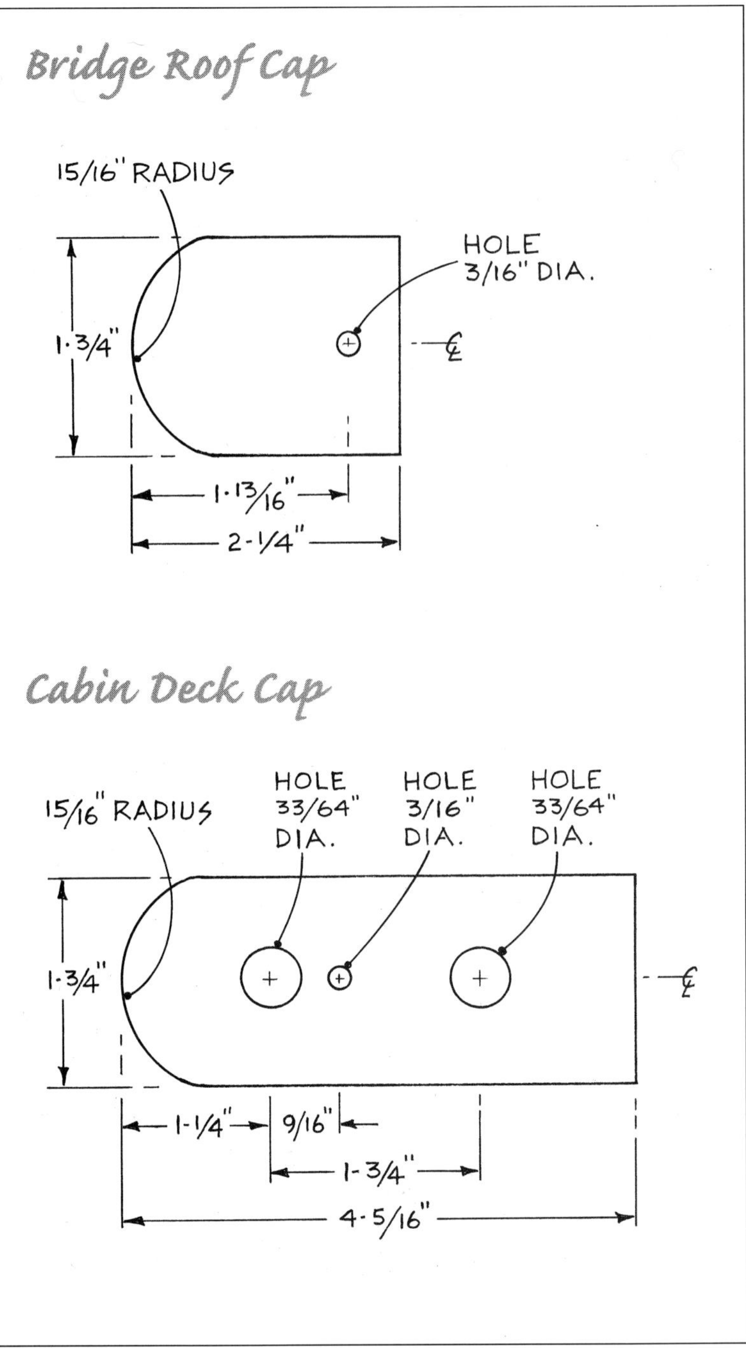

Smokestacks

Using the lathe with chuck accessories, drill centered 33⁄64-in. holes approximately 1 in. deep in each of the two 7⁄8-in.-diameter dowels. (See "Boring out dowels" on p. 15.) Cut the 15-degree top angle with the miter gauge on the table saw.

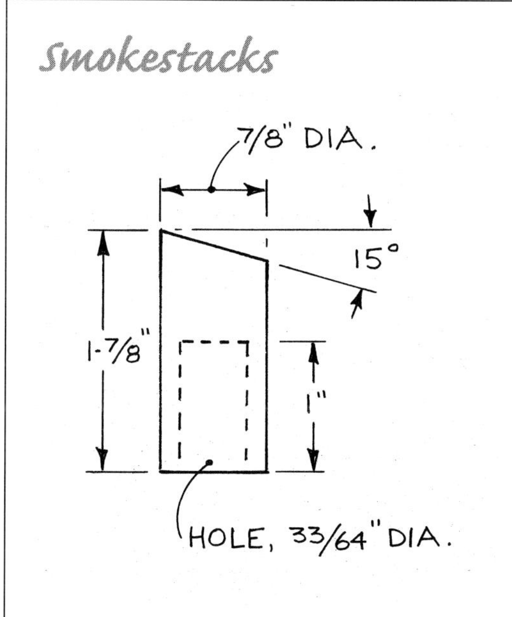

Main deck cabin

1. Cut the main deck cabin blank oversize in length by 1⁄8 in. or so.
2. Cut the 15⁄16-in. radius curve of the front end on a bandsaw, scrollsaw, or a coping saw.
3. Lay out the location of all portholes.
4. Drill 3⁄8-in. diameter holes (the depth isn't critical) for the portholes, using the spacer-block method on the drill press. Note that the rows of portholes require multiple spacer blocks. For the portholes on the back and front, clamp the workpiece to the fence to ensure a true vertical position during the drilling process (see photo D).

Photo D • *When drilling portholes into a cabin blank's end, clamp the workpiece to the fence for stability.*

5. Drill both stacking holes, again using the 1 3⁄4-in. spacer block.
6. Drill the hole for the plastic-straw flagstaff. The exact diameter of this hole will depend on the particular straw used.
7. Cut the front curve and hand-sand it smooth with a sanding block.

Cabin deck cap

1. Cut the cabin deck cap blank oversize in length.
2. Drill the stacking holes and the hole for the plastic-straw flagstaff. Note that all flagstaff holes must be aligned, as they act like stacking holes. The flagstaff will stabilize the position of the bridge cabins for the tugboat and the cabin cruiser/motorboat, which have only one main stacking hole.
3. Cut the front curve and sand smooth.

WORKING SMARTER

You can cut curves such as those on the tugboat cabins and caps on either the bandsaw or the scrollsaw. The trade-off is that while the bandsaw is faster in thicker stock, the scrollsaw is a little more accurate, so it's usually my choice for the thinner parts it can easily manage.

Bridge cabin and bridge roof cap

1. Cut the bridge cabin blank, again slightly oversize in length
2. Locate and drill the ³⁄₈-in. portholes in the cabin blank, using the spacer-block method.
3. Drill the single stacking hole and also the flagstaff hole.
4. Round off the cabin with the bandsaw.
5. Cut the bridge roof cap blank, also slightly oversize in length. Cut the front curve on the scrollsaw. Glue the cap onto the cabin, centered in all directions.
6. Drill the flagstaff hole through the cap, following through the cabin flagstaff hole.

CABIN CRUISER/MOTORBOAT

You can get several different looks with just the two basic components of this one. If you use the bridge cabin alone, it's a nice little motorboat. With both cabins stacked, any dowel in the rear position that is longer than 1¾ in. gives you a flying bridge.

Photo E • *Cabin cruiser/motorboat.*

CABIN CRUISER/MOTORBOAT

Note that all dimensions indicate a part's final size. As a rule, blanks should start oversized, as indicated in text.

PART	SIZE (IN.)	QUANTITY	MATERIAL
Cruiser deck cabin	2 x ¹³⁄₁₆ x 3¹⁄₄	1	Maple
Cruiser bridge cabin	1³⁄₄ x ¹³⁄₁₆ x 1⁷⁄₁₆	1	Maple

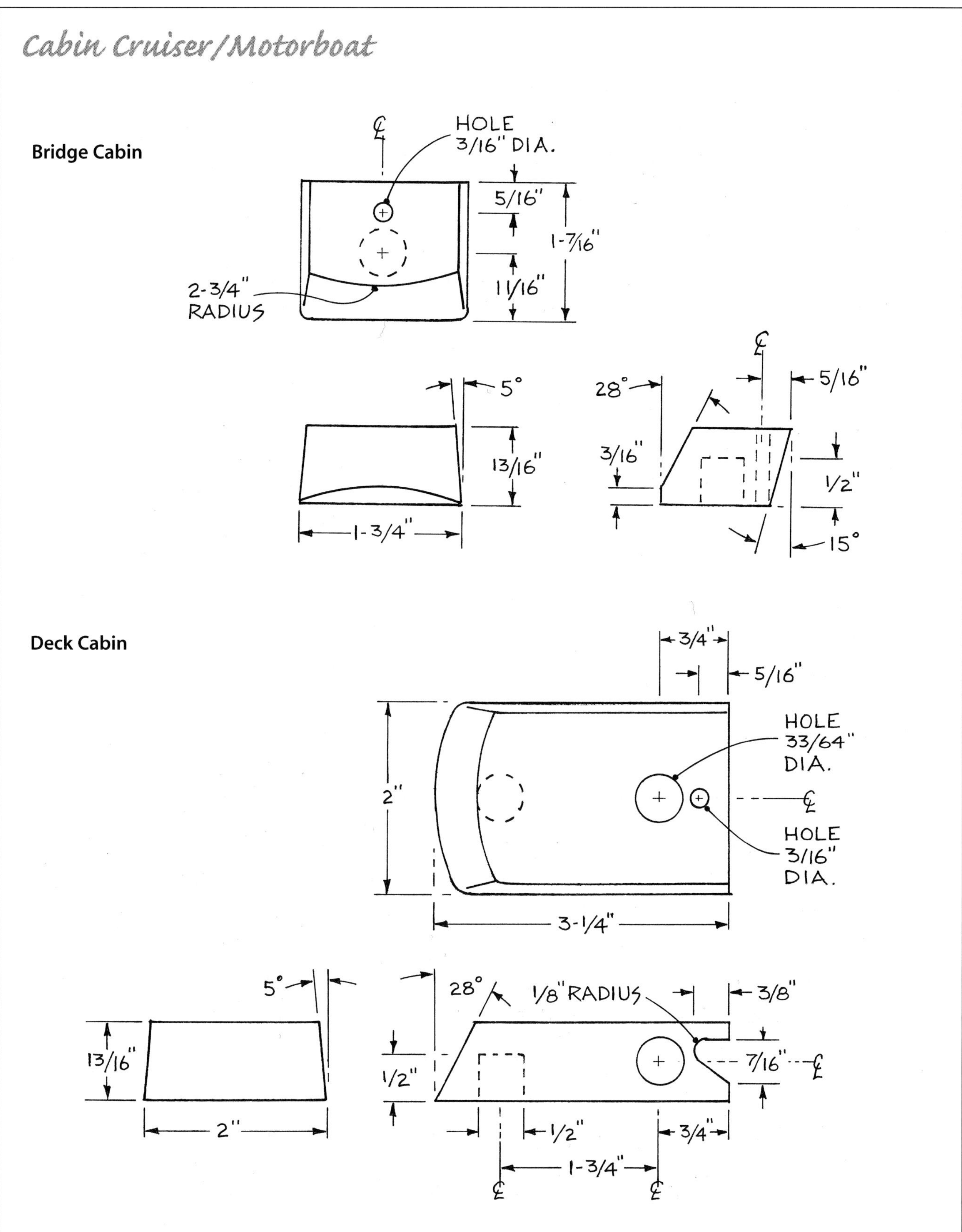
Cabin Cruiser/Motorboat
Bridge Cabin
HOLE
3/16" DIA.
5/16"
1-7/16"
11/16"
2-3/4"
RADIUS
5°
13/16"
1-3/4"
28°
5/16"
3/16"
1/2"
15°
Deck Cabin
3/4"
5/16"
HOLE
33/64"
DIA.
2"
HOLE
3/16"
DIA.
3-1/4"
5°
13/16"
2"
28°
1/8" RADIUS
3/8"
1/2"
7/16"
1/2"
3/4"
1-3/4"

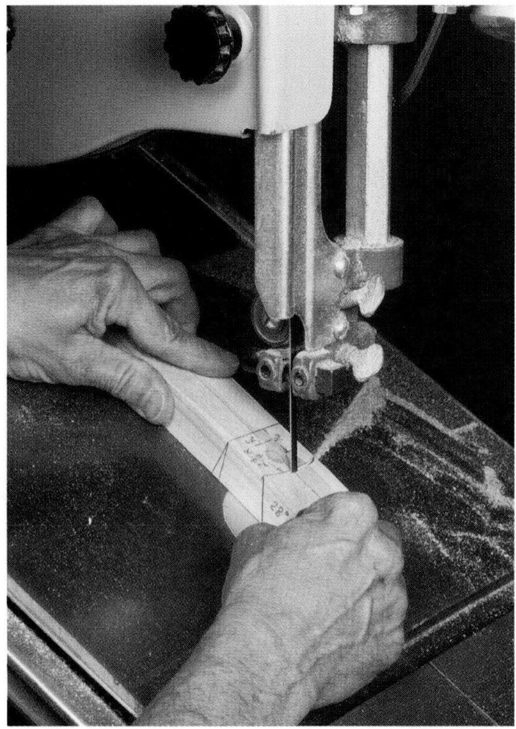

Photo F • *For safe handling while shaping on the bandsaw, use a 6-in.- to 8-in.-long blank for the cruiser bridge.*

Cruiser deck cabin

1. Cut the cruiser deck cabin blank to its final width and thickness, leaving it approximately ⅛ in. oversize in length to allow for minor adjustments when cutting and sanding.
2. Lay out both the top and side views of the cabin's curved front section on the workpiece.
3. Cut the front curve on the bandsaw, with the saw's table set at a 28-degree angle.
4. With the fence, stop block, and 1¾-in. spacer block in place on the drill press, place the workpiece (bottom side up) against the spacer and fence, and drill the rear stacking hole.
5. Remove the spacer block and slide the workpiece against the stop block to drill the partial-depth stacking hole. If you anticipate that a child younger than three will play with this toy, it's best to glue the 1-in. stacking dowel into this hole, eliminating a small loose piece that could be a choking hazard.
6. Drill the flagstaff hole.
7. Cut out the rear notched area, using a ¼-in. drill bit to create the ⅛-in. radius and the bandsaw for the finish cut.
8. Cut each side of the cabin at a 5-degree angle on the table saw.

Cruiser bridge cabin

The steps here are essentially the same as for the deck cabin, with the following exceptions.

1. Start with a blank 6 in. to 8 in. long to allow safe handling when shaping it. See photo F.
2. After cutting the front curve on the bandsaw, lightly sand the lower front of the cabin square, using a hand-sanding block. All measurements should then be taken from this end.
3. The final step is to cut the cabin to its correct length on the table saw, with the blade tilted 15 degrees.

NOAH'S ARK

Even without the animals I think old Noah would be pleased with this one.

Photo G • *Noah's ark components.*

Ark Cabin and Roof

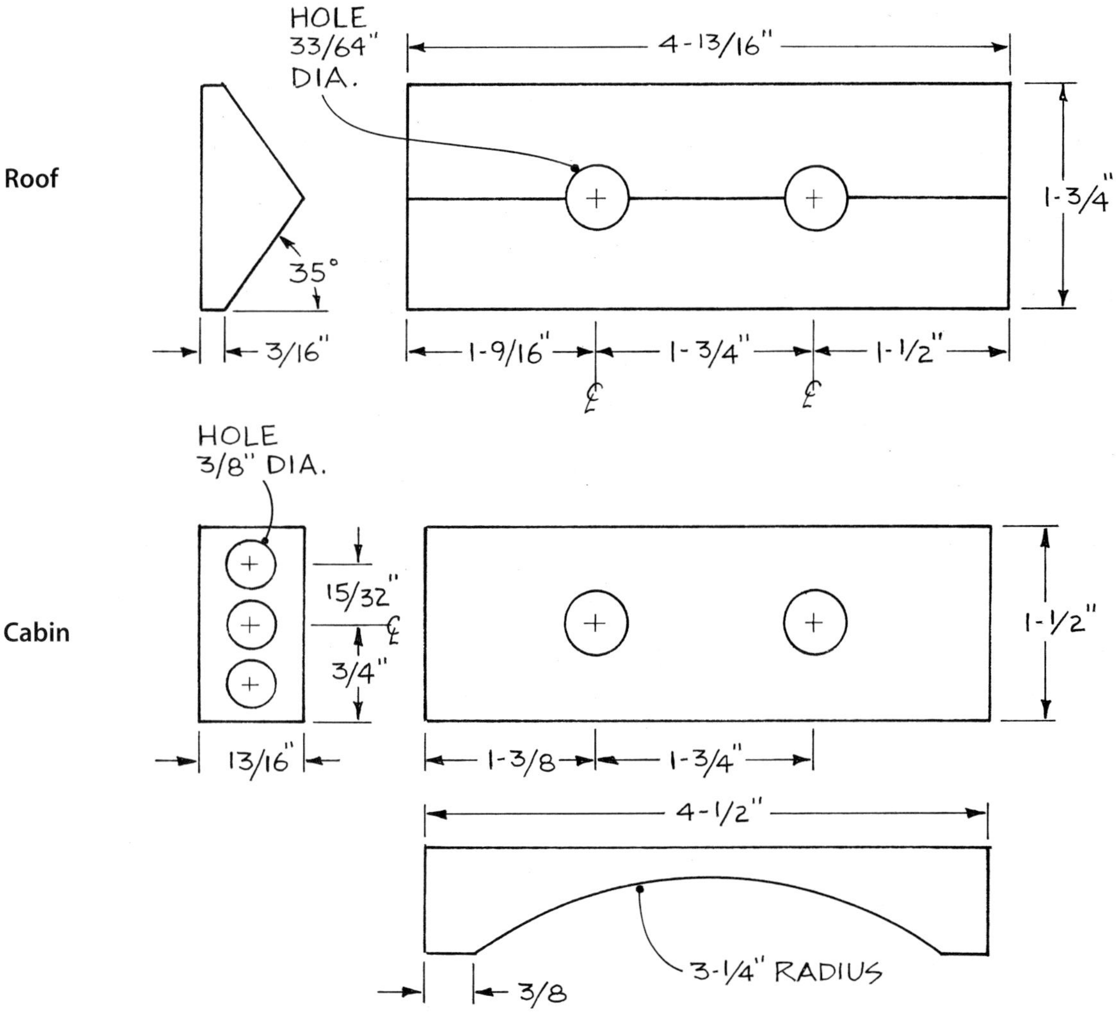

Roof

HOLE 33/64" DIA.

4-13/16"

1-3/4"

35°

3/16"

1-9/16" 1-3/4" 1-1/2"

℄ ℄

Cabin

HOLE 3/8" DIA.

15/32"

3/4"

℄

13/16"

1-1/2"

1-3/8 1-3/4"

4-1/2"

3-1/4" RADIUS

3/8

NOAH'S ARK

Note that all dimensions indicate a part's final size. As a rule, blanks should start oversize, as indicated in text.

PART	SIZE (IN.)	QUANTITY	MATERIAL
Noah's ark cabin	1½ x 13/16 x 4½	1	Maple
Gable roof	1¾ x 13/16 x 4 13/16	1	Walnut

Noah's ark cabin

1. Cut the Noah's ark cabin blank to its correct overall size.
2. Drill the portholes on both ends, using the standard stop-block drill-press setup. Clamp the workpiece to the fence for stability, as you did when drilling the end portholes of the main deck cabin.
3. Cut the large arc on the bandsaw, using a scrap block taped to the opposite side of the workpiece to help hold it securely on its side (see photos H and I).

Photo H • *A scrap block attached to the Noah's ark cabin blank with double-sided tape affords both safe handling and stability of the workpiece during the cutting of the curve.*

Photo I • *A letter opener is the perfect tool for removing the scrap block after the procedure without marking up the workpiece.*

Gable roof

1. Cut the blank to its final overall size.
2. Drill both stacking holes.
3. Make the two angle cuts on the table saw, using a piece of scrap wood (preferably pine) the same width and length as the workpiece and about 1¼ in. to 1½ in. thick taped to the workpiece. The auxiliary piece allows a sufficient work surface against the saw table. (See photo D, showing a similar process, on p. 60.) Note that the gable roof has 3⁄16-in. shoulders on both sides.

Houseboat

There are a number of combinations of components that you've already made that will give you a plausible houseboat—it all depends on your idea of a house! But I like the look of the gable roof stacked onto the main deck cabin.

Photo J • *Houseboat.*

chapter 3
TRUCKS

In this system, various components are aligned along lengths of ¾-threaded dowel and secured with wooden nuts on each end to form an assortment of buses and trucks—anything from a school bus to a full-fledged oil tanker—with friction-fitted wheels on dowel axles.

The system is so simple that I usually set kids loose on it without giving them any guidance other than an example or two to look at. And it's amazing to see what they'll come up with: One child actually thought of connecting two of the threaded rods to make an extra-long truck, something that had never occurred to me.

Although all components are intended to be secured vertically upright, they can just as easily be canted to the left and right for a cockeyed look that's often the source of much amusement.

The Trucks system is really quite simple to construct, requiring for the most part only basic drilling and cutting operations, with some optional routing.

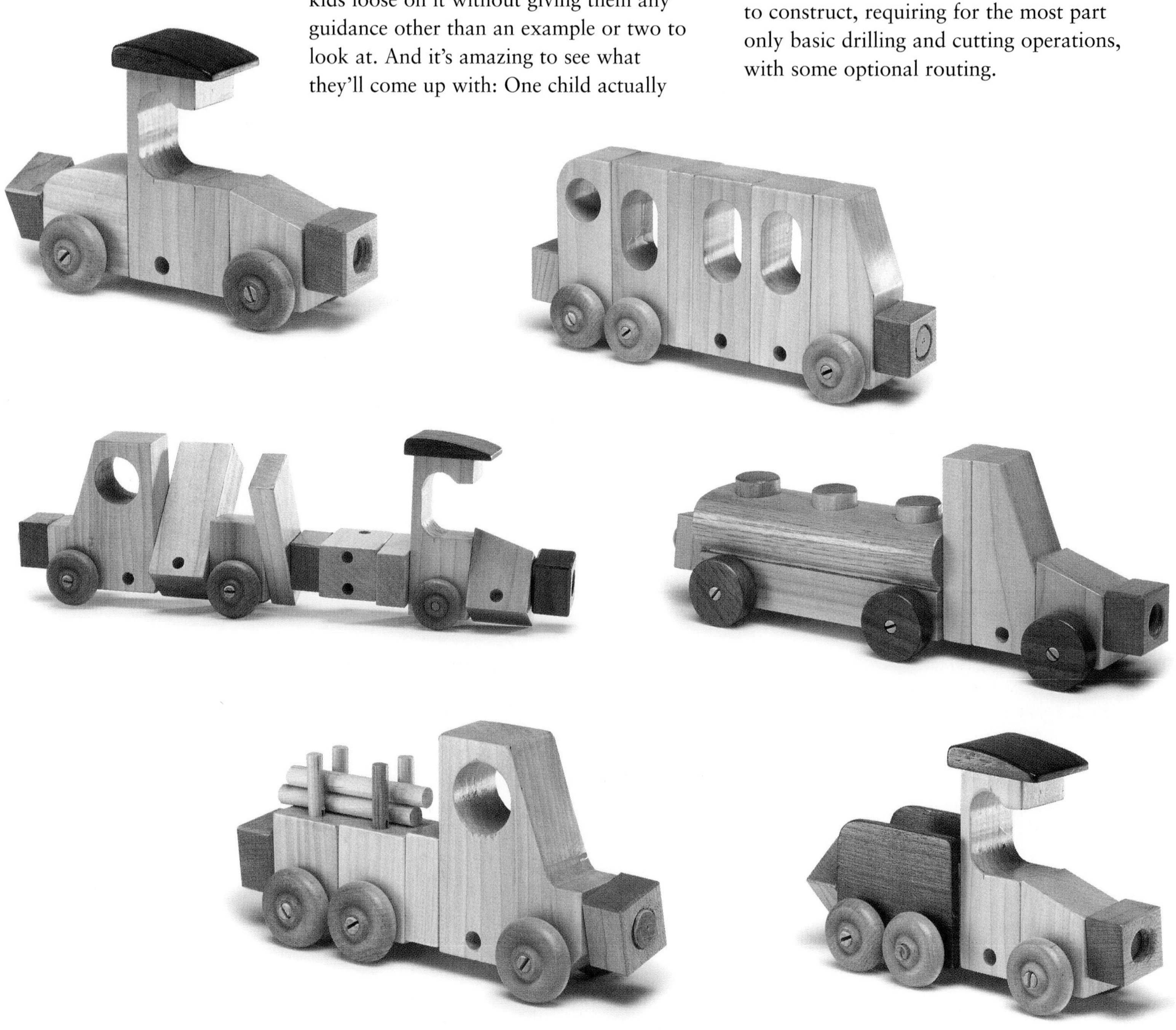

FABRICATION OF COMPONENTS

CABINS AND BODY PARTS

Photo A • *The complete parts for this system include various cabins and bodies, wheels, axles, and the threaded rods and nuts that join them.*

TRUCK PARTS

CABINS

PART	SIZE (IN.)	QUANTITY	MATERIAL
Cabin A (with hood)	$3\frac{1}{8}$ x $1\frac{5}{16}$ x 4	1	Poplar
Cabin B (standard)	$1\frac{9}{16}$ x $1\frac{5}{16}$ x 4	1	Poplar
Cabin C (with roof)	$1\frac{9}{16}$ x $1\frac{5}{16}$ x 4	1	Poplar
Cabin roof (for cabin C)	$1\frac{11}{16}$ x $\frac{7}{16}$ x $2\frac{5}{16}$	1	Walnut

BODIES

PART	SIZE (IN.)	QUANTITY	MATERIAL
Body #1 (with oval cutout)	$1\frac{9}{16}$ x $1\frac{5}{16}$ x 4	4	Poplar
Body #2 (with 1-in.-dia. cutout)	$1\frac{9}{16}$ x $1\frac{5}{16}$ x 4	1	Poplar
Body #3 (standard solid)	$1\frac{9}{16}$ x $1\frac{5}{16}$ x 4	2	Poplar
Body #4 (half vertical)	$\frac{25}{32}$ x $1\frac{5}{16}$ x 4	1	Poplar
Body #5 (hood)	$1\frac{9}{16}$ x $1\frac{5}{16}$ x 2	1	Poplar
Body #6 (coupe back)	2 x $1\frac{5}{16}$ x 2	1	Poplar
Body #7 (half & half)	$\frac{25}{32}$ x $1\frac{5}{16}$ x 2	1	Poplar
Body #8 (half body with 2 postholes)	$\frac{5}{16}$ dia. x $1\frac{1}{8}$ long	1	Dowel
Body #9 (back end)	$1\frac{9}{16}$ x $1\frac{5}{16}$ x 2	1	Poplar
Pickup bed #10 overall size is:	$2\frac{5}{8}$ x $1\frac{13}{16}$ x $3\frac{1}{8}$		
Inner body piece	$1\frac{5}{8}$ x $1\frac{5}{16}$ x $3\frac{1}{8}$	1	Poplar
Side panels	$2\frac{5}{8}$ x $\frac{1}{4}$ x $3\frac{1}{8}$	2	Walnut
Oil tanker tank	$6\frac{1}{4}$ long	1	Hand rail
Oil tanker chassis	$1\frac{1}{16}$ x $1\frac{11}{16}$ x $6\frac{1}{4}$	1	Poplar
Log posts	$\frac{5}{16}$ dia. x $1\frac{5}{8}$ long	4	Dowel

Cabins

Cabin A

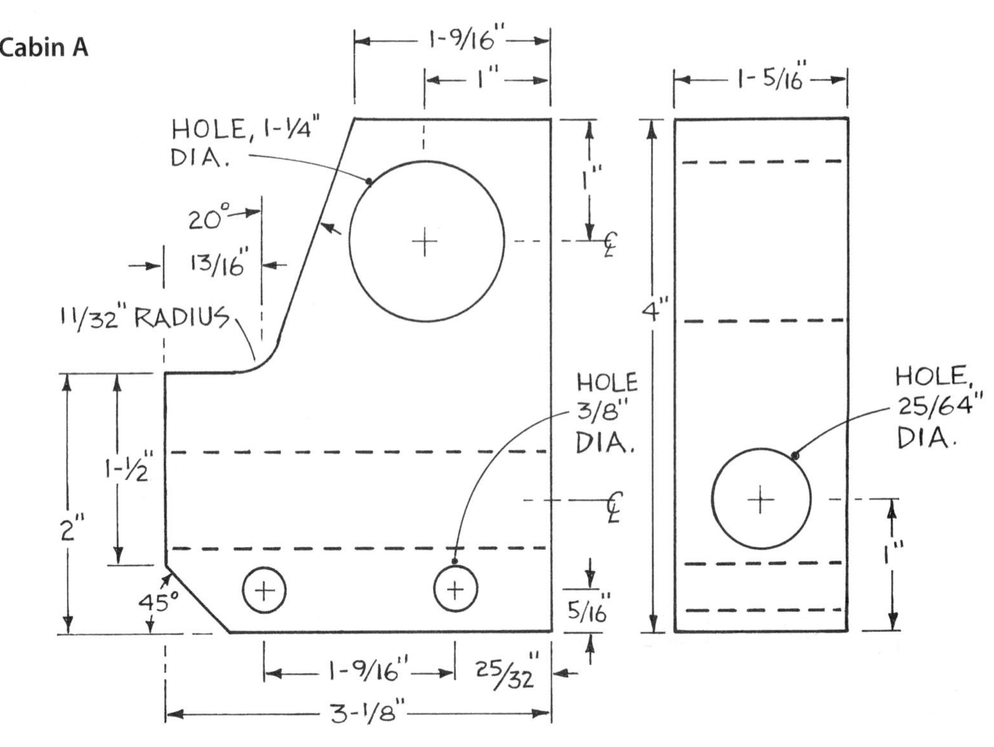

Cabin B

Cabin C

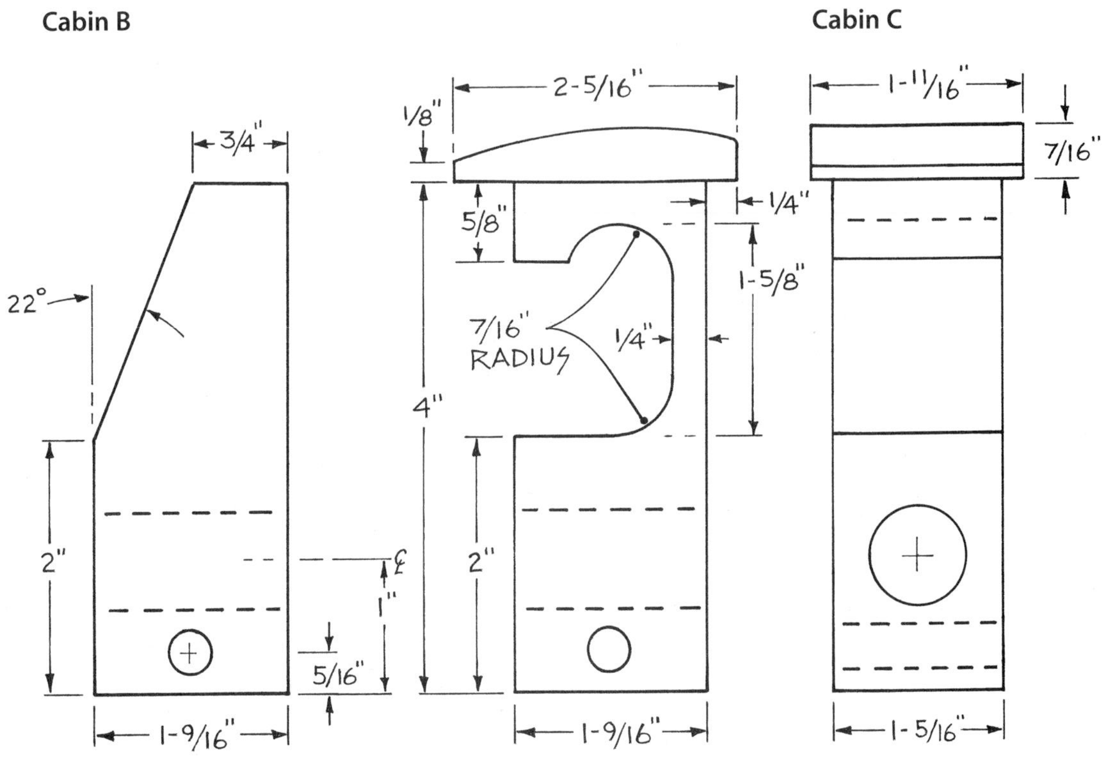

Bodies

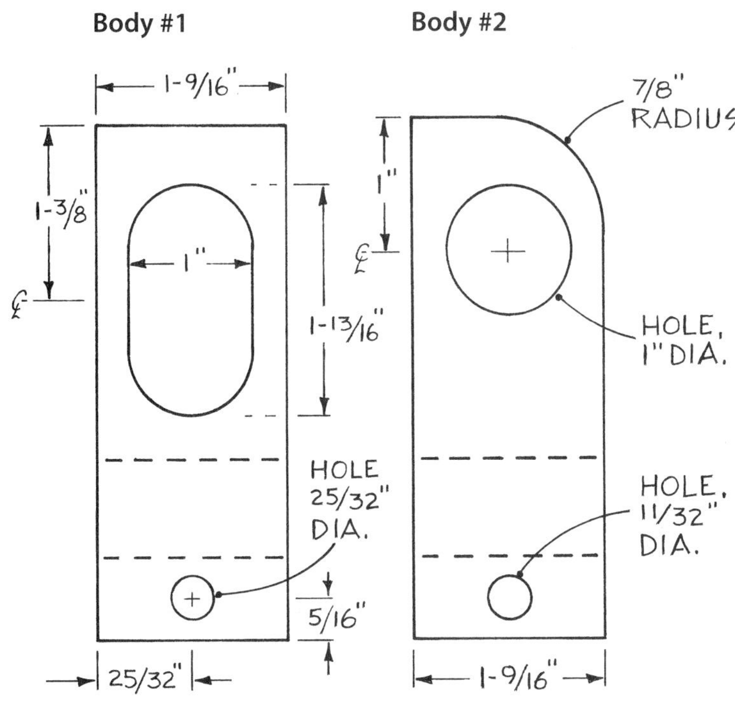
Body #1
Body #2
1-9/16"
1-3/8"
1"
1-13/16"
HOLE 25/32" DIA.
5/16"
25/32"
7/8" RADIUS
1"
HOLE, 1" DIA.
HOLE, 11/32" DIA.
1-9/16"

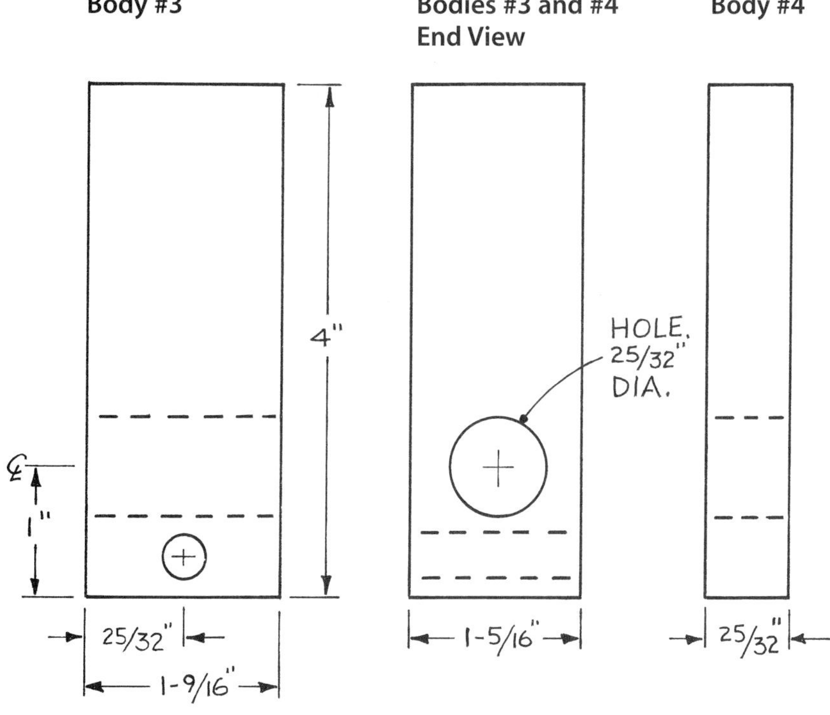
Body #3
Bodies #3 and #4 End View
Body #4
4"
1"
25/32"
1-9/16"
HOLE, 25/32" DIA.
1-5/16"
25/32"

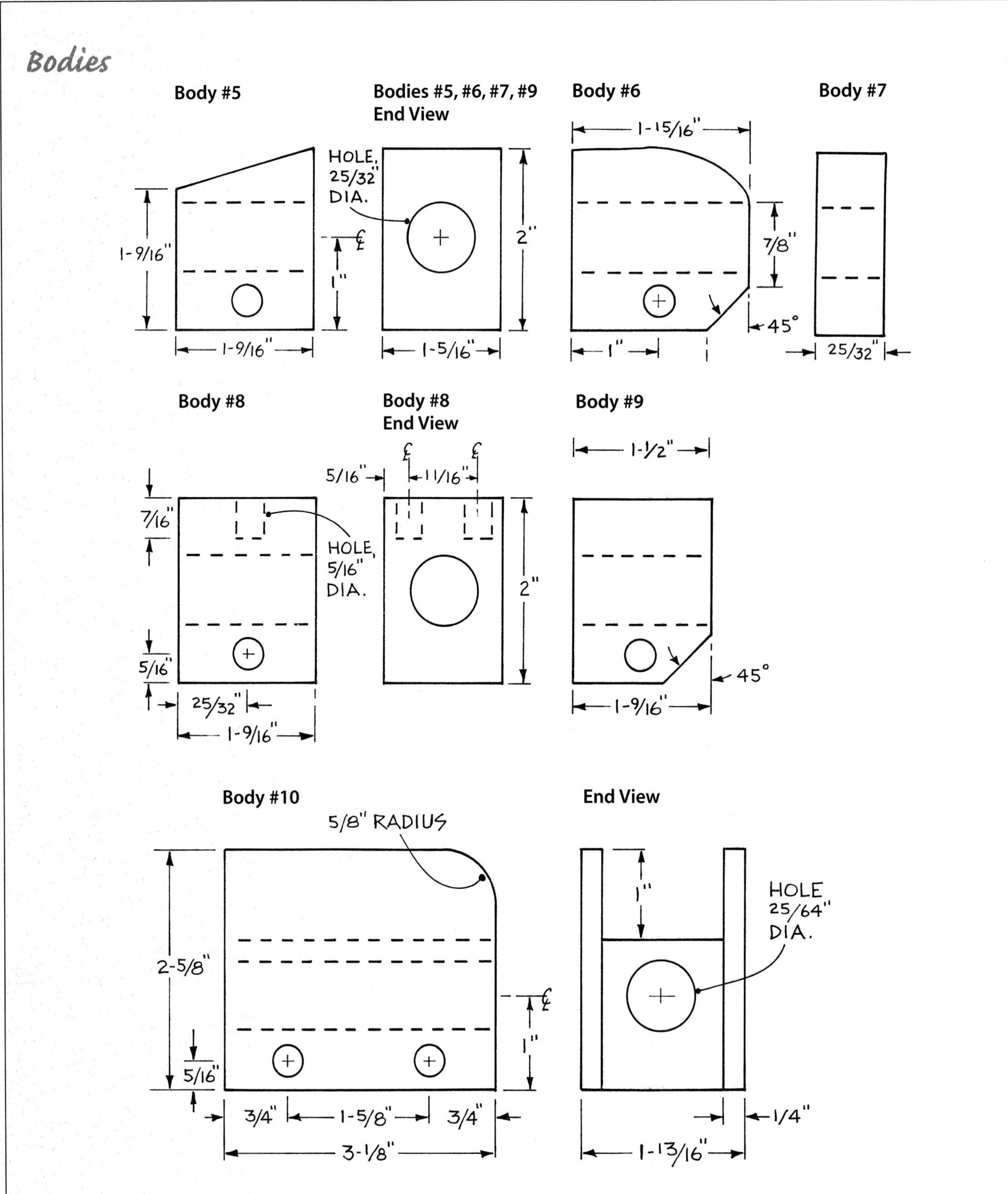
Bodies
Body #5
Bodies #5, #6, #7, #9
End View
Body #6
Body #7
1-15/16"
HOLE, 25/32" DIA.
1-9/16"
1"
2"
7/8"
45°
1-9/16"
1-5/16"
1"
25/32"
Body #8
Body #8
End View
Body #9
1-1/2"
5/16"
11/16"
7/16"
HOLE, 5/16" DIA.
2"
5/16"
45°
25/32"
1-9/16"
1-9/16"
Body #10
End View
5/8" RADIUS
1"
HOLE 25/64" DIA.
2-5/8"
1"
5/16"
3/4"
1-5/8"
3/4"
1/4"
3-1/8"
1-13/16"

Drilling for the threaded dowels

Since all cabins and body parts aside from the oil tanker body are 1⁹⁄₁₆ in. thick (including the inner piece of the truck/pickup cargo body), you can use the same drill-press setup to drill the hole for the threaded dowel in all of them.

1. Cut all cabin and body part blanks, including the inner body piece of the truck/pickup cargo body, to their final overall block sizes.
2. Set up the drill press with an auxiliary table and a fence with an adjustable sliding stop block.
3. Lay one of the 1⁹⁄₁₆-in. by 1⁵⁄₁₆-in. by 4-in. blanks on the table with a 1⁹⁄₁₆-in. side against the fence and butted against the stop block.
4. Using the center finder (see the "Tools" section on p. 7), or a brad-pointed drill bit, set the fence and stop block to locate the center point on the face of the 1⁵⁄₁₆-in.-wide face and 1 in. out from the stop block. Note that the coupe back and the inner body piece for the truck/pickup cargo body are drilled in the vertical position, all others in the horizontal. Check the plan drawings to resolve any uncertainty about the orientation of the hole in a workpiece.
5. Drill the through hole in each blank. If you're using commercial threaded dowel, the hole should be ²⁵⁄₃₂ in. in diameter. If you're making your own, which I recommend, you can drill a ³⁄₄-in. hole and hand-sand the dowel lightly for the right fit. Place a piece of scrap hardwood under each blank for a clean exit.
6. Cut the side panels for the truck/pickup cargo body to their overall size. Glue them to the 1⁵⁄₈-in. sides of the inner body piece, bottom flush.

Photo B • *All the cabin and body blanks can be drilled from the threaded dowel using the same fence and stop block.*

7. Sand the upper rear corners of the side panels to the indicated radius on the stationary sander.

Axle holes

An ¹¹⁄₃₂-in. hole should give you the right clearance to allow a properly rotating ⁵⁄₁₆-in. axle. But because of the vagaries of dowel sizing, it's a good idea to drill a test hole on scrap first.

For cabin A (with hood) and the truck/pickup cargo body, locate the two axle holes as indicated in the plan drawings. For all other components, each axle hole should be centered left to right on the part's side, ⁵⁄₁₆ in. from the bottom surface.

Again, placing a piece of scrap hardwood under the workpiece will guarantee a clean exit hole.

Window apertures and final shaping

All the round and oval body-part window cutouts are achieved with drill bits and the scrollsaw. But partial-depth windows create a nice effect. If you'd like to incorporate them, I've designed a router template to make it easy (see photo C and the drawing below). A window depth of about ⅜ in. seems to give the right look. I recommend making up several extra pieces with this feature.

1. For the round window in cabin A, simply drill a 1¼-in. hole as indicated in the plan drawing. For body #2, the hole should be 1 in.
2. For the elongated cutouts in cabin C and body #1, create the top and bottom radius with drill bits; ⅞ in. for cabin C, and 1 in. for body #1. Complete the cutout with the scrollsaw. To clean the straight surfaces of the cuts, I make a sanding board about ⅛ in. thick, ¾ in. wide, and 6 in. to 8 in. long, with 100-grit sandpaper taped to one side and 120-grit to the other.
3. Bring each component that has a final profile that is not simply rectangular to its final shape. For cabin B, use the angle jig shown in photo D and the drawing on the facing page. The ⅝-in. radius curve on the upper rear of the truck/pickup body can be obtained freehand on a stationary belt sander.

Photo C • *Clamp the template and workpiece in a vice and rout the partial-depth windows.*

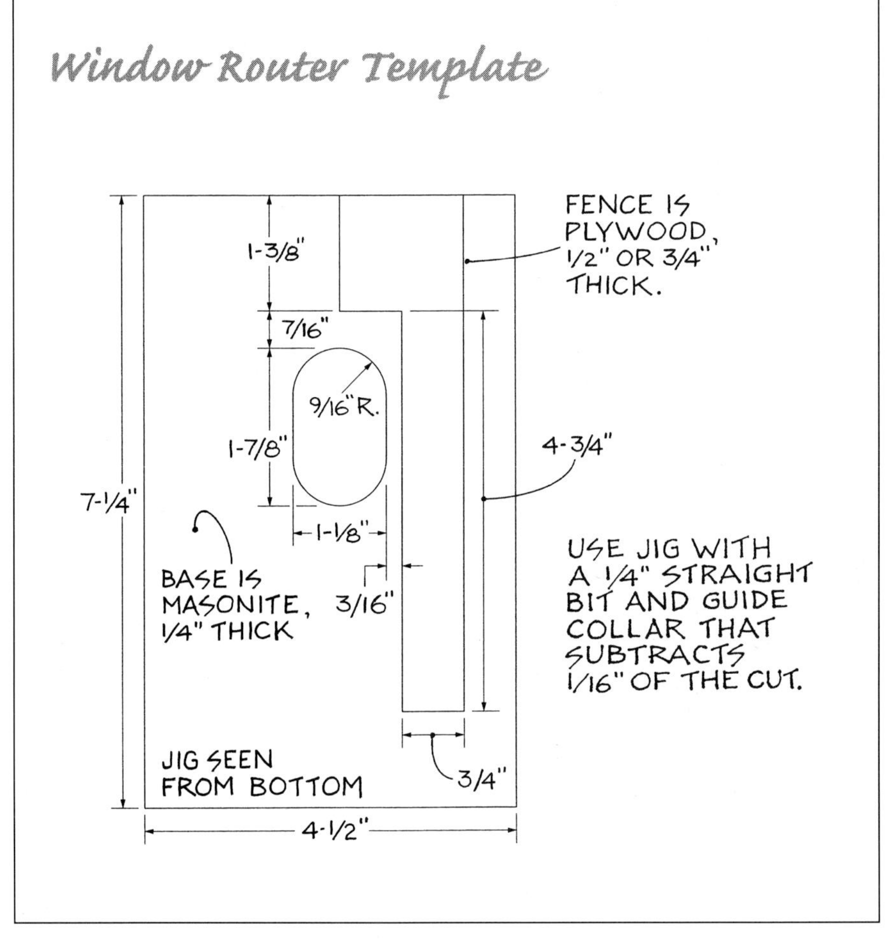

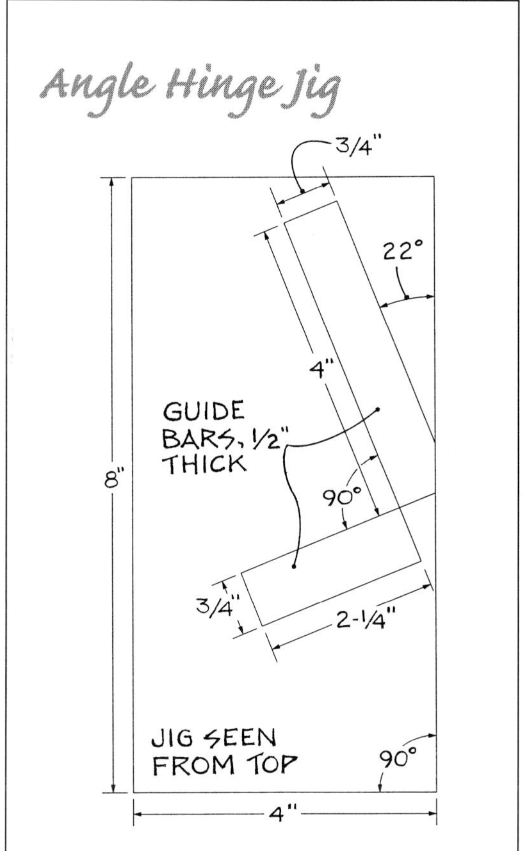

Photo D • *This simple table-saw jig gives you the 22-degree front-angle cut on cabin B. Be sure to hold the cabin in place during the cut.*

Oil tanker body

A section of handrail makes a great looking oil tanker tank, but I'm sure you don't want to purchase a full length just for this project. Check with your local lumberyard to see if they'll sell you a short piece. I've had good luck at Home Depot for this.

1. For the chassis, cut the bottom block blank to its correct final size.
2. Drill the two axle holes as indicated in the plan drawing on p. 44.
3. Make a dado cut to form a center channel 25/32 in. wide and 7/16 in. deep in the top of the bottom block.
4. For the tank, make a dado cut to form a center channel 25/32 in. wide and 11/32 in. in the bottom of the handrail section.

Photo E • *Dado cuts in the chassis and tank of the oil tanker body form the channel that accommodates the threaded dowel.*

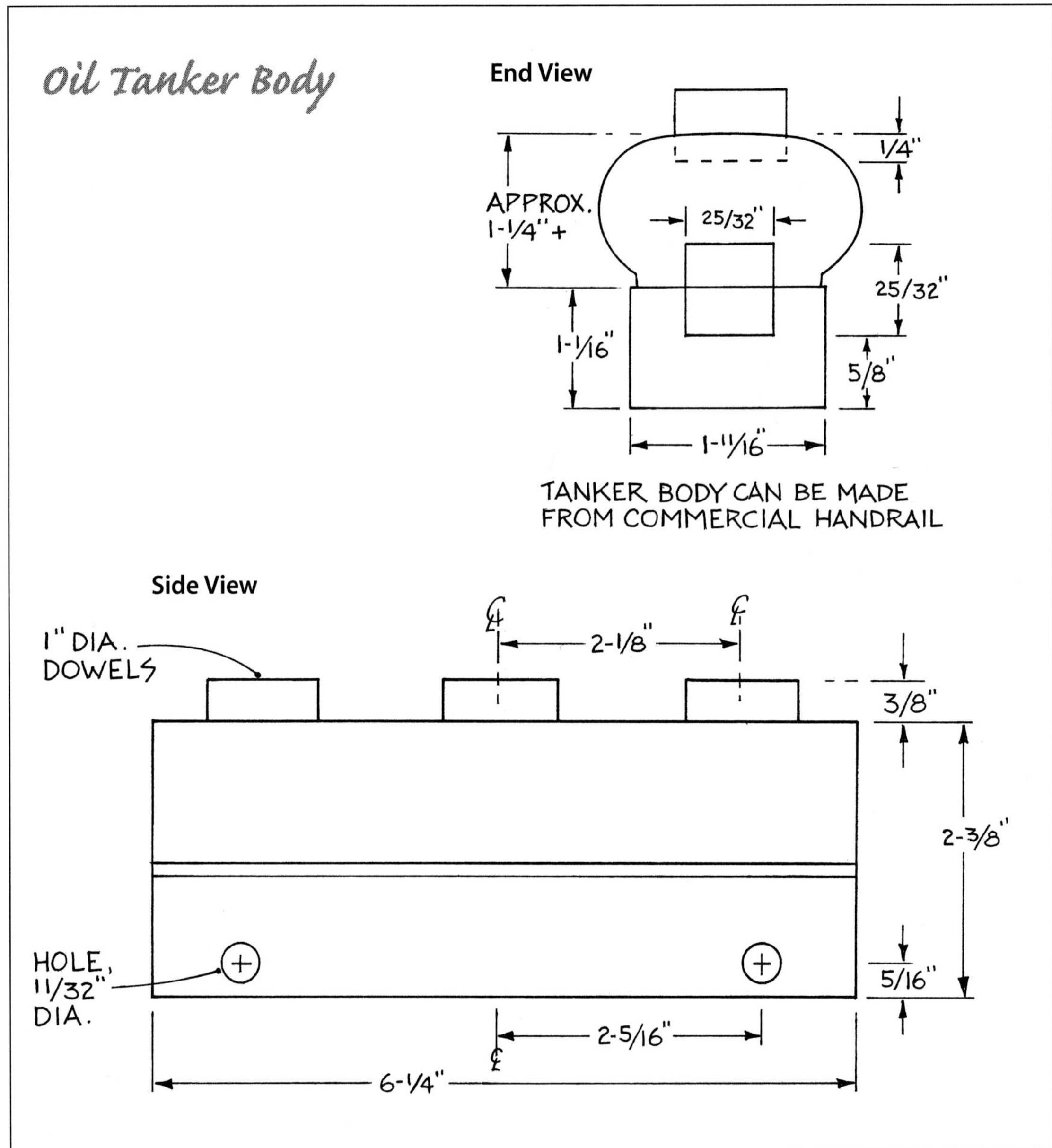

When the two pieces are joined, you'll have a $^{25}/_{32}$-in. square hole running the length of the tanker body to accommodate the threaded rod.

5. Glue the rail section and the bottom block together, making sure the sides of the square hole are properly aligned.
6. Locate and drill the 1-in. holes for the caps along its top. The holes should be about $^{1}/_{4}$ in. deep. Note that the middle hole is centered on the workpiece, and the outer ones are $2^{1}/_{8}$ in. to either side of the middle one along the centerline.
7. Cut three $^{5}/_{8}$-in. sections of 1-in. dowel for the cap blanks.
8. Apply finish to the oil tanker body before gluing the cap blanks in place. You'll get better brush strokes without the interruption of the installed caps. You may also prefinish what will be the visible portion of the cap blanks.
9. Glue the caps in place.

Roof cap for cabin C

Note that the plan drawing for cabin C includes this part.

1. Fasten the roof cap blank to an auxiliary block with double-sided tape.
2. Cut it to its final shape on the bandsaw (see photo F).

Photo F • *Fastening the roof cap blank to an auxiliary scrap block with double-sided tape makes for safe handling on the bandsaw.*

3. Glue the cap to the top of cabin C. It should be centered left to right when viewed from the front, and with the front overhang as indicated in the plan drawing.

AXLES AND WHEELS

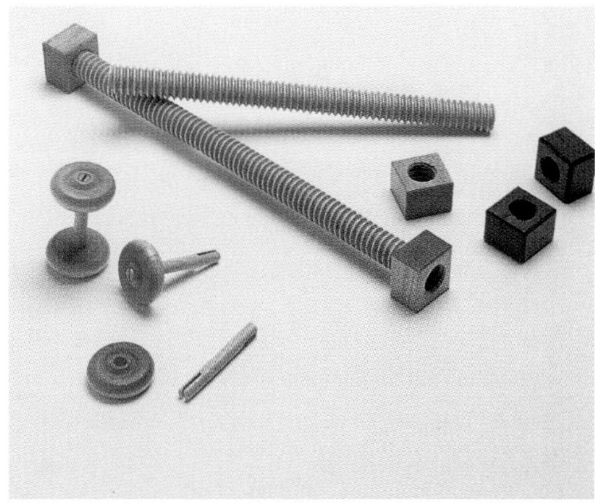

Photo G • *The wheels are pressure-fitted to dowel axles. The body parts are aligned on threaded dowels, and secured with wooden nuts.*

After you've cut the 5⁄16-in. dowels to length as indicated on p. 46, you'll need to slot their ends for the friction-fit into the wheels. The simple jig pictured in photo H and the drawing on p. 47 makes this operation a piece of cake. The dowel is positioned in the jig, and then run over the table saw.

Photo H • *A simple slotting jig ensures consistent results. The feed direction is indicated on this jig so the same side is always against the fence.*

■ AXLES, WHEELS, AND DOWELS

AXLES

PART	SIZE (IN.)	QUANTITY	MATERIAL
Axle #2	5/16 dia. x 3 long	4	Dowel
Axle #3	5/16 dia. x 3 1/2 long	4	Dowel

WHEELS (commercial or handmade)

PART	SIZE (IN.)	QUANTITY	MATERIAL
Wheels	1 1/2 dia. x 1/2 with 5/16 hole	8	Walnut

THREADED DOWELS AND NUTS

PART	SIZE (IN.)	QUANTITY	MATERIAL
Threaded 3/4-in. dowel	9 3/4, 8 1/4, 6 3/4 long	1 each	Dowel
Threaded nuts	1 1/4 x 7/8 x 1 1/4	4–6	Walnut/maple

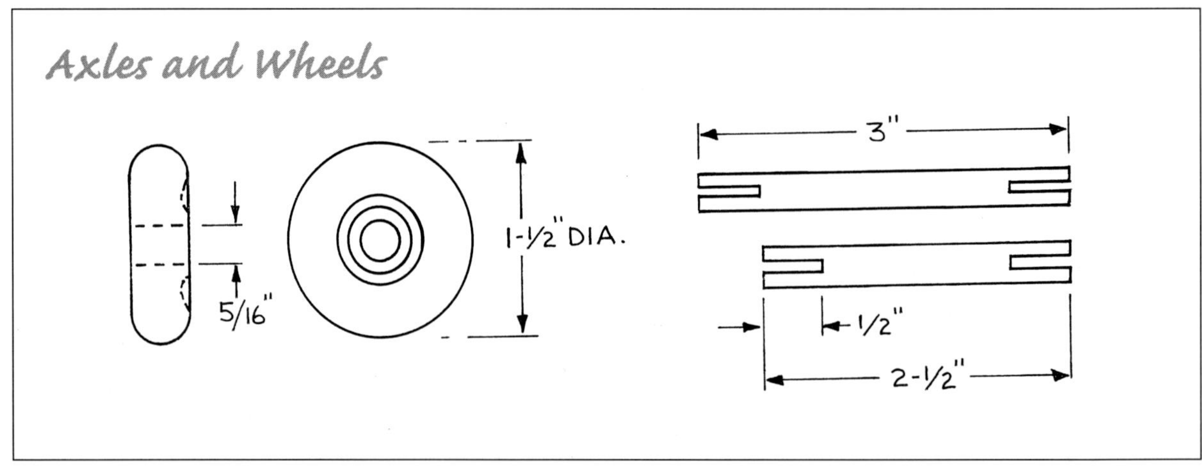

The friction-fit of the axles into the wheels will be affected by both the width and the depth of the slots. I usually cut them ½ in. deep with a narrow kerf sawblade. A standard kerf blade is okay, too, but will make for a looser fit. If you use a regular blade, you may want to cut the slot a little shallower, stiffening it up a bit.

While making the axles, also cut some 5/16-in. dowels for the log posts, but slot them on one end only. Because of the number of wheels required for this project and because the size needed is readily available (see Resources on p. 217), I've chosen to buy them ready-made. But you may wish to make your own. If so, they should be cut with a 1¾-in. hole saw and then finished to the correct diameter on the lathe, as described in the "Wheels and Axles" section on p. 16. Mount the wheels on the lathe two at a time, separated by a couple of washers, using an arbor handmade from a 5/16-in. machine bolt and a wing nut.

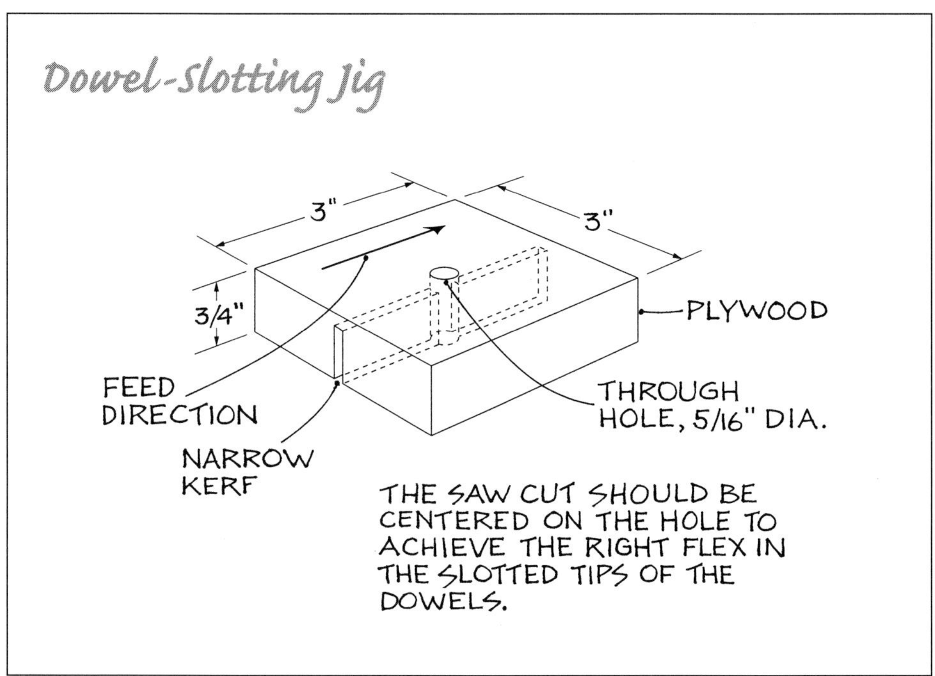

THREADED DOWELS AND MATCHING NUTS

Threaded dowels and nuts of this size are commercially available (see Resources on p. 217). I do recommend, though, that you purchase a ¾-in. wood tap-and-die set and make your own. Commercial wooden nuts are circular in shape, so you'll have to square them off to look right with the other components. I've recently found some mail-order sources (also listed in Resources) for accurately sized dowels, which are particularly desirable for the threaded parts.

To hold the dowels in the vise while I'm threading them, I drill a centered ¾-in. hole all the way through the end grain of a 1¾-in. hardwood cube, which I then cut in half, leaving two pieces with half-round cavities that accommodate the dowels without leaving jaw impressions.

Photo I • *While threading dowels, a bored-out block, cut in half, holds the dowel securely in the vise without marring its surface.*

Threaded Dowel and Nut

1-1/4"

1-1/4"

7/8"

THREADS, 7 TPI, WHOLE LENGTH

3/4" DIAMETER

LENGTHS 9-3/4", 8-1/4", 6-3/4"

Photo J • *Always tap an oversize nut blank, then cut it down to size to reduce the risk of splitting.*

Be sure to make the nut blanks oversize, to minimize potential splitting during the tapping operation. Then trim to the correct size. Neatly sanded edges on the nuts give a nice appearance and feel. The jig pictured in photo K will help you do the job quickly and precisely.

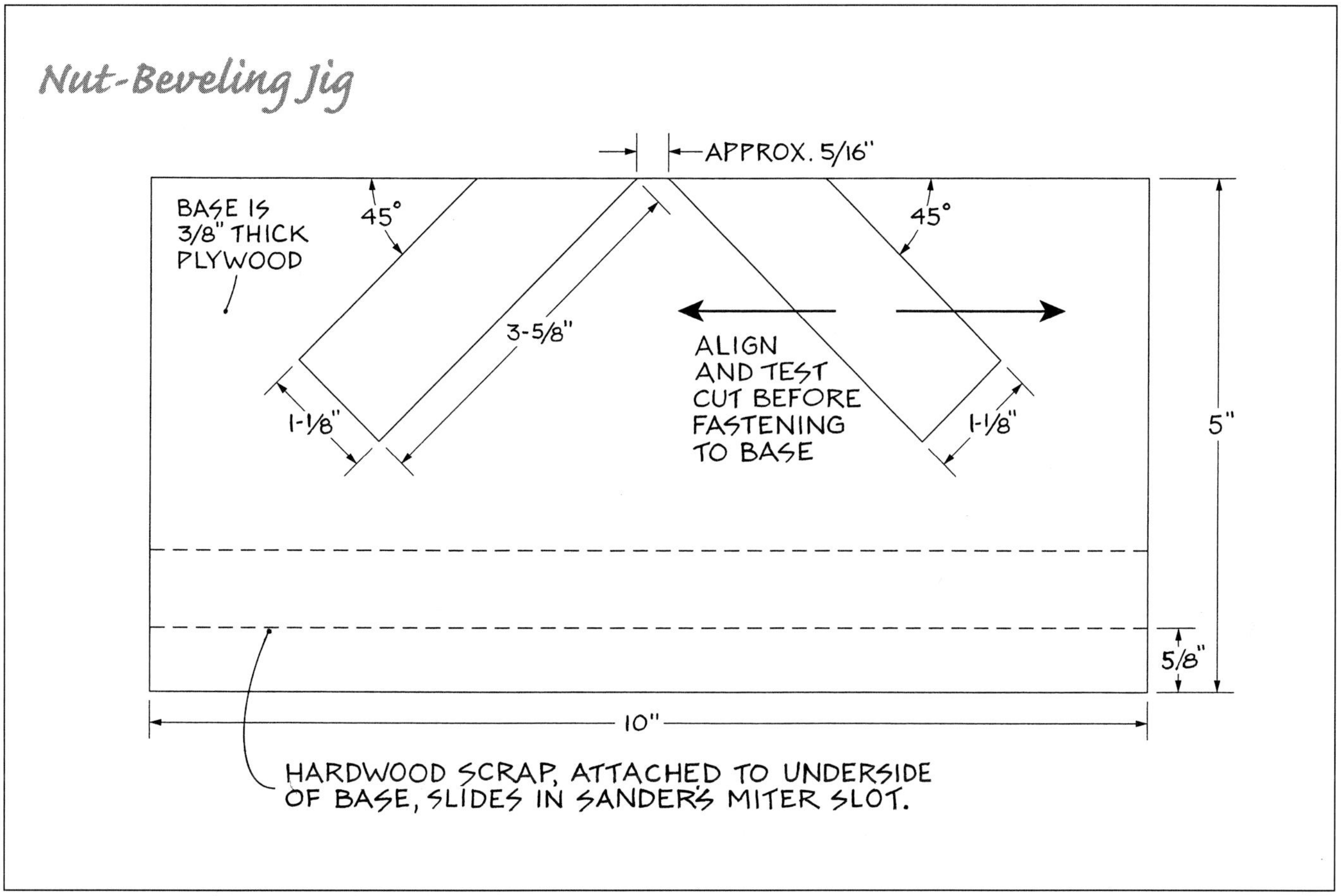

Nut-Beveling Jig

APPROX. 5/16"

BASE IS 3/8" THICK PLYWOOD

45°

45°

3-5/8"

ALIGN AND TEST CUT BEFORE FASTENING TO BASE

1-1/8"

1-1/8"

5"

5/8"

10"

HARDWOOD SCRAP, ATTACHED TO UNDERSIDE OF BASE, SLIDES IN SANDER'S MITER SLOT.

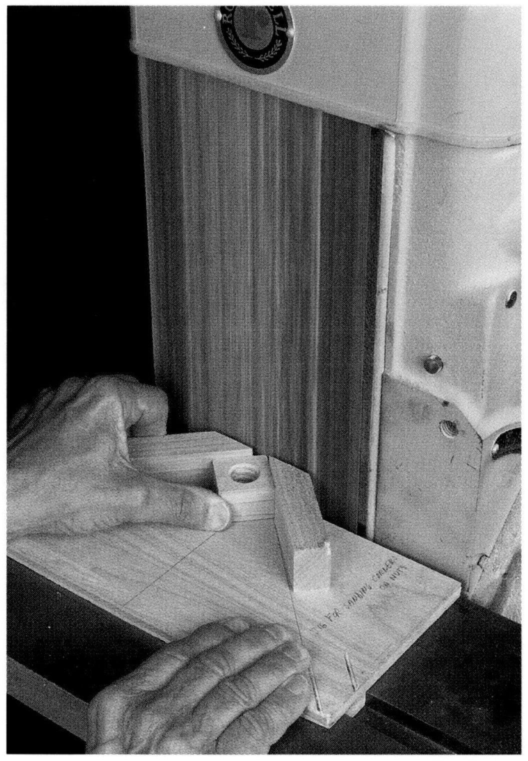

Photo K • *A beveling jig for a stationary belt sander gives you a consistent cut on all 12 edges of a square nut.*

chapter 4
HOUSES

The Houses system

incorporates a more elaborate application of the dowel stacking principle we encountered in the Boats system. In this one, various roofs, dormers, and elevation pieces are stacked alongside outdoor accessories such as trees, fences, hedges, and figures—including a small home for man's best friend—on a plywood base to form villages and complexes in any style from colonial to contemporary condo.

I actually got a lot of my ideas for this system down at the local diner, over coffee, looking through those illustrated real estate handouts and figuring out ways to combine basic design elements to suggest a wide range of architectural styles. The large number of parts in Houses makes for virtually limitless combinations, and in several months of developing the project and observing children play with it, I never saw the same house go up twice. The system's tremendous potential for engaging a

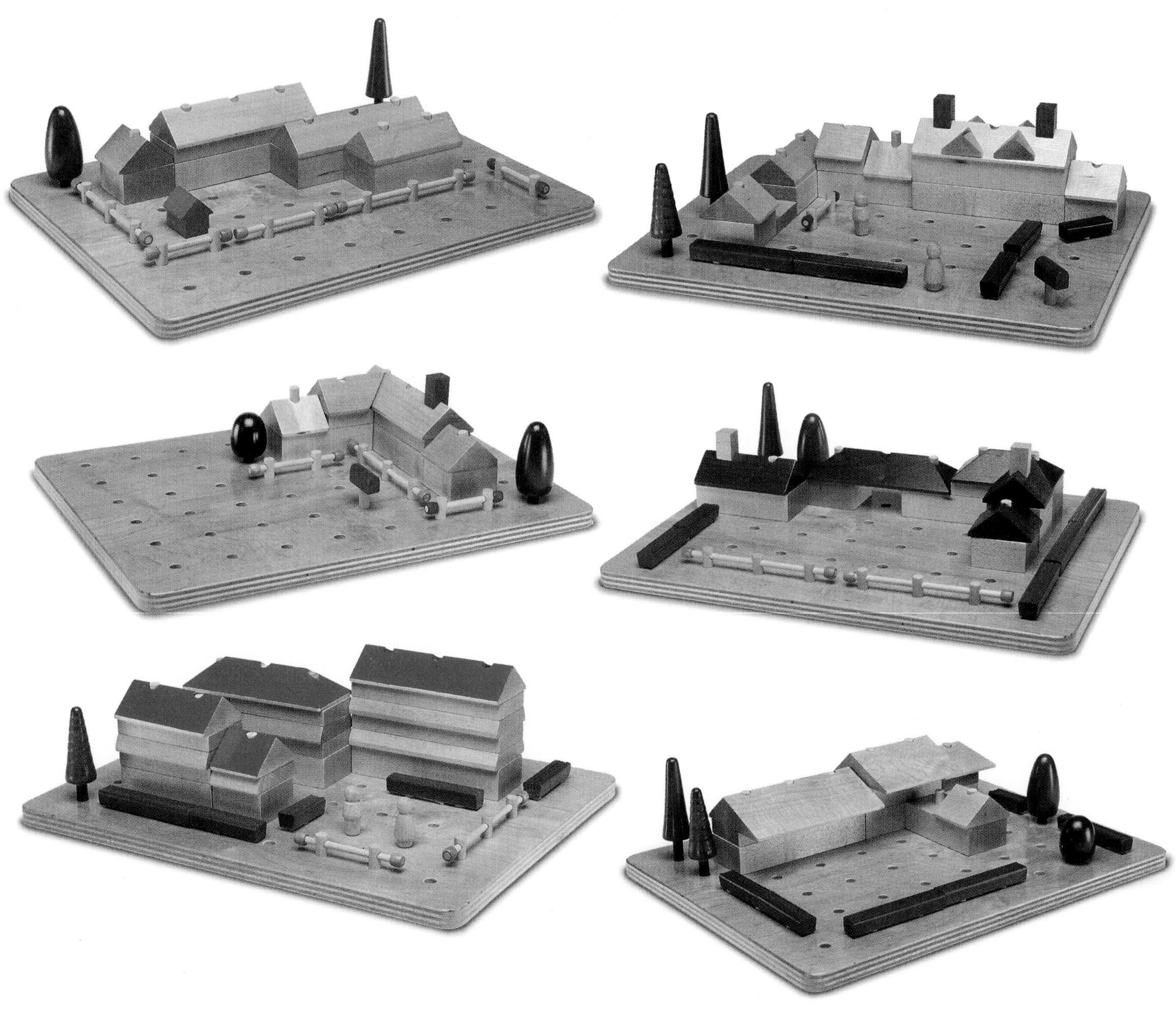

child's creative imagination has been recognized by *Parents' Choice* magazine, which gave it the Parents' Choice Award for high educational value.

Most of the pieces in the system are simple in shape and require only basic woodworking skills. The exception is the dormers, which demand special attention. It's essential that you follow the given sequence of steps carefully to make these small pieces in a safe manner.

FABRICATION OF COMPONENTS

BASIC HOUSE PARTS

PART	SIZE (IN.)	QUANTITY	MATERIAL
Some roofs may be made of walnut for contrast.			
Gable roof #1 (single)	$2\frac{5}{8}$ x $1\frac{7}{32}$ x $2\frac{1}{4}$	6	Maple
Gable roof #2 (double)	$2\frac{5}{8}$ x $1\frac{7}{32}$ x $4\frac{1}{2}$	4	Maple
Gable roof #3 (triple)	$2\frac{5}{8}$ x $1\frac{7}{32}$ x $6\frac{3}{4}$	4	Maple
Gable roof #4 (triple, for dormers)	$2\frac{5}{8}$ x $1\frac{7}{32}$ x $6\frac{3}{4}$	2	Maple
Gable roof #5 (double, for dormers)	$2\frac{5}{8}$ x $1\frac{7}{32}$ x $4\frac{1}{2}$	2	Maple
Gable roof #6 (offset)	$2\frac{7}{16}$ x $1\frac{7}{32}$ x $2\frac{1}{4}$	2	Maple
(Gable roof #6 can also be made in the $4\frac{1}{2}$ and $6\frac{3}{4}$ lengths.)			
Gable roof #7 (half)	$2\frac{5}{8}$ x $1\frac{7}{32}$ x $3\frac{1}{4}$	2	Maple
Shed roof	$2\frac{1}{4}$ x $1\frac{7}{32}$ x $2\frac{1}{4}$	2	Maple
Saltbox roof #1 (double)	4 x $1\frac{7}{32}$ x $4\frac{1}{2}$	1	Maple
Saltbox roof #2 (triple)	4 x $1\frac{7}{32}$ x $6\frac{3}{4}$	1	Maple
Hip roof #3 (triple)	$2\frac{5}{8}$ x $1\frac{7}{32}$ x $6\frac{3}{4}$	4	Maple
Hip roof #2 (double)	$2\frac{5}{8}$ x $1\frac{7}{32}$ x $4\frac{1}{2}$	4	Maple
Hip roof #1 (half)	$2\frac{5}{8}$ x $1\frac{7}{32}$ x $3\frac{1}{4}$	1	Maple
Dormers (with $\frac{1}{4}$ pins)	$1\frac{3}{4}$ x $\frac{7}{8}$ x $1\frac{1}{16}$	4	Maple
(Pins to be cut from lengths of $\frac{1}{4}$ plastic rods.)			
Elevation #1 (single/full)	$2\frac{1}{4}$ x $1\frac{1}{4}$ x $2\frac{1}{4}$	4	Maple
Elevation #2 (double/full)	$2\frac{1}{4}$ x $1\frac{1}{4}$ x $4\frac{1}{2}$	4	Maple
Elevation #3 (triple/full)	$2\frac{1}{4}$ x $1\frac{1}{4}$ x $6\frac{3}{4}$	4	Maple
Elevation #4 (single/half)	$2\frac{1}{4}$ x $\frac{5}{8}$ x $2\frac{1}{4}$	8	Maple
Elevation #5 (double/half)	$2\frac{1}{4}$ x $\frac{5}{8}$ x $4\frac{1}{2}$	4	Maple
Elevation #6 (triple/half)	$2\frac{1}{4}$ x $\frac{5}{8}$ x $6\frac{3}{4}$	4	Maple
Eaves #1 (single)	$2\frac{3}{4}$ x $\frac{5}{8}$ x $2\frac{1}{4}$	2	Maple
Eaves #2 (double)	$2\frac{3}{4}$ x $\frac{5}{8}$ x $4\frac{1}{2}$	2	Maple
Eaves #3 (triple)	$2\frac{3}{4}$ x $\frac{5}{8}$ x $6\frac{3}{4}$	2	Maple

WORKING SMARTER

Although I've found it handy to use the fence and stop-block setup that I've made for drilling holes in the base, you needn't feel obligated to follow suit. A simple board with a block clamped to it will do the job, too.

BASIC COMPONENTS

Plywood base

I recommend three sizes for the base, which should be made of high-quality ¾-in. birch or maple plywood. The reach of your drill press (as well as your ambition) will determine which one's right for you.

The smallest (pictured in the plan drawing) is 10¼ in. by 12½ in., which will give you 20 stacking holes, four rows of five holes each. Any bench-type drill press should be able to handle the drilling operation for this one.

If you have a floor-model drill press, you'll probably want to go for the next size up, 19⅝ in. by 15⅛ in., which will allow 48 holes, six rows of eight holes each. You'll need to set up a custom table and fence, as indicated in photo A.

The largest base, which will accommodate a whole village, is 24 in. square and provides 100 holes. I'd recommend having a commercial woodshop make one up for you should you decide on it.

To drill the stacking holes in the small or medium base, use the following sequence of steps.

Base

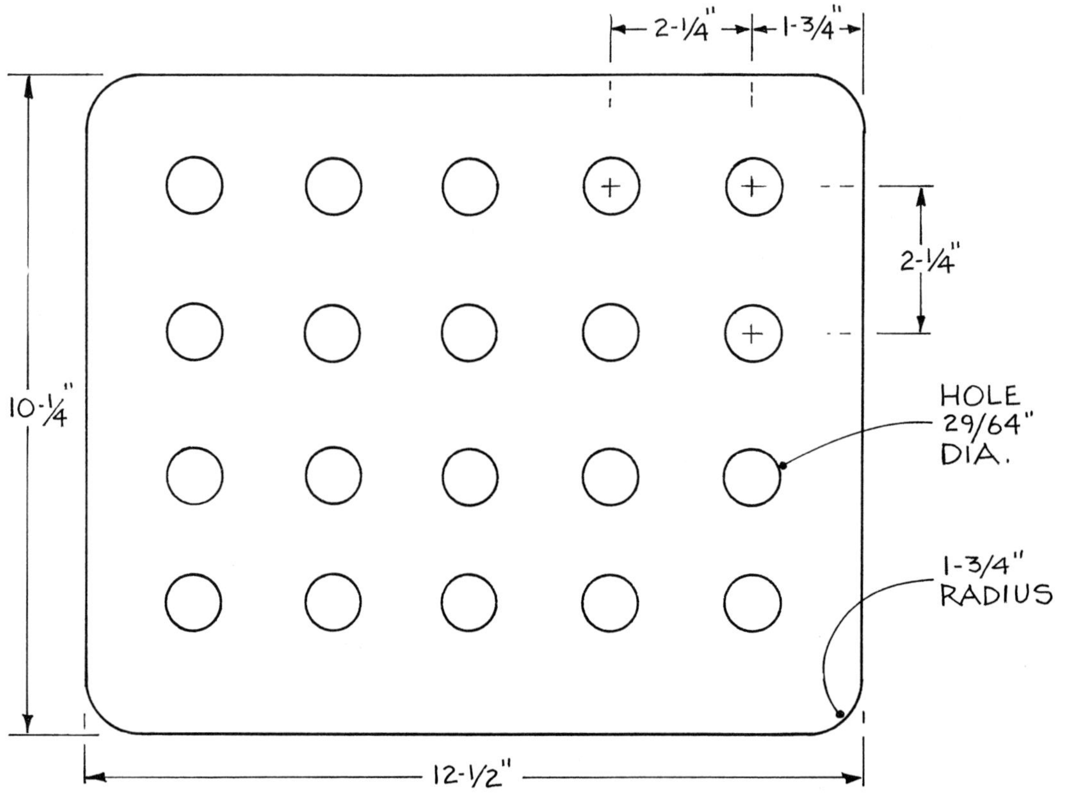

2-1/4" 1-3/4"
2-1/4"
10-1/4"
HOLE 29/64" DIA.
1-3/4" RADIUS
12-1/2"

Photo A • *A larger custom table-and-fence setup enables drilling the stacking holes in a medium-sized base on the drill press. Using the spacer blocks keeps the spacing of the holes consistent.*

1. Set up a fence with a right-side stop block on whichever drill press you are using. With one of the base's longer sides against the fence, use the center finder or a brad-point bit to position the setup for the center of the far left-hand corner hole. On the small base, this point will be $1\frac{3}{4}$ in. in from both the back and left side edges; for the medium-sized base, $1\frac{15}{16}$ in. in from both.
2. Drill the first stacking hole ($\frac{29}{64}$ in. in diameter, to receive a $\frac{7}{16}$-in. dowel). I recommend using a two-flute end mill (which will give you a nice hole with a flat bottom) and cutting to a depth of $\frac{5}{8}$ in., leaving $\frac{1}{8}$ in. of plywood. If you use a brad point or Forstner-type bit, the hole should be the maximum depth possible without breaking through the base's bottom.
3. Insert a $2\frac{1}{4}$-in. spacer block between the workpiece and stop block and drill the next hole. Repeat until the back row of holes is completed.
4. Rotate the board 180 degrees, which will position it for the right-hand hole in the new row. Drill the hole, remove a stop block, and repeat until this row is completed.
5. Reposition the fence/stop-block setup for the next row. Continue the process (including the 180-degree rotation of the board) until finished.
6. With a circle template or compass, lay out the rounded corners. I've used a $\frac{7}{8}$-in. radius, but whatever looks right to you is fine. Cut the curves on the bandsaw.
7. Sand the top edges of the base, or, if you wish, apply a minimal radius to them with a router.

Gable and hip roofs

Although the parts list specifies maple for all roof blanks, I've indicated walnut as an option for some of them to give a nice contrast. I also paint a few of the maple ones. See the end of the chapter for more on painting.

WORKING SMARTER

If you haven't used an end mill before, you should experiment with it first on scrap to get used to it. Since it doesn't have a center point to help guide its location, it has a different feel to it and the workpiece has to be clamped down.

Photo B • *Gable, hip, saltbox, and shed roofs provide a range of architectural styles. Chimneys and dormers add detail.*

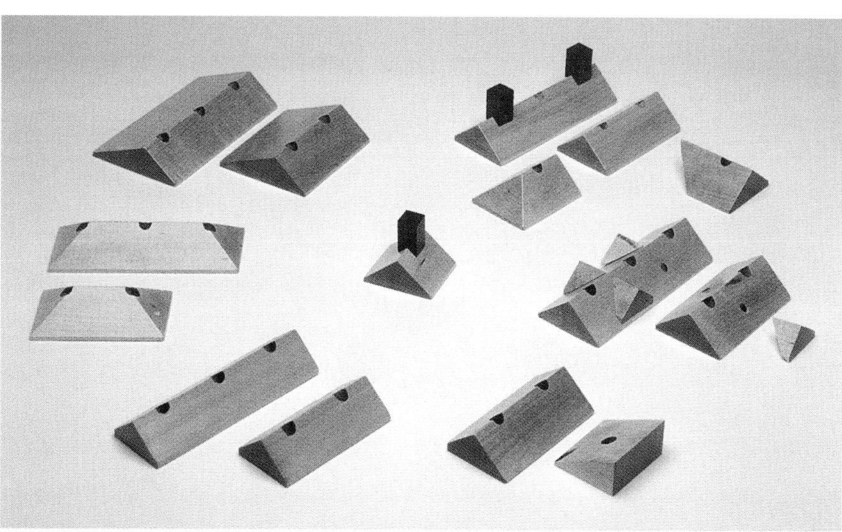

Gable Roof #7

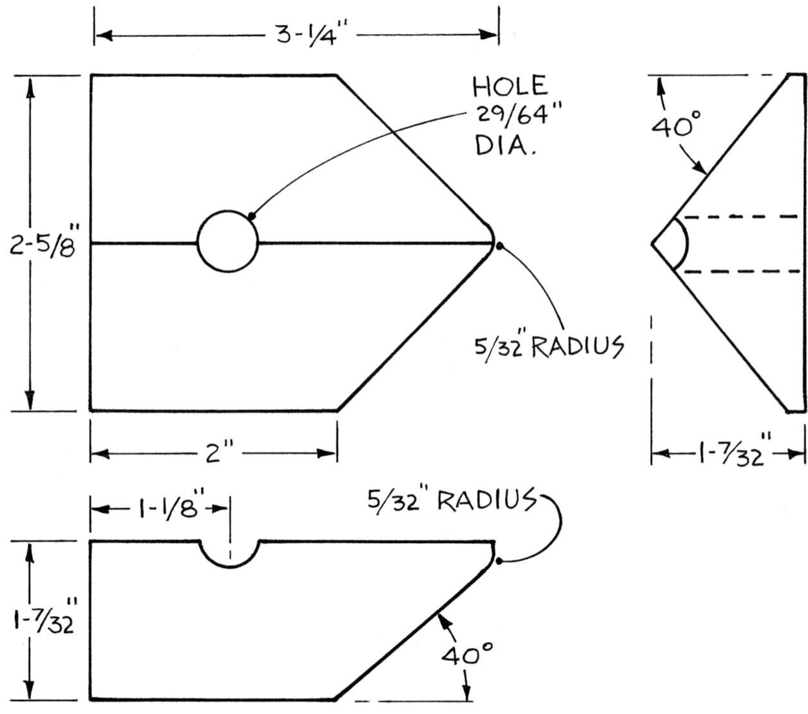
3-1/4"
HOLE
29/64"
DIA.
40°
2-5/8"
5/32" RADIUS
2"
1-7/32"
1-1/8"
5/32" RADIUS
1-7/32"
40°

Gable Roof #4

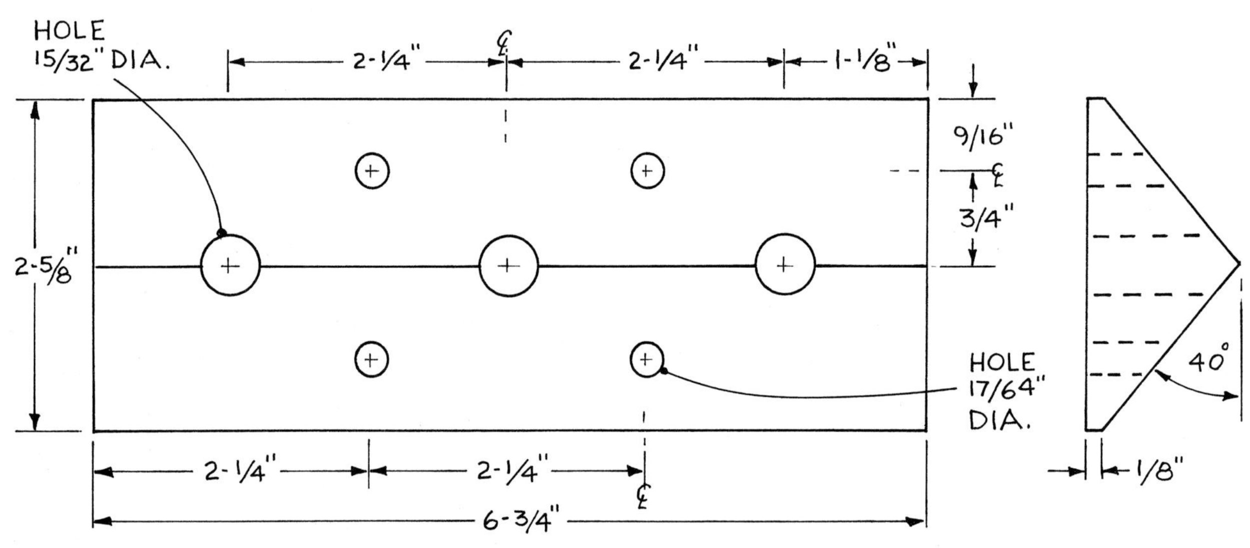
HOLE
15/32" DIA.
2-1/4"
2-1/4"
1-1/8"
9/16"
3/4"
2-5/8"
HOLE
17/64"
DIA.
40°
2-1/4"
2-1/4"
6-3/4"
1/8"

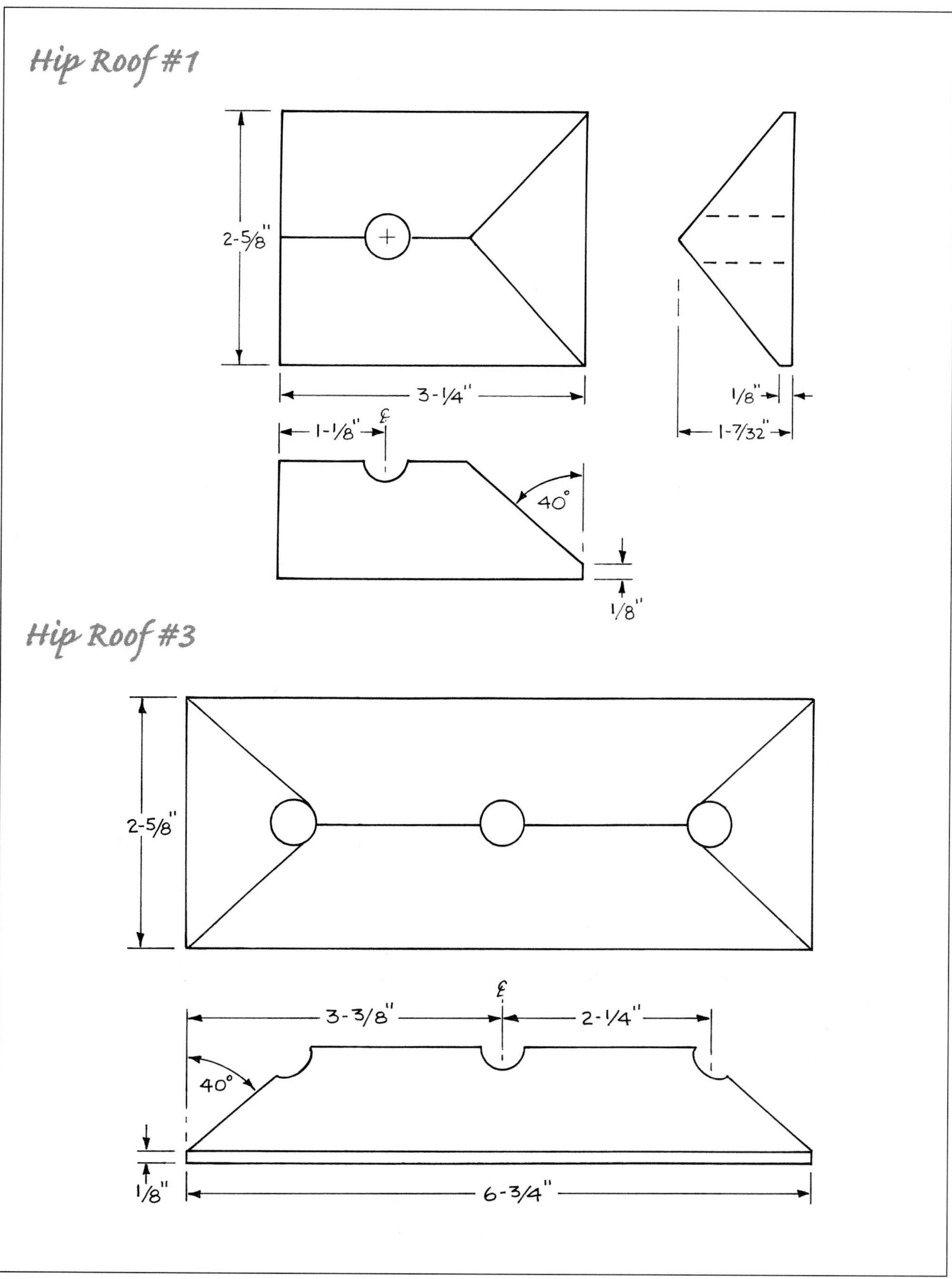
Hip Roof #1
2-5/8"
3-1/4"
1-1/8"
40°
1/8"
1/8"
1-7/32"
Hip Roof #3
2-5/8"
3-3/8"
2-1/4"
40°
1/8"
6-3/4"

Hip Roof #2

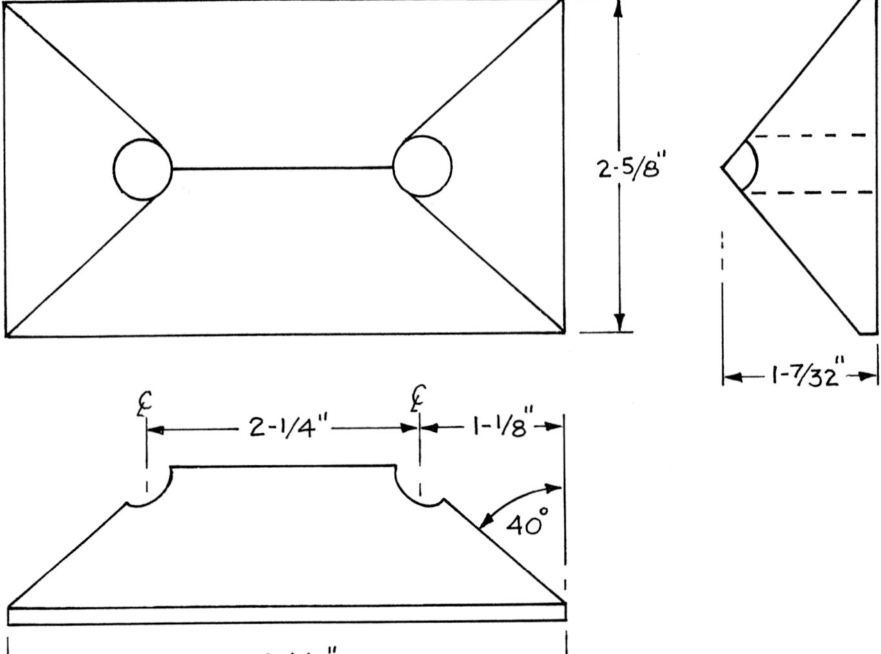

Gable Roof #3

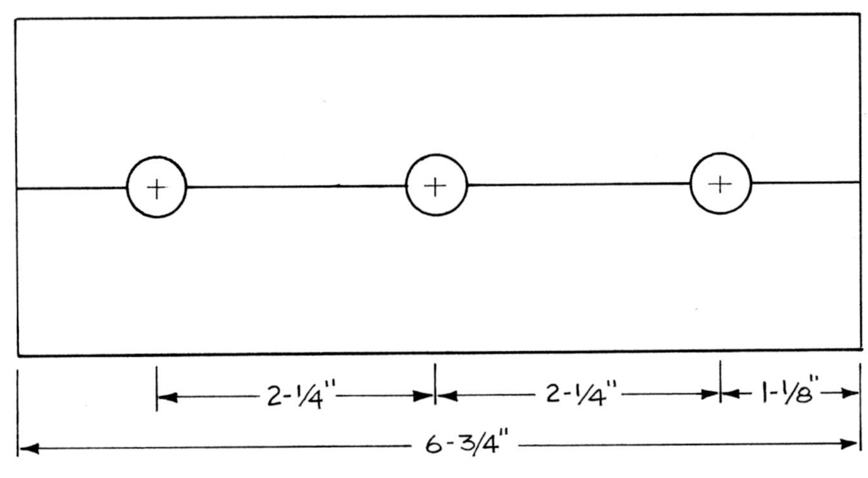

Gable Roof #2

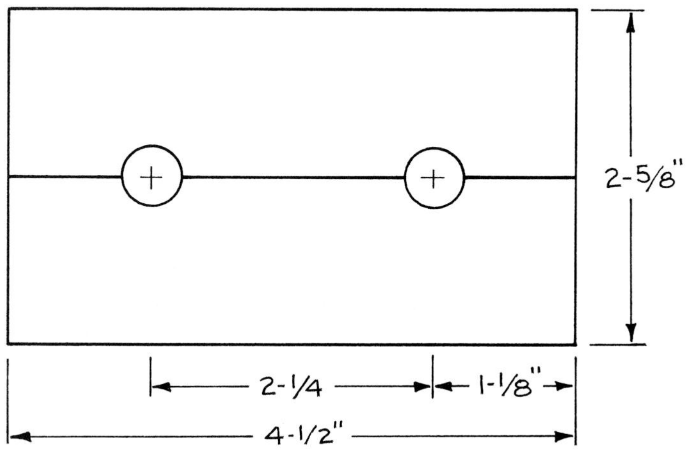

Gable Roof #1

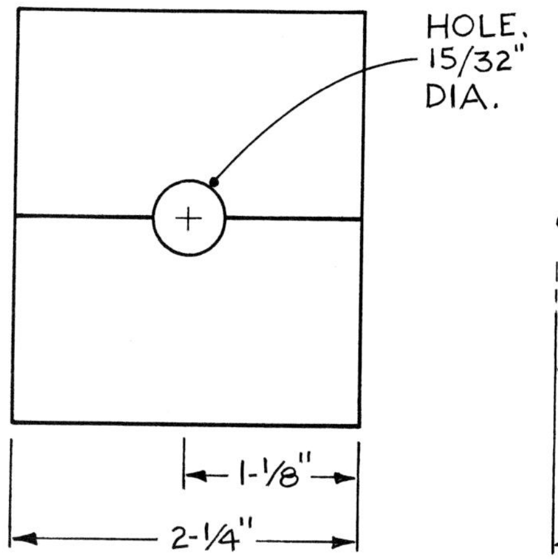

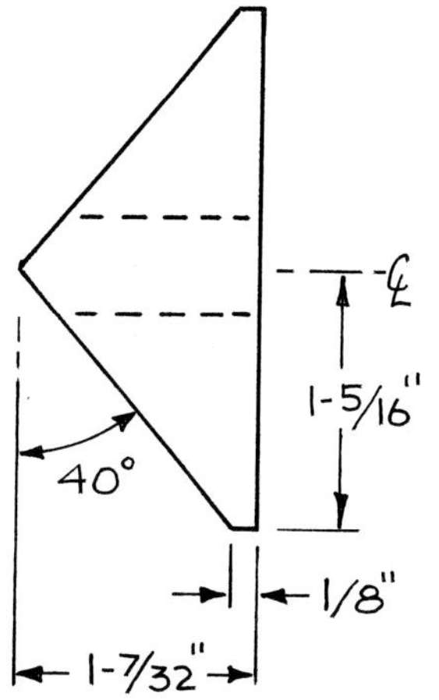

End View

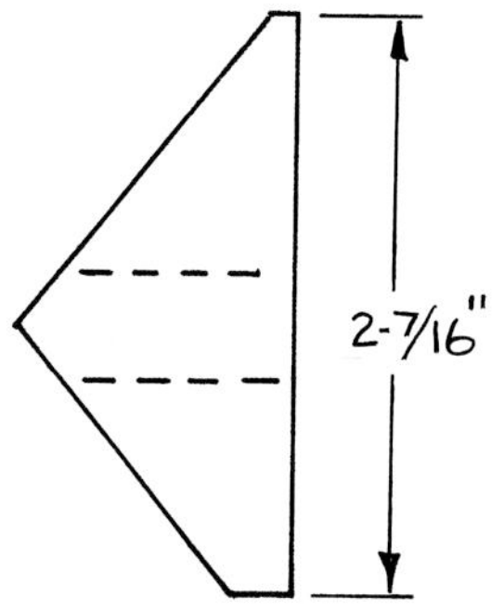

Offset Gable Roof End View

Cut all gable- and hip-roof blanks on the table saw to their final width of 2$\frac{5}{8}$ in., to a thickness of 1$\frac{9}{32}$ in. (oversize from the final dimension of 1$\frac{7}{32}$ in. to allow for sanding the ridge radius and any minor adjustments when cutting the roof angles), and to length as follows:

1. Cut hip roof #1 and gable roof #7 to their final length of 3$\frac{1}{4}$ in.
2. For the 6$\frac{3}{4}$ in. length, all other gable- and hip-roof blanks are cut to length with the miter gauge stop-block setup. For the 4$\frac{1}{2}$-in. and 2$\frac{1}{4}$-in. length pieces, insert one and then two 2$\frac{1}{4}$-in. spacer blocks.

Drill the $\frac{15}{32}$-in. roof-stacking holes, using the fence and stop-block setup on the drill press. Position for the end hole farthest from the stop block, 1$\frac{1}{8}$ in. in from the end and centered on the 2$\frac{5}{8}$ in. dimension. After drilling the first hole, insert a 2$\frac{1}{4}$-in. spacer block for subsequent holes in those pieces that have them.

Drill the $\frac{17}{64}$-in. dormer receiving holes in gable roofs #4 and #5, as indicated in the plan drawing.

Make the 40-degree end cuts on the two hip roofs, the half-hip roof, and the half-gable roof (#7), using the tenon attachment on the table saw (see photo C and the drawing p. 61).

To cut all the 40-degree pitch-roof angles, fasten each blank in turn to a block (preferably pine, easily gripped by the push bar) 2$\frac{5}{8}$ in. wide, about 1$\frac{1}{2}$ in. thick, and at least 6$\frac{3}{4}$ in. long, with double-sided tape. Set the table-saw blade for the 40-degree angle, and adjust the fence to give the workpiece a flat shoulder of approximately $\frac{1}{8}$ in., as in photo D. Simply turn the workpiece end to end to make the second cut.

Cut the offset gable-roof blanks (which are up to this point identical to #1, #2, and #3) down one side to a 2$\frac{7}{16}$-in. width,

Photo C • *A table-saw tenoning jig holds the roof blank securely in a vertical position to make the angled end cuts on the hip and half-gable roofs.*

Photo D • *An auxiliary block holds a roof blank securely on its side for the pitch angle cut, leaving a $\frac{1}{8}$-in. flat shoulder.*

leaving a higher shoulder on the cut side (see #6 profile in the plan drawing). This piece can be butted up against the side of another building. Note: Another option is to make some roofs like #6 but to then cut back the other side, too, bringing the width down to 2¼ in. These double offset roofs will fit onto the elevations with no overlap, so a series of them can be butted up for the look of a row of condos, or even a military camp.

Sand all the faces and edges. The bottom edges should receive minimal sanding, to maintain a clean look.

Saltbox roofs

The sequence of steps for these pieces is the same as above, including the use of an auxiliary block, which should be sized to the workpiece. The only difference is that the rather deep 22-degree angle cut, which produces the wider side of the rooftop, should be made in two passes—first with the blade set for a partial-depth cut and then raised to complete it. This avoids overloading the saw.

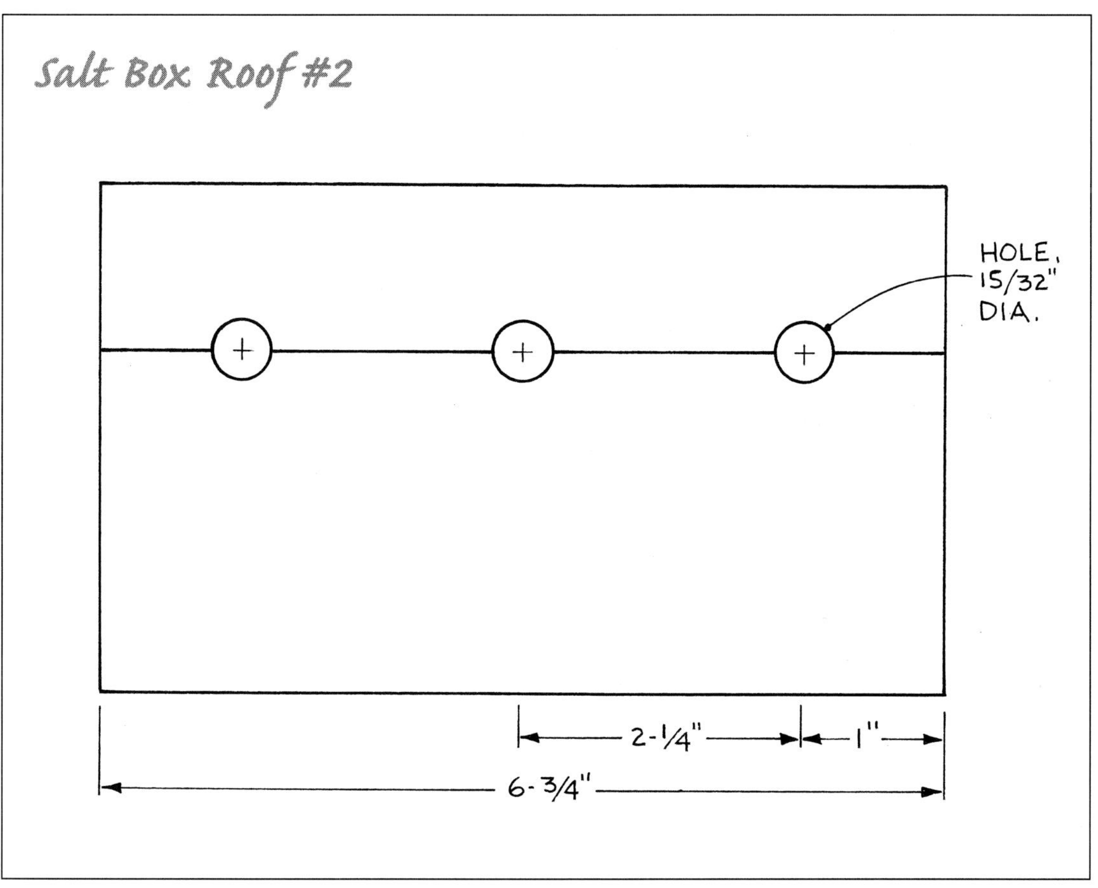

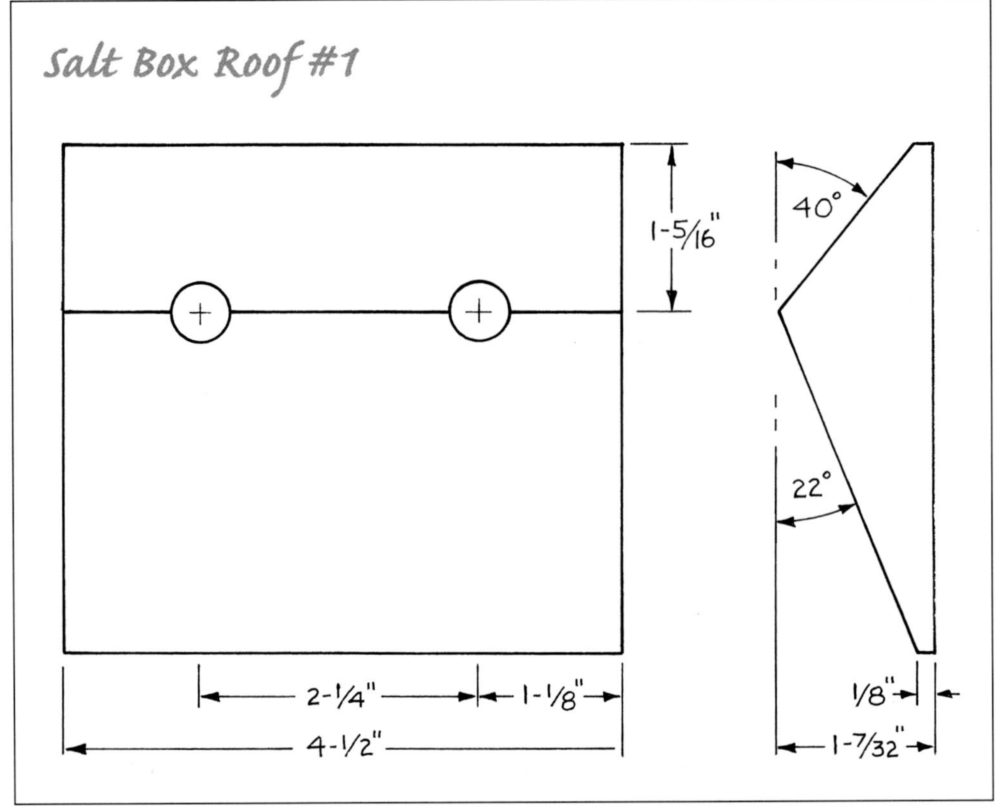

Shed roof

Again, the process is the same as above, except that the single-sided rooftop is produced by one 27-degree angle cut, with the workpiece fastened to an auxiliary block.

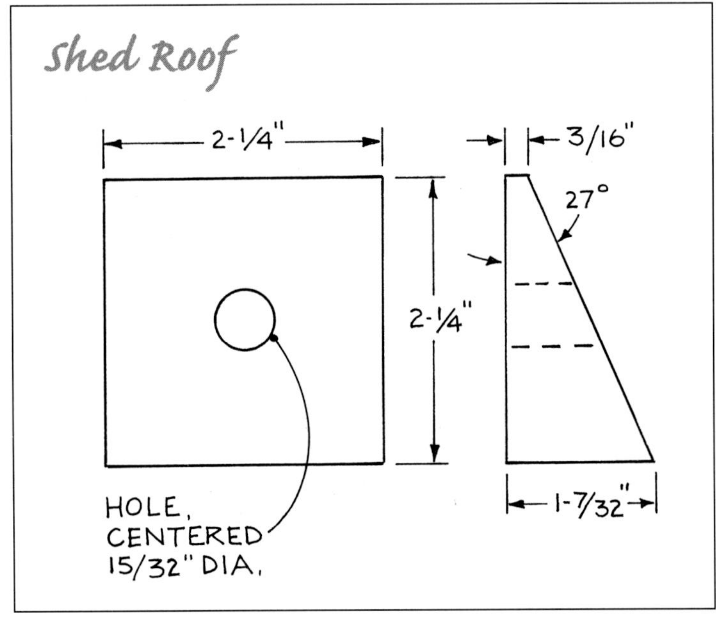

Elevations

The elevations are the blocks that provide the central mass of the houses when assembled.

These pieces are cut to their final dimension and drilled using the same spacer-block setups as for the gable and hip roofs. As before, all stacking holes are spaced 2¼ in. apart on the centerline, starting 1⅛ in. in from the ends.

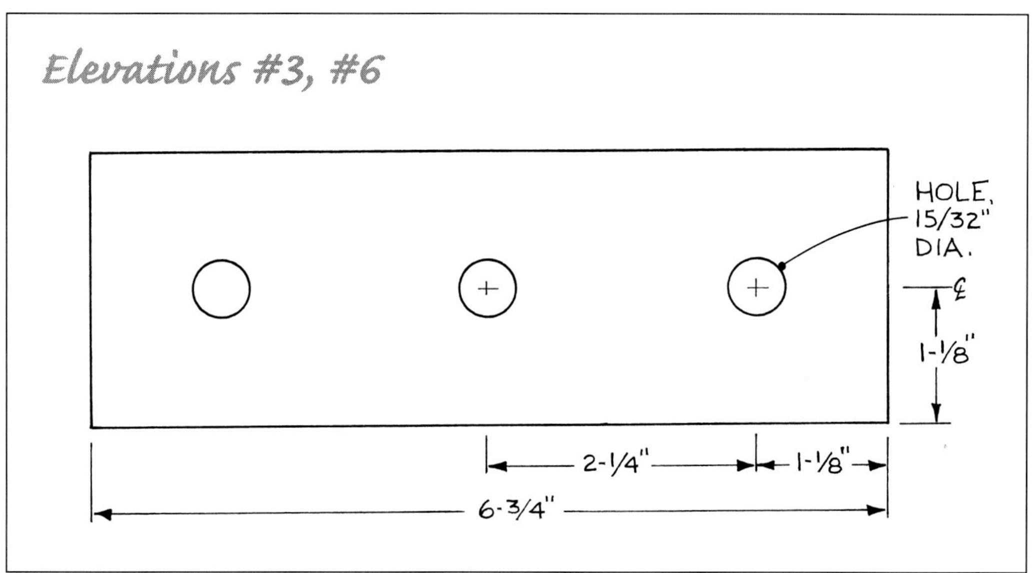

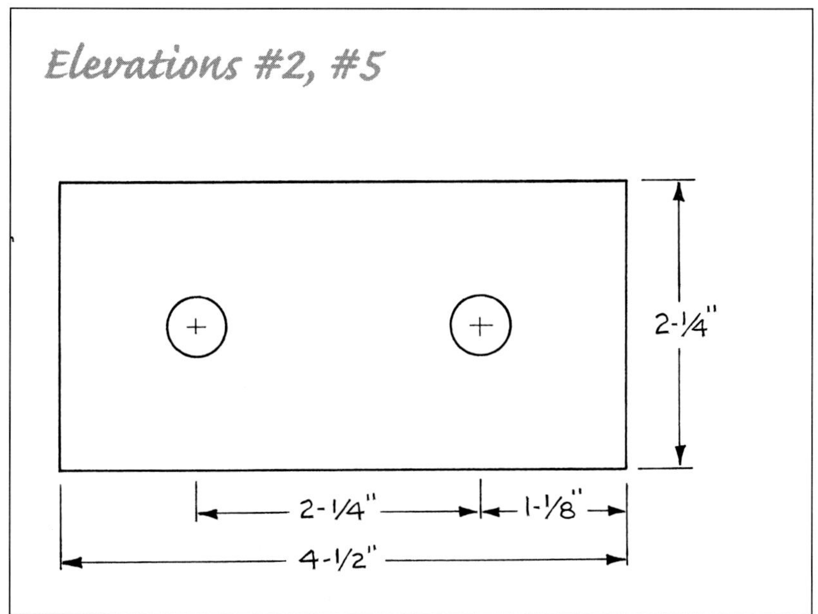

Photo E • *Elevations provide the structural mass of the houses—they act as the walls.*

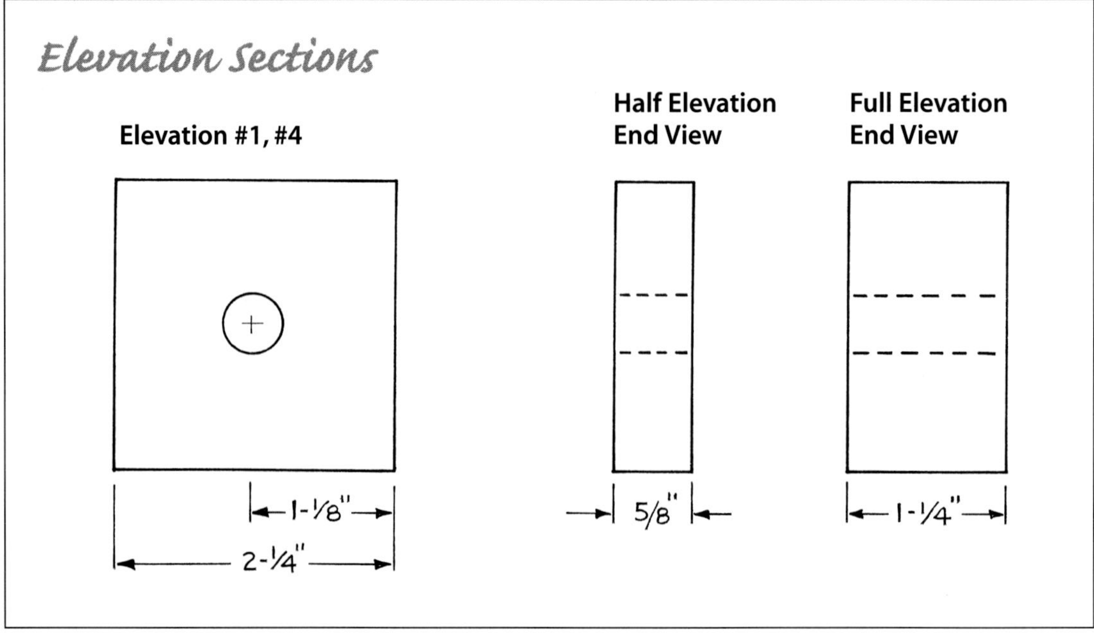

Eaves

The eaves, or flat roof pieces with an angled overhang, create a clearly delineated multilevel look, like that seen on motels and condos.

These pieces are cut and drilled in the same way as the elevations, with the addition of the 25-degree angle cut on the sides, which should be made on the table saw with the rip fence set to leave a shoulder of approximately 3⁄16 in.

Photo F • *Eaves can be stacked with the elevations to define floor levels.*

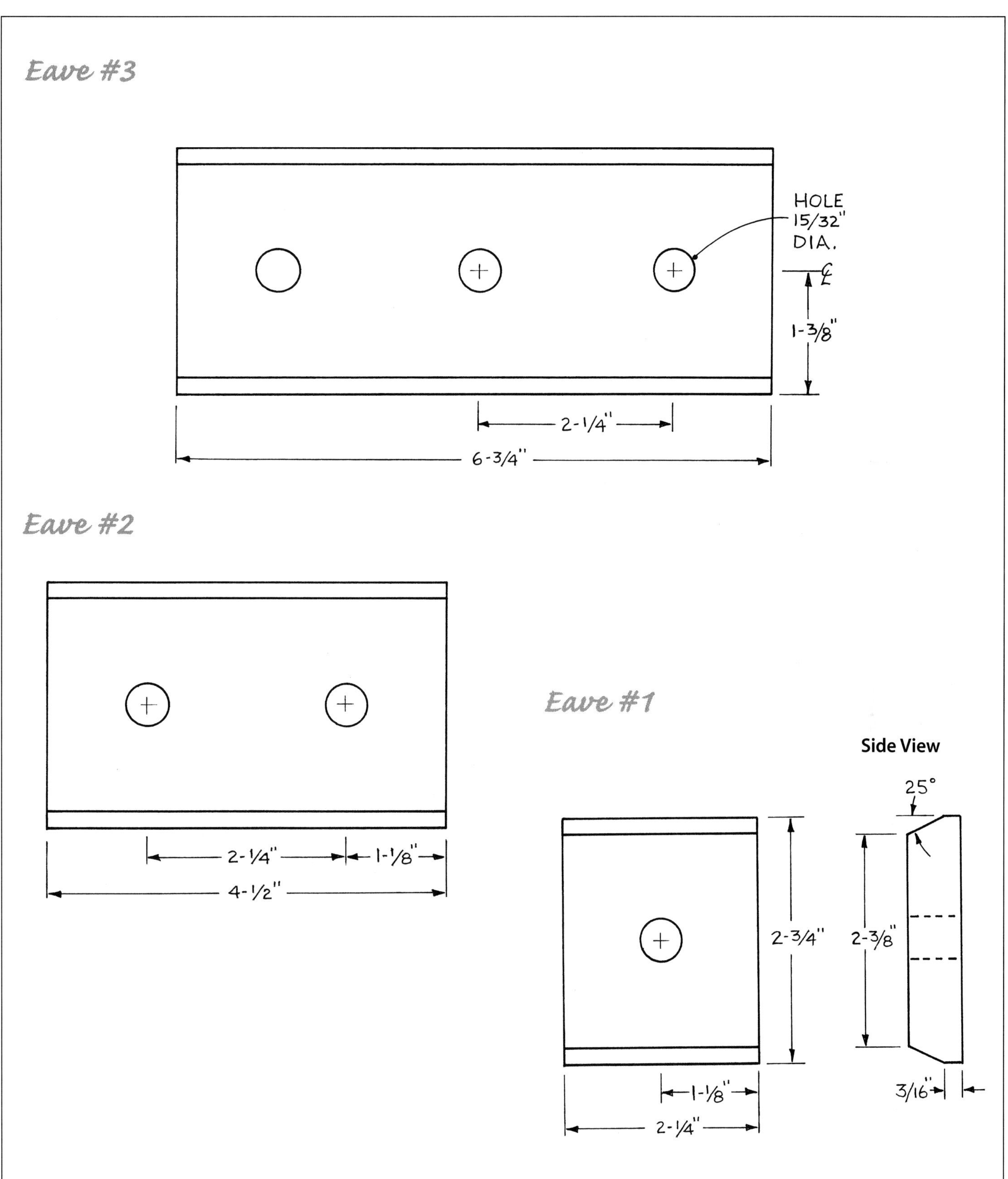
Eave #3
HOLE
15/32"
DIA.
1-3/8"
2-1/4"
6-3/4"
Eave #2
2-1/4"
1-1/8"
4-1/2"
Eave #1
Side View
25°
2-3/4"
2-3/8"
1-1/8"
2-1/4"
3/16"

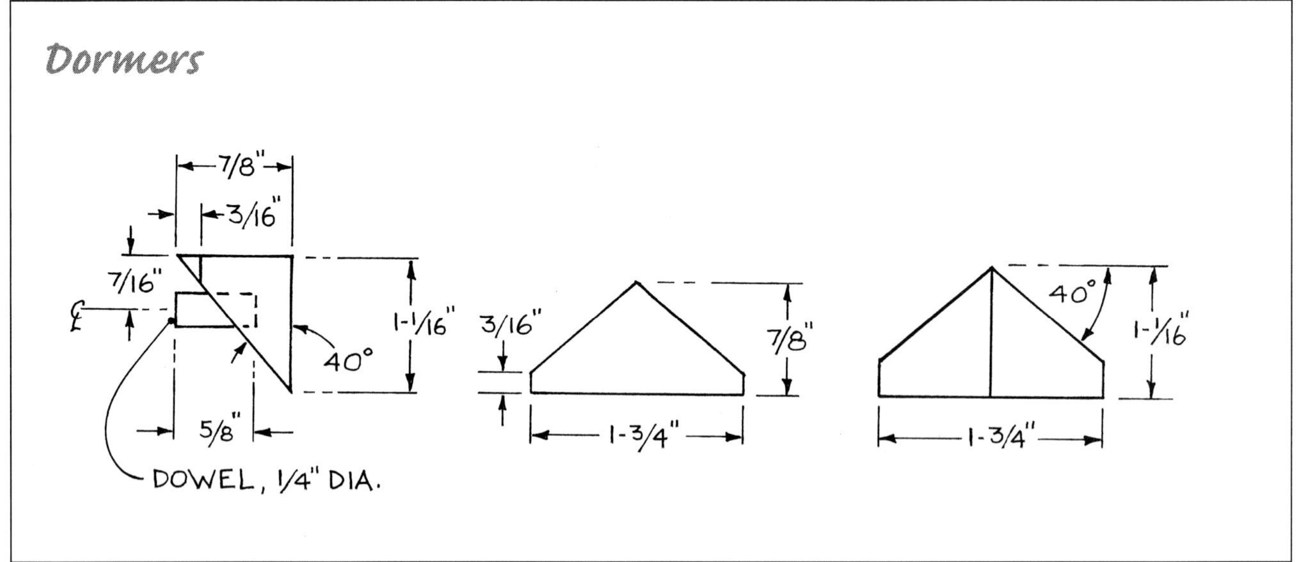

Dormers

Fabricating these pieces requires both patience and precision, so be sure to follow the sequence of steps, referring frequently to the photos.

1. Cut a blank 1¾ in. wide by approximately 12 in. long from a piece of 5/4 maple stock. The 5/4 dimension will yield the final ⅞-in. height of the dormers after the angle cuts are made.

2. Fasten the workpiece with double-sided tape to an auxiliary block 1 in. thick by 1¾ in. wide and approximately 12 in. long. Set the table-saw blade and fence to produce a 40-degree angle cut along the length of the workpiece, leaving a 3⁄16-in. flat shoulder at the base. Note that this is the same technique that was used to cut the lengthwise roof angles. Turn the workpiece end to end and repeat the cut.

3. Mill a piece of 5/4 poplar approximately 1¾ in. wide and 12 in. long (these dimensions aren't critical) to make a V-block cradle to receive the dormer workpiece.

4. To make the cuts for the sides of the V, set the table-saw blade at a 40-degree angle and lay out the V on the end of the cradle blank. Adjust the blade visually to be a little shy of the apex of the V. The cuts are made with the workpiece on its side, bringing the blade up to the correct height in subsequent passes (see photo G).

5. Tape the workpiece into this cradle, precisely flush at one end. From this end, measure in 7⁄16 in. and draw a line across the bottom of the workpiece at that point. Mark the center point of this 1¾-in. line.

6. On the drill press, adjust the table, fence, and stop-block setup to locate the center point on the 1¾-in. line with a ¼-in. brad-point drill bit.

7. Secure the assembly against the fence and stop block, and drill the partial-depth hole into the workpiece (see photo H). Reverse the workpiece in the block and repeat on the other end for the second piece. Be sure to leave the fence and stop block in place

Photo G • *With the blade set at 40 degrees, cut a V out of the center of the blank. Make the cut for the first side of the V in a couple of passes, bringing the blade up to the height of the apex.*

Photo H • *Set the drill bit visually for the depth of the holes in the dormer workpiece before clamping the assembly in place.*

after this operation, as the same setup should be used to make additional dormers.

8. Set up the table saw's miter gauge with a wooden auxiliary fence at a 50-degree angle. Remove the workpiece from the V block and make a reference mark on the roofline 1 1/8 in. in from each end.

9. Place the bottom surface of the workpiece against the auxiliary fence, with a 3/16-in. shoulder against the saw table. Visually align the mark on the roofline with the right side of the sawblade's kerf, mark the position of the near end of the workpiece on the auxiliary fence, and make the through cut (see photo I). The blade should emerge, leaving a small 3/16-in. shoulder on each side of the newly cut dormer. If it does, the pencil mark will indicate placement for subsequent cuts. If it doesn't, adjust the cut's entry point accordingly (and make a new pencil mark) for the next piece. This is a process of trial and error—the amount of shoulder isn't absolutely critical.

10. Turn the workpiece end to end to cut the next dormer.

Photo I • *Cut the completed dormers off the ends of the blank workpiece. Make sure the auxiliary fence is high enough to accommodate a through cut without jeopardizing its structural integrity.*

11. Cut the ends of the workpiece square, and repeat the drilling and cutting processes for additional dormers.

12. Glue the ¼-in.-diameter plastic pins into the dormers' holes with epoxy (the five-minute kind is fine). I use plastic, readily obtainable from hobby shops, rather than wooden dowels because the diameter is more reliable. However, I've found that there are some mail-order sources for accurately sized dowels, and if you'd like to go that route, you'll find them listed in Resources on p. 217.

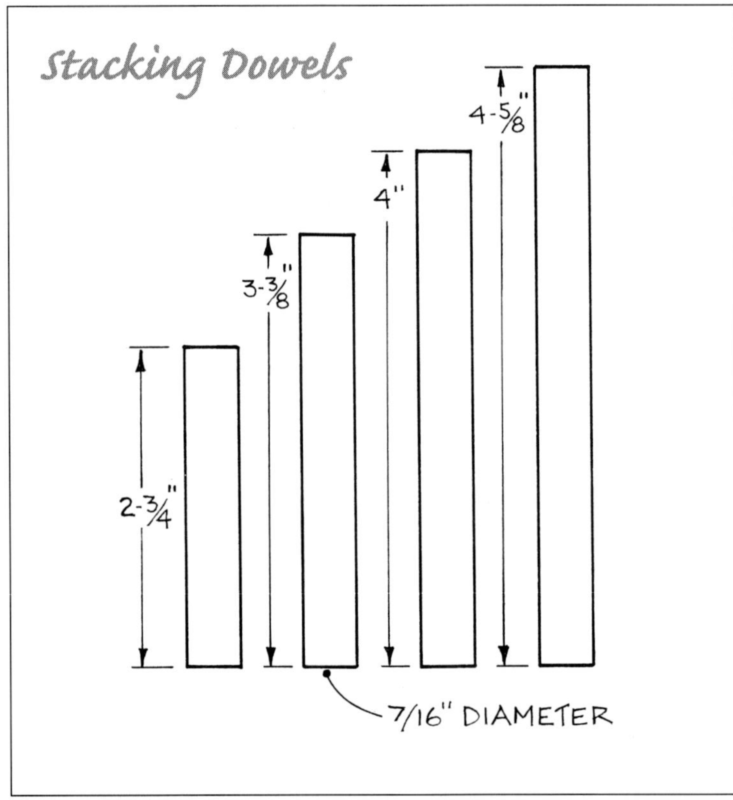

• SMALL PARTS AND SMALL CHILDREN

If it's likely that children 3 years old and under will play with this toy, some parts will need to be modified. The standard version of the Houses system involves a lot of small, loose stacking dowels that could be a choking hazard.

The solution is to glue the stacking dowels into the components, as done in the Ships system, and eliminate the base altogether. This requires having one set of elevations without any dowels, to serve as the bottom level. All the other parts will then have the dowels glued into their undersides. In order to incorporate the accessories into this version, all (except the doghouse) will have to be glued to small wooden bases to provide freestanding stability.

There's another benefit to this version: Without the imposed symmetry of the base, kids will often come up with some pretty innovative free-form city planning.

Stacking dowels

I use 7⁄16-in.-diameter dowels to stack and align the houses and roofs on the grid. The useful lengths are 2¾ in., 3⅜ in., 4 in., and 4⅝ in.

Photo J • *Accessories, including fences, trees, hedges, mailboxes, and people provide a sense of life and activity to the Houses system.*

FABRICATION OF ACCESSORIES

These parts provide the detail that really lets the imagination take hold. In addition, some of them can be painted to provide nice highlights and contrasting colors.

■ ACCESSORIES

ACCESSORIES	SIZE (IN.)	QUANTITY	MATERIAL
All accessories incorporate 7/16 dowels for insertion into the base; see plan drawing.			
Fence posts	1¼ x 3½, 4½, 6¾	2 each	Dowel
(Fence rails are made from ¼ dowel; end caps are ¼ handcrafted or commercial beads.)			
Figures	See plan drawing	1 each	Dowel
Single post hedge	1⅛ x ¾ x 2¼	As desired	Maple
Dual post hedge	1⅛ x ¾ x 4, 4½	As desired	Maple
Doghouse	1½ x 1⅜ x 1⅝	1	Maple
Mailbox (with post)	1½ x ⅝ x 2	1	Maple
Trees and bushes	See plan drawing	As desired	Dowel
Chimney	¾ x ¾ x ¼	As desired	Maple
7/16 Stacking dowels	Various lengths—see plan drawing		

Fence posts

1. Make a simple V block, with one end blocked off, sized to accommodate the 1¼-in. lengths of 7/16-in. dowel that will be used as fence posts.
2. Place one of the dowel lengths into the V block and position it against the drill-press fence and stop block to drill a 9/32-in. hole, centered 5/16 in. in from the dowel's end.
3. Clamp the block in place and drill the holes in all the posts.

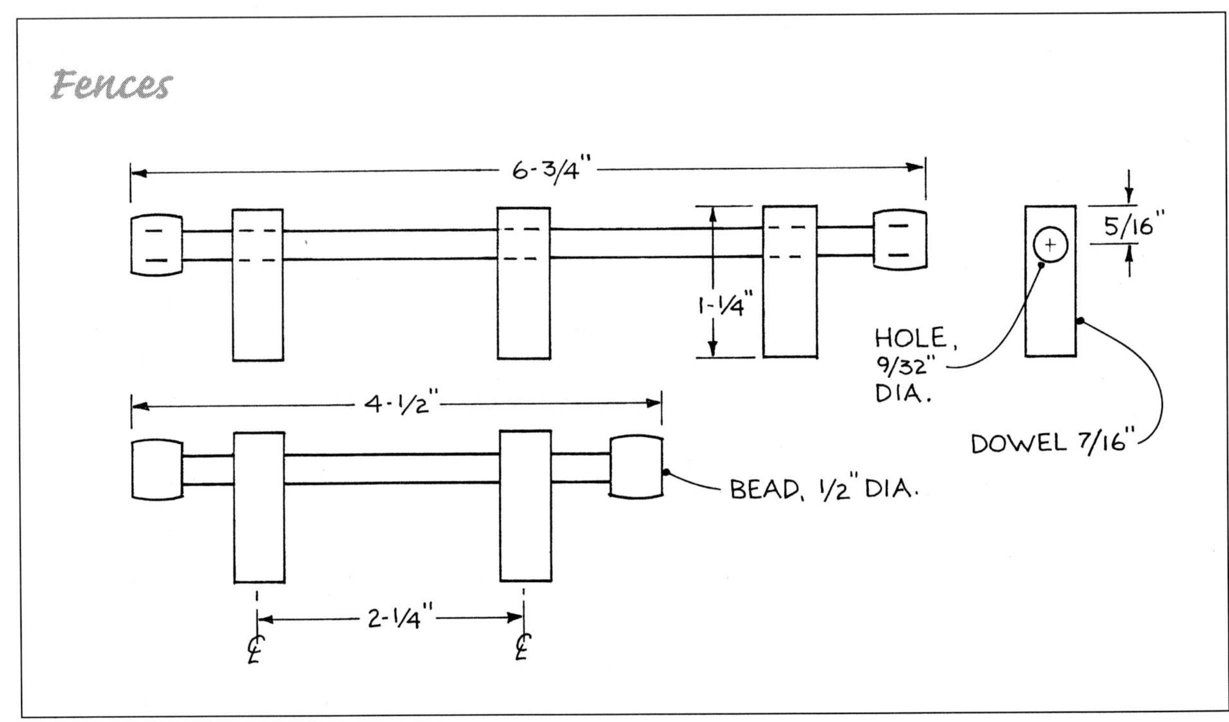

Fence rails

Dowels, ¼ in. diameter and in the three lengths indicated in the parts list, are used for the two- and three-post fences. Insert each dowel through the appropriate number of posts and glue a ¼-in. wooden bead to each end. The beads are commercially available, but you can also make your own by drilling a ¼-in. hole through a length of ½-in. dowel on the lathe and then cutting off appropriate lengths.

Hedges

Hedges can be made in whatever lengths you wish, as long as the stacking dowels are set 2¼ in. apart on center. I recommend single-post hedges 2¼ in. long, and dual-post hedges in lengths of 4 in. and 4½ in. All cuts, including the 5-degree side-angle cuts, are made on the table saw. The ridged surface of the hedge tops is created by a randomly spaced series of very shallow parallel cuts made with a thin blade set at a 30-degree angle (see photo K).

Bore the stacking holes into the bottoms of the hedge blanks as indicated in the plan drawings, and glue the ¾-in.-long, 7⁄16-in.-diameter stacking dowels in place.

Photo K • *Randomly spaced angle cuts on the table saw give the hedge tops their texture.*

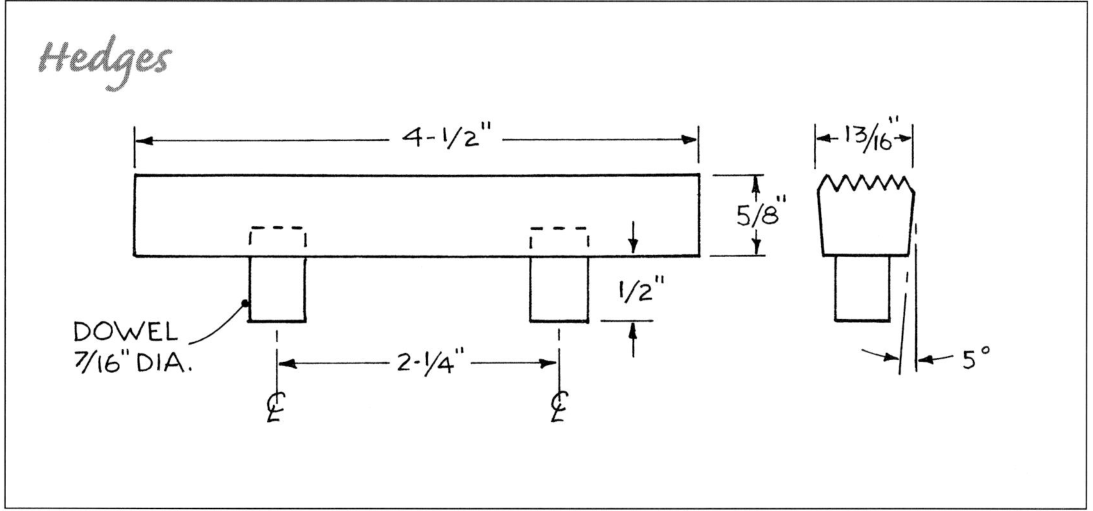

Chimneys

Several chimneys can be cut from a single blank in the following way:

1. Cut a maple blank 1¼ in. wide by ¾ in. thick by about 8 in. long. This will be enough for eight chimneys.
2. On the table saw, make a test cut partway through a piece of scrap wood with the same blade you will use to cut the individual chimneys from the main blank. Measure the kerf of this cut as accurately as possible.
3. Cut seven spacer blocks at a width of ¾ in. plus the width of the measured kerf.
4. Set up the drill press with fence and stop block, positioned to center the first 15⁄32-in.-diameter hole ⅜ in. from the end of the workpiece in the center of a ¾-in. side (see photo L).

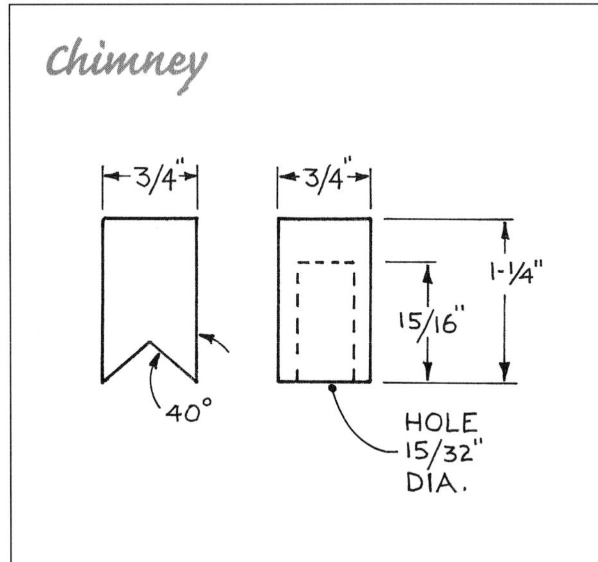

Photo L • *Spacer blocks are used to drill the chimney blank for the stacking dowels. The width of the saw cut for each individual chimney (drawn here on the workpiece) must be accounted for in centering the holes.*

5. Drill the hole 15⁄16 in. deep. Insert a spacer block and drill the next hole; repeat for all holes.
6. Set the table-saw blade at a 40-degree angle and make a lengthwise V cut into the bottom of a piece of scrap ¾ in. thick (the length and width aren't critical). This V should mate the peak angle of the roofs exactly, and the apex of the V should be clean. Getting the blade angle and height just right is another trial-and-error process.
7. When the setup is correct, make a lengthwise V cut in the drilled bottom of the workpiece, as in photo M. Lightly sand the bottom of the workpiece to take the sharpness off the two edges.
8. Set up the miter gauge with auxiliary fence and stop blocks on the table saw and, using the spacer blocks you used for drilling the stacking holes, cut the individual chimneys from the workpiece (see photo N).

Photo M • *The V cut in the bottom of the chimney block is made with the workpiece on its side, after the blade angle and height have been checked on a scrap block.*

Photo N • *The individual chimneys are cut from the workpiece using the same spacer blocks as for drilling the stacking holes.*

Trees and bushes

The trees and bushes are all turned from various-sized dowels, and the largest is 1½ in. in diameter. The drawings on p. 74 indicate shapes I've used, but feel free to improvise on them. The technique is to predrill the dowel lengths for the 7⁄16-in. stacking dowels on the lathe, as shown in the section "Boring out dowels" on p. 15. Then glue the appropriate length 7⁄16-in. dowel into the hole. Chuck the 7⁄16-in. dowel into the lathe for the turning operation.

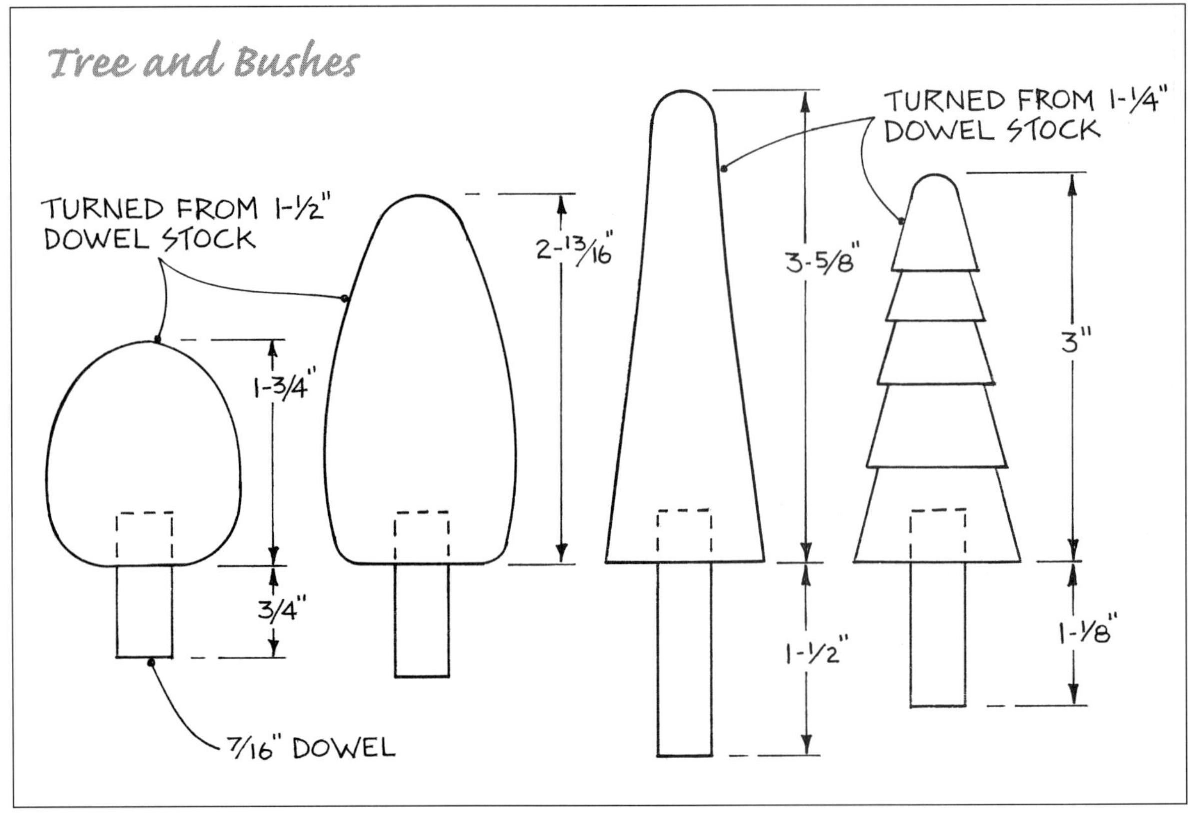

Figures

The technique here is the same as for the trees but uses ⅞-in. dowel lengths.

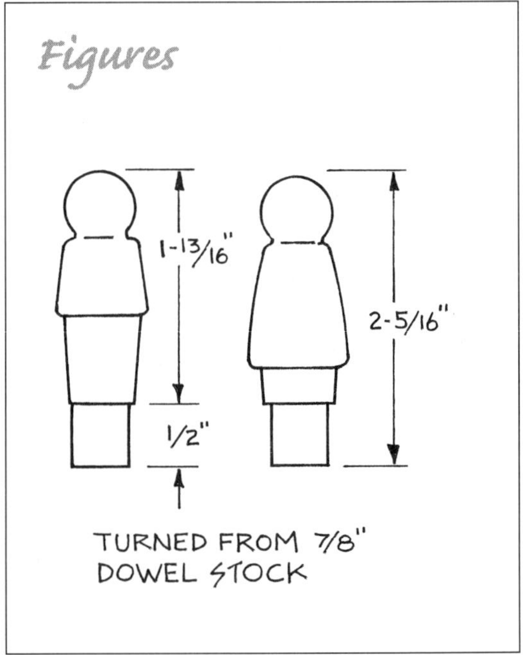

Doghouse

All cuts for this piece are made on the table saw.

1. Cut the workpiece to its overall block size as indicated on the plan drawing.
2. Drill the bottom 7/16-in. stacking hole for the stacking dowel.
3. Cut both sides of the gable roof at a 45-degree angle.
4. Make a cut about 3/16 in. deep on each side, just below the 45-degree cuts.
5. Make a vertical cut on each side to meet the 3/16-in.-deep cuts, leaving the roof with an overhang.
6. Glue in the 7/16-in. stacking dowel.

Mailbox

1. Cut the blank to the correct block size of 1½ in. by 11/16 in. by 5/8 in.
2. Locate and drill the centered 7/16-in. hole ¼ in. deep to receive the dowel.
3. Tape the bottom of the workpiece to an auxiliary block and sand the top on a stationary sander to visually match the curve indicated on the plan drawing. You can also use a radius gauge if you wish; the radius is approximately 5/16 in.
4. Glue in the 19/16-in.-long by 7/16-in. dowel.

PAINTING THE ACCESSORIES

You can brighten up the look of some parts of the Houses system nicely with a little judiciously applied paint. I use any good quality high-gloss, oil-based paint that's nontoxic when dry.

For the trees, bushes, and hedges, I use forest green. For the chimneys, mailbox, and some of the fence-rail beads, I use a nice red. I leave the mailbox post and some of the rail beads natural. The doghouse could be anything, but I've used bright blue for a little contrast.

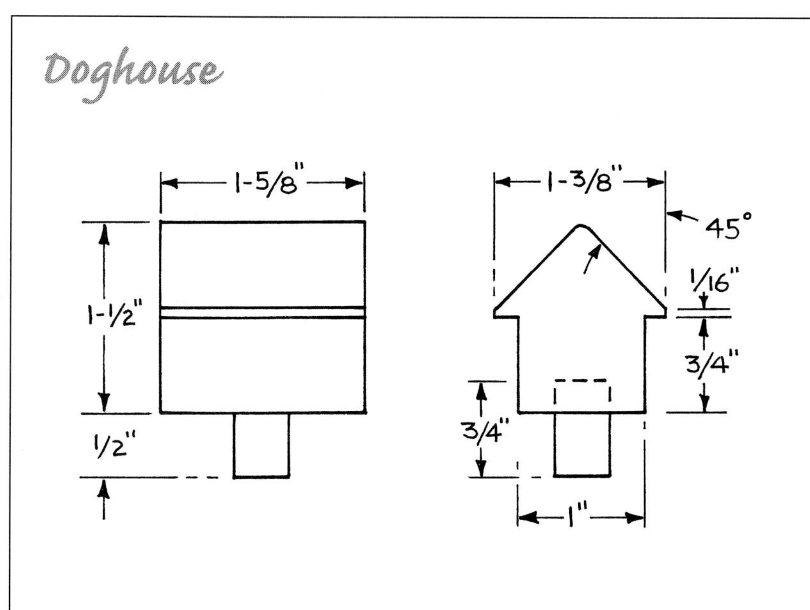

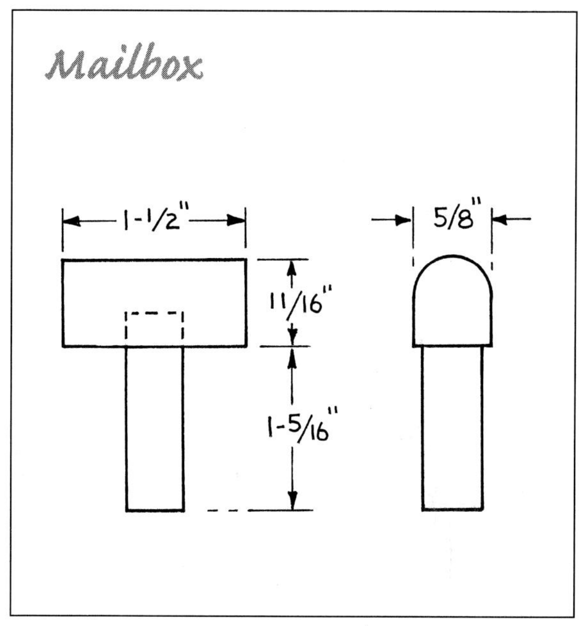

chapter 5
PLANES

The Planes system combines wooden nuts and bolts with friction-fittings (like those found in Tinker Toys) to attach a variety of elements to a generic fuselage, allowing the assembly of everything from a vintage biplane to a supersonic military jet.

The fuselage is also designed so that front and back parts can be reversed, enabling your young pilot to fly some uniquely fantastic creations in addition to the jetliners, seaplanes, and other recognizable types that are possible.

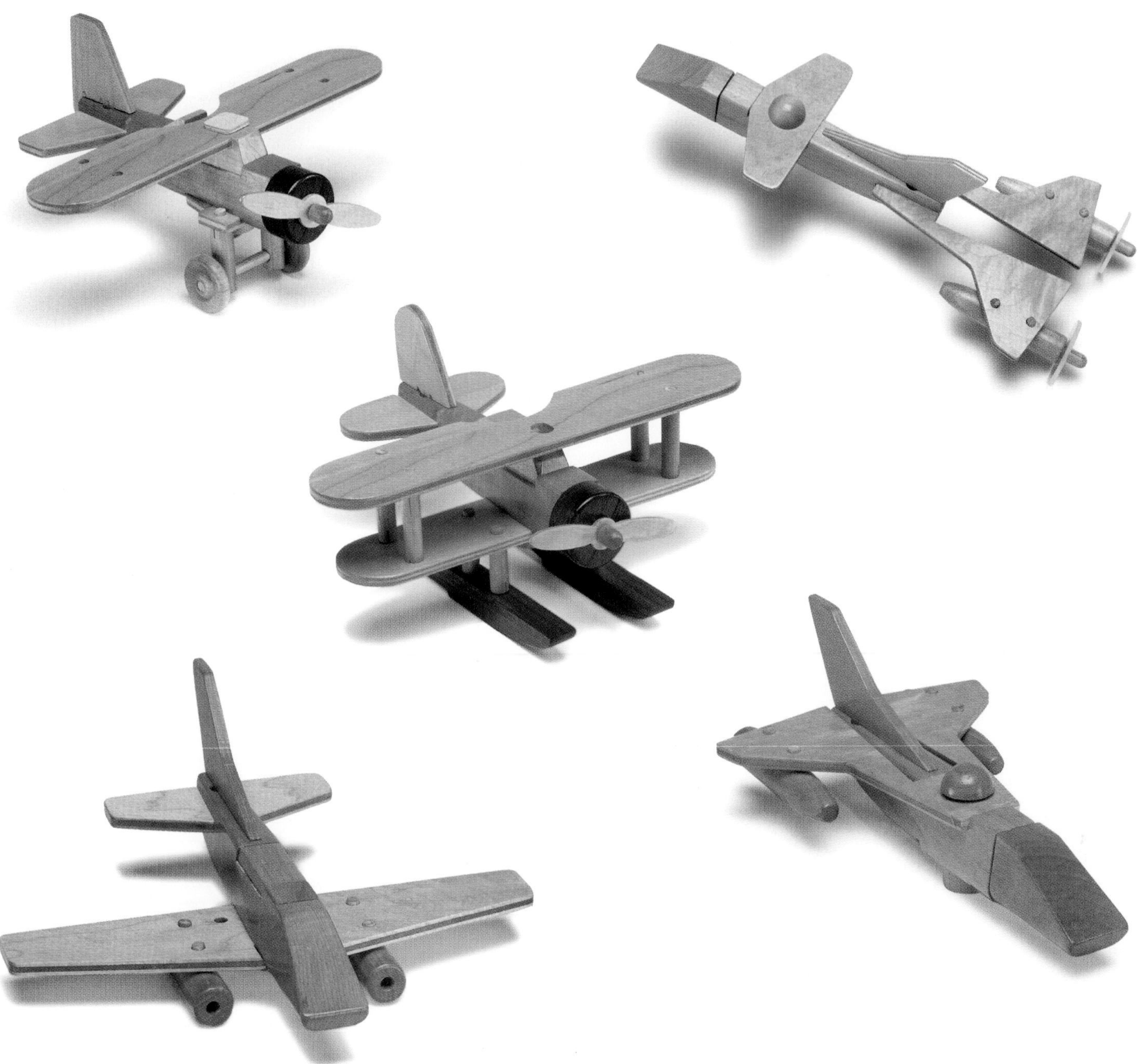

Photo A • *The reversibility of components makes for some combinations that Orville and Wilbur never dreamed of.*

FABRICATION OF COMPONENTS

■ FUSELAGE AND DELTA NOSE

PART	SIZE (IN.)	QUANTITY	MATERIAL
Fuselage	1 1/4 x 1 3/8 x 6 3/4	1	Maple
Delta nose	1 1/4 x 1 3/8 x 2 1/2	1	Maple
Bottom filler plate	1 1/32 x 1/4 x 1 7/8	1	1/4 maple plywood
Top filler plate	29/32 x 1/4 x 1 7/8	1	1/4 maple plywood

With its many angled parts, this project calls for considerable precision, and as we go along, I'll show you several jigs and fixtures that will ease the way.

■ FUSELAGE AND DELTA NOSE

I'm going to give you two construction methods for the fuselage and the delta nosepiece. Each has its pros and cons: You be the judge of which to use.

One way is to form the fuselage and nose as one piece, then separating them and drilling for the dowel that will again unite them. The advantage here is that the contours match perfectly, but to preserve that match after the separation, you need to be extremely precise about locating the hole in each piece.

The other way is to make the parts separately. This way, you can make up extra nose blocks and fall back on trial and error for aligning the two components.

Two-piece construction of fuselage

I'll give you the two-piece method first.

1. Cut the fuselage block to its final width of 1 3/8 in. and final length of 6 3/4 in. Cut the thickness to 1 5/16 in., which is 1/16 in. oversize to allow for adjustments further along.
2. Lay out the top and side views on the workpiece.
3. Draw two lines across the top of the workpiece, one 1 13/16 in. from the front end, the other 15/16 in. from the back end. Mark the center point of each line, locate these points on the drill press, and drill the two 13/32-in. through holes.
4. Locate the center point of the front view of the fuselage (the 1 3/8 in. by 1 5/16 in. surface).
5. With the workpiece clamped in the vertical position to an auxiliary fence on the drill press, position for this point and drill a 3/8-in.-diameter hole approximately 9/16 in. deep, as in photo B.

Photo B • *A clamp holds the fuselage workpiece securely upright for drilling the 3/8-in.-diameter hole.*

Fuselage and Delta Nose

End View

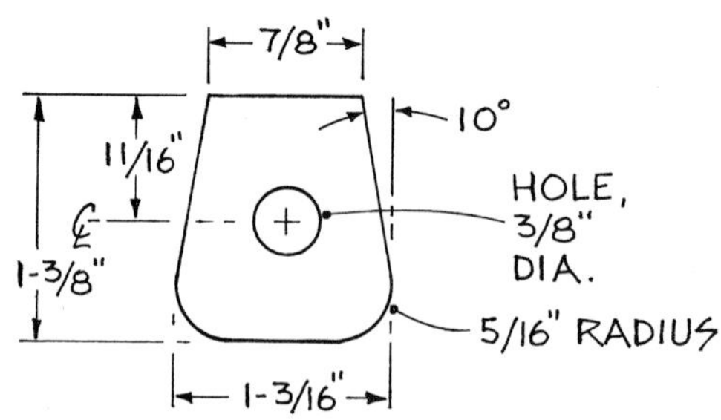

Side View

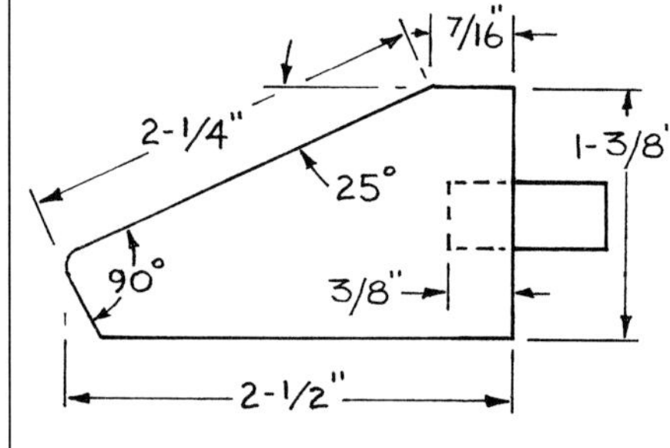

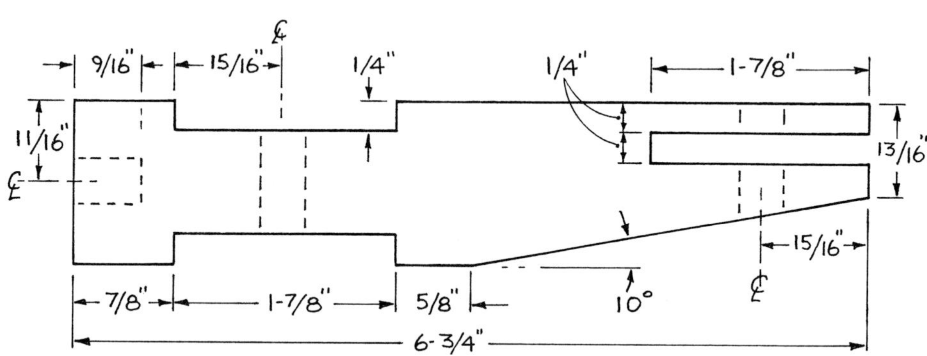

Top View

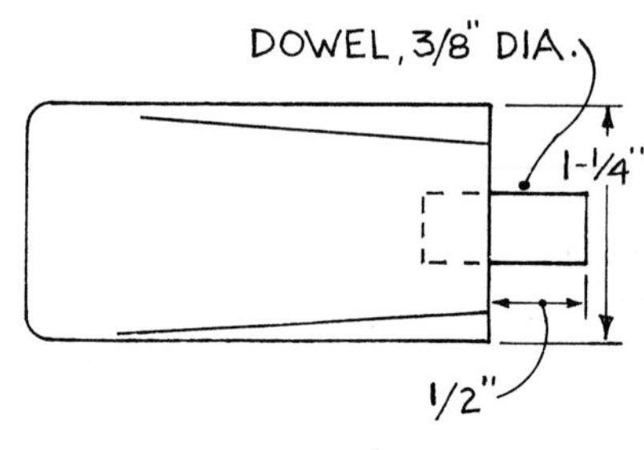

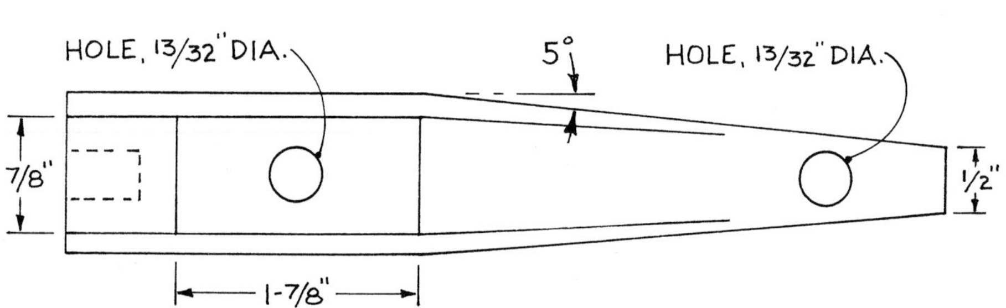

Two-Piece Fuselage Construction

1. DRILL HOLES IN FUSELAGE BLANK.

2. CUT TOP AND BOTTOM DADOES AND REAR SLOT.

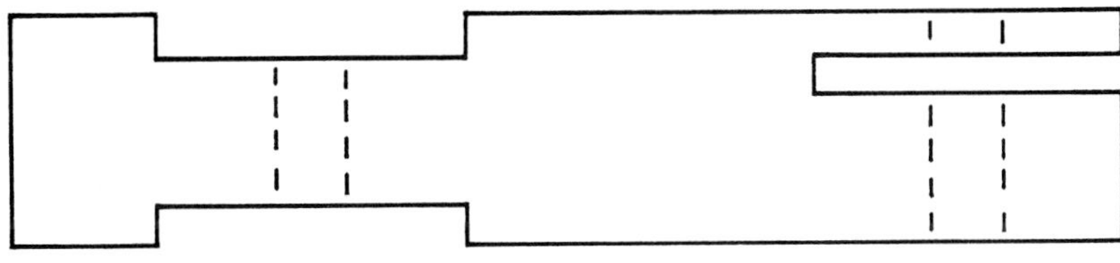

3. CUT REAR TAPER AT 10°.

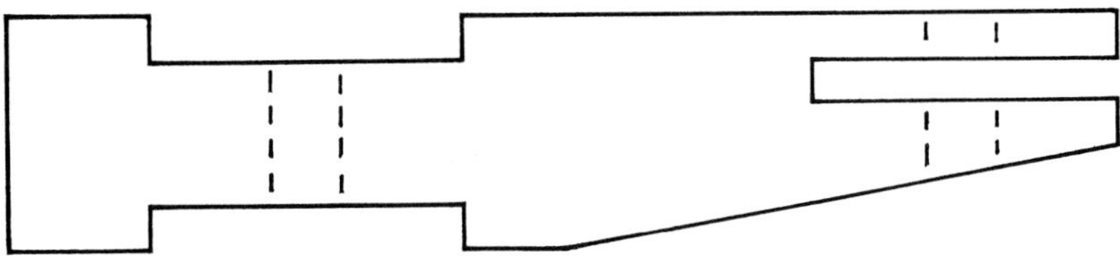

4. DRILL DOWEL ALIGNMENT HOLES IN NOSE BLOCK BLANKS AND FUSELAGE.

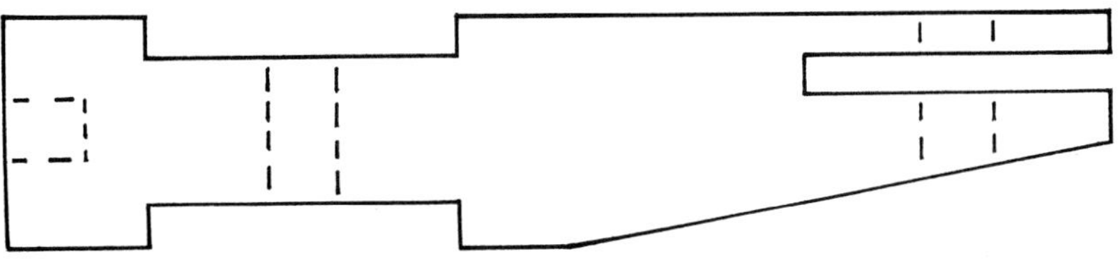

Fuselage Construction

5. CUT ANGLES ON NOSE WHILE POSITIONED ON FUSELAGE.

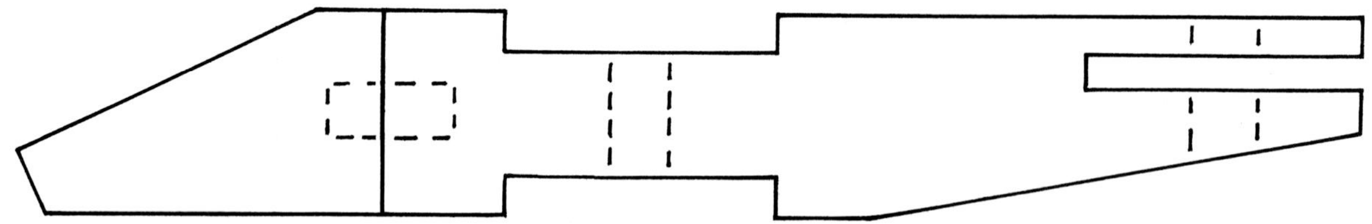

6. CUT 5° TAPER ON BOTH SIDES OF FUSELAGE AND NOSE.

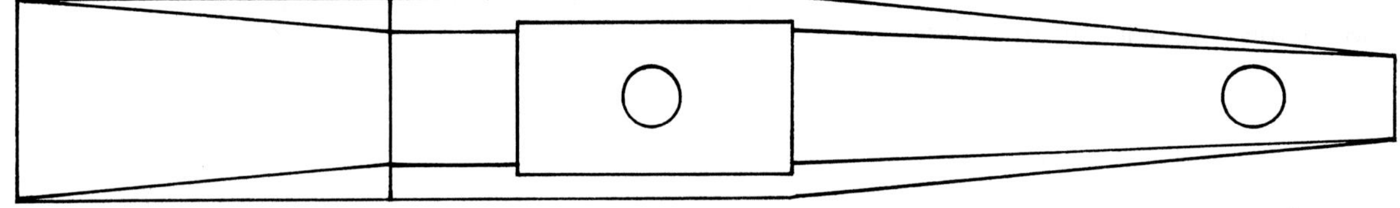

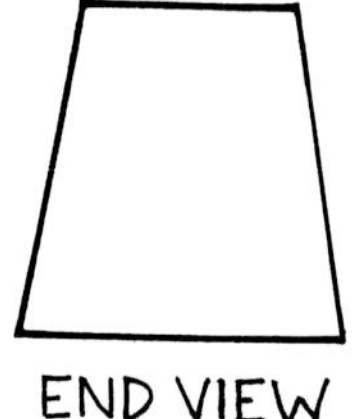

END VIEW

6. Cut the top and bottom dados on the table saw, 1/4 in. deep by 1 7/8 in. long, starting 7/8 in. back from the front end of the fuselage. I recommend using the auxiliary fence and stop block technique for this procedure.

7. Line up one of the end cuts (front or back) visually, set the stop block for that point, and make the cut. Flip the workpiece over for the corresponding cut on the other side. Repeat the process for the other two end cuts. The cuts to remove the remaining wood can be made freehand.

8. Using the tenon attachment on the table saw, cut the rear 1/4-in. by 1 7/8-in. slot, 1/4 in. from the top surface of the workpiece. The cut can be made with multiple passes of the regular blade.

9. Cut the bottom back taper approximately 10 degrees, using a simple angle-cutting jig (see photo C). For details on the construction of this type of jig, see the "Angle-Cutting Strategies" section on p. 13. If you've a steady hand, you can make this cut freehand on the bandsaw. Either way, save the cutoff piece; it'll come in handy in step #13.

10. Cut three delta nose block blanks, 1 7/16 in. by 1 5/16 in. by 2 5/8 in. These dimensions are all oversize to allow for adjustments in fitting the nose to the fuselage. You'll only need one piece, but the other two will allow for the trial-and-error process of alignment.

11. Drill a centered 3/8-in.-diameter hole approximately 3/8 in. deep into one of the 1 3/8-in. by 1 5/16-in. faces of a nose block blank. Check for alignment with the fuselage by inserting a short 3/8-in.-diameter dowel between the parts. If the alignment is correct, temporarily join the two parts using double-sided tape, with the dowel in place (see photo D). In this fashion we will shape the two as a single workpiece from this point on.

12. With the assembly held in a vertical position by the tenon attachment on the table saw (see photo E on p. 84), cut the top surface of the delta nose at a downward 25-degree angle, leaving a 7/16-in.-wide flat surface on top. Cut the bottom angle at 90 degrees to the 25-degree-angled surface, as indicated in the plan drawing, using the miter gauge with auxiliary fence.

Photo C• *A simple jig makes cutting the fuselage's bottom back taper an easy job.*

Photo D • *The contours of the fuselage and the delta nose must match when the two pieces are joined.*

Photo E • *The tenoning jig secures the workpiece for the top angle cut on the delta nose block.*

13. Affix the cutoff piece from step #9 back into position, aligned to the bottom surface of the fuselage, with double-sided tape. This will help stabilize the workpiece during the next cutting operation.

14. Cut the full length of both sides of the fuselage workpiece at a 10-degree angle on the table saw, leaving the bottom surface about 1 1/4 in. wide and the top 7/8 in. wide.

15. With the bandsaw table tilted for an outward 5-degree angle, make the rear taper cut on each side of the fuselage, starting from the rear end of the fuselage. The angle of this taper is approximately 2 1/2 degrees. It's important that the tail finishes at least 1/2 in. wide to provide sufficient support around the 13/32-in. through hole. Blend the back taper and angled side cuts with a sanding block.

16. If you have an overhead router, rout the bottom edges with a 5/16-in.-radius bit. If not, file and sand for the radius indicated in the front-view plan drawing. If you have a miniature spokeshave, that will do the job, too. Remove the cutoff piece and sand to blend all angles and radii.

17. Separate the fuselage and nose block and glue a 7/8-in. length of 3/8-in. dowel into the nose block.

One-piece construction of fuselage

1. Cut a single blank for the fuselage and delta nose block, 1 3/8 in. by 1 5/16 in. by 9 1/2 in. The length is oversize to allow for the later cut that will separate the two pieces.

2. Follow all the same procedures for the cutting and for the drilling of the two 13/32-in. through holes as in the first method.

3. Separate the nose block and the fuselage on the table saw.

4. Make a cross-section template to exactly locate and drill the centered 3/8-in.-diameter hole on the two pieces. The alignment is critical, but if it's just slightly off, sand the two parts to match.

5. Glue the 7/8-in. length of 3/8-in. dowel into the nose block.

Filler plates and filler-plate bolt

The filler plates fit into the dado areas on the top and bottom of the fuselage when another component is not filling the space. Wooden bolts secure these parts.

1. Cut both filler plates to size on the table saw. For the side bevels, set the blade at a 10-degree angle, as indicated in the plan drawing.

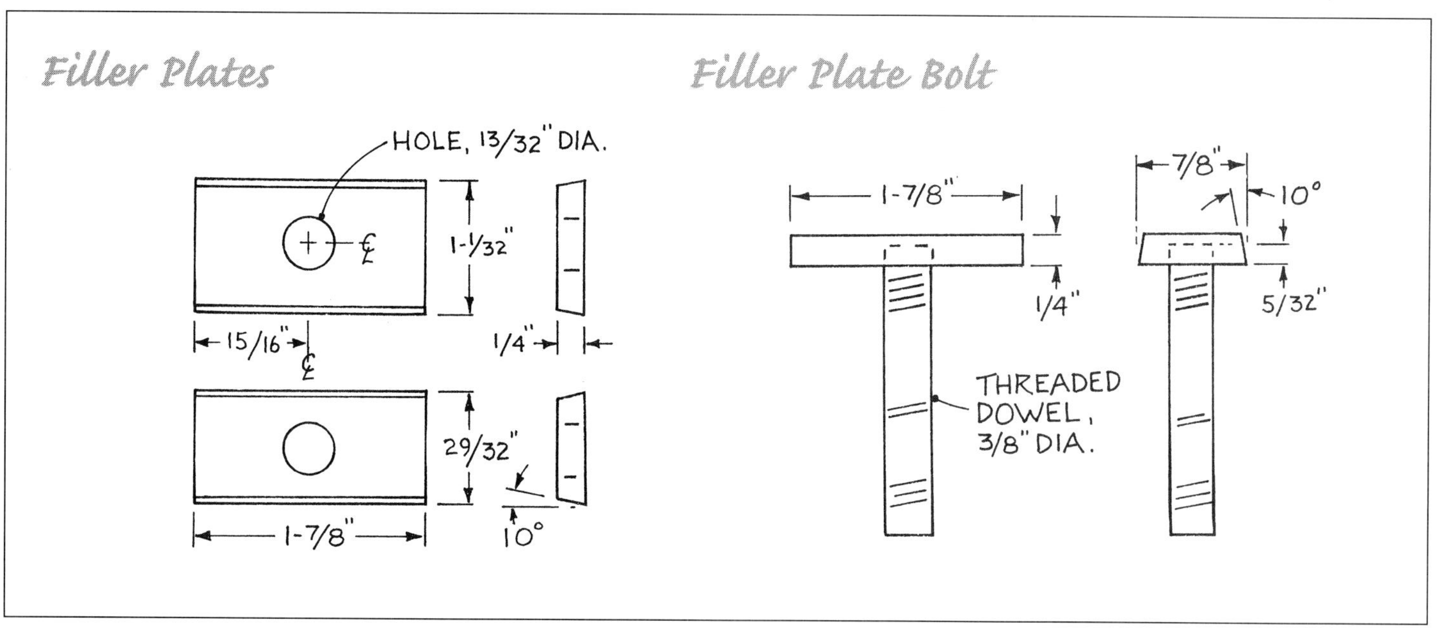

2. Locate and drill the $^7/_{16}$-in. hole in each workpiece.
3. Cut the plate for the filler-plate bolt in the same fashion. Drill a centered $^{13}/_{32}$-in. hole approximately $^5/_{32}$ in. deep into the plate to receive a length of $^3/_8$-in. threaded dowel (test-drill on a piece of scrap first to make sure the diameters of the hole and dowel match).
4. Glue the dowel into place, leaving $2^1/_8$ in. of thread exposed.

WINGS, RUDDERS, AND STABILIZERS

Delta wing

The construction of the delta wing entails a fairly involved series of angle cuts, so I've provided the drawing on p. 87 that should help clarify it.

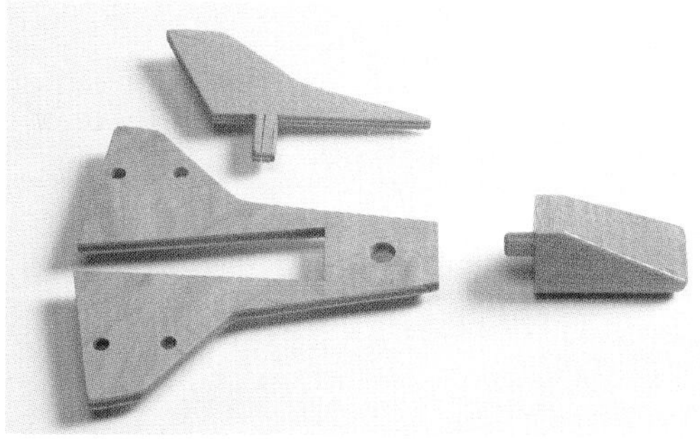

Photo F • *The delta wing, delta rudder, and delta nose are the key elements of a military-type supersonic jet.*

1. Cut a blank of high quality (preferably maple) $^1/_4$-in. plywood, 6 in. wide by $6^1/_8$ in. long. The $6^1/_8$-in. dimension, which is $^1/_8$ in. oversize, should correspond to the grain direction.
2. Draw the full layout on the workpiece, with the leading edge on the 6-in. dimension.
3. Locate and drill all holes, as indicated in the plan drawing.

WORKING SMARTER

When fabricating a piece with several angle cuts, like the delta wing, I usually stop each cut short of completion, maintaining the original straight edges of the workpiece as long as possible for referencing against fences and jigs. I also recommend cutting with the table-saw blade set at maximum height (which I know is an unorthodox approach—*use your judgment!*) to minimize undercutting into the junction with the next cut.

■ WINGS, RUDDERS, AND STABILIZERS

PART	SIZE (IN.)	QUANTITY	MATERIAL
Biplane top wing (#1)	2 x 1/4 x 10	1	1/4 maple plywood
Biplane lower wing (#2)	1 7/8 x 1/4 x 9	1	1/4 maple plywood
Combination wing (#3)	2 1/2 x 1/4 x 10	1	1/4 maple plywood
Delta wing (#4)	6 1/8 x 1/4 x 6	1	1/4 maple plywood
Combination stabilizer	1 7/8 x 1/4 x 4 1/2	1	1/4 maple plywood
Biplane stabilizer	2 x 1/4 x 4	1	1/4 maple plywood
Combination rudder	2 3/16 x 1/4 x 2 5/8	1	1/4 maple plywood
Biplane rudder	2 x 1/4 x 2 5/8	1	1/4 maple plywood
Delta rudder	2 3/4 x 1/4 x 4 3/4	1	1/4 maple plywood

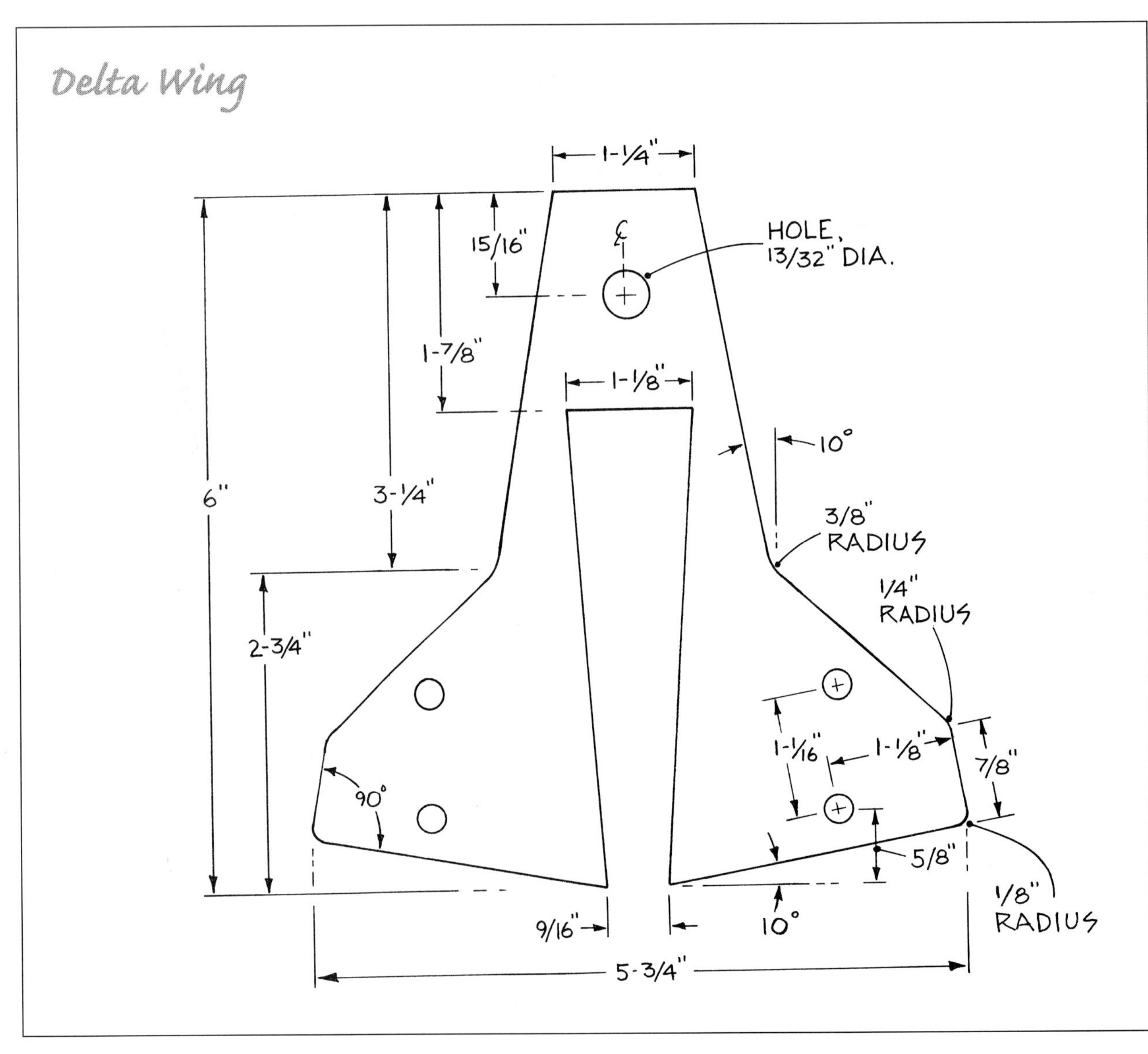

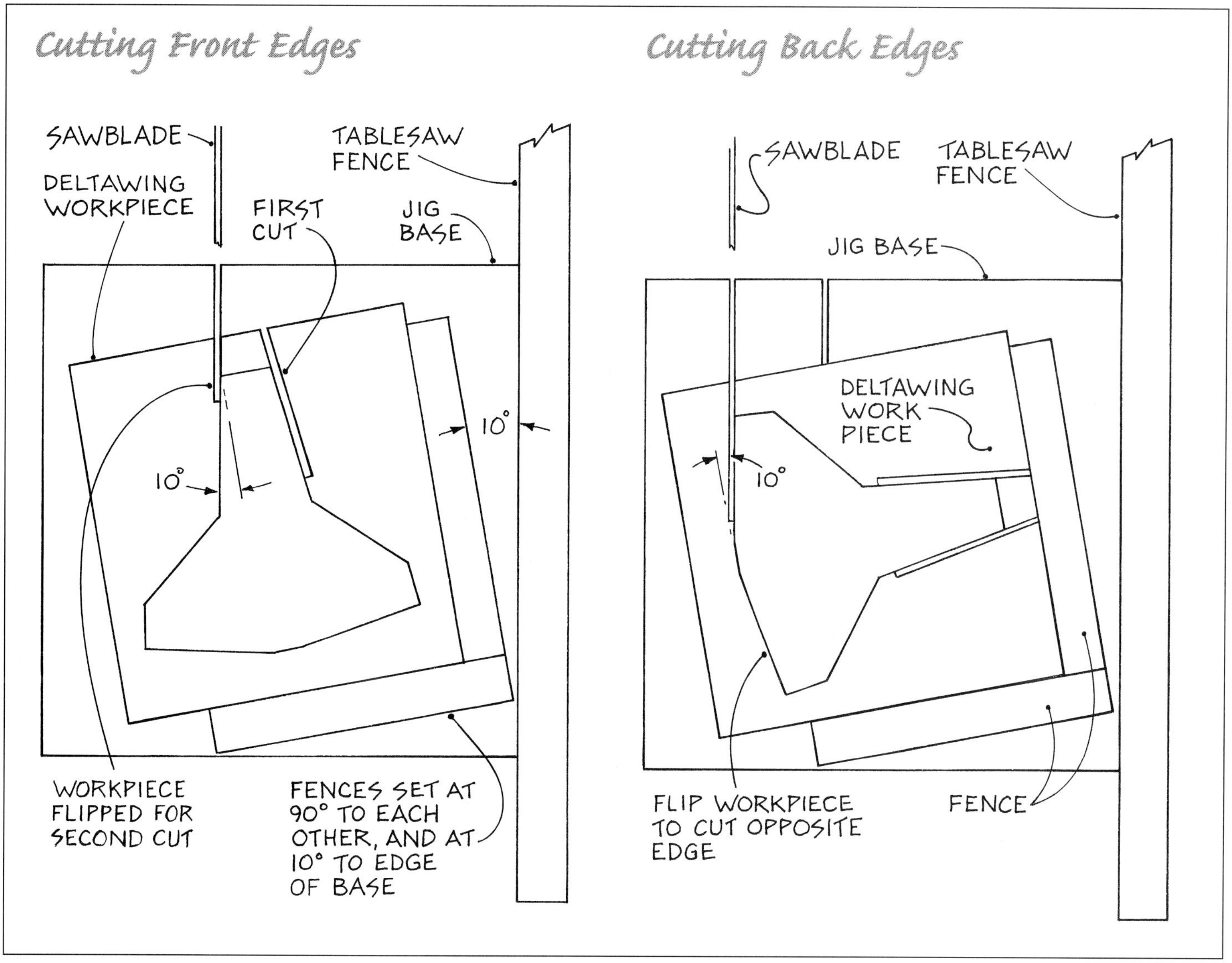

Cutting Front Edges

SAWBLADE
TABLESAW FENCE
DELTAWING WORKPIECE
FIRST CUT
JIG BASE
10°
10°
WORKPIECE FLIPPED FOR SECOND CUT
FENCES SET AT 90° TO EACH OTHER, AND AT 10° TO EDGE OF BASE

Cutting Back Edges

SAWBLADE
TABLESAW FENCE
JIG BASE
DELTAWING WORK PIECE
10°
FLIP WORKPIECE TO CUT OPPOSITE EDGE
FENCE

4. Using a simple 10-degree angle jig, make the first forward side cut, stopping short of the junction with the 40-degree cut (see photo G) and the first view of the sequence drawing. Simply flip the workpiece over for the second cut.

5. Also with a simple angle jig, make the first 40-degree angle cut on the wing's leading

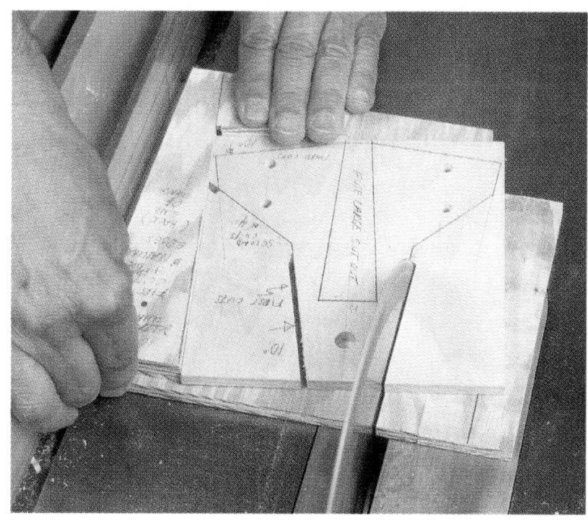

Photo G • *Cut the delta wing on the table saw, using a jig to secure its position. Flip the jig and workpiece over to make opposite, symmetrical cuts. Double-sided tape helps secure wing blanks in the jigs for all angle cuts.*

edge, again stopping short of completion (see photo H). Flip the workpiece for the second cut.

6. Cut both trailing edges 10 degrees on the table saw, using the same jig as in step #4 (see photo I) and the second view of the sequence drawing.

7. On the scrollsaw, complete all the angle cuts, make the interior cut, and finish the wing tips.

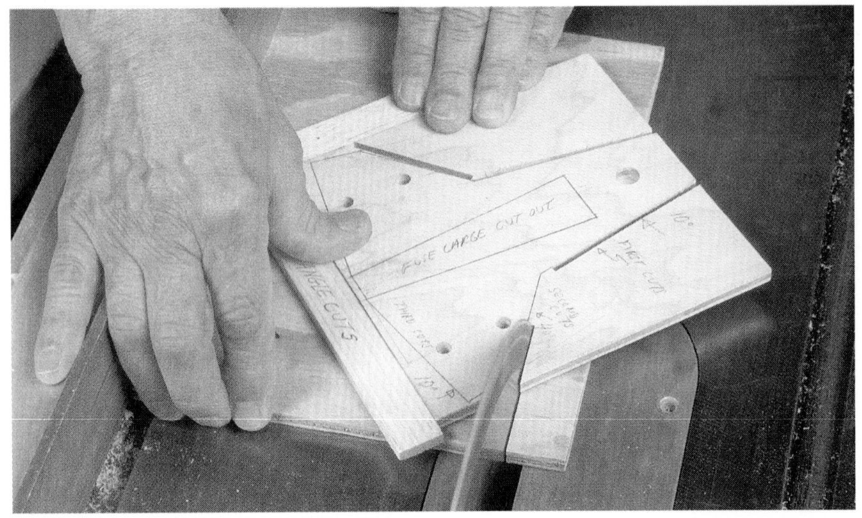

Photo H • *A second jig enables the second series of cuts and completes the front part of the wing. Leave them shy of completion so the circular blade does not cut into the finished wing underneath.*

Photo I • *The third and final cut on the rear edge completes the wing. The same jig used to cut the forward side cuts on the delta wing provides the 10-degree angle for the trailing edges.*

Biplane wings

The biplane wings are also made of ¼-in. plywood.

1. Cut the blanks for the upper and lower wings to their correct overall size.
2. Lay out all curves and holes as indicated in the plan drawing. It's essential that the holes be accurately placed to provide the proper alignment of the wings on the connecting struts.
3. Drill all the ¼-in. holes in the two blanks and the 13/32-in. hole in blank #2.
4. Cut the end curves on the scrollsaw.

Photo J • *Biplane wings, the corresponding rudder and stabilizer, and the cowl and propeller give a vintage look.*

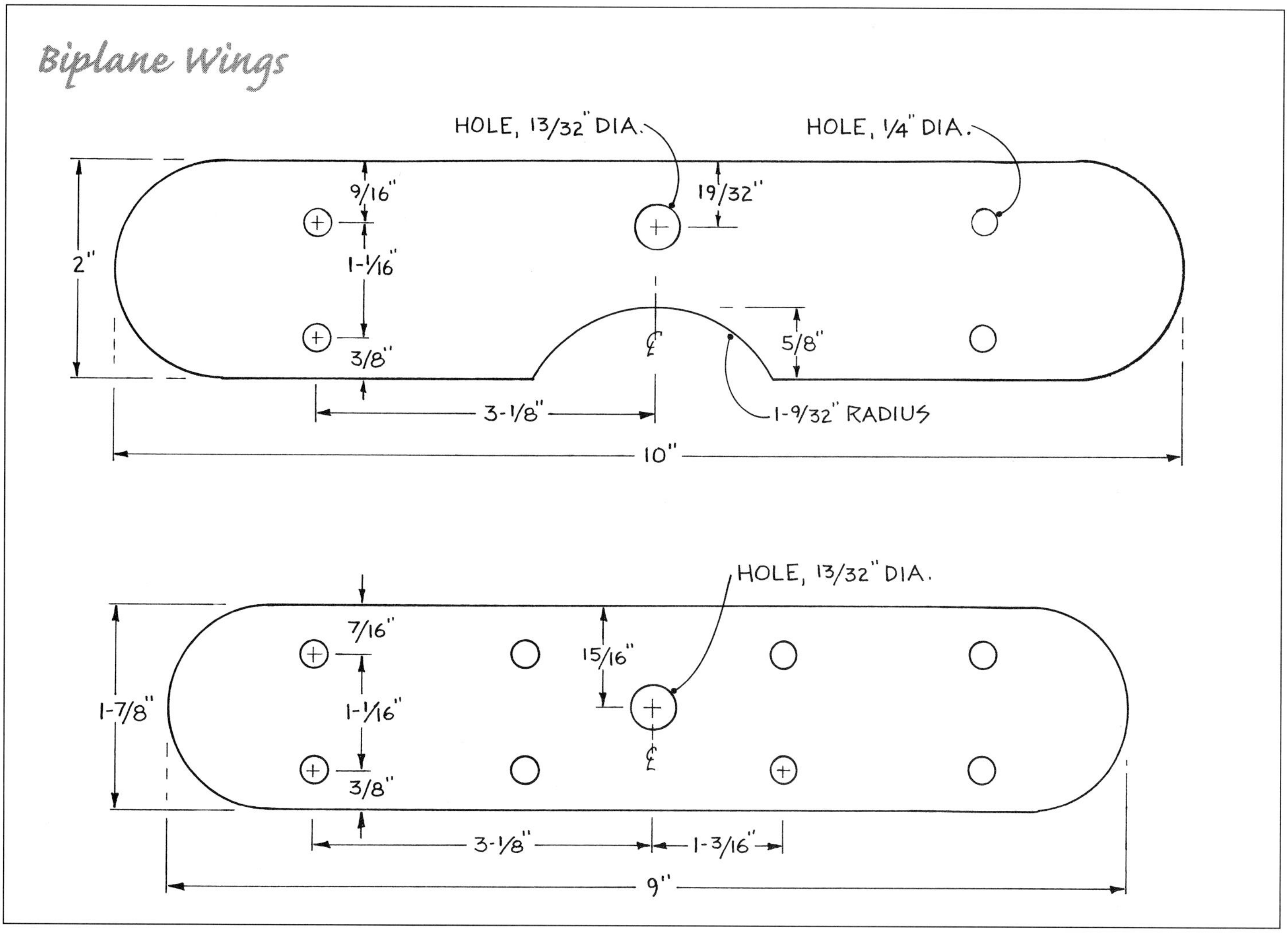

Biplane Wings

HOLE, 13/32" DIA.
HOLE, 1/4" DIA.
9/16"
19/32"
2"
1-1/16"
5/8"
3/8"
3-1/8"
1-9/32" RADIUS
10"

HOLE, 13/32" DIA.
7/16"
15/16"
1-7/8"
1-1/16"
3/8"
3-1/8"
1-3/16"
9"

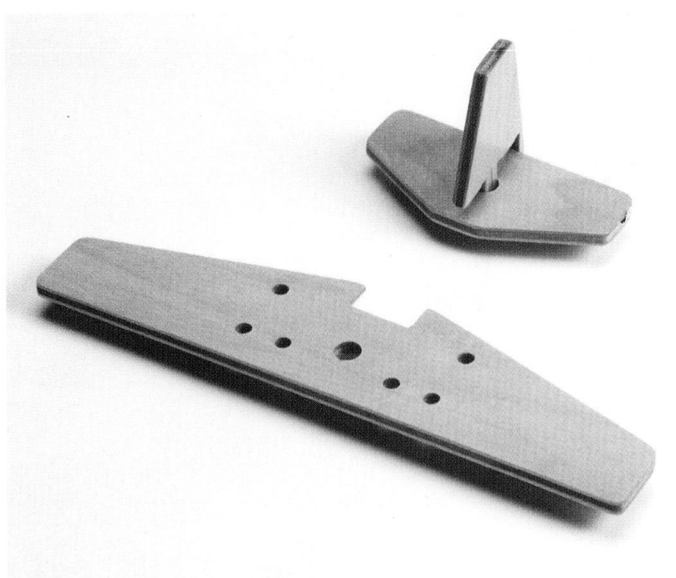

Photo K • *The combination wing with combination rudder and stabilizer are used to make up a single-engine monoplane. Reverse the wing to assemble a twin-engine jet.*

Combination wing

1. Cut the blank to its correct overall size.
2. Lay out and drill all holes.
3. Make the two leading-edge 15-degree angle cuts with a simple angle jig. Alternately, you can make these cuts freehand on the scrollsaw and true them up with a sanding block.
4. Make the cutout on the scrollsaw.

Note that with the 15-degree edge leading, the combination wing gives the look of a jet. Reverse it so the straight edge leads and it can be used to assemble a single-engine propeller plane.

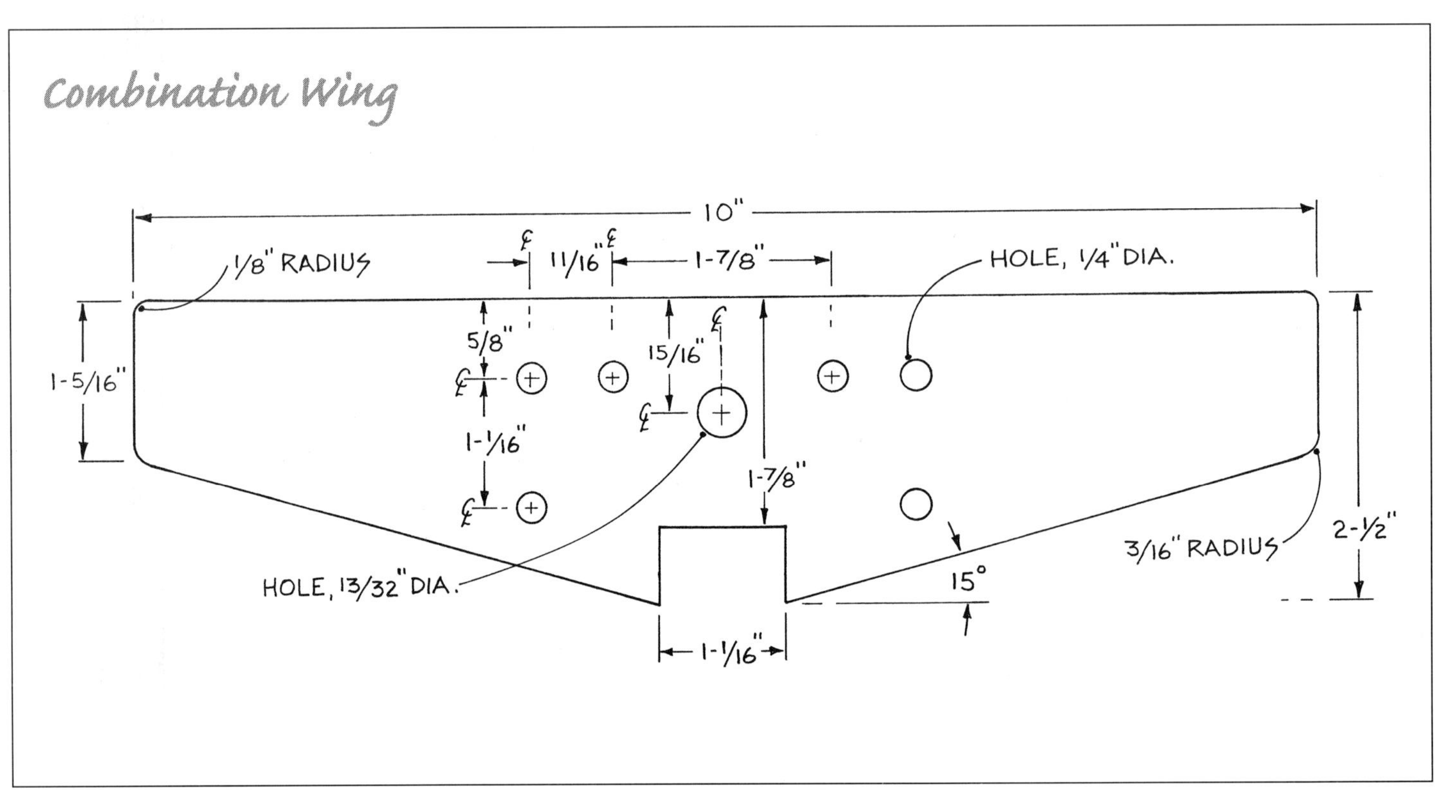

Rudders and Stabilizers

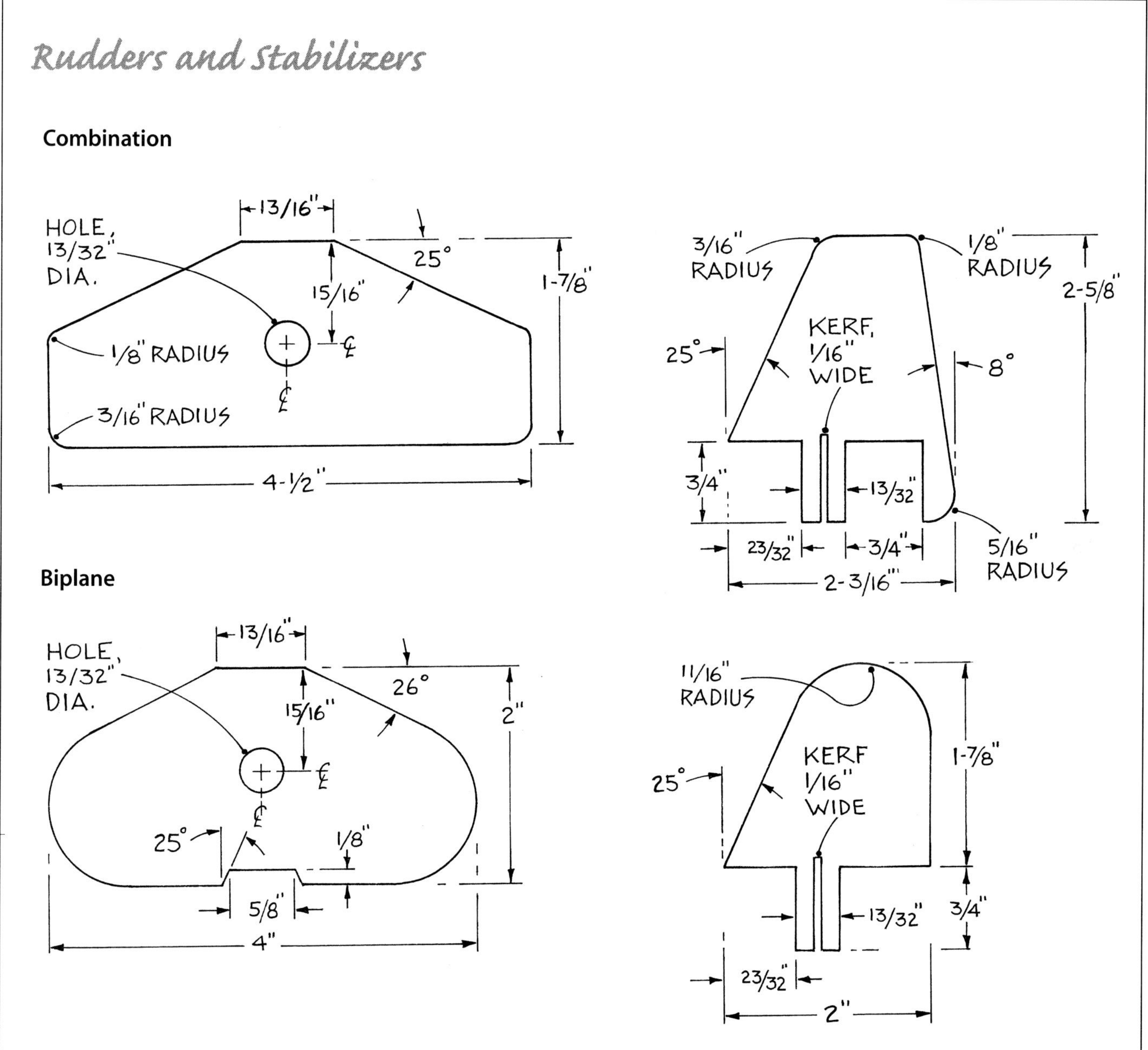

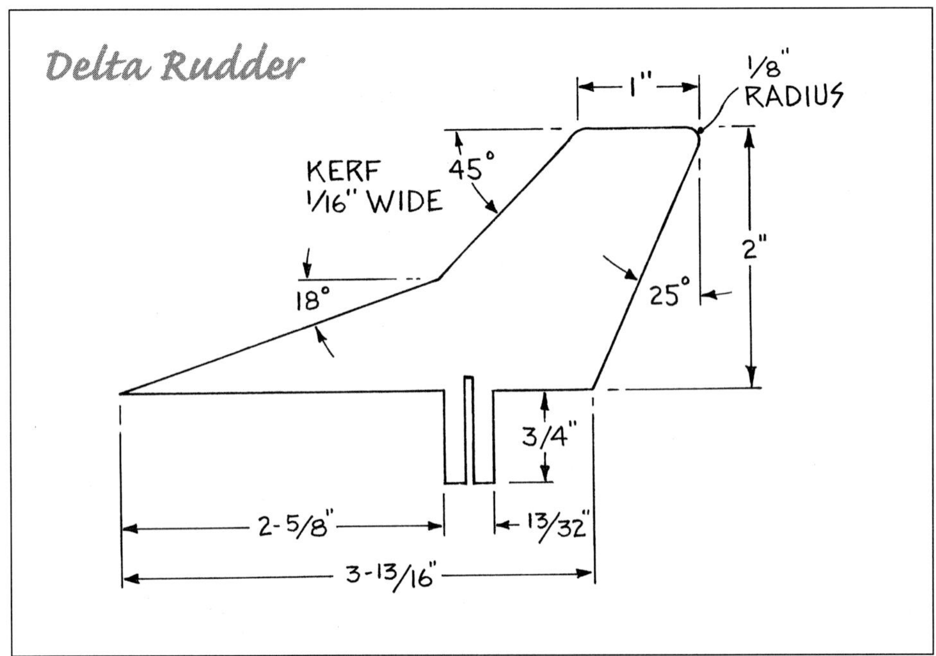

Rudders

All the rudders (and stabilizers) are also made from ¼-in. plywood. They all have at least one 25-degree angle, which can all be cut with one jig.

1. Cut the three blanks to their correct overall sizes, as indicated in the parts list.
2. Lay out the appropriate pattern on each blank.
3. Switch to a thin blade on the table saw, with a kerf of less than ⅛ in.

Photo L • *The sides and central slot of the rudder insertion tabs are cut on the table saw with the workpiece in an upright position against the auxiliary fence.*

4. With the workpiece upright and flat against an auxiliary fence on the miter gauge, make the three vertical cuts in each of the three blanks that will form the sides and central slot of the insertion tab, as in photo L.
5. For the combination rudder, there will be a fourth such cut, marking the back of the rear cutout area. Note that the slot cuts are slightly deeper than the others to provide the tabs with a little more flexibility for friction-fitting.
6. Make the 18-degree and then the 45-degree angle cuts in the delta rudder workpiece, using simple jigs and stopping the cuts shy of their junction.
7. Make the rear 25-degree angle cut in the workpiece, this time cutting all the way through the workpiece.
8. On the scrollsaw, complete the 18-degree and 45-degree angle cuts and make the two straight bottom cuts that will isolate the tab. True the bottom edge with a sanding block.
9. Make the 25-degree angle cuts in the other two rudder blanks and then finish

cutting the perimeter of each on the scrollsaw. Sand all cuts by hand to smooth out any irregularities.

10. File or sand all of the rudder insertion tabs to friction-fit into the 13/32-in. stabilizer and the rear fuselage holes. A 13/32-in. hole drilled through a piece of 1/4-in. hardwood plywood makes a useful gauge for testing the fit.

Stabilizers

1. Cut the two blanks to their correct over–all sizes.
2. Lay out the appropriate pattern on each blank.
3. Drill the 13/32-in. hole in the blank for the combination stabilizer, as indicated in the plan drawing.
4. Make the two 25-degree angle cuts in the workpiece, and hand-sand to round the corners.
5. Drill the 13/32-in. hole in the blank for the biplane stabilizer.
6. Make the 25-degree angle cuts in the workpiece.
7. Finish the piece by cutting the radius curves and rear notch on the scrollsaw.

MISCELLANEOUS PARTS

Landing-gear plate

The landing-gear plate supports the landing gear. The wheels ride on a dowel and are connected to the plate with two other dowels. I recommend using commercial wheels for this project (see Resources on p. 217). You'll need two of them, 1¼ in. diameter by ⅜ in. thick, with a ¼-in. axle hole.

Photo M • *The landing-gear plate bolts to the underside of the fuselage on a top wing, Piper Cub-type plane.*

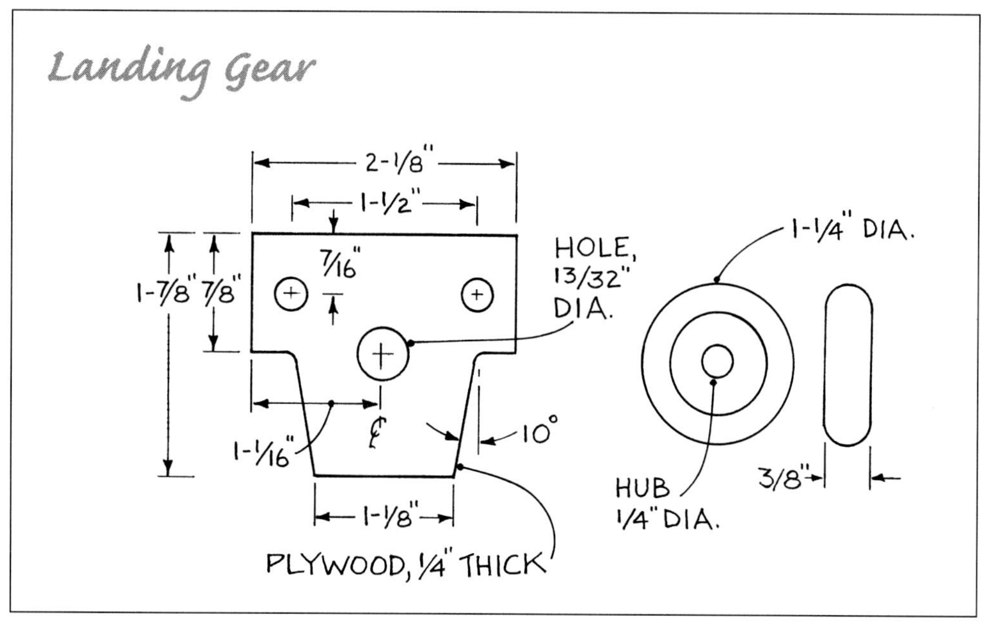

■ MISCELLANEOUS PARTS

PART	SIZE (IN.)	QUANTITY	MATERIAL
Combination engines	3/4 x 3 5/8	2	3/4 dowel
Slotted engine mounts	1/4 x 11/16	4	1/4 dowel
Pontoons	11/16 x 5/8 x 5 3/4	2	Cherry
Landing gear struts	1/2 x 1 7/8	2	1/2 dowel
Pontoon struts	3/8 x 1 11/16	4	3/8 dowel
Wing struts	3/8 x 2 3/16	4	3/8 dowel
Wheels	1 1/4 x 3/8	2	Commercial
Landing gear plate	1 7/8 x 1/4 x 2 1/8	1	1/4 maple plywood
Propeller #1	1/2 x 1/8 x 4 3/8	1	1/8 maple plywood
Propeller #2	7/16 x 1/8 x 3 1/2	1	1/8 maple plywood
Open cockpit	13/16 x 13/16 x 2 7/8	1	Maple
Closed-in cockpit	13/16 x 13/16 x 2 7/8	1	Maple
Threaded mounting dowel (for closed-in cockpit)	3/8 x 1 7/8	1	Commercial
Cowl (w/3/8 dowel pin)	1 5/8 x 5/8	1	Walnut
Prop spinners	3/8 x 7/8	2	Dowel
"Spinning" props	1 7/8 x 1/8 (or 1/16)	2	1/8 Plexiglas
All bolts are fitted with lengths of commercial 3/8 threaded dowel; see plan drawing.			
Bolt w/half-round head	1-in. ball	1	Commercial
Bolt w/full-round head	7/8-in. ball	1	Commercial
Filler plate bolt	1 7/8 x 1/4 x 7/8 (plate dimension)	1	1/4 maple plywood
Bolt w/flat head	3/4 x 1/8 x 3/4 (head dimension)	1	1/8 maple plywood
Nut	1 dia. x 1	1	Commercial
(To be turned down to a 7/8 diameter and cut into sections 1/4 to 5/16 in thickness; see plan drawing.)			
Slotted axles	1/4 dia. x 3 1/4, 3 1/2	1 each	Dowel
Slotted axles	1/4 dia. x 2 7/8	2	Dowel

1. Cut the blank to its overall size.
2. Locate and drill all holes.
3. With the workpiece in an upright position against an auxiliary fence on the table saw, make the 10-degree angle cuts.
4. Make the cuts from the sides of the workpiece to the top of the angle cuts on the scrollsaw.

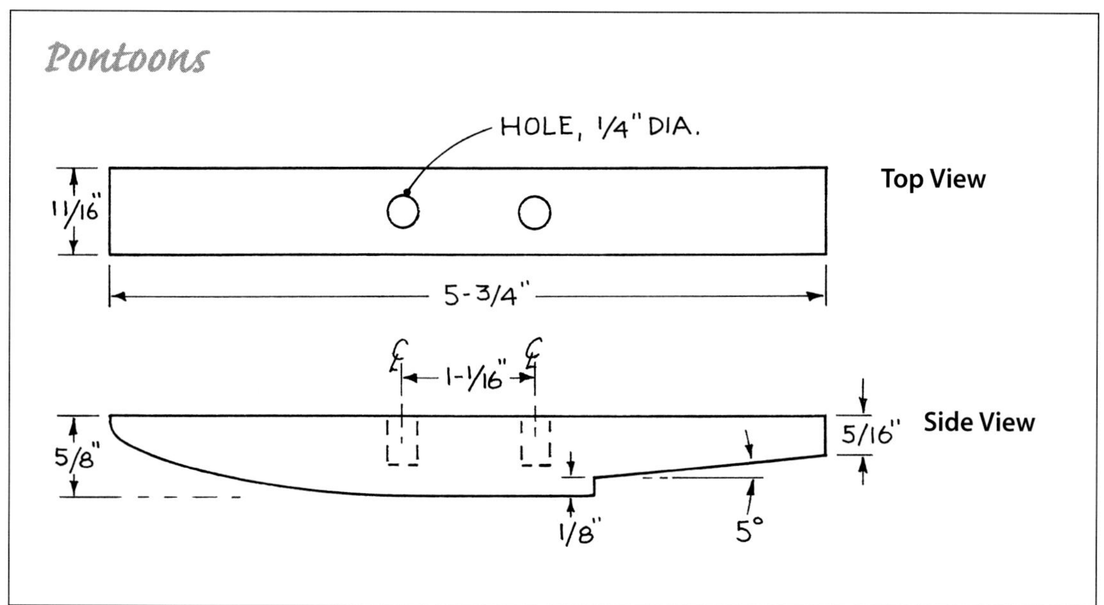

Photo N • *Friction-fit struts fasten the pontoons to the undersides of wings.*

Pontoons

The pontoons are held in place with two struts, described on p. 99.

1. Cut the blanks to size.
2. Drill the partial-depth holes in the pontoon blanks 3⁄8 in. deep.
3. Fasten the blanks together with double-sided tape to cut the profile as indicated in the full-size template on the scrollsaw.

Cockpits

The closed and open cockpits are made in the same way. The only difference is that the closed cockpit does not have a dado on its top.

1. Cut the blank for the open cockpit to its correct overall size.
2. Drill the 13⁄32-in. through hole as indicated in the plan drawing, centered on the 13⁄16-in. dimension when looking down at the top of the workpiece. Test-drill in scrap first to make sure the hole diameter matches the dowel.
3. Cut the front and back of the top dado on the table saw, using a regular rip blade. Since this is a small piece, it's safer to cut out the waste on the scrollsaw. Omit this step for the closed cockpit.

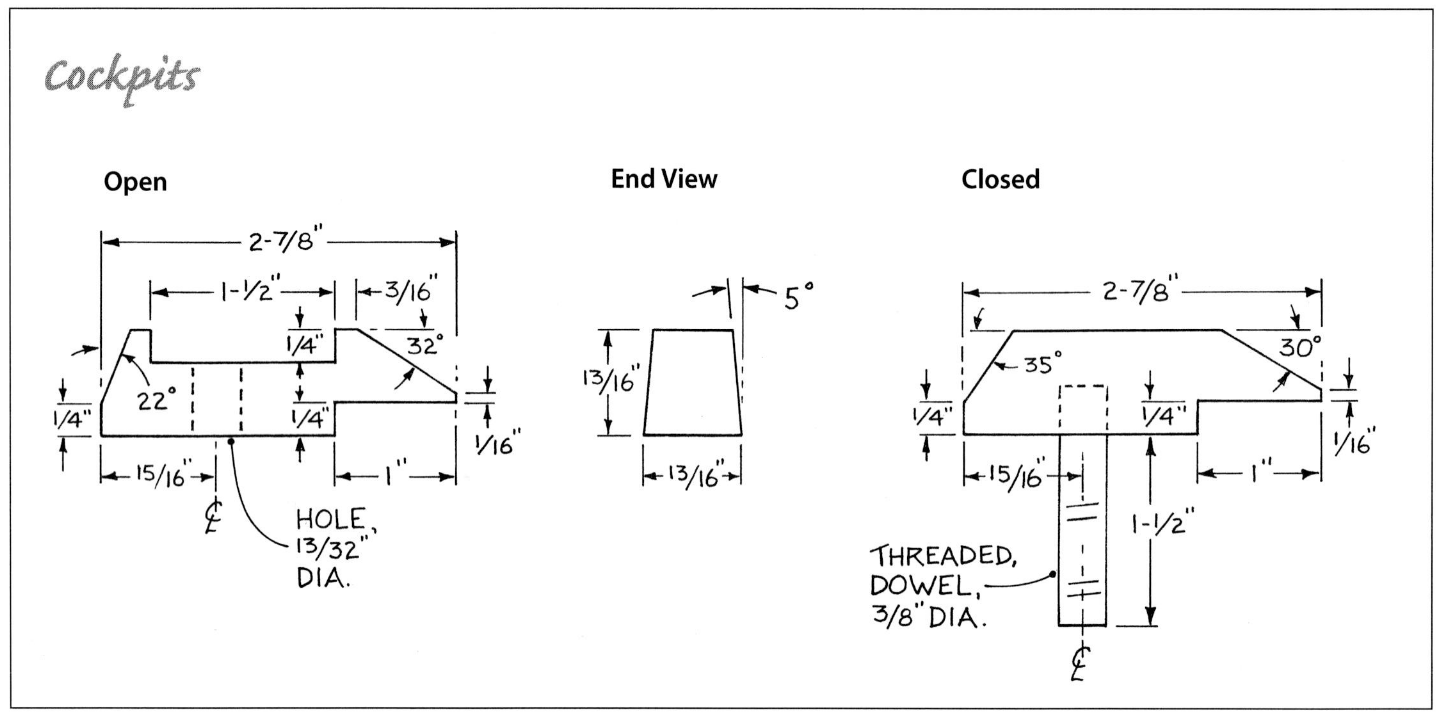

Photo O • *Open and closed cockpit variations. The round head bolt represents a pilot's head while securing the open cockpit to the fuselage.*

4. Cut out the rabbet on the end on the table saw, with the workpiece fastened to an auxiliary block in a vertical position for the longer of the two cuts.
5. Make the 22-degree and 32-degree angle cuts on the table saw, using the miter gauge with an auxiliary fence, or freehand on the scrollsaw, if you prefer.
6. Cut both sides of the workpiece to an inward 5-degree angle.
7. Glue and insert a 1⅞-in. threaded dowel in the hole on the bottom. In practice I often leave this dowel oversize by about ¼ in., which allows the stacking of an additional wing, or any other combination that strikes your fancy.

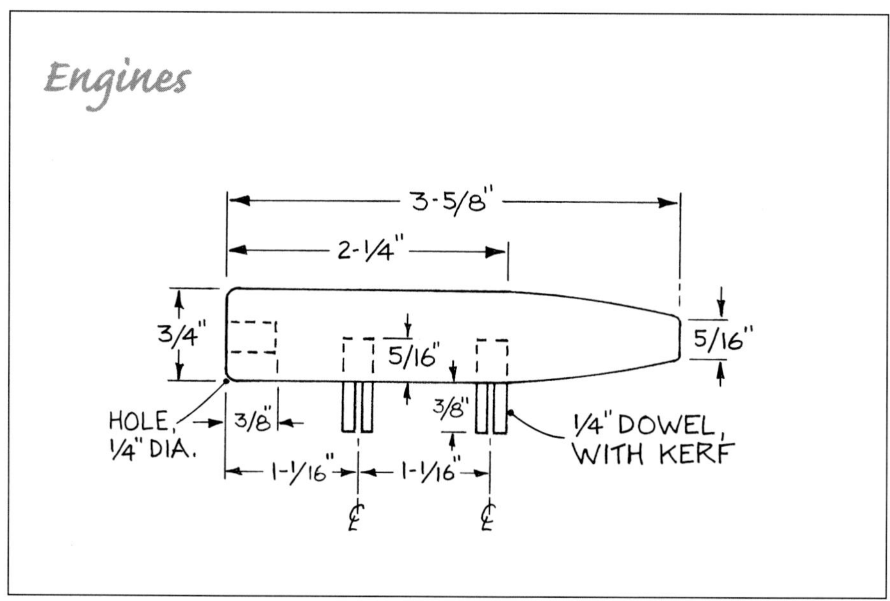

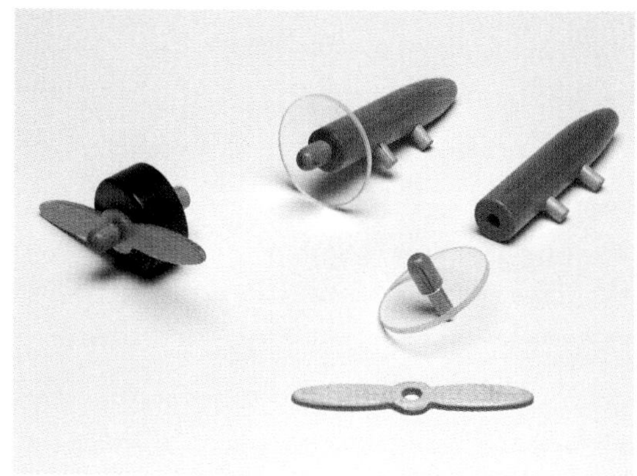

Photo P • *Engines: Friction-fit prop spinners affix the propellers to the cowl and the "spinning" discs to the combination engines. Unadorned, the combination engines double as jet engines.*

Engines

The combination engines can be fitted with propellers or left as they are to provide convincing-looking jet engines. They are made as follows:

1. Chuck a 3⅝-in. length of ¾-in. dowel into the lathe and drill a centered ¼-in. hole ⅜ in. deep into one end (see the "Boring out dowels" section on p. 15). This hole can either receive a prop spinner or be left open to be a jet intake.
2. Reverse the workpiece in the lathe and turn the rear section to the shape indicated in the plan drawing.
3. Using a V block and a single spacer block, locate and drill the two holes for the ¼-in. mounting dowels in each engine (see photo Q).

Photo Q • *A spacer block ensures accurate placement of the mounting dowel holes in the combination engines.*

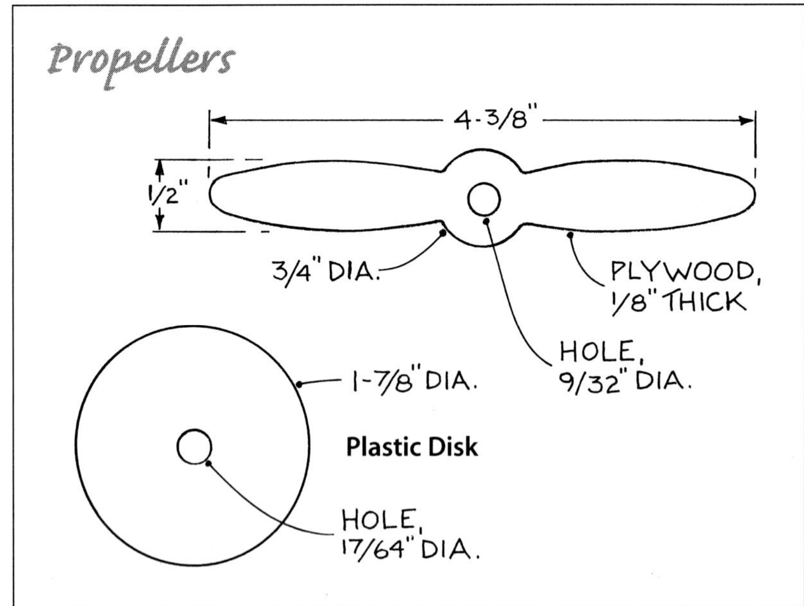

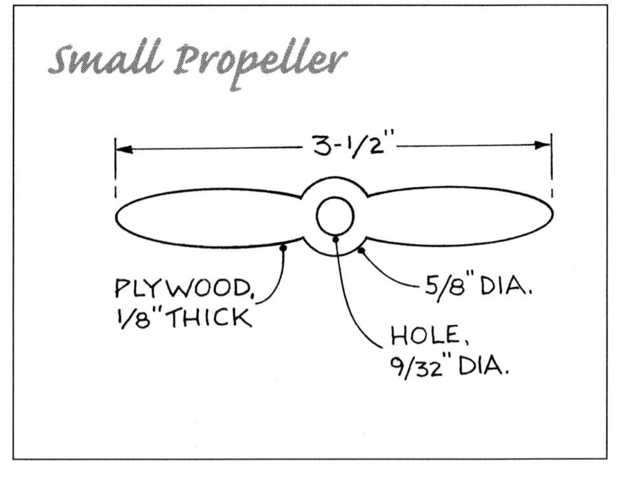

Propellers

The two propellers should be cut to the indicated patterns from high-quality ⅛-in. plywood blanks after the centered 9⁄32-in. mounting holes have been drilled.

A Plexiglas (or any other clear plastic) disk 1⅞ in. in diameter, either ⅛ in. or 1⁄16 in. thick, provides the look of a spinning propeller. Drill a centered ¼-in. hole to allow mounting on a prop spinner.

Prop spinner

1. Chuck a ½-in. length of ⅜-in.-diameter dowel into the lathe and drill a ¼-in. hole about ¼ in. deep.
2. Glue in a ⅝-in. length of ¼-in. dowel.

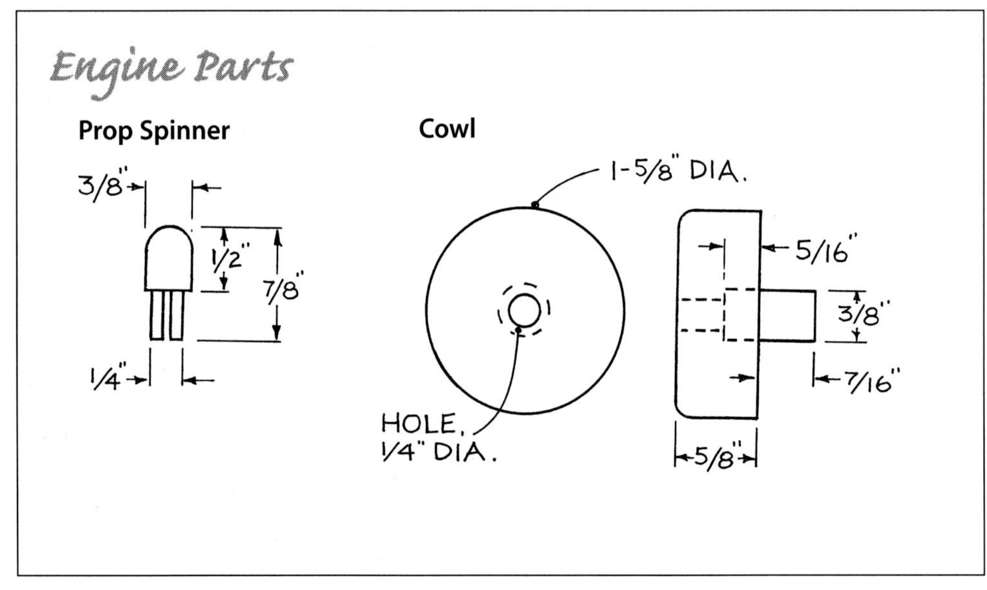

3. Turn the radius on the lathe. Alternately, it can be formed by sanding or filing with the workpiece chucked into the drill press.

I recommend slotting this piece by hand, because it's so small; an X-Acto razor saw works well for this.

Cowl

The cowl is inserted into the fuselage to receive the propeller for a vintage look. To make one:

1. Cut a walnut blank that is slightly oversize from the finished 1⅝-in. diameter with a hole saw (which will also create a ¼-in. center hole).
2. Mount the workpiece on the lathe with a ¼-in. arbor bolt and finish it as you would a wheel. (See the "Wheels and Axles" section on p. 16.)
3. Drill the partial depth ⅜-in. hole about ¼ in. deep, and glue in an 11/16-in. length of ⅜-in. dowel for mounting on the fuselage. The ¼-in. hole on the other side will receive the prop spinner.

Landing gear and pontoon struts

There are friction-fit struts for attaching the landing gear and the pontoons to the underside of the various planes and for connecting the upper and lower biplane wings. The fabrication procedure is essentially the same for all three types; refer to the parts list and plan drawing for dimensions.

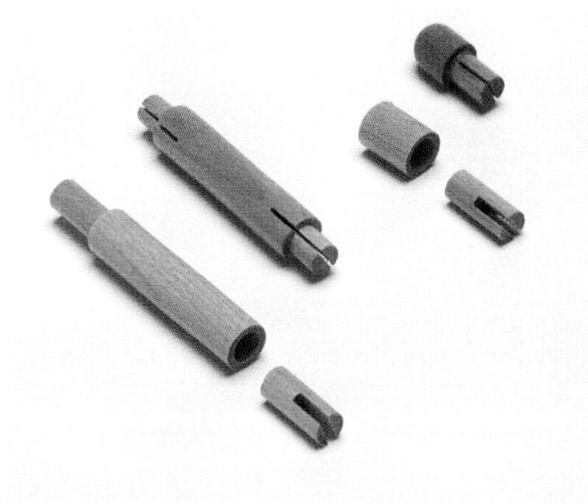

Photo R• *Strut shoulders can be formed either on the lathe or by the insertion of a section of smaller diameter dowel.*

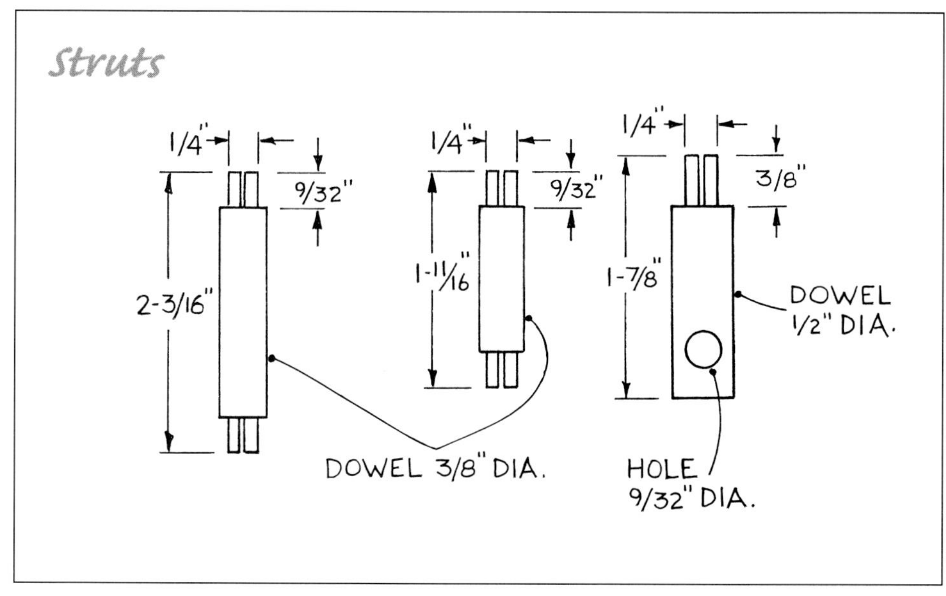

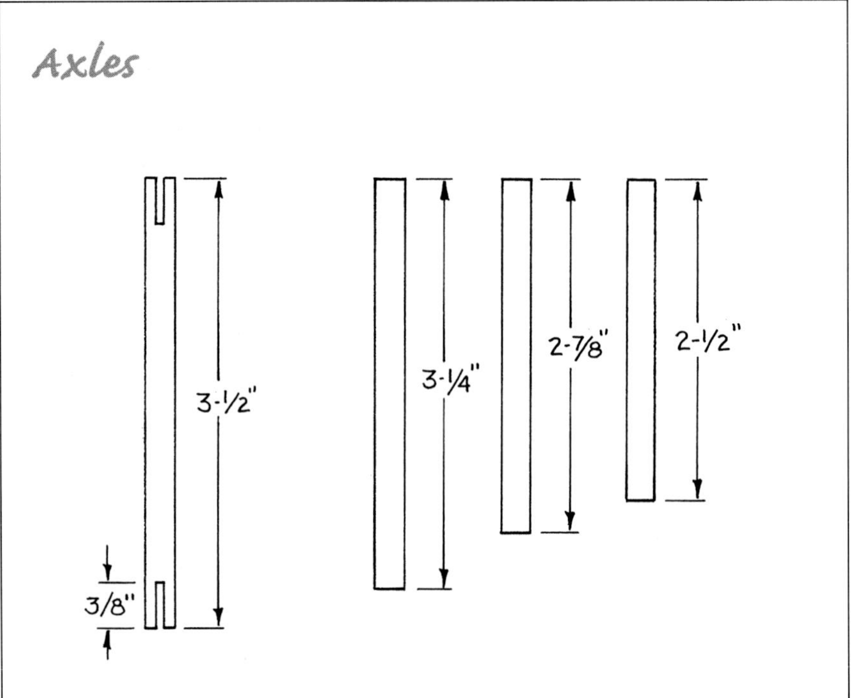

1. Chuck one of the ½-in. dowel lengths into the lathe (either wood or metal).
2. Turn a ¼-in., ⅜-in. shoulder in the dowel's end.
3. Cradle the workpiece in a V block and drill the other end for a 9/32-in. axle hole, as indicated in the plan drawing.

The wing and pontoon struts are made of lengths of ⅜-in. dowel, with a 9/32-in. shoulder turned in at each end. Slot each shoulder for friction-fitting. I recommend doing this by hand, as we did for the prop spinners. If a lathe is not available, the dowel ends can be drilled to receive a length of ¼-in. dowel that is glued in place to form the shoulder.

Axles

Axles are simply lengths of ¼-in. dowel, slotted at each end. The shortest one allows the attachment of the landing-gear struts to the landing-gear plate, and the other two sizes provide for underwing mounting of the struts on the different wing types.

Nuts and bolts

These parts are made up of commercially available components (see Resources on p. 217). They are used to fasten all forward wings to the fuselage.

To make the half-round bolt head, split a 1-in. diameter ball with a matte knife so that one piece is slightly more than half size. Sand the revealed surface flat on a sanding block.

The flat-top bolt is like the half-round bolt, but with a ¾-in.-square head made of ⅛-in. hardwood plywood.

To drill the ¼-in.-deep hole for the threaded dowel into the half-round head, drill a ¾-in. hole into a scrap block and seat the half ball into it on the drill-press table. To drill the corresponding hole in the ⅞-in. ball, chuck it into the lathe. Again, be sure to verify on a piece of scrap that the drill bit matches the actual diameter of the ⅜-in. threaded dowel before drilling into a workpiece.

Nuts are commercially available to be cut down as indicated in the plan drawing.

As an option, the lengths of threaded dowel can be replaced with ⅜-in. N/C machine bolts. Cut off the bolt heads to glue the threaded lengths to the wooden heads with epoxy, and drill out sections of 1-in. dowel to receive the corresponding nuts, also glued in place with epoxy.

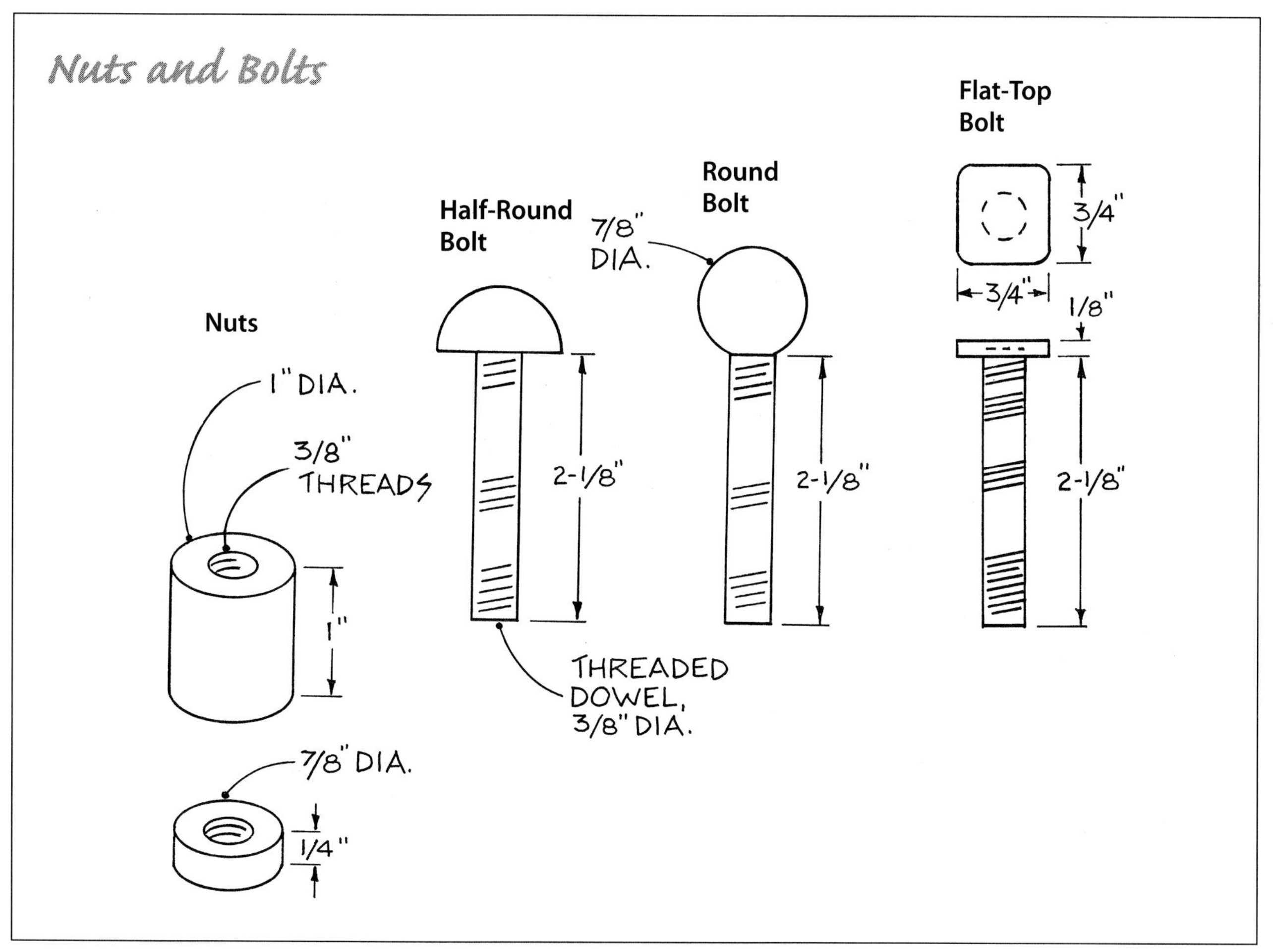

chapter 6
VEHICLES

As much as we adults are fascinated by cars, so are kids. Your young driver can take an imaginary spin in a sedan or a coupe, or do some delivery work with a pickup or van. And if he's feeling sporty, he can gad about in a dune buggy powered by a hefty V-6, or even break the double-century mark in a supercharged Indy 500 wedge.

Although you can construct just about any type of truck or car imaginable with the many interchangeable components in this chapter, the assembly system is extremely simple. Selected parts are fitted to a generic chassis and secured by a front-to-back rod that is attached to the front bumper. The rear bumper pressure-fits to the rod.

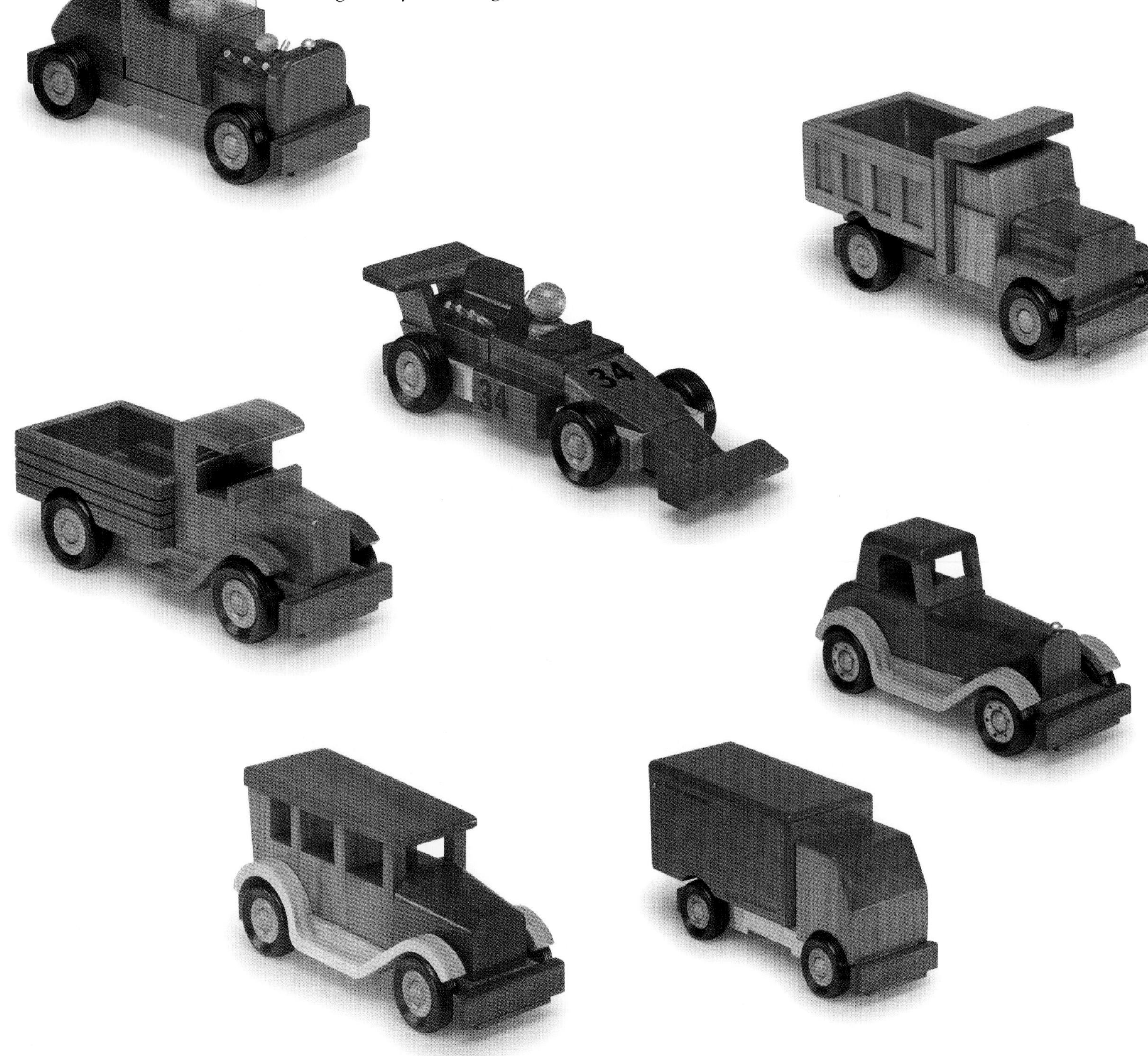

Fabrication of Components

This chapter is organized a little differently from the previous ones. Instead of discussing the components of each version all in one place, all the components of a similar type are together. You'll find, for example, all the hoods described in one section, instead of all the parts used to make a milk truck. I've done it this way because many of the components are very similar, and discussing them together saves a lot of words and space.

This project calls for both skill and patience. The front end and rear foil of the Indy 500 racer involve numerous angle cuts, the fenders require a lot of freehand scrollwork, and the small exhaust pipes of the exposed dune buggy and racer engines can be finicky to handle.

I've provided photos and illustrations that, along with the text and the plan drawings, should make it easy to understand both the sequence of steps and the way the components work together.

CHASSIS

The chassis is the heart of the system, and it must be dimensionally precise to receive the various parts in the proper alignment. Since the same chassis is used for all vehicles, I recommend making up at least three or four of them, so several different vehicles can be assembled at the same time.

Photo A • *The chassis and locking assembly rod are the basis for every vehicle variation.*

CHASSIS

Quantities given are for fabrication of a single component (or paired set of components). See text for suggested numbers of components.

PART	SIZE (IN.)	QUANTITY	MATERIAL
Chassis sides	$\frac{1}{2}$ x $\frac{3}{8}$ x $5\frac{1}{8}$	2	Cherry
Chassis pins	$\frac{1}{8}$ dia. x $\frac{3}{8}$	2	$\frac{1}{8}$ dowel
Front and back end pieces	$\frac{1}{2}$ x $\frac{3}{8}$ x $1\frac{1}{2}$	2	Cherry
Wheels	$1\frac{1}{4}$ dia. x $\frac{7}{16}$	4	Commercial
Axle pegs (to match selected wheels)	$\frac{1}{4}$	4	Commercial

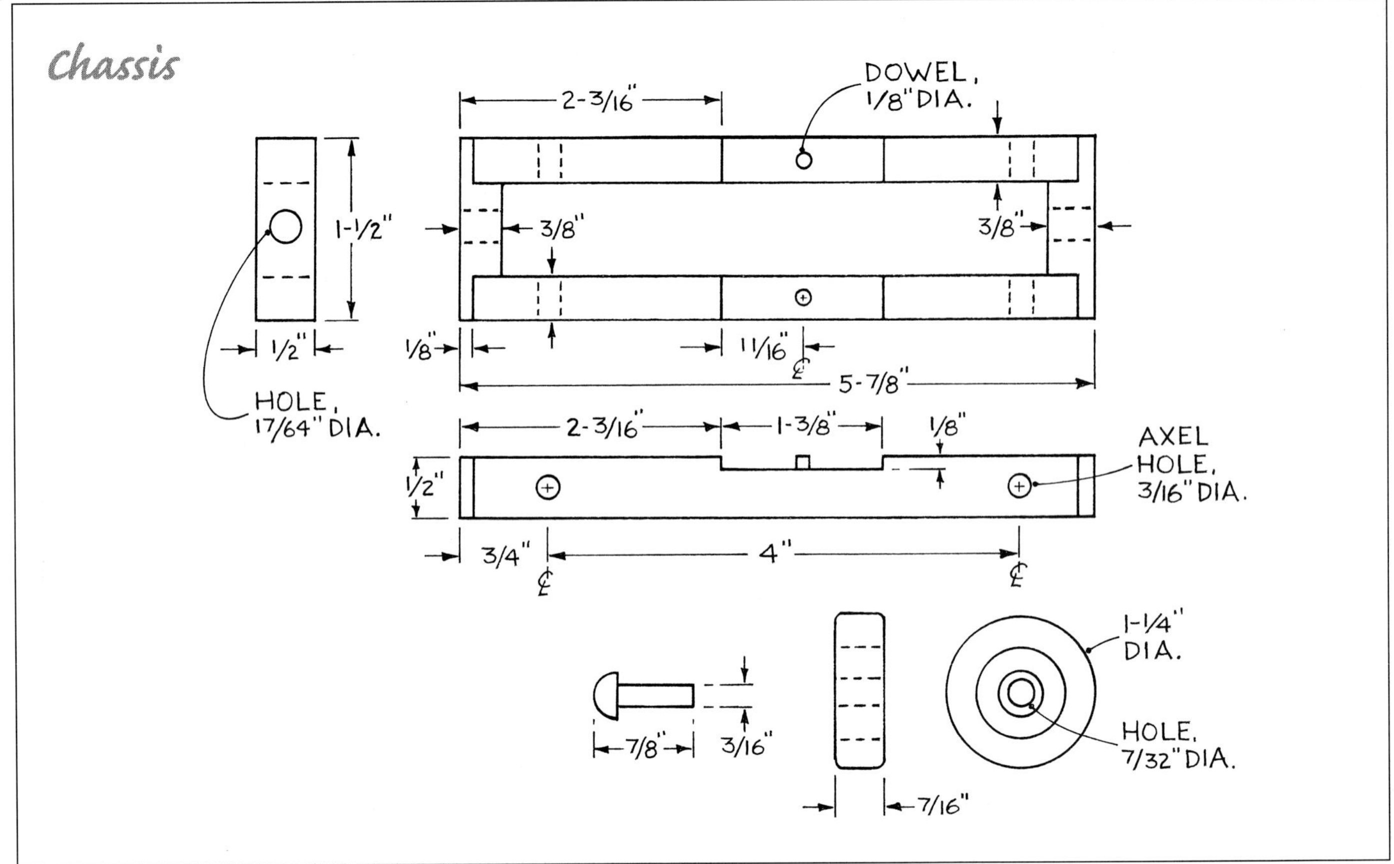

1. Cut a blank for the chassis sides 5⅞ in. long by ½ in. wide by 1 in. thick. The last dimension is just over twice the finished thickness, so that you can resaw the blank into two matched parts. Do this only after making the dado cuts and drilling the axle holes.
2. Make the dado cutout on the workpiece, referring to the plan drawing for correct placement along its length. Do this on the table saw, using a miter gauge to guide the piece.
3. Drill the 3⁄16-in. peg-axle holes as indicated in the plan drawing. Since there may be some fluctuation in the actual peg diameter, test-drill on scrap first to check the fit. Do not drill the ⅛-in. pinholes at this time. This will be done with the fenders in place to ensure their correct alignment.
4. With the 1-in. dimension on the table, rip the blank and trim the two resulting pieces to the final thickness of ⅜ in. on the table saw.
5. Cut an oversize double-width blank for the two end pieces.
6. Cut the rabbet on the two ends of the blank, again referring to the plan drawing. Fasten the blank to an auxiliary block with double-sided tape for the vertical cuts.
7. Rip the block in two equal widths, and trim the two pieces to their final ⅜-in. width.
8. Drill a centered 17⁄64-in. through hole in each end piece to receive the locking assembly rod.
9. Glue the sides and ends together, using a rubber band wrapped around the perimeter for clamping pressure (see photo B).

Photo B • *A rubber band makes a fine clamp for gluing up the chassis, equalizing the pressure around the perimeter.*

10. Assemble the wheels and peg axles and glue them into the peg-axle holes. For a touch of realism, I recommend using #262 rubber wheels, $1\frac{1}{4}$ in. diameter by $\frac{7}{16}$ in. thick, available from Cherry Tree (see Resources on p. 217). Should these be unavailable, be sure to check the peg diameter of any substitutes before drilling the corresponding chassis holes. Note also that $1\frac{1}{4}$ in. is the maximum wheel diameter that will work with the fender design as given.
11. Draw a forward-pointing arrow in one of the dado areas to facilitate the correct orientation of the fenders for assembly.

■ LOCKING ASSEMBLY ROD

This part is used for every vehicle except the Indy 500 racer. Again, I recommend making up several of them, though the total number should be one less than the number of chassises. However, the racer does use the same rear bumper as the others, so be sure to make up enough of them. The rear bumper is the same as the front bumper, but has a $\frac{1}{4}$-in. hole drilled through.

1. Cut the blanks for the two bumpers and bottom plates. The bottom plates will engage under the chassis in assembly and prevent rotation of the rod.
2. Drill a centered $\frac{1}{4}$-in. hole to a partial depth of $\frac{3}{16}$ in. in the front bumper and completely through the rear one.
3. Glue a length of $\frac{1}{4}$-in. dowel into the front bumper hole, a little oversize from the indicated $5\frac{7}{8}$-in. dimension, to be adjusted during final assembly.
4. After you've cut the dowel to the final length, slot it either by hand with a saw, or with a jig like the one featured on p. 45.
5. Glue the two bottom plates to the bumpers, positioned as indicated in the plan drawing on p. 108.

WORKING SMARTER

Whenever I have identical pieces that call for dado or rabbet cuts, like the chassis sides and ends, I perform the procedure on a single blank that is slightly more than double the width (or thickness, as the case may be) of the finished piece. I then rip the blank into two equal-sized parts on the table saw, guaranteeing the absolute symmetry of the two and saving time as well.

■ LOCKING ASSEMBLY ROD

Quantities given are for fabrication of a single component (or paired set of components). See text for suggested numbers of components.

PART	SIZE (IN.)	QUANTITY	MATERIAL
Rod	$\frac{1}{4}$ dia. x $5\frac{7}{8}$	1	$\frac{1}{4}$ dowel
Front bumper	$\frac{1}{2}$ x $\frac{1}{4}$ x $2\frac{1}{8}$	1	Walnut
Locking bar	$\frac{3}{8}$ x $\frac{3}{32}$ x $1\frac{1}{2}$	1	Walnut
Rear bumper	$\frac{1}{2}$ x $\frac{1}{4}$ x $2\frac{1}{8}$	1	Walnut

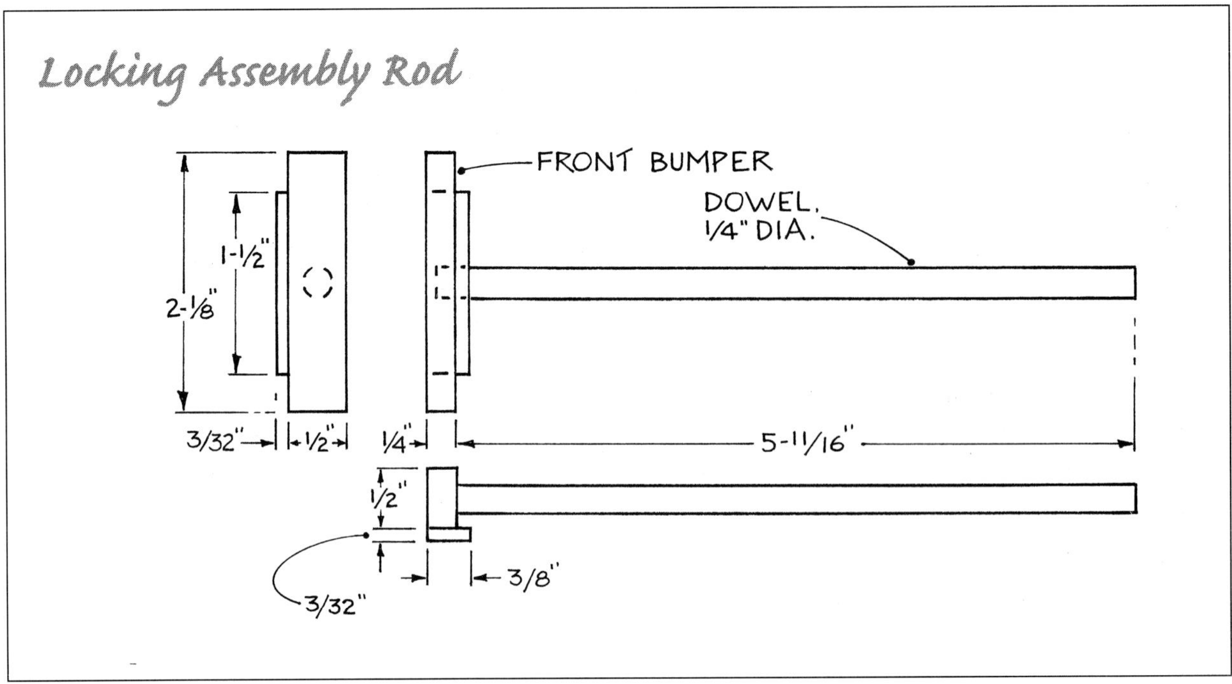

WORKING SMARTER

Although I'm a big fan of double-sided tape, when I fasten together a pair of blanks for delicate matched parts like the fenders, I prefer spot-gluing. That way, there's no chance of the breakage that can occur when separating the two if tape is used. Of course, it's essential that you don't put glue within the layout lines, or your fenders will be stuck together.

FENDERS

I recommend working with an oversize blank, allowing the layout of the circles that will be drilled out to form the wheel wells (see photo C).

1. Spot-glue together two blanks of $^3/_8$-in. maple plywood, about 6 in. long and at least 1$^3/_4$ in. wide, applying the glue along the edges and making sure no glue gets within the layout lines for the fenders.

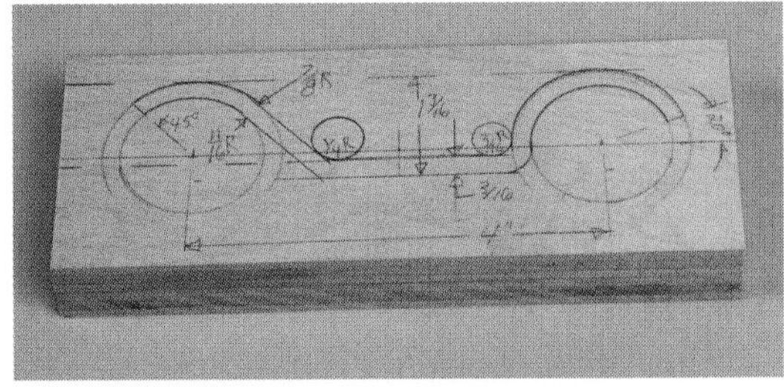

Photo C • *Fasten together the two plywood fender blanks to guarantee that the finished shapes are symmetrical. Use oversize blanks to allow the layout of the holes that will form the wheel wells.*

FENDERS

Quantities given are for fabrication of a single component (or paired set of components). See text for suggested numbers of components.

PART	SIZE (IN.)	QUANTITY	MATERIAL
Fenders (full size)	1$^3/_{16}$ x $^3/_8$ x 5$^{15}/_{32}$	2	Maple plywood
Fender supports	$^1/_2$ x $^3/_{32}$ x 2$^9/_{16}$	2	Maple
Flanges	$^3/_8$ x $^1/_8$ x 1$^3/_8$	2	Maple
Fenders (half size)	1$^3/_{16}$ x $^3/_8$ x 3$^7/_{16}$	2	Maple plywood
Fender supports	$^1/_2$ x $^3/_{32}$ x 2	2	Maple
Flanges	$^3/_8$ x $^1/_8$ x 1$^3/_8$	2	Maple
Optional filler flanges	$^3/_8$ x $^1/_8$ x 1$^3/_8$	2	Maple

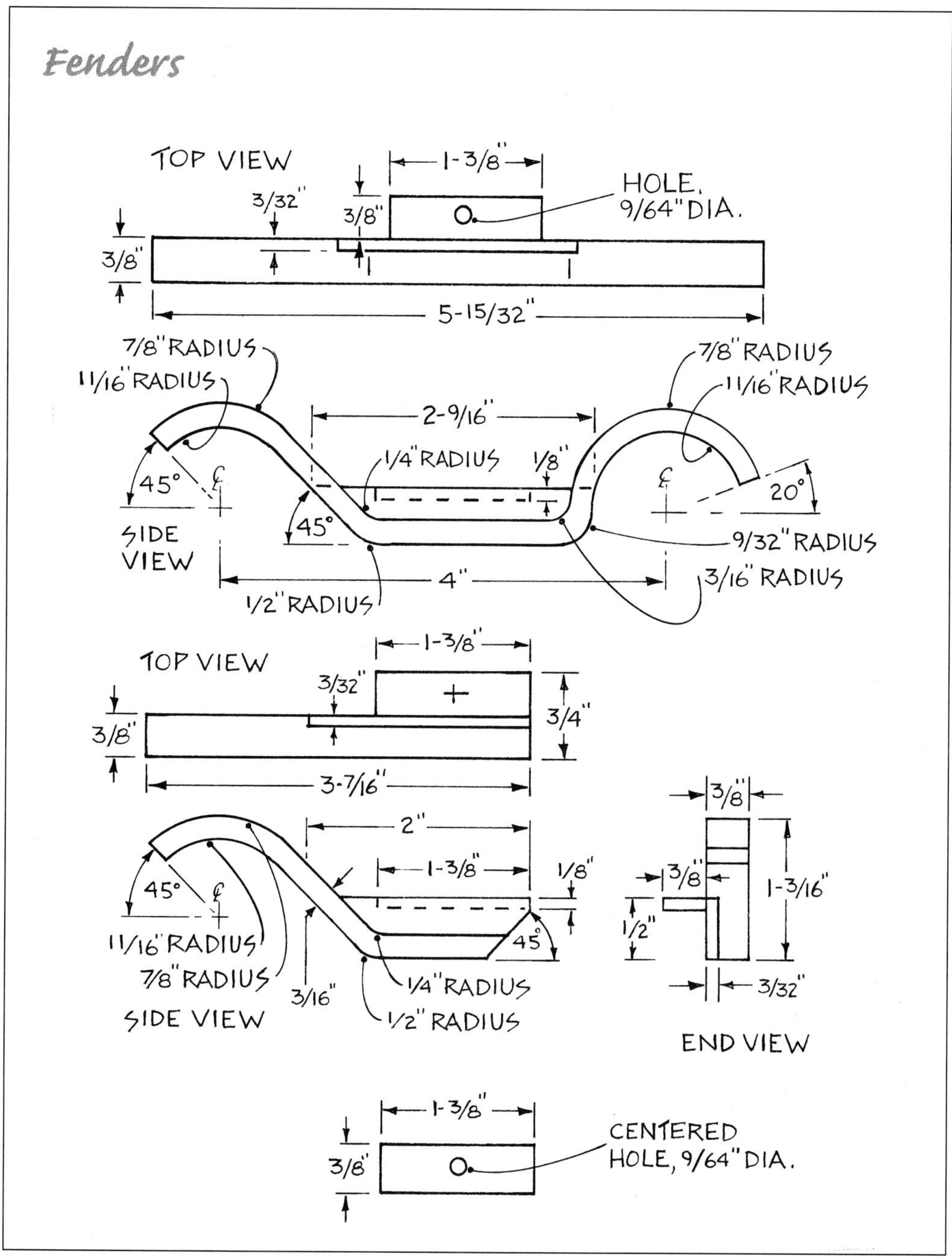

2. Drill the two 1⅜-in. holes for the wheel-well radius curves and also a ½-in.-diameter hole and a ⅜-in.-diameter hole to form, respectively, the ¼-in.- and 3⁄16-in.-radius curves at the top juncture of the front and rear fenders with the running board (see photo D on p. 110).

3. Complete the fender top profile on the scrollsaw (see photo E on p. 110).

4. Cut off the excess stock at the bottom of the workpiece on the table saw.

5. Separate the two fender blanks. To cut the 3⁄32-in. by ½-in. rabbet on the table saw, tape each workpiece to an auxiliary block, as in photo F on p. 110. Note that the two cuts are on opposite sides of the two workpieces, in mirror-image symmetry. Again, if you're not comfortable working

Photo D • *Drill 1⅛-in.-diameter holes in the blanks to create the interior wheel-well curves on the stacked fender blanks.*

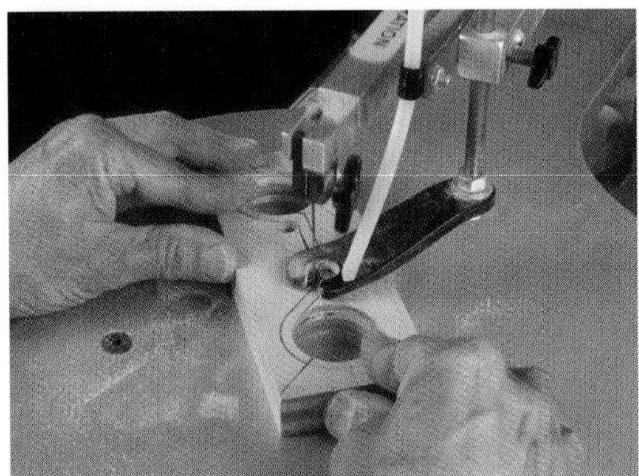

Photo E • *Patience is the key to cutting the fender profile accurately and smoothly on the scrollsaw.*

Photo F • *An auxiliary block secures each workpiece for cutting the mirror-image fender rabbets. Use a thicker block if you're uncomfortable working this close to the blade.*

on the table saw in this way, make a larger jig from a thicker board that keeps your hands farther from the blade.

6. Cut the two maple fender supports, ½ in. by ⅛ in. by about 2¾ in. long. Glue them into the rabbets, bottom edges flush with the running-board undersides. Trim the waste to match the fender profile.

7. Cut the two flanges to the dimensions indicated in the parts list, to fit the ⅛-in. by 1⅜-in. dado in each side frame of the chassis. Temporarily spot-tape the flanges into place on the chassis.

8. Position a fender with the underside of the running board flush with the bottom of the chassis. Slide it back and forth until it is centered between the wheels, making sure there's clearance for wheel rotation. Mark the top edge of the fender support and the flange to give a reference for alignment.

9. Remove the flange from the chassis and glue it to the fender support, aligned as marked.

10. Replace the fender assembly on the chassis and drill a ⅛-in.-diameter pinhole through the center of the flange portion and about ¼ in. into the chassis (see photo G).

Photo G • *Drilling the mounting pinhole through the fender flange into the chassis ensures the alignment of the components.*

11. Remove the fender assembly and redrill the flange hole to $^{9}/_{64}$ in. diameter, to provide clearance. Glue the $^{1}/_{8}$-in.-diameter dowel pin into the chassis and trim so that it sticks out $^{1}/_{8}$ in.
12. Repeat this process with the other fender.

The half-section fenders are made in the same way.

CHASSIS LOCKING CHANNELS

These pieces are glued to the undersides of all components to accommodate the locking assembly rod. The exact length varies from component to component. They are cut to the required lengths from oversize pieces. Gluing on the chassis locking channel is the last step in the fabrication of any part that utilizes it.

1. Cut a blank (any hardwood will do, since this piece is only visible on the underside of a vehicle) $^{3}/_{4}$ in. by $^{1}/_{2}$ in. by about 18 in. long. If you plan to make extra components, increase the length accordingly.
2. Cut a centered channel $^{9}/_{32}$ in. wide by $^{25}/_{64}$ in. deep running the length of the workpiece. I use a round-nose, $^{1}/_{4}$-in. endmill or router bit for this operation, which can be done with an overhead router, a handheld router, or on the drill press. However, since the channel will work with a square bottom, it can also be formed by parallel cuts on the table saw, or with a dado blade shimmed to cut $^{9}/_{32}$ in. wide.

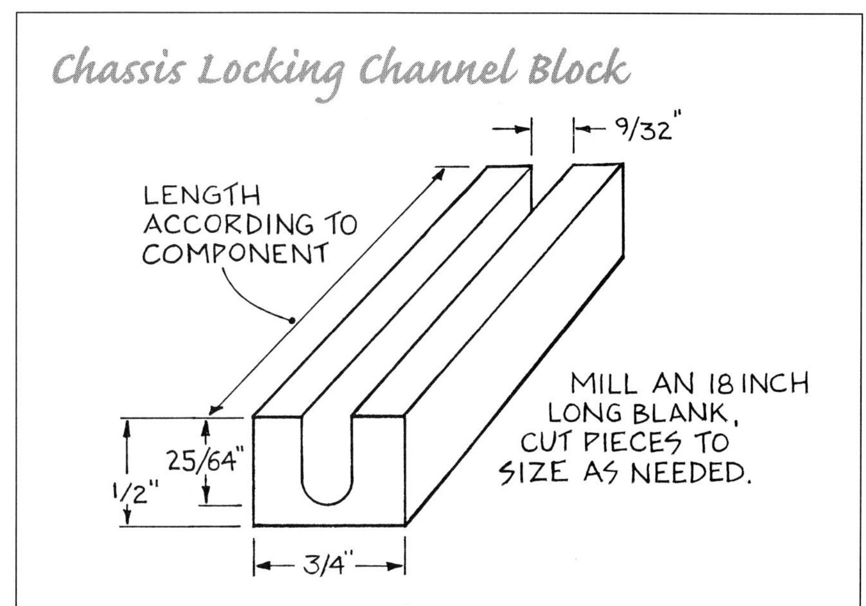

HOODS

There is a large selection of hoods to choose from. Some are very simple to make and do not have detailed step-by-step instructions.

■ HOODS

Quantities given are for fabrication of a single component (or paired set of components). See text for suggested numbers of components.

PART	SIZE (IN.)	QUANTITY	MATERIAL
Hood #1 (w/1 in. locking channel)	1 3/8 x 1 x 1 3/8	1	Cherry
Hood #2 (w/1 7/16 locking channel)	1 1/2 x 1 3/16 x 1 3/4	1	Cherry
Hood #3 (w/1 3/8 locking channel)	1 1/2 x 1 3/16 x 1 3/8	1	Cherry
Hood #4 (w/2 21/32 locking channel)	1 1/2 x 1 x 2 17/32	1	Cherry
Radiator (for hood #4)	1 x 3/16 x 1 1/16	1	Walnut
Aluminum rivet for radiator	1/8 dia.	1	Commercial
Hood #5 (1 3/16 locking channel)	1 3/8 x 1 1/8 x 1 1/2	1	Cherry
Fenders (for hood #5)	5/8 x 11/32 x 1 1/2	2	Cherry
Hood #6	1 5/16 x 17/32 x 1 5/8	1	Cherry

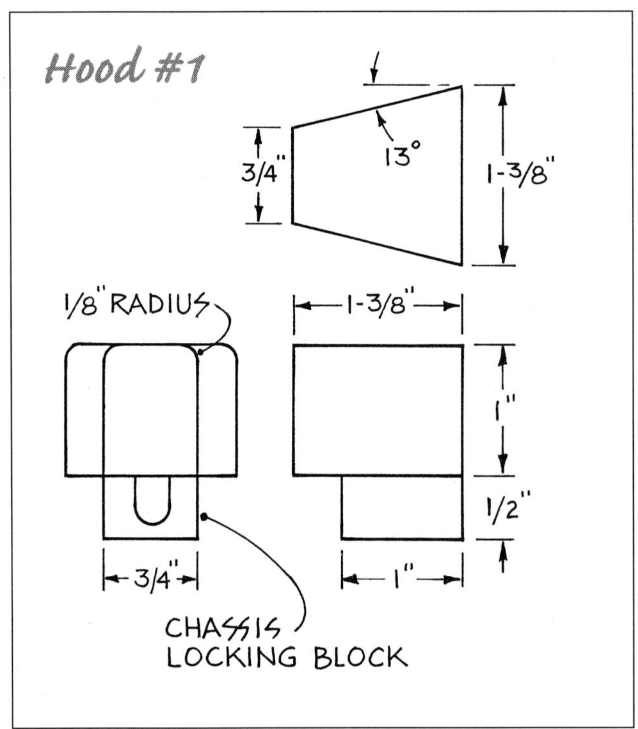

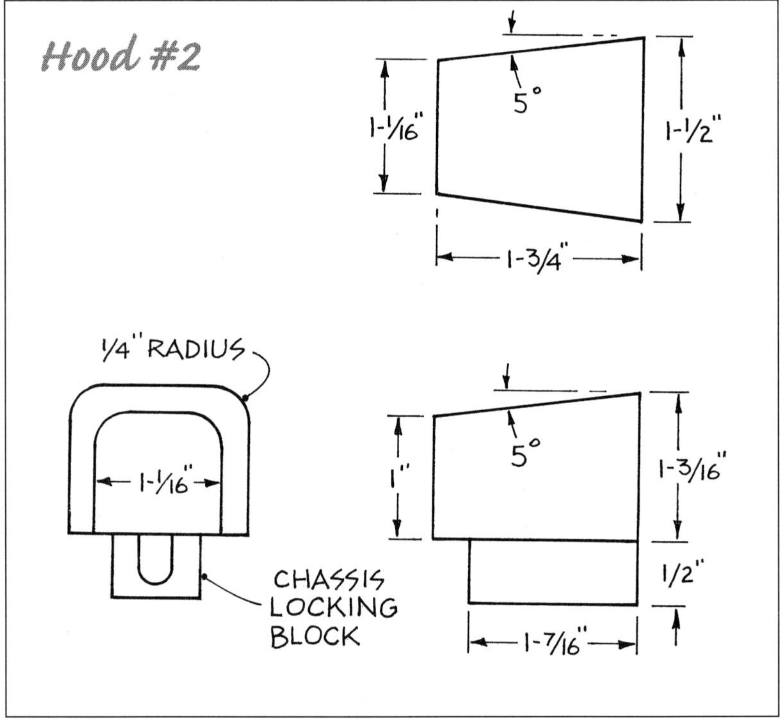

Hood #3

1-1/2"
1-3/16"
1/4" RADIUS
CHASSIS LOCKING BLOCK
1-3/8"

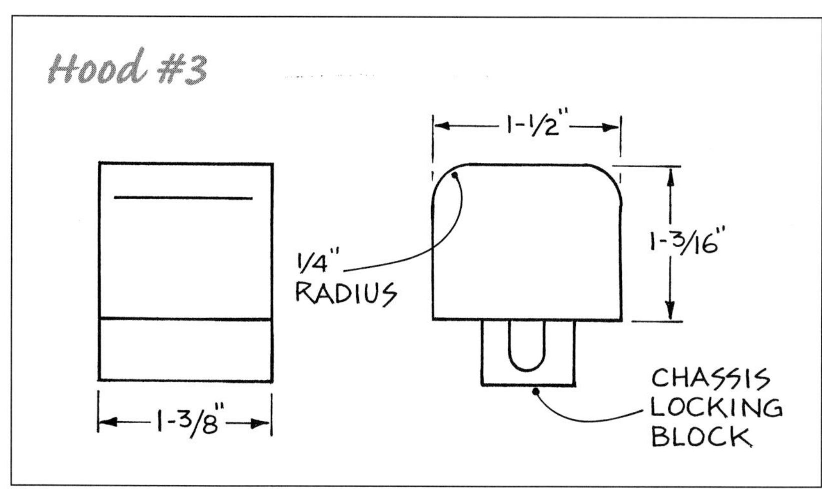

Hood #4

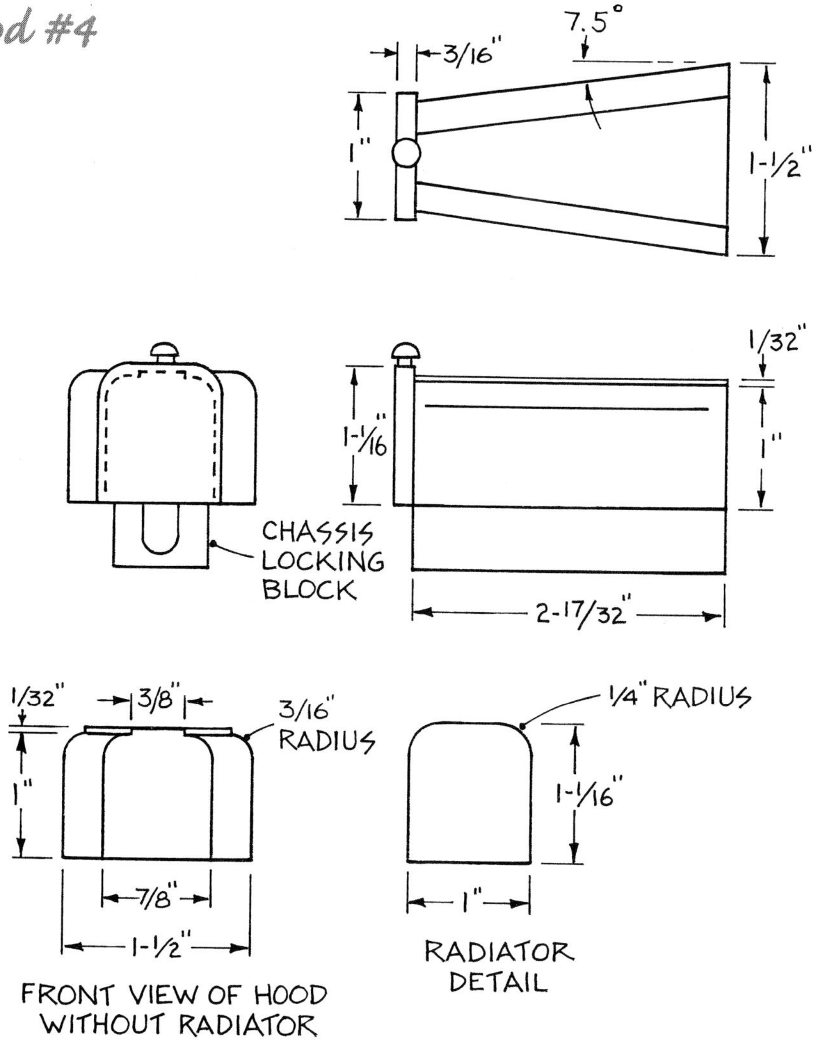

7.5°
3/16"
1"
1-1/2"
1/32"
1-1/16"
1"
CHASSIS LOCKING BLOCK
2-17/32"
1/32"
3/8"
3/16" RADIUS
1"
7/8"
1-1/2"
FRONT VIEW OF HOOD WITHOUT RADIATOR
1/4" RADIUS
1-1/16"
1"
RADIATOR DETAIL

WORKING SMARTER

At my age, my hand isn't quite as steady as it once was, so I prefer cutting the kind of angles found in the hoods mechanically, using jigs on the table saw. However, they can also be cut on the bandsaw and then smoothed out with a sanding block.

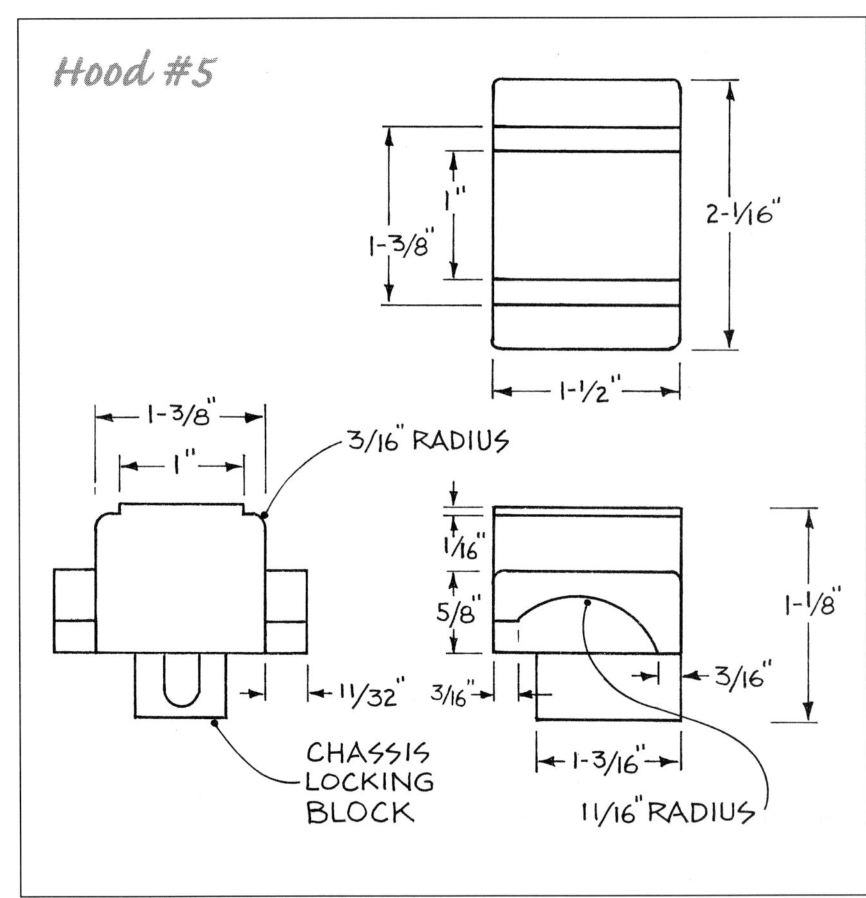

Hoods #1, #2, and #4

These hoods all have side taper cuts that can be made with the same type of simple angle jig after the blanks have been cut to overall block size (see photo H). You'll need a different jig for each hood since the angles are different, as indicated in the drawings.

The radius on the top sides of these three hoods can be formed on an overhead router with a roundover bit (see photo I), on a router table with a different type of jig, or by hand with a miniature spokeshave, as in photo J.

Photo H • *A simple jig gives you the side angles on hoods #1, #2, and #4.*

1. For hood #4, cut the walnut radiator to shape, as indicated in the plan drawing, on the table saw; the radius curves can be cut on the scrollsaw.

Photo I • *The top-edge radius on hoods #1, #2, and #4 is most easily cut with an overhead arm router with a roundover bit.*

Photo J • *To cut the radius on the hoods, a miniature spokeshave will also do the trick.*

2. Glue it to the front of the hood, flush at the bottom and centered side to side. A 1/8-in. peg painted with silver paint or, better yet, a small aluminum rivet set into the top center makes a nice looking radiator cap.

Hoods #3 and #5

These hoods require no angle cuts. Hood #3 is simply cut to its overall size (see the plan drawing), and the top radius on each side is then formed as described above.

1. For hood #5, cut the central piece to its overall block size on the table saw.
2. Lay out the two fenders on 11/32-in.-thick stock and cut them to shape on the scrollsaw. Smooth the curves with sandpaper fastened to a dowel with double-sided tape.
3. Create the top radius (which is slightly recessed, forming a lip in the top surface of 1/16 in.) on the overhead router with a roundover bit. Alternately, this feature can be made by first cutting a 1/16-in. by 3/16-in. rabbet on the table saw and then shaping the curve with a file or sandpaper (the lip prevents using the miniature spokeshave here).

Photo K • *Hood #5's recessed top edge curve, with its shallow lip, can be formed either on the overhead router or as a rabbet that is then rounded by hand. This can also be performed on a router table.*

4. Glue the fenders to the central piece, positioned as indicated in the plan drawing.
5. Cut and glue locking channels onto all the hoods, centered left to right. Lengths are given both in the parts list and the plan drawing.

There is a sixth hood, but it's covered below in the section on the Indy 500 racer.

CABS

There are more cabs than any other component type, and some of them are reasonably involved in construction.

CABS

Quantities given are for fabrication of a single component (or paired set of components). See text for suggested numbers of components.

PART	SIZE (IN.)	QUANTITY	MATERIAL
Cab #1 (locking channel $1\frac{3}{16}$)	$1\frac{1}{2}$ x $1\frac{3}{16}$ x $1\frac{3}{4}$	1	Cherry
Cab #2 (locking channel $1\frac{1}{4}$)	$1\frac{5}{8}$ x $1\frac{1}{4}$ x 2	1	Cherry
Cab #3 (locking channel 1)	2 x 1 x $1\frac{7}{8}$	1	Cherry
Cab #4 (locking channel $1\frac{11}{32}$)	2 x $1\frac{3}{4}$ x 2	1	Cherry
Cab #5 (locking channel $1\frac{3}{4}$)	$2\frac{1}{8}$ x $1\frac{5}{8}$ x $1\frac{3}{4}$	1	Cherry
Roof	$1\frac{5}{8}$ x $\frac{1}{4}$ x $1\frac{15}{16}$	1	Walnut
Cab #6 (locking channel $1\frac{3}{4}$)			
Front panel	$1\frac{1}{2}$ x $\frac{1}{4}$ x $2\frac{1}{8}$	1	Walnut
Back panel	$1\frac{1}{4}$ x $\frac{1}{4}$ x $2\frac{1}{8}$	1	Walnut
Side panels	$1\frac{5}{8}$ x $\frac{1}{4}$ x $2\frac{1}{8}$	2	Walnut
Roof	$1\frac{5}{8}$ x $\frac{1}{4}$ x $1\frac{15}{16}$	1	Walnut
Floor panel	$1\frac{1}{4}$ x $\frac{1}{2}$ x $1\frac{3}{8}$	1	Cherry
Cab #7 (locking channel $1\frac{1}{4}$)	$1\frac{5}{8}$ x 2 x $1\frac{1}{4}$	1	Cherry
Windshield	$\frac{3}{16}$ x $\frac{5}{32}$ x $1\frac{5}{8}$	1	Cherry
Cab #8 (locking channel $1\frac{3}{4}$)			
Front panel	$1\frac{3}{8}$ x $\frac{1}{4}$ x $1\frac{3}{16}$	1	Cherry
Back panel	$1\frac{3}{8}$ x $\frac{1}{4}$ x $2\frac{1}{8}$	1	Cherry
Side walls	$1\frac{3}{4}$ x $\frac{1}{4}$ x $2\frac{1}{8}$	2	Cherry
Floor panel	$1\frac{1}{4}$ x $\frac{1}{2}$ x $1\frac{5}{16}$	1	Cherry
Windshield	$1\frac{3}{8}$ x $1\frac{1}{16}$	1	$\frac{1}{16}$ clear plastic
Driver	$\frac{7}{8}$ dia. x $2\frac{3}{8}$	1	Commercial
Cab #9 (locking channel $1\frac{25}{32}$)	2 x $1\frac{1}{8}$ x $1\frac{25}{32}$	1	Cherry
Windshield	$\frac{3}{8}$ x $\frac{1}{4}$ x $1\frac{1}{4}$	1	Walnut
Driver	$\frac{5}{8}$ dia. x $1\frac{3}{16}$	1	Commercial
Cab #10 (locking channel $1\frac{15}{16}$)			
Body	$1\frac{1}{2}$ x 1 x $2\frac{15}{16}$	1	Cherry
Windshield	$1\frac{3}{8}$ x $\frac{1}{4}$ x $\frac{3}{4}$	1	Cherry
Bottom back block	$1\frac{1}{2}$ x $\frac{1}{2}$ x $\frac{5}{8}$	1	Cherry
Top piece	$1\frac{3}{8}$ x 1 x $1\frac{7}{8}$	1	Cherry
Cab #11 (locking channel $1\frac{7}{8}$)	$1\frac{1}{2}$ x $2\frac{9}{16}$ x $1\frac{3}{4}$	1	Cherry
Roof	$1\frac{5}{8}$ x $\frac{5}{16}$ x $4\frac{1}{8}$	1	Cherry

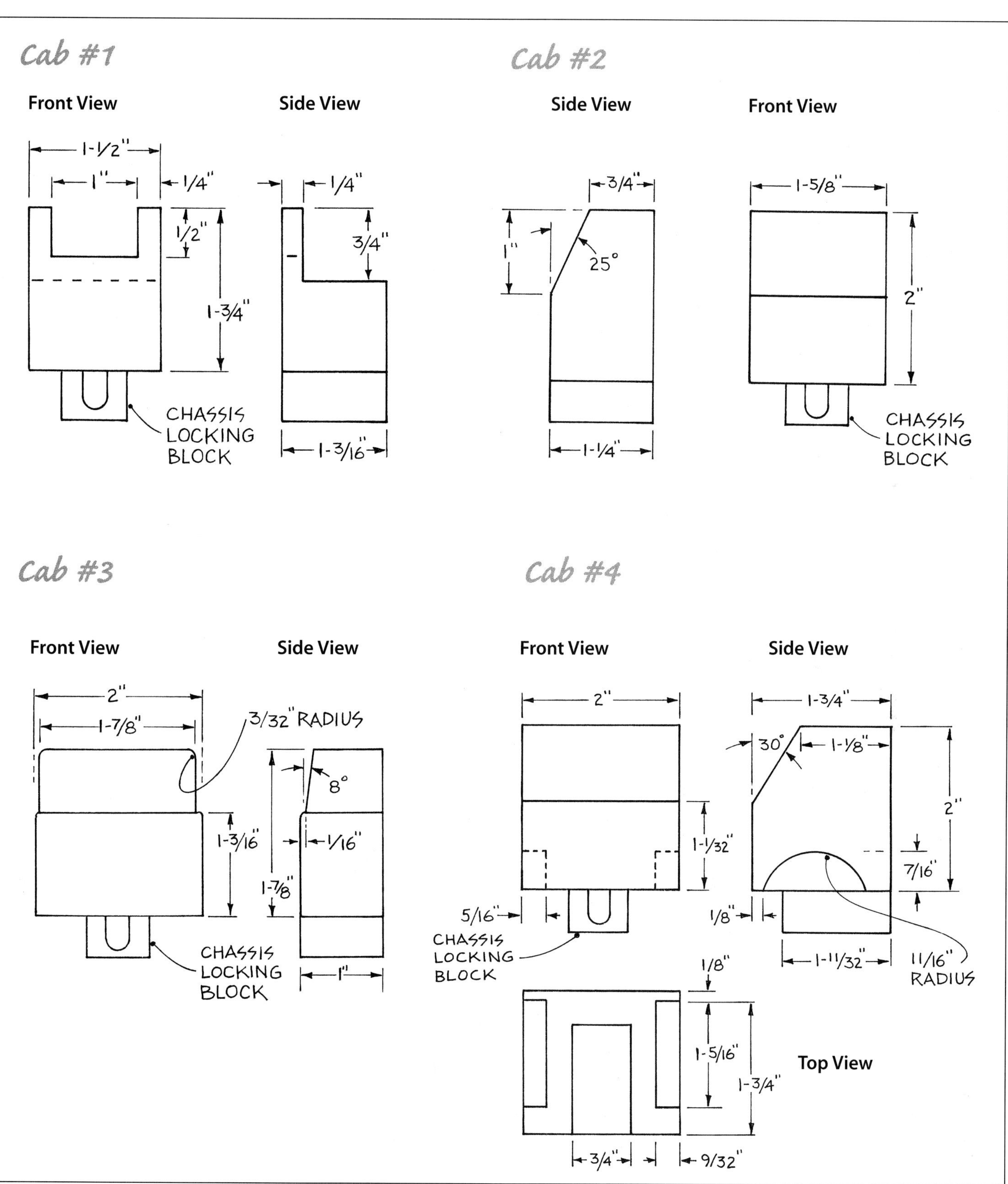

Cab #1
Front View
Side View
1-1/2"
1"
1/4"
1/4"
1/2"
3/4"
1-3/4"
CHASSIS LOCKING BLOCK
1-3/16"
Cab #2
Side View
Front View
3/4"
1"
25°
1-1/4"
1-5/8"
2"
CHASSIS LOCKING BLOCK
Cab #3
Front View
Side View
2"
1-7/8"
3/32" RADIUS
8°
1-3/16"
1/16"
1-7/8"
CHASSIS LOCKING BLOCK
1"
Cab #4
Front View
Side View
2"
1-3/4"
30°
1-1/8"
2"
1-1/32"
7/16"
5/16"
1/8"
CHASSIS LOCKING BLOCK
1-11/32"
11/16" RADIUS
1/8"
1-5/16"
1-3/4"
Top View
3/4"
9/32"

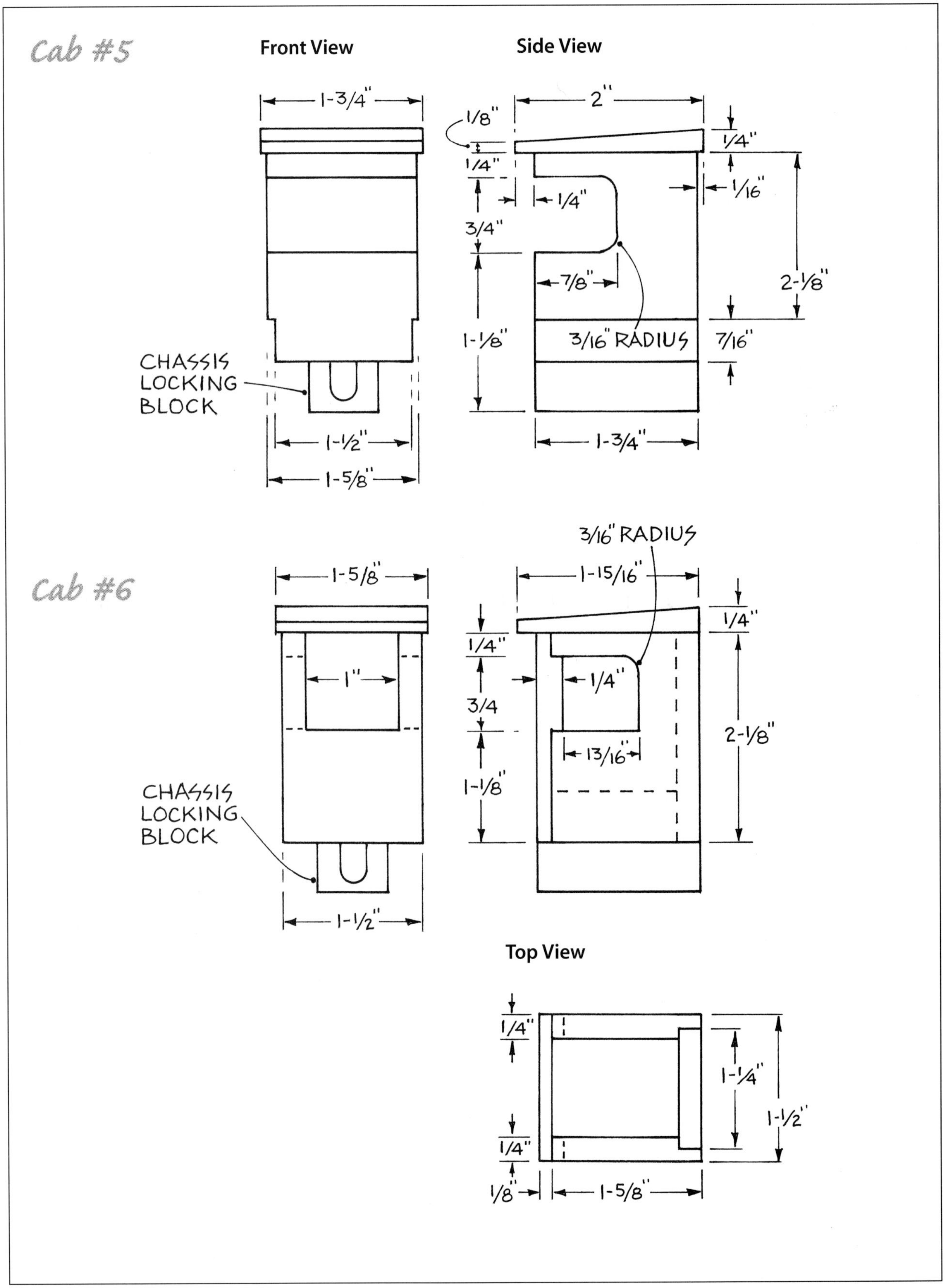

Cab #5

Front View

Side View

Cab #6

Top View

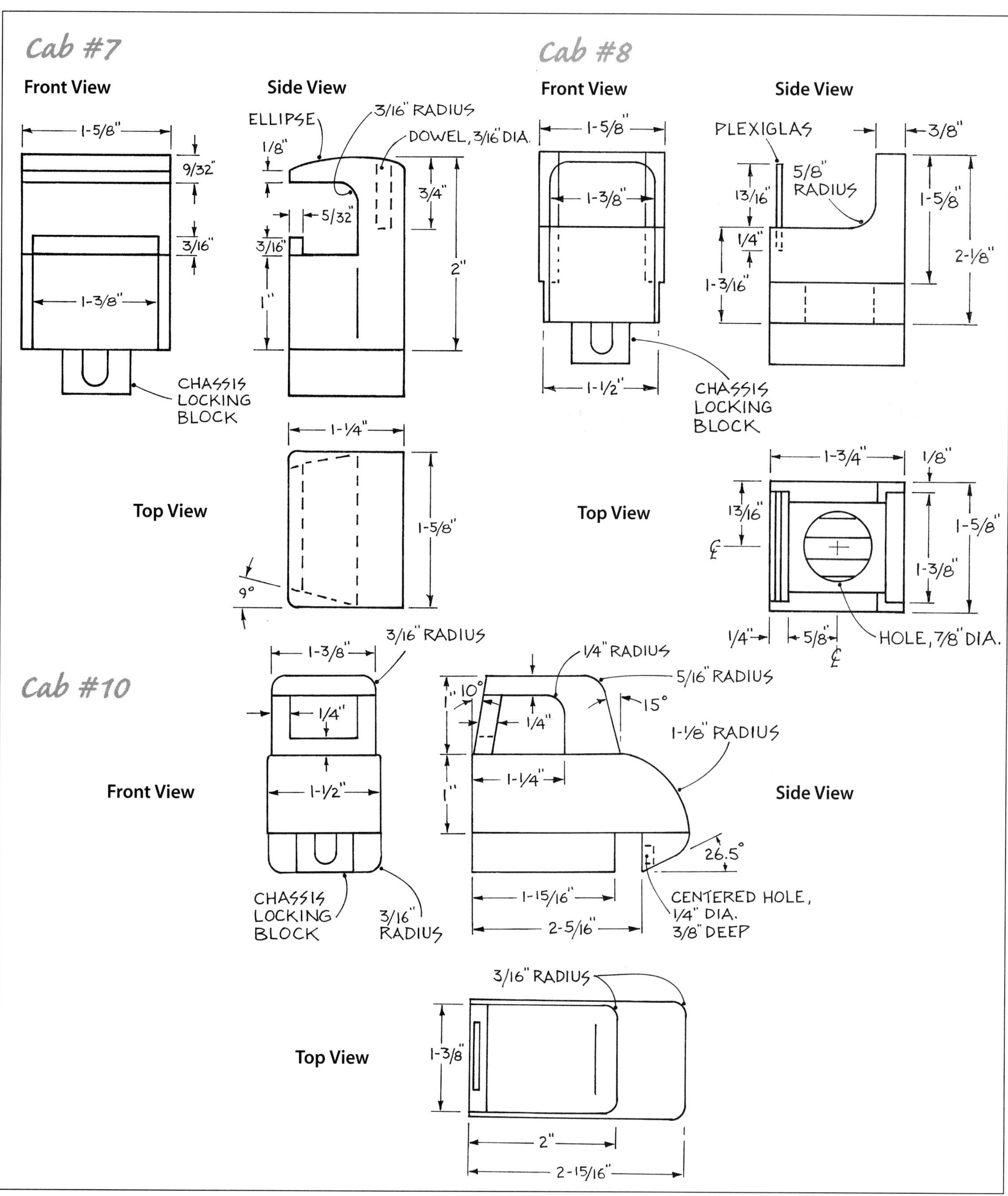
Cab #7
Front View
Side View
1-5/8"
9/32"
3/16"
1-3/8"
CHASSIS LOCKING BLOCK
ELLIPSE
3/16" RADIUS
DOWEL, 3/16" DIA.
1/8"
3/4"
5/32"
3/16"
2"
1"
1-1/4"
Top View
1-5/8"
9°
Cab #8
Front View
Side View
1-5/8"
1-3/8"
1-1/2"
CHASSIS LOCKING BLOCK
PLEXIGLAS
3/8"
13/16"
5/8" RADIUS
1-5/8"
1/4"
1-3/16"
2-1/8"
Top View
1-3/4"
1/8"
13/16"
1-5/8"
1-3/8"
1/4"
5/8"
HOLE, 7/8" DIA.
Cab #10
1-3/8"
3/16" RADIUS
1/4"
1-1/2"
Front View
CHASSIS LOCKING BLOCK
3/16" RADIUS
1/4" RADIUS
5/16" RADIUS
10°
15°
1/4"
1"
1-1/8" RADIUS
1-1/4"
1"
Side View
26.5°
1-15/16"
2-5/16"
CENTERED HOLE, 1/4" DIA. 3/8" DEEP
3/16" RADIUS
Top View
1-3/8"
2"
2-15/16"

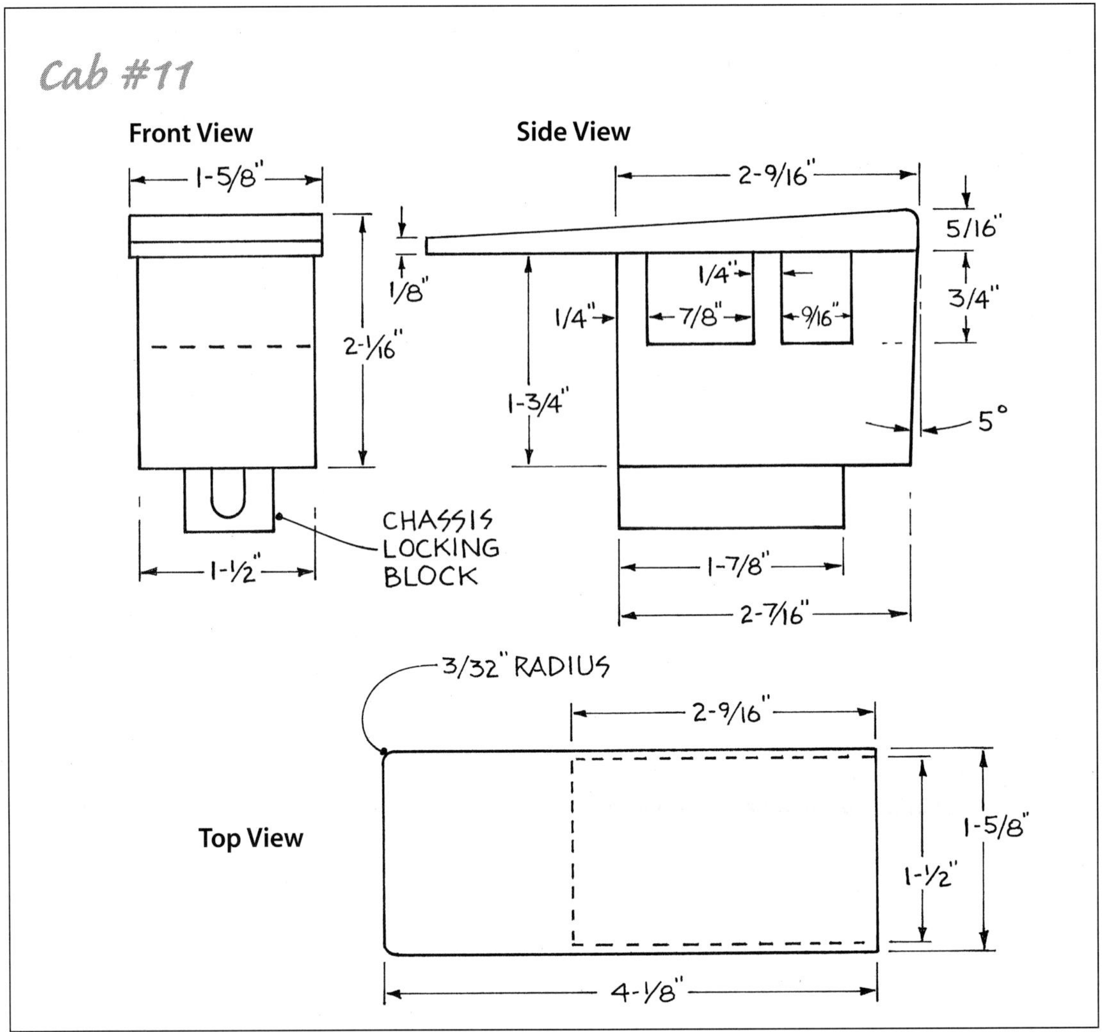

Cab #1

This cab can be combined with cab #11 to make a sedan. It is a simple part, which could be made in a number of ways. Here's one that I've used:

1. Cut the blank to its overall block size.
2. Create the "L" profile (see the plan drawing) with two cuts on the table saw.
3. Cut out the window area on the scrollsaw.

Cab #2

1. Cut the blank to overall block size.
2. Make the 25-degree angle cut on the bandsaw or, alternately, on the table saw with the workpiece taped to an auxiliary fence on the miter gauge.

Cab #3

1. Cut the blank to the correct overall block size.
2. Cut the $^{1}/_{16}$-in. by $^{11}/_{16}$-in. rabbet that wraps around the front and sides.

3. Lay out the 8-degree angle and cut it on the bandsaw, or on the table saw with an auxiliary block.

Cab #4

1. Cut a piece of stock to the overall block size and fasten a piece of scrap with double-sided tape to the bottom of the workpiece.
2. Drill the four holes that will form the wheel wells.
3. Make the 30-degree angle cut on the table saw to finish shaping the part.

Cab #5

1. Cut the block to size and drill the two 3/8-in. holes to form the 3/16-in.-radius curves at the back of the cutout area.
2. Complete the cutout on the bandsaw, using a narrow blade. I recommend starting the cut in the waste area, cutting into the hole, and then exiting from it along the final edge; it's much easier than trying to hit it right on the way in. Alternately, the two entry cuts can be made on the table saw with the workpiece facedown.
3. To cut the shallow angle of the walnut roof cap, fasten it with double-sided tape to an auxiliary block with one side cut to a 3-degree angle, as in photo L.

Cab #6

This cab consists of six pieces that are cut to shape and then glued together to enclose the cab's inner space. To help you see how this works, I've added a perspective drawing of the components on p. 122. To make this part:

1. Cut all pieces to their correct overall sizes, as indicated in the parts list.
2. Cut the upper and lower rabbet cuts on the inside of the front panel, as indicated in the plan drawing. The vertical cuts are made on the table saw with the workpiece in a vertical position on an auxiliary block, and the two shallow horizontal cuts are made on the scrollsaw. These recesses will receive the side panels.

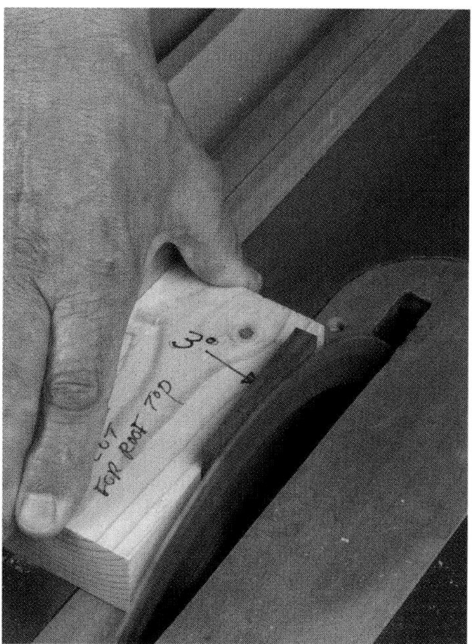

Photo L • *The walnut roof cap for cab #5 is secured with double-sided tape to a slightly tapered block for the shallow angle cut.*

3. Cut the inside bottom rabbets on the side panels, to receive the floor panel. Then cut the inside back edge rabbet that will receive the back panel.
4. Drill a 3/8-in.-diameter hole in each side panel to form the indicated 3/16-in. radius in the window area. I recommend a Forstner bit if you have one.
5. Working on the scrollsaw, cut out the window areas in the side panels and also the windshield area of the front panel.
6. Cut out the roof blank and make the angle cut as for the roof of cab #5.
7. Glue the floor and perimeter panels together. I've found Quick-Grip clamps to be handy for this procedure, but rubber bands will work, too.
8. Glue the roof in place.

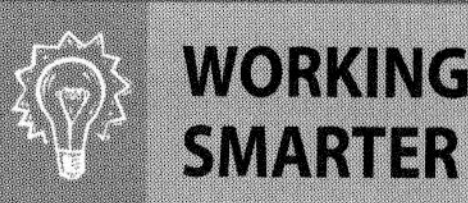

WORKING SMARTER

When I'm drilling to form a radius curve in a thin piece like one of the side panels of cabs #6 and #8, my first choice is a Forstner bit, for the clean edge it leaves. But because Forstner bits tend to overheat in thicker stock, I'll opt for a regular brad-point bit in a solid piece like cab #5.

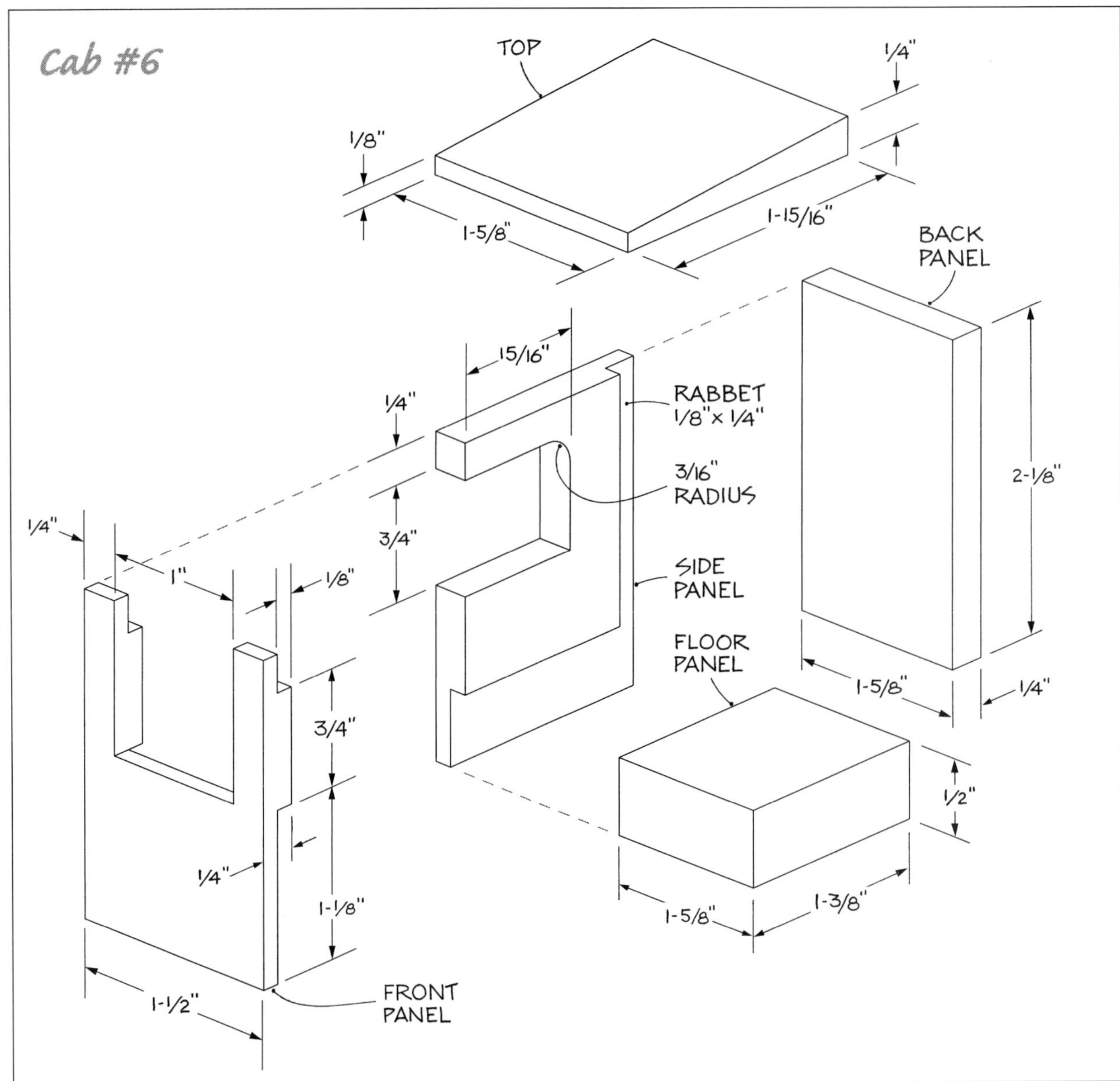

Cab #7

1. Cut a blank to the correct overall block size, as indicated in the parts list.
2. Lay out the front and side views on the workpiece for reference purposes.
3. Locate and drill a hole $3/4$ in. deep into the top of the workpiece, $1/4$ in. from the back edge and centered left to right. Glue in a length of $3/16$-in. dowel and trim it flush. This will add strength to the overhanging top of the cab, helping to prevent its shearing off in the event of an acciden–tal blow.
4. Drill a hole into the side of the workpiece with a $3/8$-in. bit to create the $3/16$-in. radius at the top rear of the cutout area, as indicated in the plan drawing.
5. With the workpiece facedown on the table saw, make a cut to form the bottom of the cutout area. Repeat for the top inside cut, stopping short of the hole. Complete the cutout on the bandsaw.
6. Cut the windshield strip to size and glue it into place at the front of the cutout area.

7. Raise the table-saw blade to a height of $1\frac{3}{8}$ in. and rotate the miter gauge (fitted with an auxiliary fence) 9 degrees in a clockwise direction. Align the workpiece on the fence facing forward, with the blade just clearing the line on the front right, and make the cut to produce the front right taper (see photo M). It's essential that the blade not exceed the indicated height, to keep it clear of the cab's roof.

Photo M • *To cut the angle on each side of the cab, set the miter gauge to 9 degrees.*

8. Rotate the fence counterclockwise to 9 degrees off square and, working on the other side of the saw blade, make the corresponding cut on the left side of the workpiece. The cab's front should now be $1\frac{3}{8}$ in. wide. Clean up the cuts with a sanding block.

Cab #8

This cab is a component of the dune buggy and consists of a series of panels cut to fit and glued together, like cab #6. The drawing below should be helpful. This one also incorporates a clear plastic windshield.

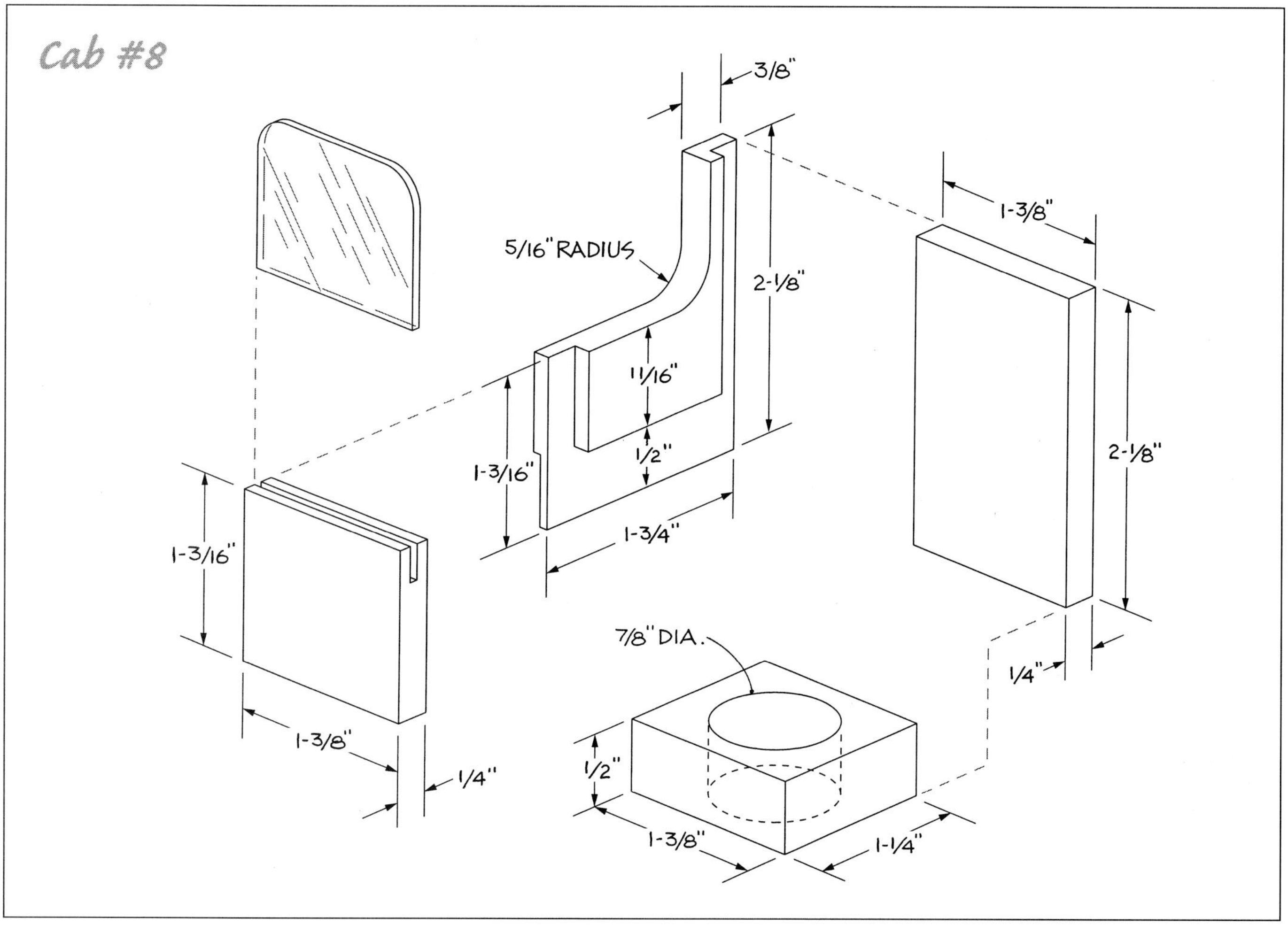

Cab #8

3/8"
5/16" RADIUS
2-1/8"
1-3/8"
11/16"
1/2"
1-3/16"
1-3/4"
2-1/8"
1-3/16"
7/8" DIA.
1/4"
1-3/8"
1/4"
1/2"
1-3/8"
1-1/4"

1. Cut the front panel, the back panel, the floor panels, and the two side panels to their correct overall sizes as indicated in the parts list.
2. On the table saw, cut a slit approximately $\frac{1}{4}$ in. deep in the top edge of the front panel to receive the clear plastic windshield. This plastic comes in both $\frac{1}{8}$ in. and $\frac{1}{16}$ in. thicknesses; either is fine—just be sure to use a blade with the appropriate kerf. Glue the windshield in place with epoxy.
3. Cut the mirror-image rabbets into the inside front and back edges of the side panels, as indicated in the plan drawing. Cut the indicated rabbets along the inside bottom edges to receive the floor panel. If you wish, cut the indicated $\frac{1}{16}$-in. by $\frac{1}{2}$-in. rabbets. They're for appearance only.
4. Drill a $\frac{5}{8}$-in.-diameter hole into each side panel to form the $\frac{5}{16}$-in.-radius curve. Complete cutting the panels to shape on the scrollsaw.
5. Drill a centered $\frac{7}{8}$-in. through hole in the floor panel to receive the commercially made figure indicated in the parts list.
6. Glue the components together as for cab #6.

Cab #9

Cab #9 is covered below in the section on the Indy 500 racer.

Cab #10

The body and top piece of cab #10 are both formed from blanks that are about 6 in. oversize in length to allow their safe handling during the bandsaw cuts and radius-forming operations.

1. Cut the main body blank to its correct width and thickness as indicated, leaving the length oversize at about 9 in.
2. Cut the bottom back block to its indicated size. Locate the center point on one of the $\frac{1}{2}$-in. by $1\frac{1}{2}$-in. faces and drill a $\frac{1}{4}$-in.-diameter hole $\frac{3}{16}$ in. deep to receive the assembly rod.
3. Glue the bottom back block to the rear underside of the main body blank (see the drawings for placement). Make sure the hole faces the cab's front end.
4. Cut the workpiece to its correct profile on the bandsaw (see photo N).

Photo N • *Shape the #10 cab profile on the bandsaw. An oversize blank makes it easy and safer to handle the workpiece while cutting the profile.*

5. Radius the trunk area (including the bottom block) on the overhead router, as in photo O. This step can also be executed on a router table.
6. Cut the workpiece to its correct final length of $2\frac{15}{16}$ in.
7. Cut a blank for the top piece, also about 6 in. oversize in length.
8. Cut the 15-degree angle at the rear of the top piece on the table saw, as in photo P. Form the external curve on a stationary belt sander.
9. Drill a $\frac{1}{2}$-in.-diameter hole to form the $\frac{1}{4}$-in. radius at the rear of the cutout area. Complete the cutout on the bandsaw, as in photo Q.

Photo O • *Use a $^{3}/_{16}$-in. router bit to contour the trunk area of cab #10. This operation can also be performed on a router table.*

Photo P • *The external curve of cab #10's top piece is first cut on the table saw.*

Photo Q • *After drilling to form the rear radius, bandsaw out the waste. Keeping the workpiece oversize at this time makes this work possible.*

10. Radius the top and rear edges as you did the trunk area of the main body blank. Cut the workpiece to its correct final length of 1$^{7}/_{8}$ in., with the table saw set to produce the 10-degree front edge angle.
11. Cut the windshield blank to its correct overall size; note that the top and bottom edges are cut at a 10-degree parallel angle. Make the cutout on the scrollsaw.
12. Glue the components together, using a single clamp top-to-bottom to apply pressure while holding the windshield in place.

Cab #11

1. Cut the blank to its overall dimensions.
2. On the table saw, make the four vertical cuts, $^{3}/_{4}$ in. deep, that form the fronts and backs of the window areas. Complete cutting out the windows on the scrollsaw.
3. Cut the cab's 5-degree back angle on the table saw.
4. Cut the roof blank to its overall size.
5. Using the same technique as for the roofs of cabs #5 and #6, cut the roof blank at an angle to produce a taper of $^{5}/_{16}$ in. to $^{1}/_{8}$ in., rear to front. Form the radius curve of the top rear edge with a sanding block.
6. Glue the roof in place, flush rear.

All cabs

Cut and glue locking channels onto all the cabs, centered left to right. Note that the channels for cabs #10 and #11 are mounted flush with their front ends. All channel lengths are given both in the parts list and the plan drawings.

■ TRUCK PARTS

Quantities given are for fabrication of a single component (or paired set of components). See text for suggested numbers of components.

PART	SIZE (IN.)	QUANTITY	MATERIAL
Bed #1 (locking channel $1\frac{3}{8}$)			
Side panels	$1\frac{1}{4}$ x $\frac{1}{4}$ x $2\frac{1}{14}$	2	Cherry
End panels	$1\frac{1}{4}$ x $\frac{1}{4}$ x $1\frac{3}{4}$	2	Cherry
Floor	$1\frac{3}{4}$ x $\frac{1}{2}$ x $1\frac{3}{4}$	1	Cherry
Bed #2 (locking channel $2\frac{5}{16}$)			
Side panels	1 x $\frac{1}{4}$ x $3\frac{1}{4}$	2	Cherry
End panels	1 x $\frac{1}{4}$ x $2\frac{1}{4}$	2	Cherry
Floor	2 x $\frac{1}{4}$ x $3\frac{1}{4}$	1	Cherry
Wheel covers	$\frac{5}{16}$ x $\frac{1}{4}$ x $1\frac{5}{16}$	2	Cherry
Bed #3 (locking channel $2\frac{1}{8}$)			
Side panels	$1\frac{3}{8}$ x $\frac{1}{4}$ x $3\frac{1}{4}$	2	Cherry
End panels	$1\frac{3}{8}$ x $\frac{1}{4}$ x 2	2	Cherry
Floor panel	2 x $\frac{1}{4}$ x 3	1	Cherry
Floor Chassis	$1\frac{7}{16}$ x $\frac{11}{32}$ x 3	1	Cherry
Ribs	$\frac{1}{4}$ x $\frac{1}{16}$ x $3\frac{1}{4}$	4	Cherry
Ribs	$\frac{1}{4}$ x $\frac{1}{16}$ x $1\frac{3}{8}$	4	Cherry
Ribs	$\frac{1}{4}$ x $\frac{1}{16}$ x $\frac{7}{8}$	12	Cherry
Ribs	$\frac{1}{4}$ x $\frac{1}{16}$ x 2	2	Cherry
Cabin canopy (locking channel $\frac{1}{4}$)			
Top	$2\frac{1}{4}$ x $\frac{1}{4}$ x 1	1	Cherry
Back	$2\frac{1}{4}$ x $\frac{1}{4}$ x $2\frac{1}{2}$	1	Cherry
Van compartment (locking channel $3\frac{1}{4}$)			
Side panels	$2\frac{3}{16}$ x $\frac{1}{4}$ x $4\frac{1}{2}$	2	Cherry
Front panel	$2\frac{3}{16}$ x $\frac{1}{4}$ x $2\frac{1}{4}$	1	Cherry
Top panel	$2\frac{1}{4}$ x $\frac{1}{4}$ x $4\frac{5}{8}$	1	Cherry
Floor	2 x $\frac{5}{8}$ x $4\frac{3}{8}$	1	Cherry
Door	$1\frac{3}{4}$ x $\frac{3}{8}$ x 2	1	Cherry
Chassis	$1\frac{1}{2}$ x $\frac{7}{32}$ x $3\frac{9}{16}$	1	Cherry
Oil tank #1 (locking channel $1\frac{3}{8}$)	$1\frac{5}{8}$ dia x $1\frac{13}{16}$	1	Dowel
Oil tank #2 (locking channel $1\frac{13}{16}$)	$1\frac{5}{8}$ dia. x $1\frac{13}{16}$	1	Dowel
Tank caps	$\frac{3}{4}$ dia. x $\frac{1}{2}$	2	Dowel

■ TRUCK COMPONENTS

Beds

Beds #1 and #2 are for a short and a long pickup truck, respectively, and #3 can be used to make up a contractor's truck. I'd call it a dump truck, except that it lacks a dumping mechanism—maybe you can come up with one!

Photo R • *Hood #1, cab #7, bed #2, and the half fenders make up the pickup truck.*

Photo S • *Cab #3, hood #5, the cabin canopy, and bed #3 make up the contractor's truck.*

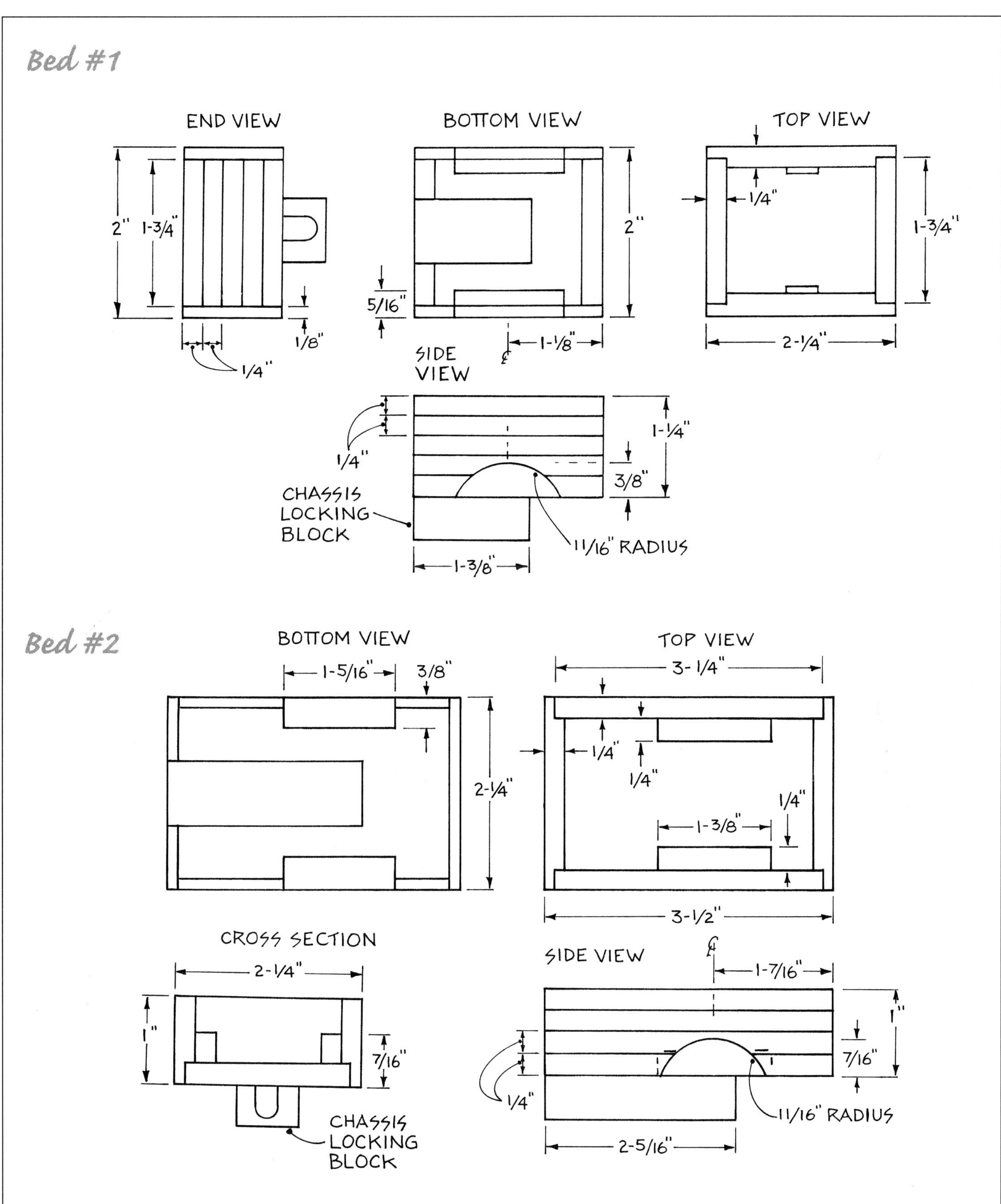
Bed #1
END VIEW
BOTTOM VIEW
TOP VIEW
2"
1-3/4"
1/8"
1/4"
2"
5/16"
1-1/8"
1/4"
1-3/4"
2-1/4"
SIDE VIEW
1/4"
1-1/4"
3/8"
CHASSIS LOCKING BLOCK
11/16" RADIUS
1-3/8"
Bed #2
BOTTOM VIEW
1-5/16"
3/8"
2-1/4"
TOP VIEW
3-1/4"
1/4"
1/4"
1/4"
1-3/8"
3-1/2"
CROSS SECTION
2-1/4"
1"
7/16"
CHASSIS LOCKING BLOCK
SIDE VIEW
1-7/16"
1"
7/16"
1/4"
11/16" RADIUS
2-5/16"

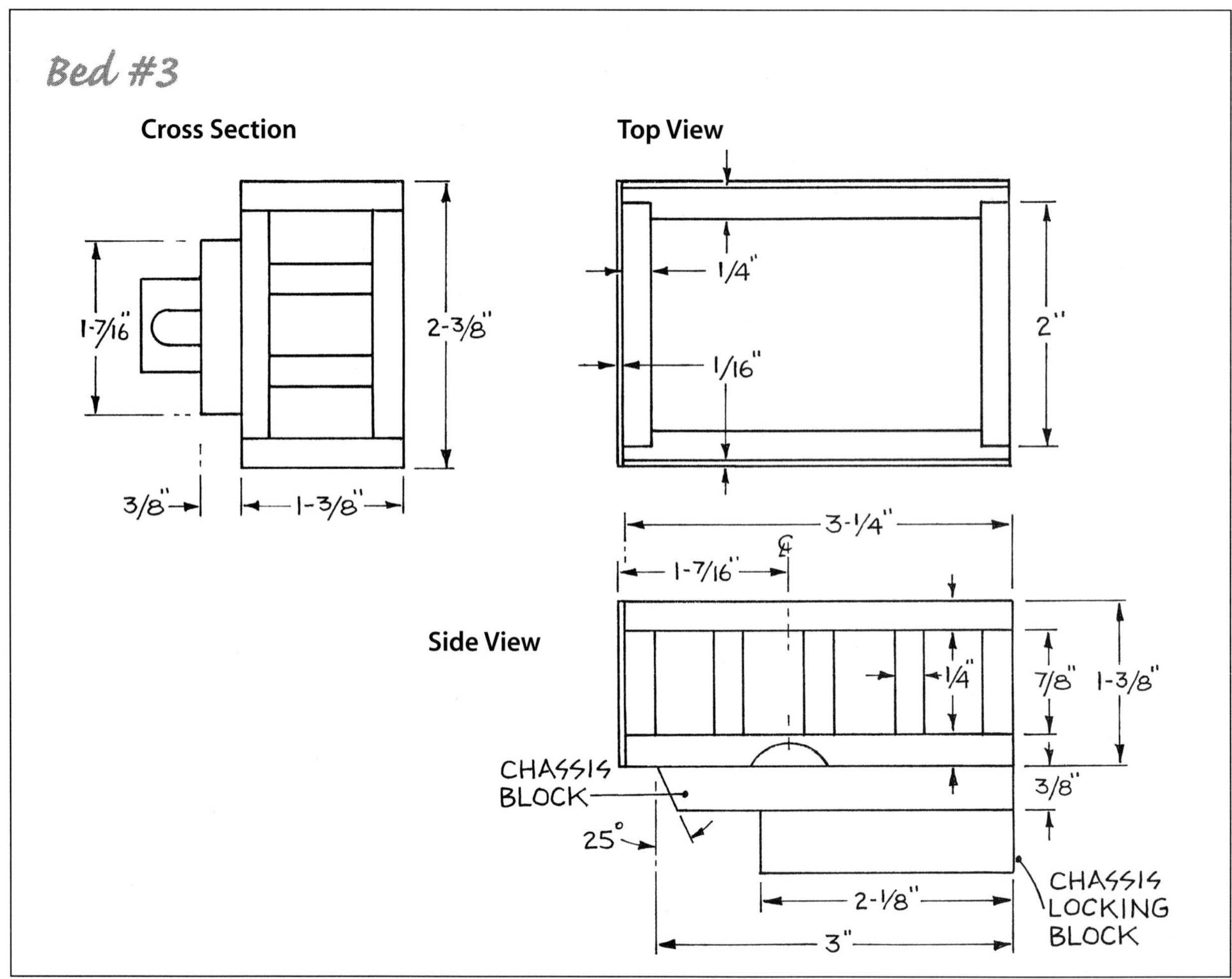

Bed #1

1. Cut all panels to size as indicated in the parts list.
2. Working on the table saw fitted with a very thin blade and the rip cut spacer-block setup, make the parallel cuts that delineate the "slats" on the side and end panels; see photos T and U.
3. Cut the $\frac{1}{8}$-in. by $\frac{1}{4}$-in. rabbets on the inside vertical edges of the side panels, to receive the end panels and a $\frac{1}{8}$-in. by $\frac{1}{2}$-in. rabbet on the inside bottom edge of each to receive the floor panel.
4. Glue the floor and perimeter panels together.
5. Cut an auxiliary block to measure $2\frac{1}{4}$ in. by $1\frac{1}{2}$ in. by 2 in. and fasten it to the bottom of the workpiece with double-sided tape. This block will provide a surface for the center point of the $1\frac{3}{8}$-in. wheel-well hole on each side, and prevent tearout during the drilling operation as well. Locate the center point of these holes as indicated on the plan drawing, and drill each one $\frac{5}{16}$ in. deep. Remove the auxiliary block with a letter opener.
6. Cut and glue a locking channel onto the bed, centered left to right and flush front. Lengths are given both in the parts list and the plan drawing.

Photo T • *To make the consistent parallel cuts that form the "slats" on the panels of beds #1 and #2, use a rip-fence stop and spacer blocks to align the workpiece for the cut. Note: This jig does not guide the workpiece through the cut.*

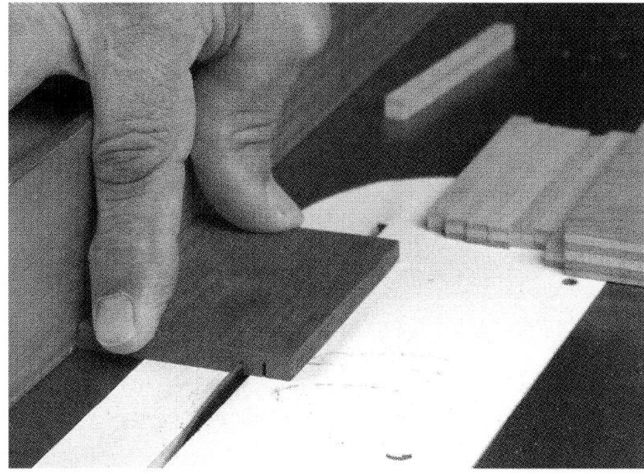

Photo U • *After each cut, remove a spacer block and slide the rip fence closer to the blade as much space as for the next cut. Note the spacer blocks are used for position only. You move the rip fence for each cut.*

Bed #2

This bed is essentially a larger version of #1, with some minor variations.

1. Cut all parts to size, as indicated in the parts list.
2. Cut a 1/8-in. by 1/4-in. rabbet in the bottom inside edge of the side and end panels. This will accommodate the floor panel.
3. Cut a 1/8-in. by 1/4-in. rabbet in each inside vertical edge of the two end panels. These will receive the side panels.
4. Glue the floor and perimeter panels together.
5. Cut the two internal wheel-well covers to correct block size and glue them in place, as indicated on the plan drawing.
6. Cut an auxiliary block 3 1/2 in. by 1 1/2 in. by 2 1/4 in. Fasten it to the bottom of the workpiece and locate and drill the wheel-well holes as you did for bed #1.
7. Again using the table-saw rip cut spacer-block setup, make the parallel cuts that define the "slats" in the side and end panels.
8. Cut and glue a locking channel onto the bed, centered left to right and flush front. Lengths are given both in the parts list and the plan drawing.

Bed #3

This bed is a little more involved because of the substantial number of small pieces that form the raised ribs, but it's really not any more difficult to fabricate. Here's the sequence:

1. Cut all pieces to size as indicated in the parts list, with the exception of the ribs. Note the 25-degree angle at the back of the chassis block, as indicated in the plan drawing.
2. Cut a couple of long strips to the width and thickness of the ribs. Prefinish these strips before cutting to the correct rib lengths; you'll get nice smooth brush strokes much more easily this way.
3. Cut a 1/8-in. by 1/4-in. rabbet in the bottom inside edge of the side and end panels to receive the floor panel.
4. Cut a 1/8-in. by 1/4-in. rabbet in each inside vertical edge of the two side panels to receive the end panels.
5. Glue the floor and perimeter panels together.
6. As for beds #1 and #2, fasten an auxiliary block about 1 1/2 in. thick to the underside of bed #3 to locate and drill the wheel-well holes.

7. Glue the chassis block into place as indicated in the plan drawing, flush front and centered left to right.
8. Glue all raised ribs in place as indicated in the plan drawing. For the two bottom side ribs, precut the indicated wheel-well sections on the scrollsaw.
9. Cut and glue a locking channel onto the bed, centered left to right and flush front. Lengths are given both in the parts list and the plan drawing.

Cabin canopy

The cabin canopy protects the cabin roof when rocks or debris are loaded by crane into the bed of a truck.

1. Cut the top panel to its overall dimensions.
2. Cut the back panel to its correct width and thickness, leaving it about ½ in. oversize in length. Cut one end at a 6-degree angle and then trim the other end square to bring the length to 2½ in.
3. Make the bottom corner back panel cutouts on the table saw with the workpiece mounted on an auxiliary fence, upright for the vertical cuts and on its side for the horizontal ones.
4. Lay out the locking channel cutout area on the workpiece. Drill a starter hole and make the cutout on the scrollsaw.
5. Glue the two panels together and then sand the back of the top panel flush with the back panel on a sanding block.
6. Fasten the workpiece to a machinist's square block with double-sided tape.
7. With a center punch, mark for two holes to receive ⅛-in. support dowels, ⅛ in. in from the back edge of the workpiece top and ½ in. in from each side. Hand hold the workpiece on the drill-press table and drill the holes ⅝ in. deep. The mass and precision of the machinist's block will give you the stability you need for this operation.
8. Glue the support dowels in place and trim them flush.

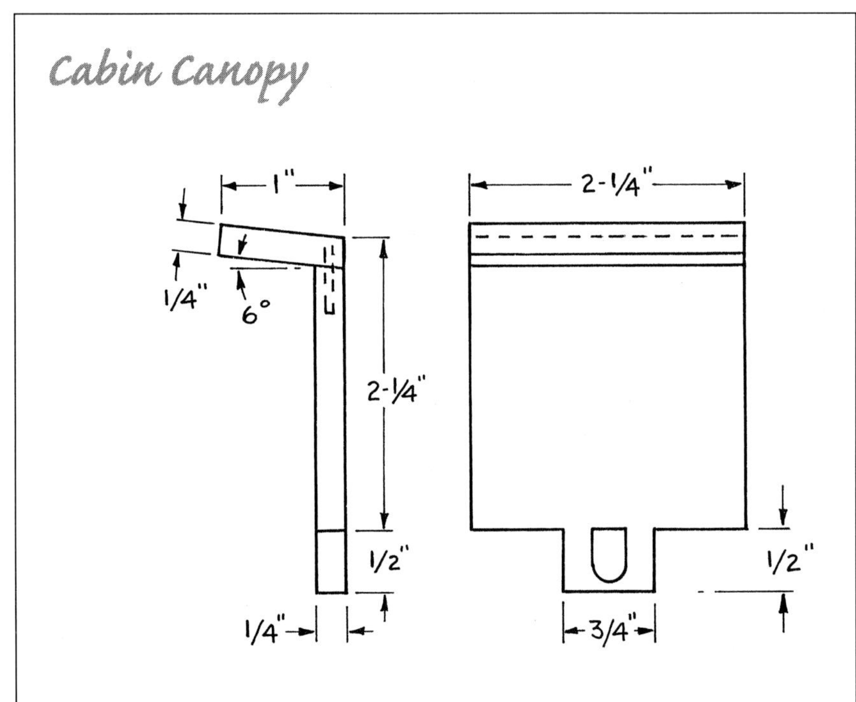

Photo V • *The notched-out area in the underside of the van compartment's floor and the recess in the door enable swiveling the door open on its pin hinges with one finger.*

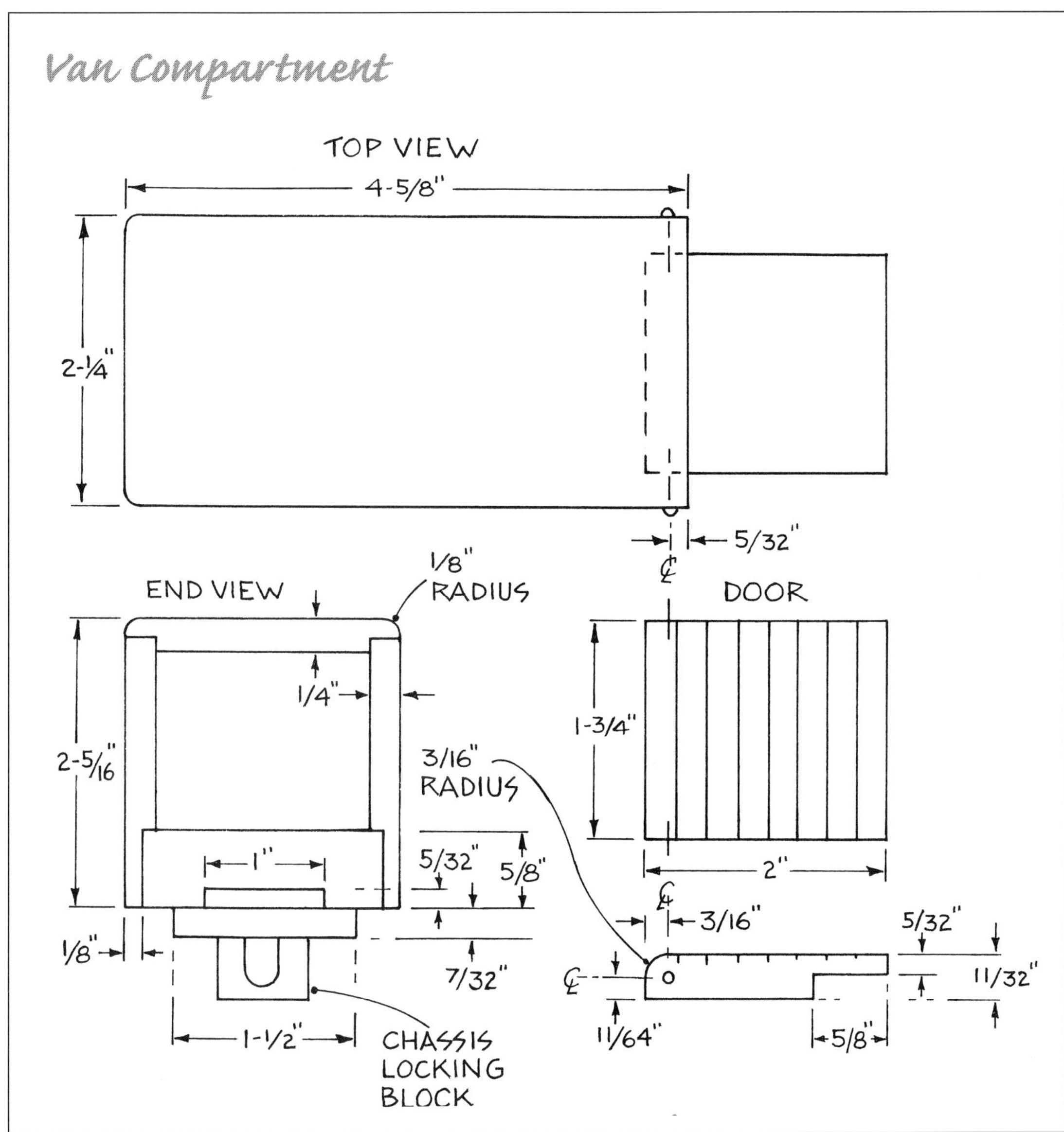

Van compartment

The van compartment combines with cab #4 for the look of a typical van.

1. Cut the side, top, and front panels and the floor to size as indicated.
2. Cut a 1/8-in. by 5/8-in. rabbet into the inside bottom edge of the two side panels to receive the floor.
3. Cut a 1/8-in. by 1/4-in. rabbet into the bottom side edges and the bottom front edge of the top panel to receive the side panels.
4. Cut 1/8-in. by 1/4-in. rabbets into the inside side edges of the front panel to receive the side panels, and a 1/8-in. by 5/8-in. rabbet into its bottom inside edge to receive the floor.
5. Rout out the area indicated in the plan drawing at the rear underside of the floor. This will facilitate opening the gate with a finger.
6. Glue together all panels and the floor, using one clamp side to side and one end to end.

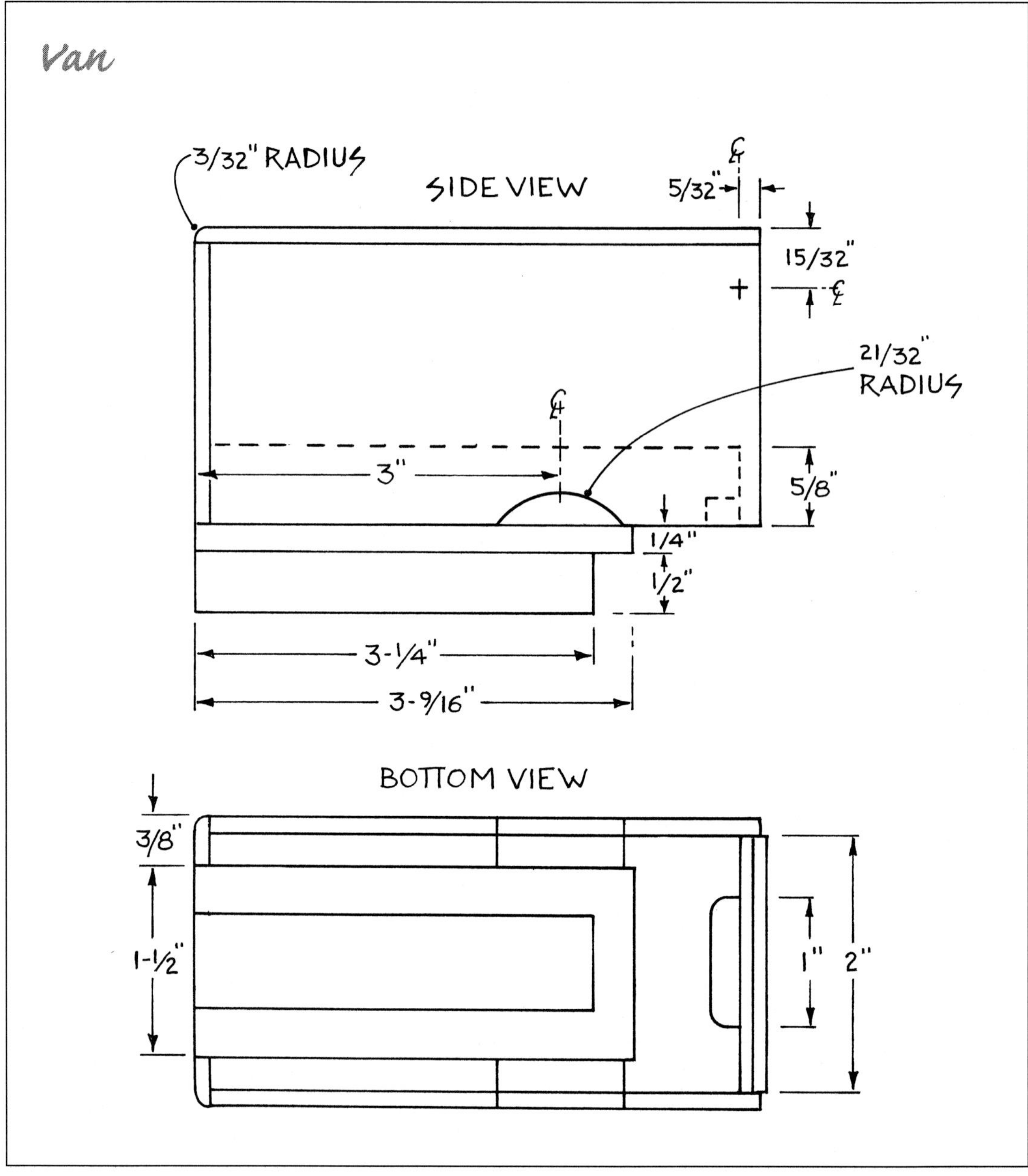

7. Using the same auxiliary block method as for the three truck beds, locate and drill the 1¼-in.-diameter wheel-well holes ⅜ in. deep, as indicated in the plan drawing.

8. Cut the chassis block to size and glue it to the compartment's underside, flush front and centered left to right.

9. Cut the door to size, leaving it just a hair oversize in width to allow for friction-fitting with a sanding block. Add the planking grooves, using the same spacer-block setup as for beds #1 and #2.

10. Radius the top edge of the door as indicated in the plan drawing, using a sanding block.

11. Sand the sides of the door to fit snugly into the compartment. Locate and drill the indicated pinholes through the side panels and into the door to receive a brass escutcheon pin on each side.

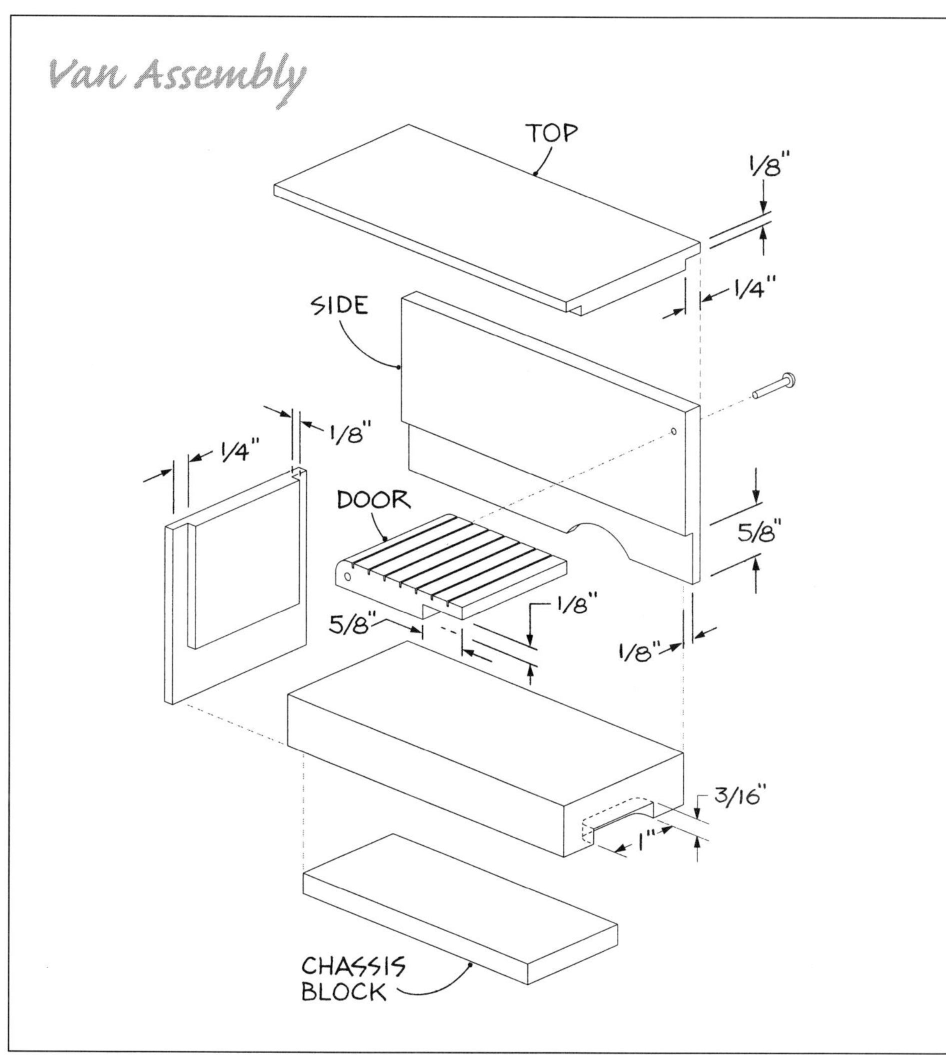

12 Cut and glue the locking channel to the compartment's underside, flush front and centered left to right.

Oil tanks

The two oil tanks can be used in tandem with cab #4 for a full-length tanker or singly with a hood and cab for a smaller version. They are essentially lengths of 1⁵⁄₁₆-in. dowel fitted with filler caps that are cut from ¾-in. dowel and glued into ½-in.-deep receiving holes.

1. Cut two square scrap blocks (the thickness isn't critical) with a side length equal to the actual diameter of the 1⁵⁄₁₆-in. dowel you will be using for the tanks.
2. Glue a block to each end of a 4½-in. length of the dowel, making sure the block sides are in the same plane.
3. Using the block sides as a guide against the table and fence of the table saw, cut the workpiece down to a width of 1½ in. The resulting flat surface on the dowel will receive the locking channels.
4. Slice off the ends of the workpiece near the joints with the scrap blocks, and cut the dowel into two pieces of the correct length.

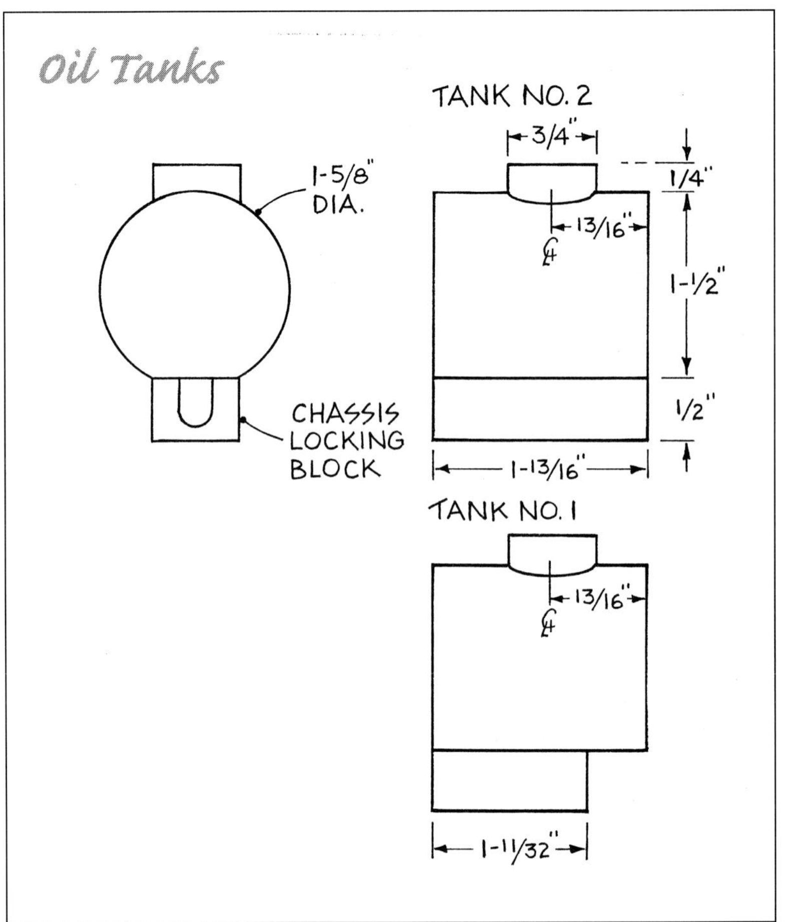

5. Drill the two blanks for the filler caps and glue them in place.

6. Cut and glue locking channels onto the two tanks. Note that they are not identical.

DUNE BUGGY COMPONENTS

Engine

1. Cut the engine-block blank and the two manifold blanks to their overall sizes.

Photo W • *The dune buggy consists of its own engine, cab #8, and the coupe back.*

■ DUNE BUGGY

Quantities given are for fabrication of a single component (or paired set of components).

PART	SIZE (IN.)	QUANTITY	MATERIAL
Dune buggy engine (locking channel 1 3/8)			
Block	1 x 27/32 x 1 1/2	1	Cherry
Exhaust manifolds	3/8 x 1/16 x 1 1/2	2	Walnut
Radiator	1 5/8 x 5/16 x 1 3/16	1	Cherry
Aluminum rivet for radiator	1/8 dia.	1	Commercial
Carburetor	1/4 peg	1	Commercial
Exhaust pipes	1/8 dia. x 7/16	8	Aluminum pins
Coupe back (locking channel 1 3/8)	1 1/2 x 1 3/16 x 1 15/16	1	Cherry
Driver		1	Commercial

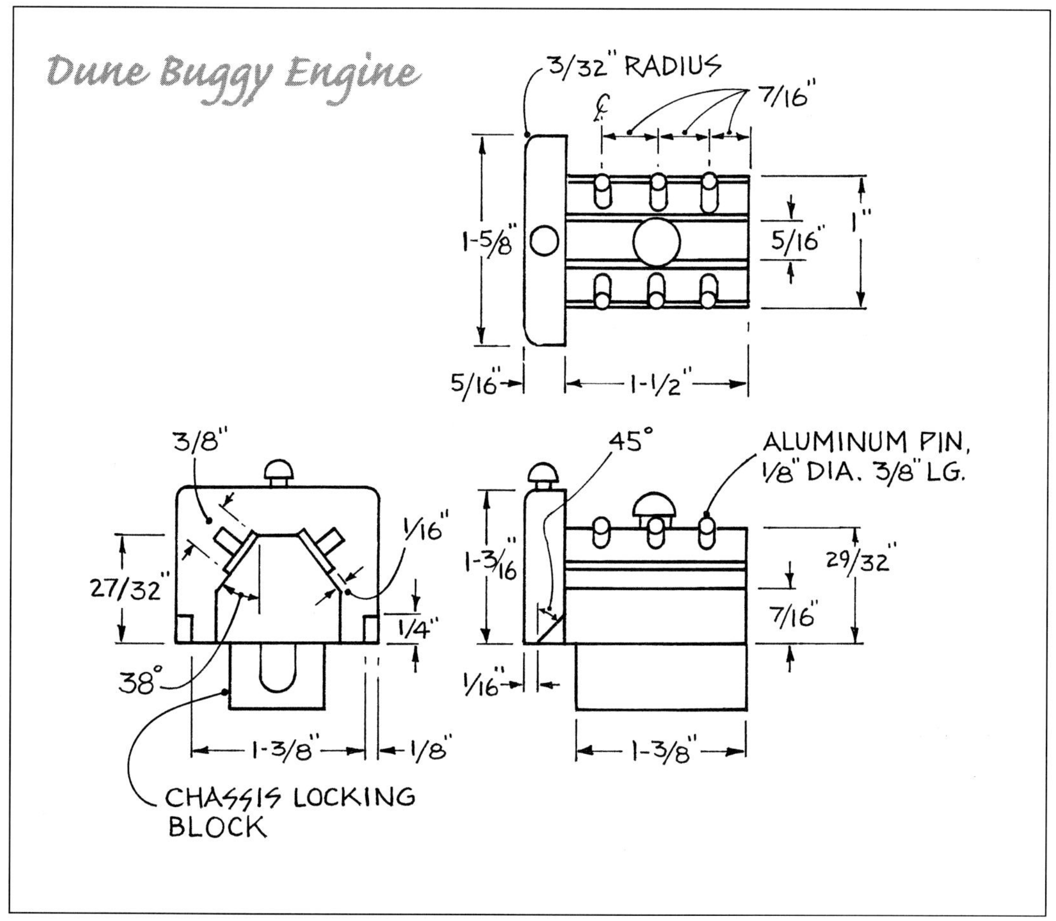

2. Cut both sides of the engine block at a 38-degree angle, as indicated in the plan drawing. Use the same type of jig as for the vertical and angle cuts in the Indy 500 engine (see the illustrations for that section, starting on p. 139).

3. Glue the manifolds to the angled surfaces, their edges lining up with the flat top area of the engine block.

4. Drill a hole in the top center of the engine block to receive a 1/4-in. commercial peg

(see the parts list) for the carburetor. The exact depth of this hole will depend on the peg you use.

5. Drill three evenly spaced holes through each manifold, using the special V block (see the drawing below), 1/8 in. diameter by 3/16 in. deep. These holes will receive the aluminum pins or painted dowel lengths as exhaust pipes. As always, if you're using wooden dowels, be sure to check actual diameter before drilling.
6. Cut the radiator blank to its overall size. Locate and drill the 1/8-in. hole centered on the top to receive a 1/8-in. aluminum rivet as the cap.
7. Round the front top and sides and also the top corners of the radiator blank at a 1/8-in. radius. This can be done either on the overhead router with a 1/4-in. roundover bit (with the workpiece fastened to a scrap block) or by hand-sanding. Notch the back bottom corners at a 45-degree angle and about 1/8 in. deep as indicated for wheel clearance.
8. Glue the radiator to the engine block, centered left to right and flush at the bottom.
9. Cut and glue the 1 3/8-in. locking channel to the engine's bottom, centered left to right and flush at the rear.

Coupe back

The coupe back is a component of the dune buggy, but it can be used in other ways—even as a hood.

1. Cut the blank to the correct width and thickness, leaving it about 6 in. long to facilitate its handling during the routing operation.
2. Cut the workpiece profile on the bandsaw.
3. Form the 3/8-in.-radius curved edges along the top and rear of the workpiece, using either the overhead or stationary router. This is similar to the process used for cab #10 (see p. 124).
4. Cut the workpiece to its final length on the table saw.
5. Cut and glue on the locking channel, flush front.

Driver

See p. 145 for the dune buggy driver.

INDY 500 COMPONENTS

I've included all the Indy 500 components in one section, since they are specific to this particular vehicle (although of course it's possible to combine them with others).

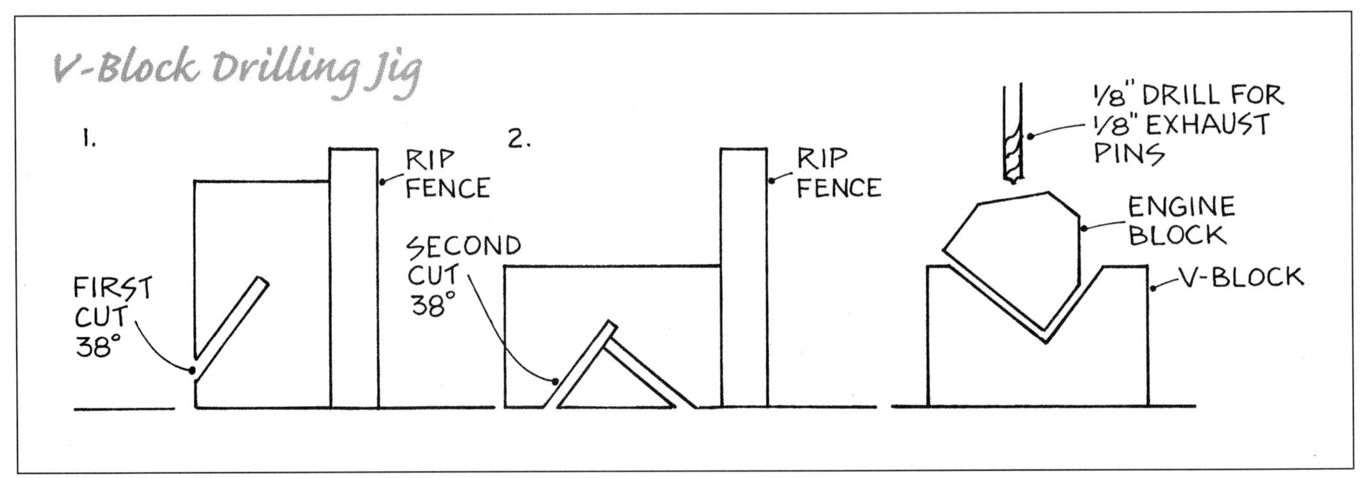

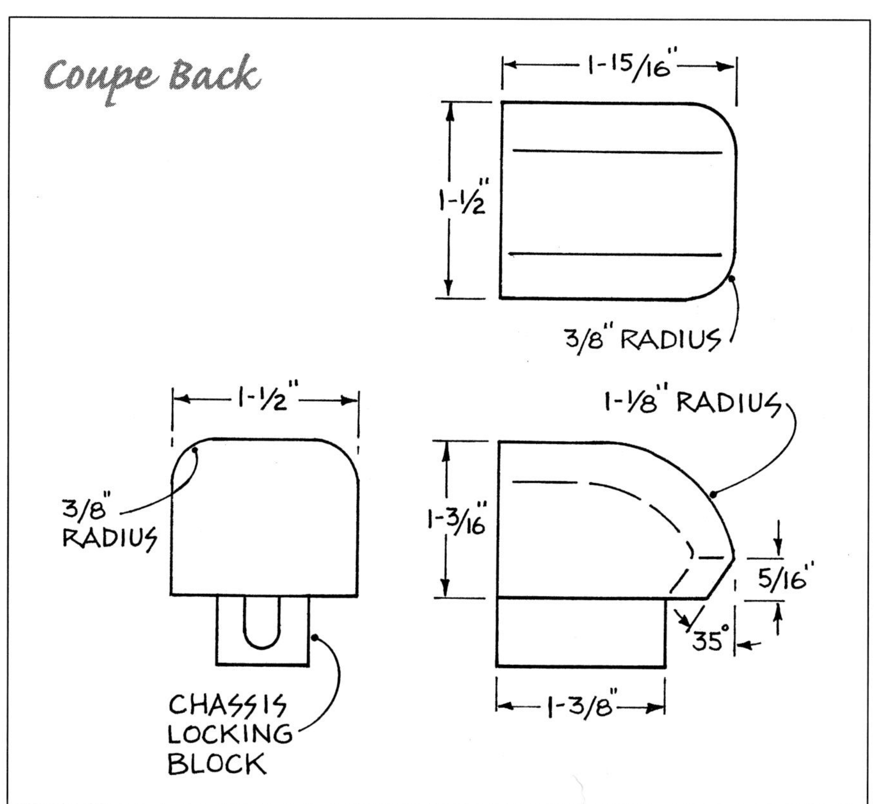

■ INDY 500

Quantities given are for fabrication of a single component (or paired set of components).

PART	SIZE (IN.)	QUANTITY	MATERIAL
Assembly rod			
Rod	1/4 dia. x 5 7/8	1	1/4 dowel
Nose	1 x 9/16 x 7/8	1	Cherry
Wing	3/4 x 1/4 x 2 1/8	1	Cherry
Locking bar	5/16 x 1/16 x 1	1	Cherry
Engine (locking channel 1 1/8)			
Block	1 1/4 x 1 1/8 x 1 1/2	1	Cherry
Exhaust pipes	1/8 dia. x 7/16	8	Aluminum pins
Rear foil assembly (locking channel 3/8)			
Support block	1 1/4 x 7/8 x 17/16	1	Cherry
Rear foil	15/16 x 3/16 x 2	1	Cherry
Driver		1	Commercial

Engine

The engine is the most complex part, requiring a series of cuts on the table saw with jigs.

1. Cut the block to its overall dimensions and lay out the front view for reference purposes.

2. Locate and drill the two 5/16-in. holes through the 1 1/8-in. dimension to create

Photo X • *The Indy 500 racer consists of its own locking rod, cab #9, hood #6, its own engine, and the rear foil assembly.*

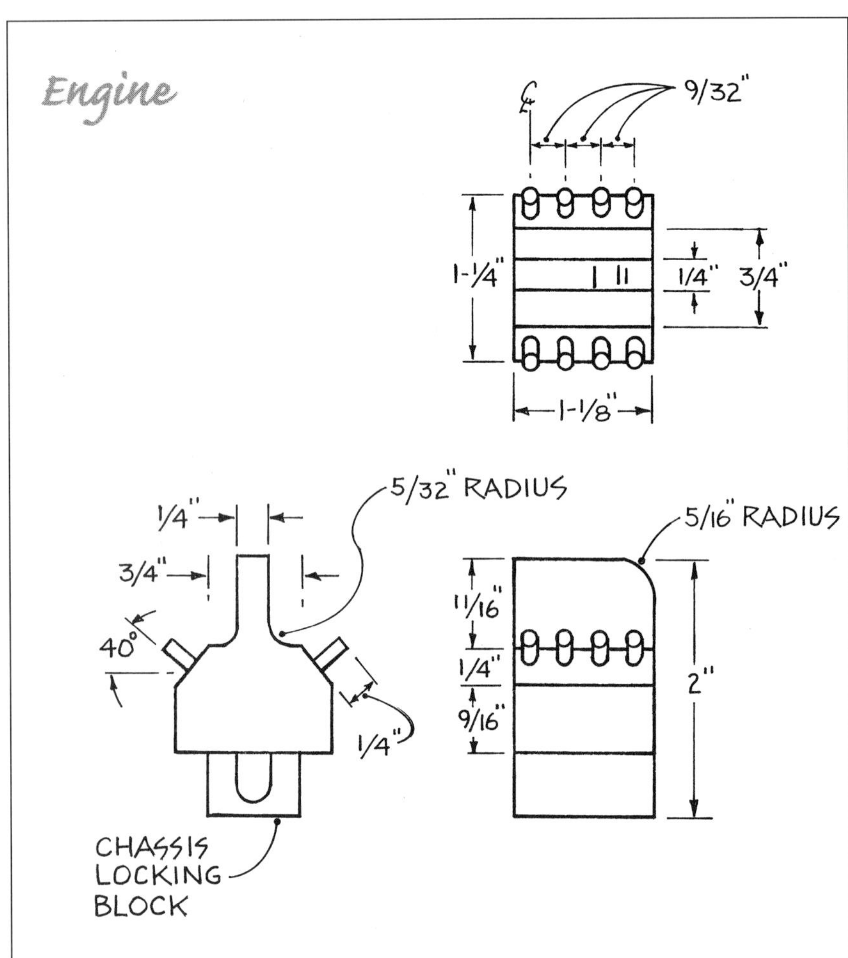

the 5/32-in. radii at the air intake base (see view #1 in the drawing at right.

3. Form the 5/16-in. top back radius on the air intake, either on the bandsaw or the stationary sander (see view #2).

4. With double-sided tape, mount the workpiece upside down on a simple jig, securing it to both the Masonite base and the wood fence, to make the first of the two vertical table-saw cuts that isolate the air intake and lead into the 5/16-in. holes. See view #3 and photo Y. Reverse the workpiece right to left for the second cut.

5. Mount the workpiece right side up on the jig, again taping it both on the bottom and on the side against the jig's fence. Make the 40-degree angle cut that intersects the hole, as shown in view #4 and photo Z. Reverse the workpiece right to left for the second cut.

6. Mount the workpiece in a V cradle as shown in view #5 to drill the four 1/8-in.-diameter holes in each side, as indicated in the plan drawing (see photo AA). The holes should be 3/16 in. deep to receive 7/16-in.-long aluminum or painted wooden pins that are glued in place. Epoxy should be used for the aluminum pins.

7. Cut and glue the 1 1/8-in. locking channel to the bottom of the engine.

Indy 500 assembly rod

1. Cut the wing blank to size, and draw the top-view layout onto the workpiece, including the two inward slanting 10-degree angle lines indicated on the plan drawing that delineate the protruding tip section. These lines should be 3/4 in. apart at the rear edge.

Indy 500 Engine Fabrication

VIEW NO. 1 VIEW NO. 2 VIEW NO. 3 VIEW NO. 4 VIEW NO. 5

Photo Y • *A simple jig holds the Indy 500 engine block for the two vertical cuts at the sides of the air intake.*

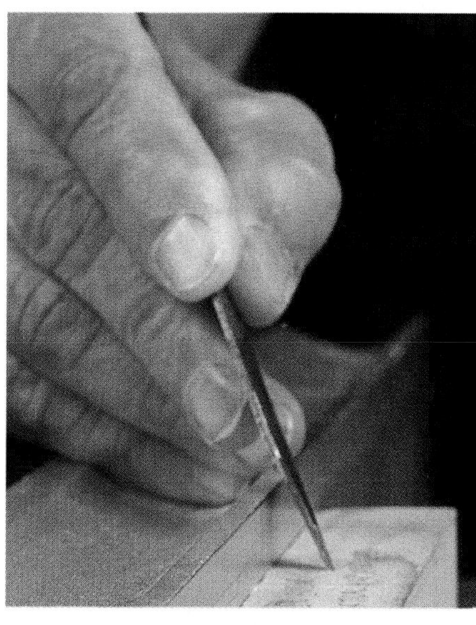

Photo Z • *The same jig is used for the 40-degree angle cuts as well.*

Photo AA • *Aluminum or painted wooden pins inserted into 1/8-in. holes drilled into the engine block provide the exhaust pipes.*

2. On the table saw, cut back the front edge 1/8 in. on either side of the tip section. Cut in from one side, stopping short of the tip area, and then flip the piece over end to end and repeat, leaving the wing width at 5/8 in. Raising the saw blade will minimize undercutting into the tip area, but use caution. If you're uncomfortable doing this on the table saw, this operation can be done on a scrollsaw.

3. Cut the nose block to its overall size. Locate the center point on one of the 9/16-in. by 1-in. faces of the workpiece and drill a hole 7/32 in. deep to receive the 1/4-in. dowel locking bar. Do not exceed this depth to ensure that the hole doesn't break through the top surface of the piece after the downward angle is cut.

4. Cut both sides at the 10-degree angle indicated in the plan drawing.

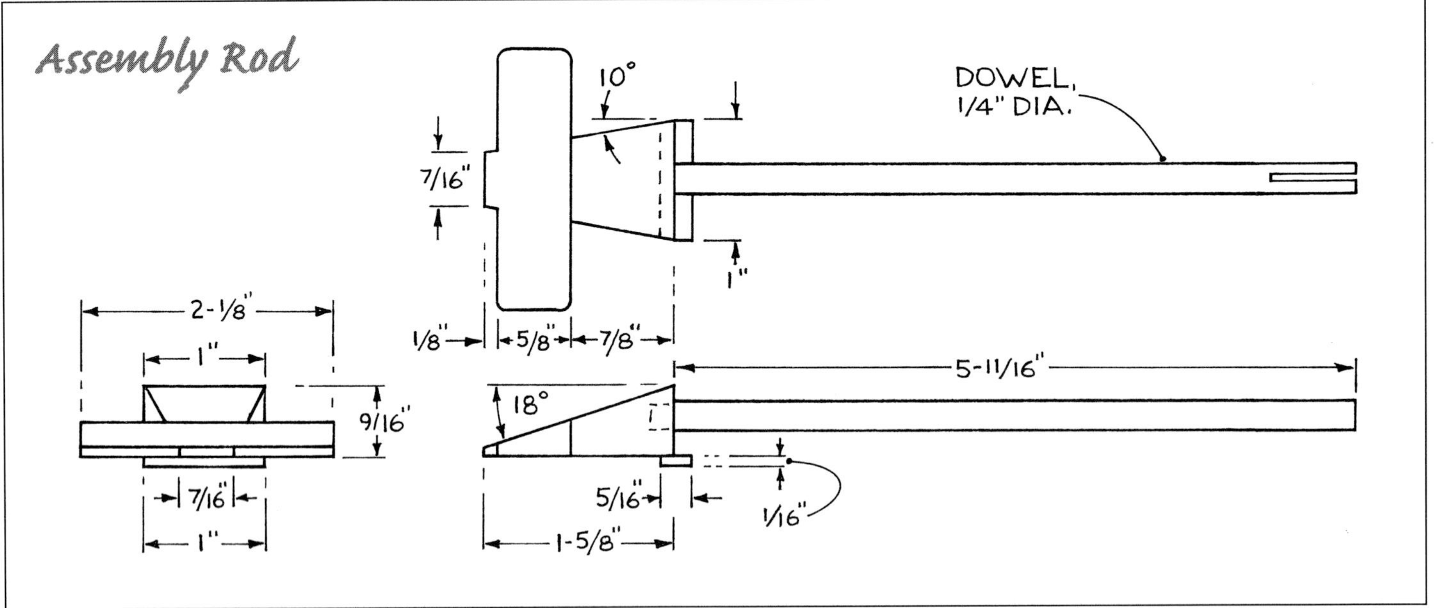

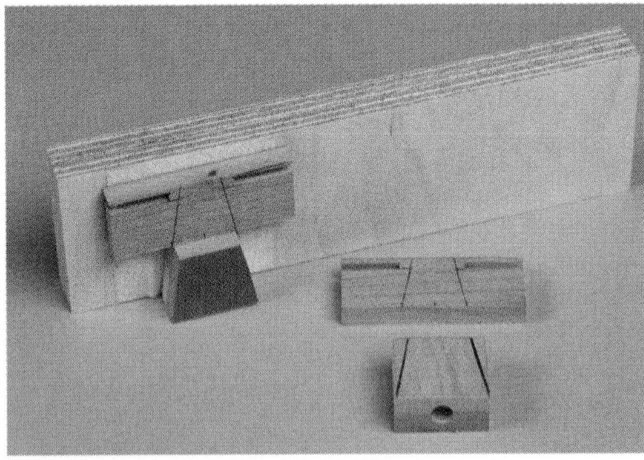

Photo BB • *The Indy 500 front foil wing and nosepiece are cut from separate blanks. The hole in the rear of the nose receives the locking rod.*

Photo CC • *The wing and nose blanks are glued together before being mounted on an auxiliary block for the top angle cut.*

5. Line up the wing and the nosepiece on a flat surface and glue them together with the nose centered on the wing.
6. Tape the workpiece onto a scrap block and cut the downward 18-degree angle on the top (see photo CC).
7. Cut the lock bar to size and glue it to the bottom back edge of the nose as indicated in the plan drawing.
8. Hand-trim the front end to its final shape.
9. Glue the ¼-in. dowel locking bar in place. As in the regular locking assembly rod, this dowel should be slotted and left slightly oversize in length until final assembly.

This assembly rod uses the same rear bumper as the regular assembly rod.

Hood #6

1. Cut the blank to its overall size.
2. Using a jig as indicated in photo DD, make the 10-degree side angle cuts tapering toward the front of the workpiece, as indicated in the plan drawing.

Photo DD • *The Indy 500 hood blank has been flipped over in the simple jig for the second side angle cut.*

3. Fasten the workpiece to an auxiliary block with double-sided tape to make the 18-degree top angle cut (see photo EE).
4. If necessary, hand-sand the surfaces of the hood to align with the nose.
5. Cut and glue the 1¼-in. locking channel to the bottom of the hood, flush with the rear.

Photo EE • *The top angle cut on the Indy 500 hood is made with the workpiece in a vertical position, fastened to an auxiliary block with double-sided tape.*

Cab #9

1. Cut the blank to its overall size.
2. Locate and drill the ⅝-in.-diameter hole indicated in the plan drawing. The depth is ⅜ in. to receive a commercial figure (see the parts list).
3. Make the horizontal cuts for the side rabbets on the workpiece.

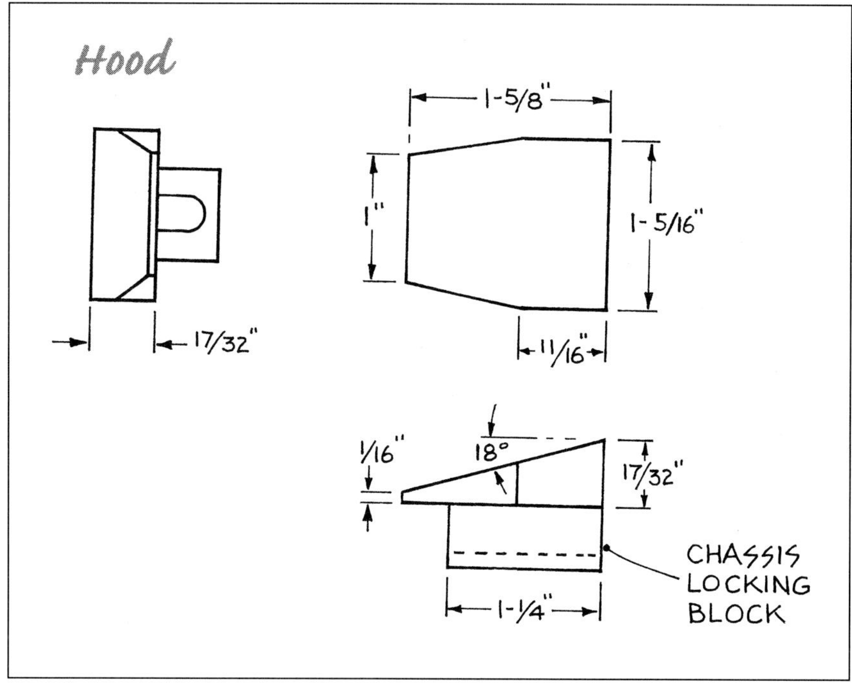

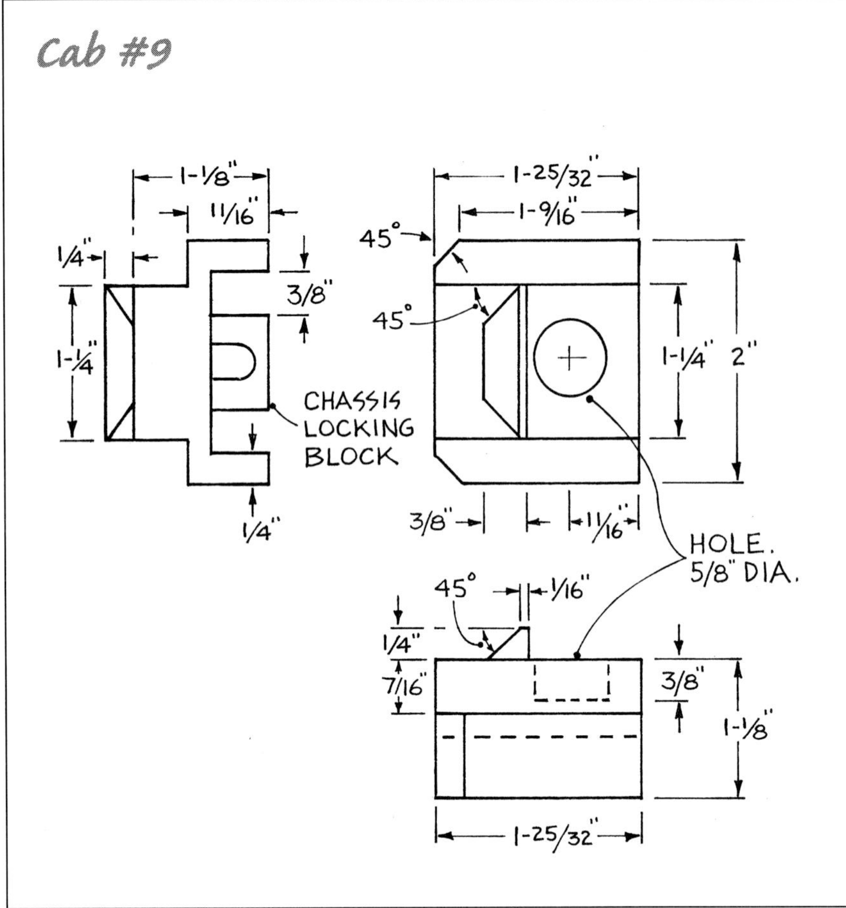

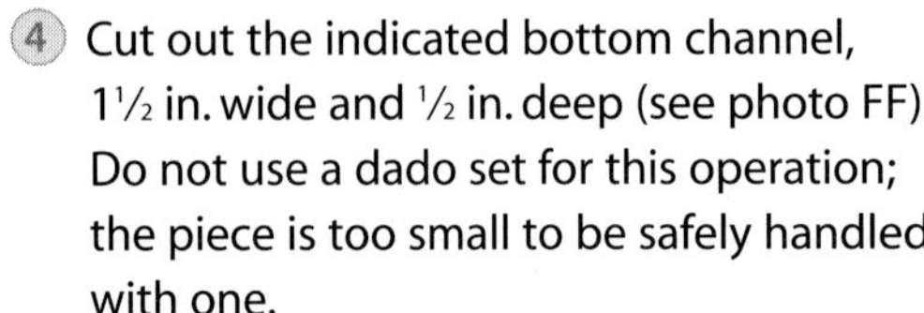

Photo FF • *The channel on the underside of cab #9 is formed by a series of parallel cuts on the table saw after the horizontal cuts for the side rabbets have been made.*

Photo GG • *Vertical cuts complete the side rabbets after the channel is cut.*

4. Cut out the indicated bottom channel, $1\frac{1}{2}$ in. wide and $\frac{1}{2}$ in. deep (see photo FF). Do not use a dado set for this operation; the piece is too small to be safely handled with one.
5. Make the vertical cuts to complete the side rabbets (see photo GG).
6. Make the indicated 45-degree angle cuts at the front corners of the workpiece. Note that they should leave untouched an area approximately $\frac{1}{8}$ in. wide at either side of the channel's front; see the plan drawing.
7. Cut the windshield blank, $\frac{3}{8}$ in. by $\frac{1}{4}$ in. by $1\frac{1}{4}$ in. I recommend using a razor saw to make this part.
8. Fasten the workpiece to an auxiliary block with double-sided tape to make the 45-degree front angle cut along the $1\frac{1}{4}$-in. dimension of the windshield blank, leaving a $\frac{1}{16}$-in. flat area on top. Make the indicated 45-degree side angle cuts.
9. Glue the windshield in place on the cab.
10. Cut and glue the $1\frac{25}{32}$-in. locking channel to the bottom of the cab.

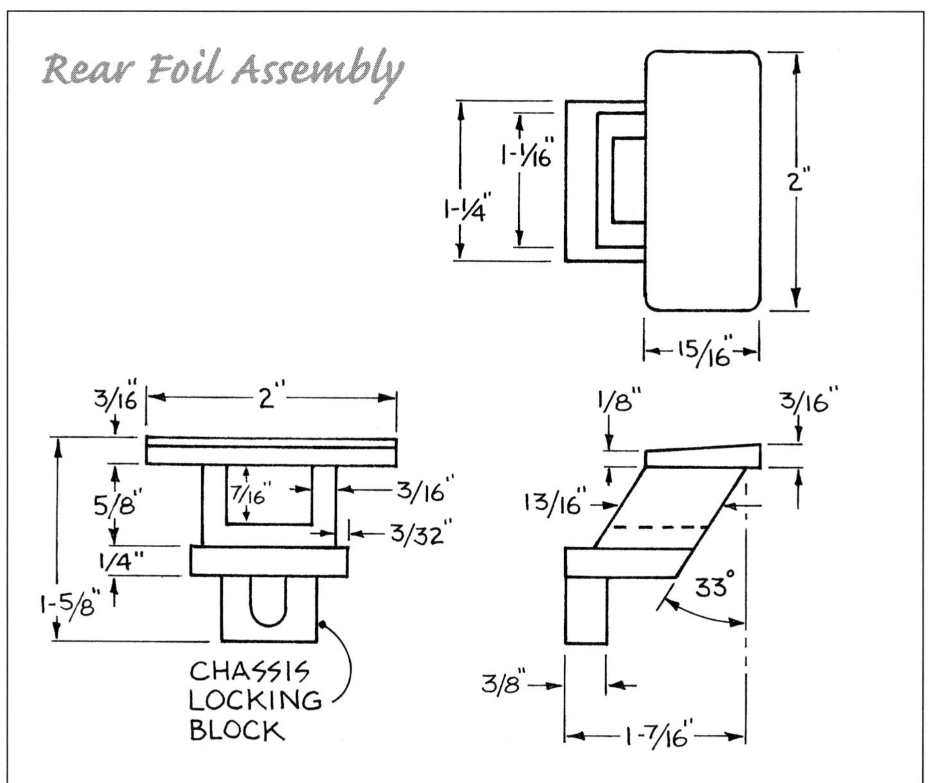

Rear foil assembly

The rear foil support block is another part that is a little complicated to make, so I've included a sequential drawing in perspective (see p. 144) as well as some photos to help clarify it.

1. Cut the rear foil support block to its overall width and thickness, and an oversize length of around 3 in. to facilitate its safe handling (see view #1 of the drawing).
2. Make the interior 33-degree angle cut 5/8 in. deep, as shown in view #2.
3. Make the 33-degree end cut (see photo HH), and also view #2).
4. Make the two cuts running the length of the workpiece's sides, 1/4 in. up from the bottom surface and 3/32 in. deep, as indicated in view #3.

Photo HH • *The rear angle cut is made on the foil support block after the interior angle cut is made.*

5. Cut the channel with a series of parallel passes on the table saw (see photo II on p. 144 and view #4).
6. Make the cuts along the workpiece's sides (indicated in view #5) to meet the third set of cuts, completing the 3/32-in. by 5/8-in. rabbets, as in photo JJ on p. 144.

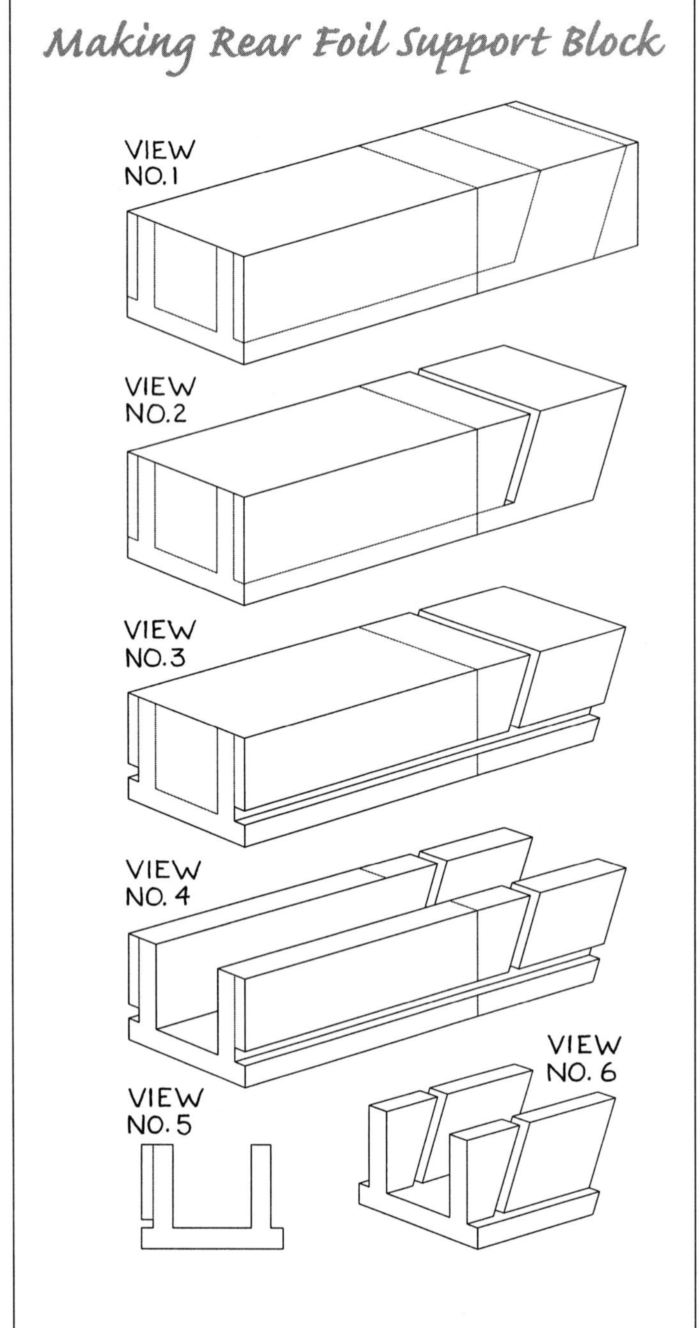

Photo II • *The second in the series of parallel cuts that form the support block's channel.*

Photo JJ • *Table saw cuts along the side complete the support block rabbets.*

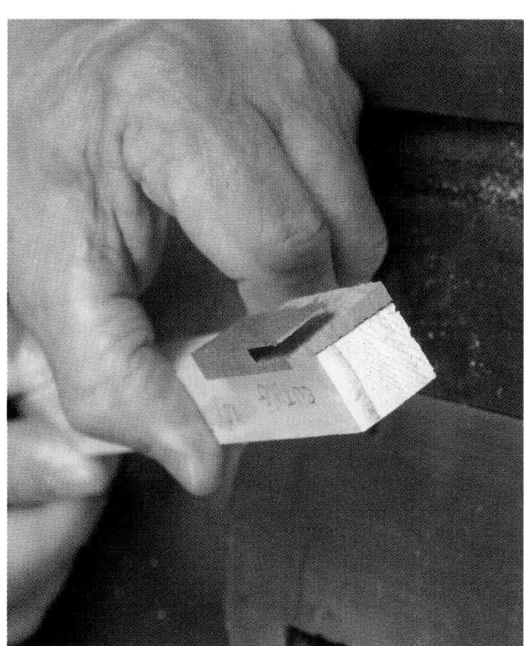

Photo KK • *The rear foil's taper is cut with the workpiece fastened to a scrap block with double-sided tape.*

7. Fasten the workpiece to an auxiliary block to cut it to its final length.
8. Using a razor saw, cut along the flat surface to remove the two small islands visible in view #6.
9. Cut the rear foil blank to its overall size.
10. Tape the foil blank to a scrap block for the top taper cut, as in photo KK.
11. Glue the foil to the support block.
12. Cut and glue the ³⁄₈-in. locking channel to the bottom of the support block, flush with the front.

Drivers

I use commercial figures (see Resources on p. 217) as drivers, the larger is for the dune buggy, the smaller for the Indy 500 racer.

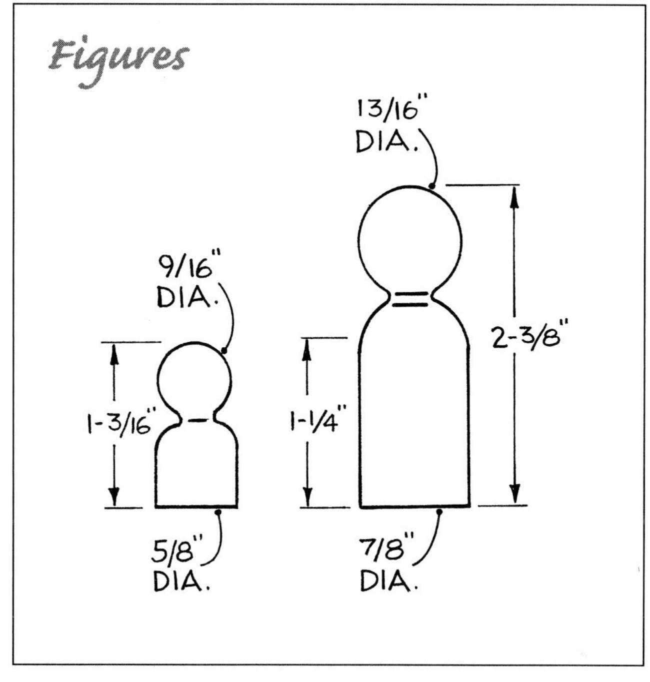

chapter 7
SHIPS

True to my word, I've kept the biggest system (I won't say the best—you be the judge of that!) for last. The large number of parts calls for extensive precision cutting and drilling—and patience. If you're looking for a challenge, you've found it.

The Ships system consists of a variety of components, most of which incorporate nesting lugs (glued-in sections of plastic rod) on the underside and receiving holes on top, to allow stacked assembly onto a generic hull. Although there's some overlap with the Boats system (both feature a tugboat, for example), the Ships

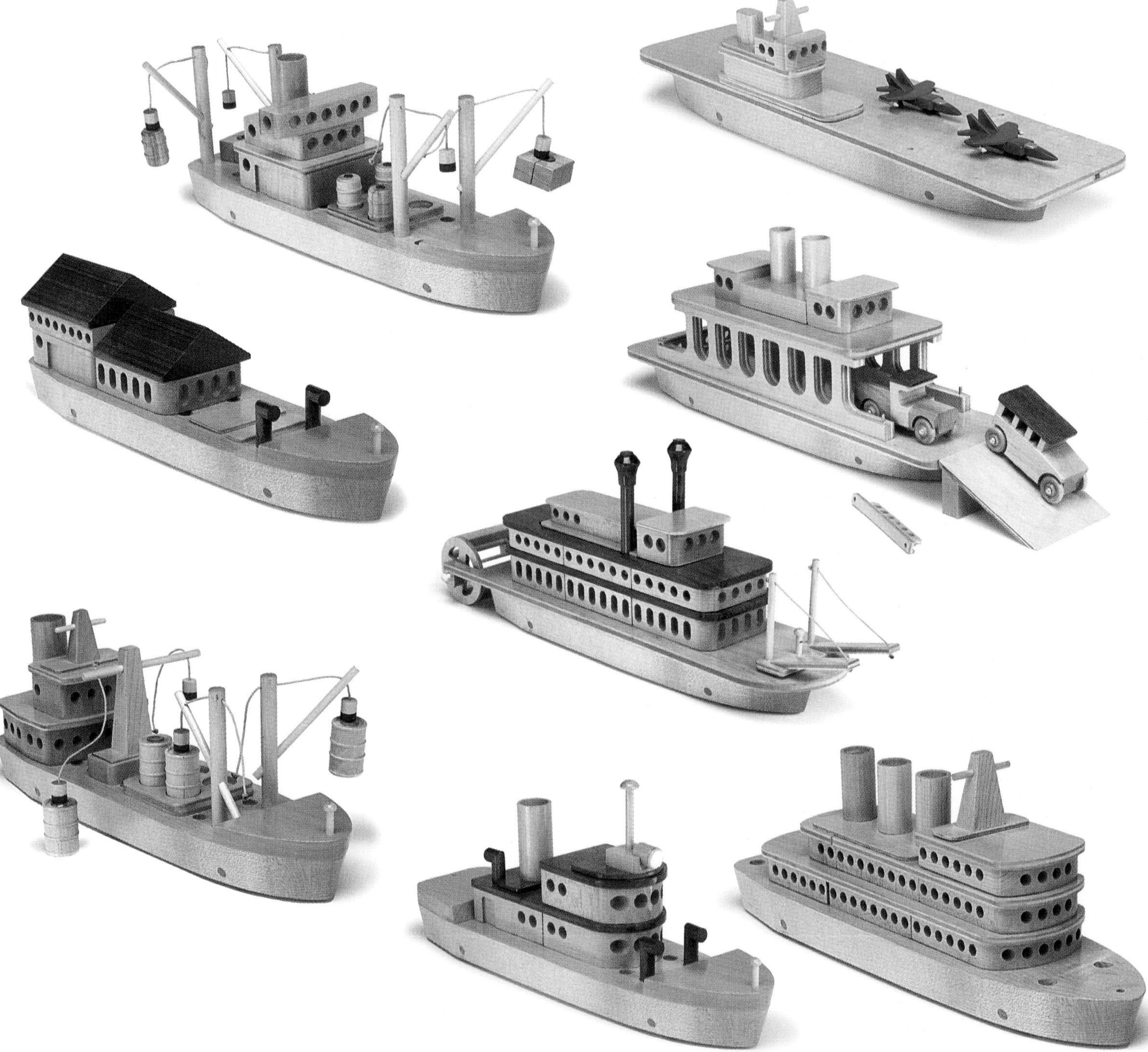

parts are substantially larger and offer more options.

This system, perhaps more than any other, has been inspired by impressions gathered over many years. I've spent a lot of time on Staten Island visiting relatives, and it's a great place to watch ships. There's a hill just north of the Verrazano Narrows Bridge from which you can view the whole New York harbor. I've always been taken by the intrinsically toylike quality of tugboats at work, dwarfed by their loads. Then there was a trip to New Orleans, where I was charmed by the vintage look and smooth ride of a paddle wheeler. And when I saw the airplanes on the deck of the aircraft carrier *Intrepid* docked off the West Side of Manhattan, I said, "I've gotta make some of those!"

You'll find all of them, and a good deal more, in Ships.

FABRICATION OF COMPONENTS

■ BASIC SHIP PARTS

PART	SIZE (IN.)	QUANTITY	MATERIAL
Hull	$4\frac{1}{2}$ x $1\frac{7}{16}$ x 17	1	Maple
Rear hull rollers	$1\frac{1}{8}$ dia. x $1\frac{5}{8}$	2	$1\frac{1}{8}$ dowel
Front hull roller	$1\frac{1}{8}$ dia. x $2\frac{1}{2}$	1	$1\frac{1}{8}$ dowel
Washers	$\frac{5}{16}$	5	Commercial
Axles	$\frac{5}{16}$ dia. x $4\frac{1}{2}$	2	$\frac{5}{16}$ dowel
Forward deck riser	4 x $\frac{5}{8}$ x $3\frac{3}{8}$	1	Maple
Aft deck riser	$4\frac{1}{2}$ x $\frac{5}{8}$ x $3\frac{1}{2}$	1	Maple
Deck plate #1	$1\frac{11}{16}$ x $\frac{1}{8}$ x $2\frac{7}{8}$	1	$\frac{1}{8}$ maple plywood
Deck plate #2	$1\frac{1}{4}$ x $\frac{1}{8}$ x $2\frac{7}{8}$	1	$\frac{1}{8}$ maple plywood
Deck plate #3	$\frac{3}{4}$ x $\frac{1}{8}$ x $2\frac{7}{8}$	1	$\frac{1}{8}$ maple plywood
Deck plate #4	$1\frac{11}{16}$ x $\frac{1}{8}$ x $2\frac{7}{8}$	1	$\frac{1}{8}$ maple plywood
Deck plate #5	$1\frac{3}{8}$ x $\frac{1}{8}$ x $2\frac{7}{8}$	1	$\frac{1}{8}$ maple plywood
Smokestack #1	$1\frac{1}{4}$ dia. x $2\frac{5}{8}$	2	$1\frac{1}{4}$ dowel
Removable pins for stack #1	$\frac{1}{2}$ dia. x $1\frac{1}{2}$	2	Plastic rod
Smokestack #2	$1\frac{1}{8}$ dia. x 2	1	$1\frac{1}{8}$ dowel
Smokestack #3	1 dia. x 2	3	1 dowel
Removable pins for stack #3	$\frac{1}{2}$ dia. x $1\frac{1}{2}$	3	Plastic rod
Smokestack #4	$1\frac{1}{8}$ dia. x 2	2	$1\frac{1}{8}$ dowel
Base for stack #4	$1\frac{3}{8}$ x $\frac{1}{8}$ x $2\frac{7}{8}$	2	$\frac{1}{8}$ maple plywood
Smokestack #5	$1\frac{1}{8}$ dia. x 2	3	$1\frac{1}{8}$ dowel
Base for stack #5	3 x $\frac{1}{8}$ x $2\frac{7}{8}$	3	$\frac{1}{8}$ maple plywood
Smokestack #6	$1\frac{1}{4}$ dia. x $2\frac{3}{4}$	2	$1\frac{1}{4}$ dowel
Base for stack #6	$1\frac{3}{8}$ x $\frac{1}{8}$ x $2\frac{7}{8}$	2	$\frac{1}{8}$ maple plywood
Smokestack #7	1 dia. x $1\frac{1}{2}$	1	1 dowel
Tower #1 A block	$1\frac{1}{4}$ x $\frac{13}{16}$ x 2	1	Maple
Cross arm	$\frac{3}{16}$ dia. x 2	1	$\frac{3}{16}$ dowel
Base	1 x $\frac{1}{8}$ x $2\frac{7}{8}$	1	$\frac{1}{8}$ maple plywood
Tower #2 A block	1 x $\frac{7}{8}$ x $1\frac{5}{8}$	1	Maple
Cross arm	$\frac{3}{16}$ dia. x 2	1	$\frac{3}{16}$ dowel
Base	1 x $\frac{1}{8}$ x $2\frac{7}{8}$	1	$\frac{1}{8}$ maple plywood
Funnels	$\frac{1}{2}$ x $2\frac{1}{4}$	2	$\frac{1}{2}$ walnut dowel
Funnels	$\frac{1}{2}$ x $1\frac{7}{8}$	2	$\frac{1}{2}$ maple dowel
Peg	$\frac{1}{4}$ dia. w/$\frac{5}{8}$-dia. head x $2\frac{1}{2}$	1	Commercial
Peg	$\frac{5}{16}$ dia. w/$\frac{1}{2}$-dia. head x $1\frac{7}{8}$	1	Commercial
Peg	$\frac{1}{4}$ dia. w/$\frac{3}{8}$-dia. head x $1\frac{3}{16}$	1	Commercial

Nesting lugs are cut to size from ½ plastic rod; a 3-foot length should be sufficient. Alternately, accurately sized wooden dowel may also be used; see Resources on p. 217.

WORKING SMARTER

I've always used plastic lugs for this system because of their dimensional dependability. But now that accurately sized dowels are available (see Resources on p. 217), wooden lugs are a viable option.

GENERIC COMPONENTS

Several components are shared by most of the ships, so I'll cover those first.

Nesting lugs

All the large parts fit together with nesting lugs. You'll cut holes and fit a fair number of them for every version, so I'll talk about this task here to avoid repetition.

The lugs are cut from lengths of ½-in.-diameter plastic rod and glued into place with epoxy. I recommend a 33⁄64-in.-diameter size for all receiving holes. But if you find alignment problematic at this tolerance level, the holes for all components except the hull may be increased to 17⁄32 in.

I recommend using a two-flute center-cut end-mill bit for drilling the ½-in.-diameter lug cavities, particularly the shallow ones in the thin plywood pieces, because of the nice flat hole-bottom it leaves. I often use one for the receiving holes, too. But if you're not experienced with this tool, I'd advise practicing on scrap first to get the feel of it, since it doesn't have a point to guide it into the workpiece.

Gluing the lugs in place is the final step in the fabrication of all components that incorporate them. But beforehand, I chuck each lug into the lathe and lightly file a slight radius onto the end to help guide it in place during the assembly of a ship. If you have a metal lathe, a ½-in. collet will do the job, too.

Except where noted, the nesting lugs protrude ⅝ in. from the workpiece surface. The lug cavities should be at least ¼ in. deep wherever possible. For pieces made of ¼-in. plywood, this depth should be ⅛ in. to 3⁄16 in., and for those made of ⅛-in. plywood, 1⁄16 in.

All paired lugs and receiving holes are spaced 2 in. apart from centerline to centerline. With a few exceptions, pieces that have a single pair of lugs and/or receiving holes will have them centered on both their length and width.

Whenever a lug and a receiving hole are in direct alignment on a component (that is, one is over the other), you can guarantee accuracy and save time with the jig shown in photos A and B. To make the jig:

1. Cut a piece of plywood ½ in. to ¾ in. thick, about 4 in. wide and long enough to be clamped securely at each end to the drill-press table.
2. Drill a hole with a ½-in. end mill as deep into the plywood as possible without breaking through.
3. Insert a ½-in. lug into the hole, protruding about ¼ in.

Photo A • *This simple jig guarantees the accurate alignment of receiving holes that are directly above lugs on a component.*

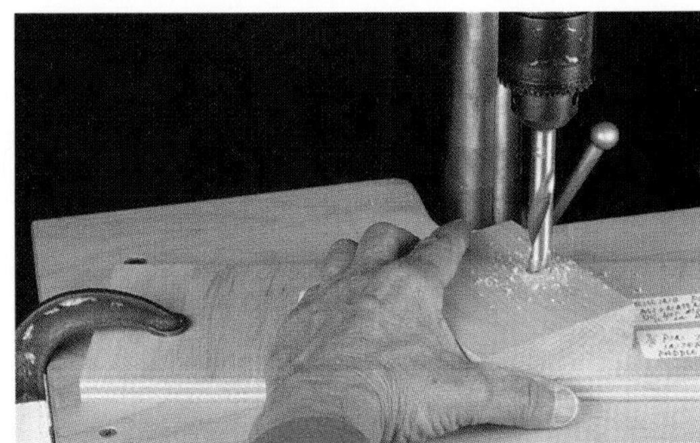

Photo B • *To drill an aligned receiving hole, the lug cavity on the workpiece is seated over the lug in the jig.*

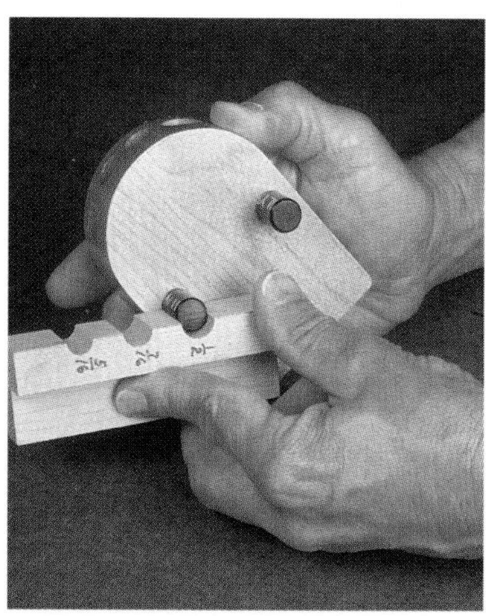

Photo C • *Slide this jig up against a lug to make sure it's square to the component's surface before the glue sets.*

4. Place the appropriate lug cavity of the workpiece onto this lug to drill an aligned 33/64-in. receiving hole. I strongly recommend not moving this jig once it's set up, so you may wish to plan to drill all receiving holes at one time.

The simple jig in photo C guarantees that lugs are glued perfectly square to the surface of components.

Portholes

Several of the cabins in Ships, like those in Boats, require the drilling of numerous portholes, and again, I recommend the stop-block spacer-block setup on the drill press to expedite this procedure, shown in photo D.

Hull

The hull, which is the basis of all the ships in the system, incorporates front and back rollers in its underside for mobility.

1. Cut the hull blank to its overall dimensions, leaving it about 1/8 in. oversize in length to accommodate cutting the front curve.

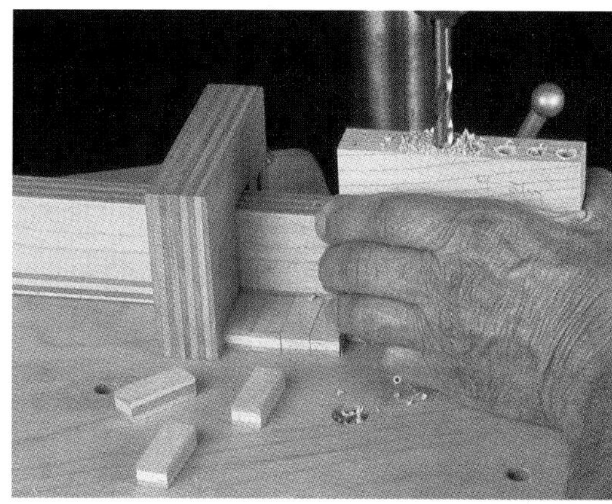

Photo D • *The stop-block spacer-block setup on the drill press provides speed and accuracy in drilling the many portholes on components like the cruise ship cabins.*

2. Working on the drill press, with an auxiliary table and fence and using 1-in. spacer blocks, drill the two rows of 33/64-in. nesting lug holes in the workpiece as indicated in the plan drawing. Hole depth should be 3/4 in.
3. Lay out the roller wells on the bottom of the workpiece. Draw two lines across the 4 1/2-in. dimension, centered on the 1 1/4-in. dimension of the roller wells. Continue these lines up the sidewalls and mark a point 3/8 in. from the bottom on each to locate the center of the axle holes.
4. Drill the four 5/16-in. axle holes, making sure each penetrates the well area.
5. Rout out the two roller wells as indicated. It's possible to do this freehand, but you may want to use a template fastened to the workpiece with double-sided tape. The final depth is achieved in progressive passes.
6. On the top of the hull blank, lay out all curves, angles, and radii (see photo E on p. 154).
7. On the bandsaw, cut the front curve with an inward 15-degree angle. Sand to blend in at about the third set of deck holes.

Hull

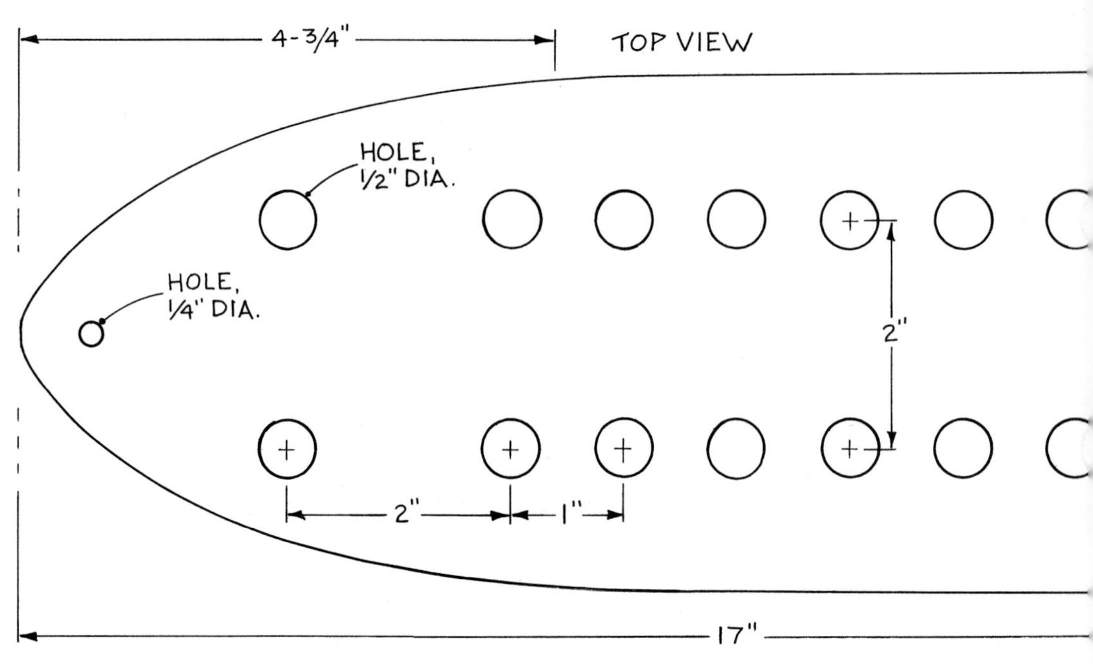

Side View

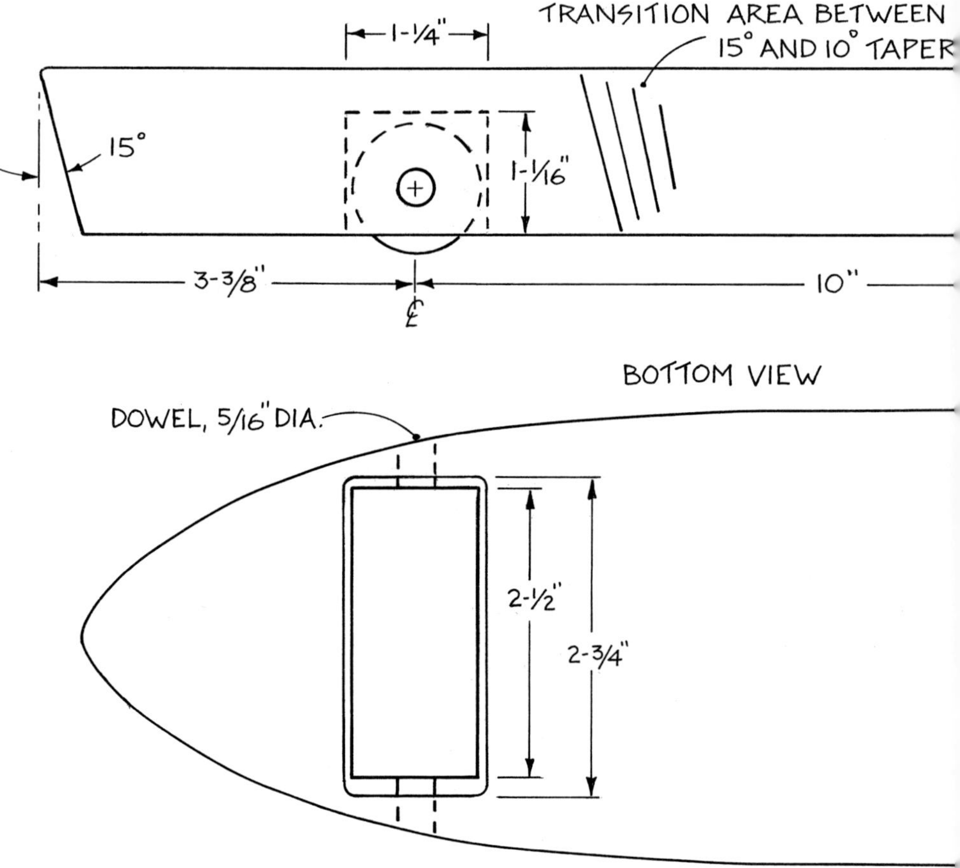

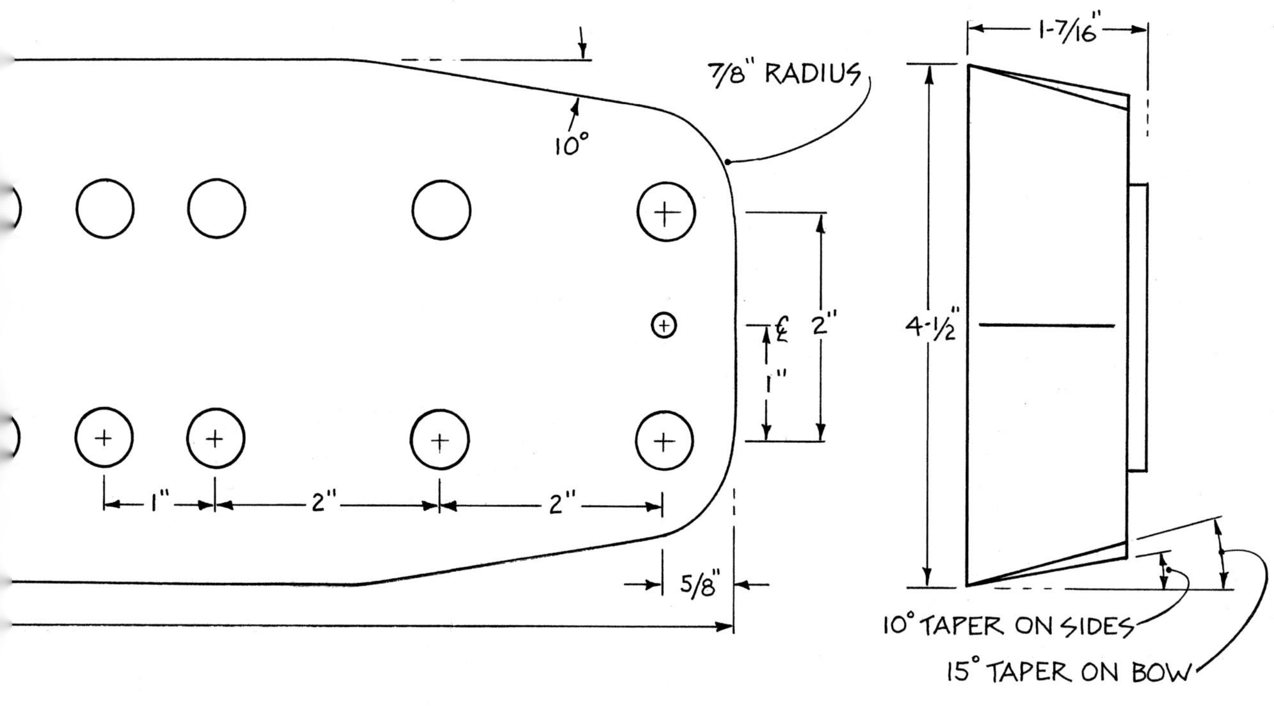
7/8" RADIUS
10°
1-7/16"
4-1/2"
2"
1"
1"
2"
2"
5/8"
10° TAPER ON SIDES
15° TAPER ON BOW

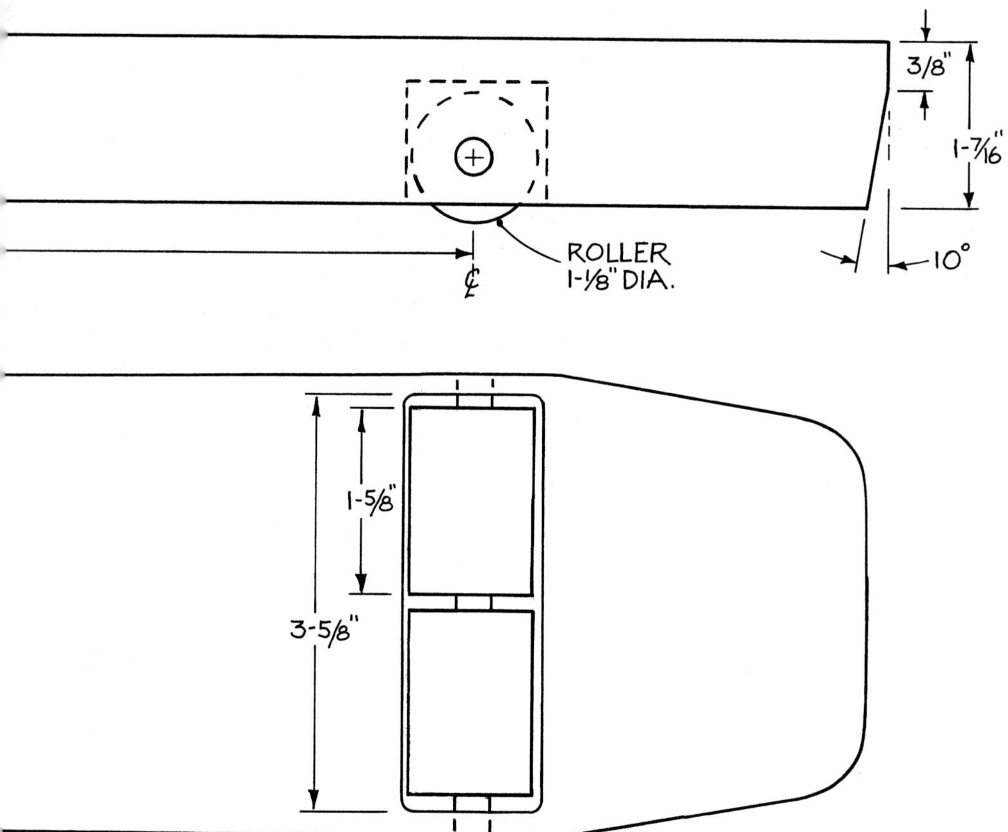
3/8"
1-7/16"
ROLLER
1-1/8" DIA.
10°
1-5/8"
3-5/8"

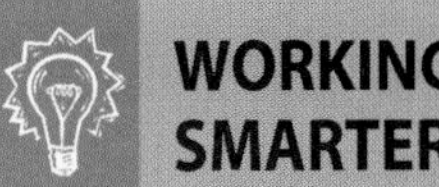

WORKING SMARTER

You'll have an easier time getting a nice smooth finish on the lugged components if you apply the finish *before* gluing the lugs in place. Just be sure not to get any finish into the lug cavities.

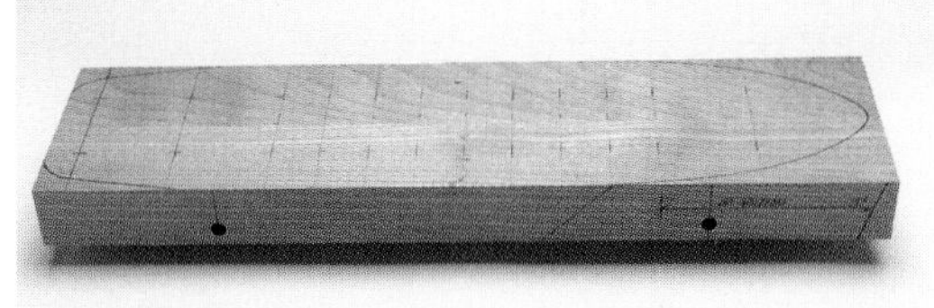

Photo E • *Start with a hull blank slightly oversize in length to facilitate cutting the front curve.*

8. Cut both sides and the rear at a 10-degree inward angle. As indicated in the plan drawing, leave the top 3/8 in. of the rear surface untouched by this cut. Sand all curves and radii to blend.
9. Cut the three indicated lengths of 1 1/8-in.-diameter dowel for the rollers. On the lathe, drill an 11/32-in. axle hole through each one, using the technique described in the "Boring out dowels" section on p. 15. Two rollers are used at the rear to avoid having to bore out a single longer piece.
10. Assemble the rollers in the wells with the 5/16-in. washers, one between the rear two and one where each roller meets a well wall (see photo F).
11. Insert the 5/16-in. dowel axles, oversize in length, into the axle holes on one side of the hull, threading them partway through the rollers in the wells. Place glue in the opposite axle holes, and then onto the portion of each axle still outside the hull, near its end, so that final insertion carries the glue into the first hole. This avoids the inadvertent gluing of the moving parts. Trim the axles flush to the hull with a razor saw.

Photo F • *Rollers fitted to the underside of the hull allow the toy to move.*

Deck risers

The deck risers give a characteristic look to a ship, although not all ships incorporate them. They also have the esthetic function of breaking the line of the hull's flat surface.

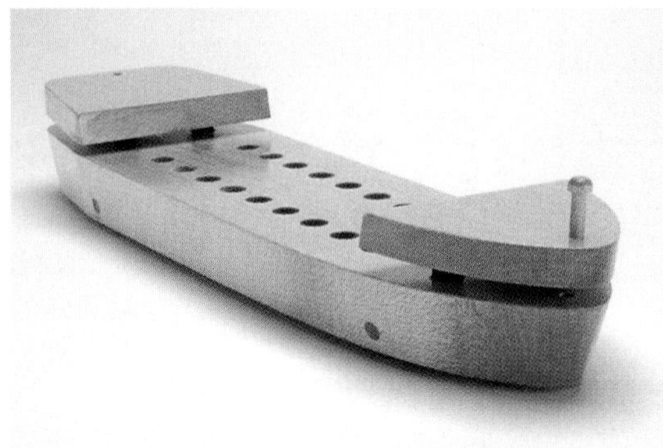

Photo G • *The forward and aft risers are shaped to match the hull's sides.*

1. Cut the forward riser blank to its overall size, leaving it about 1/8 in. oversize in length to allow for cutting the front curve.
2. Make a 15-degree angle cut along the 4 1/4-in. dimension.
3. Working from the bottom edge of this angle cut, locate and drill the two lug cavities 1/4 in. deep. Spot-tape lugs into the cavities (they should protrude 5/8 in.) and insert the riser in place on the deck.
4. Trace the hull perimeter onto the bottom of the riser. Remove the riser, remove the lugs, and cut the drawn curve with an outward 10-degree angle to match the perimeter of the hull. Sand to neutralize any misalignment.
5. Follow the same procedure to make the back riser. Note, however, that the back riser perimeter has no taper.

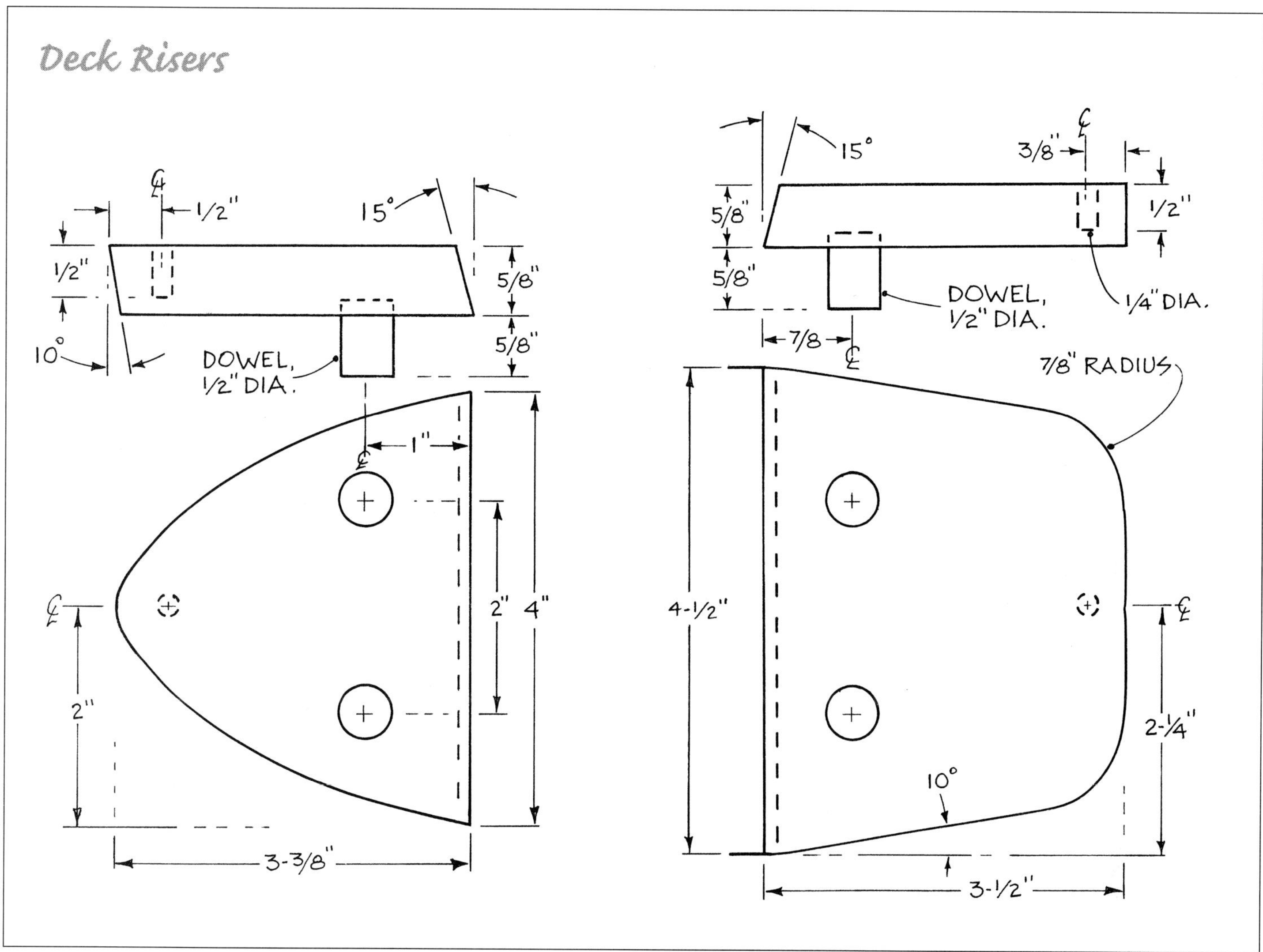

Deck plates (fillers)

These parts are used to fill some unused holes in the hull. Some have a specific stacking function as well.

1. Cut the five plates to size, as indicated in the parts list and the plan drawing. Note that all plates are made from maple plywood, 1/4 in. thick for #4 and 1/8 in. thick for the rest.
2. Round the corners by hand-sanding or on a stationary sander.
3. Drill the lug holes in plate #1, at the locations indicated in the drawing. Plate #1 is one of the exceptions to the rule regarding centered lug placement. Here, the centers of the cavities should lie 3/8 in. back from one of the 2 7/8-in. edges of the blank, with the usual 2-in. spacing centered on the width of the piece.
4. Drill the lug holes in plates #2 and #3. They have two lugs on the underside, centered on the width and length.
5. Drill the lug holes in plate #4. It has a pair of holes only. It can be used to raise up a cabin or to add space between two stacked cabins.
6. Drill the lug holes in plate #5. This plate is used for mounting chimneys with receiving holes, and has a pair of lugs on one side and a single centered one on the other side.

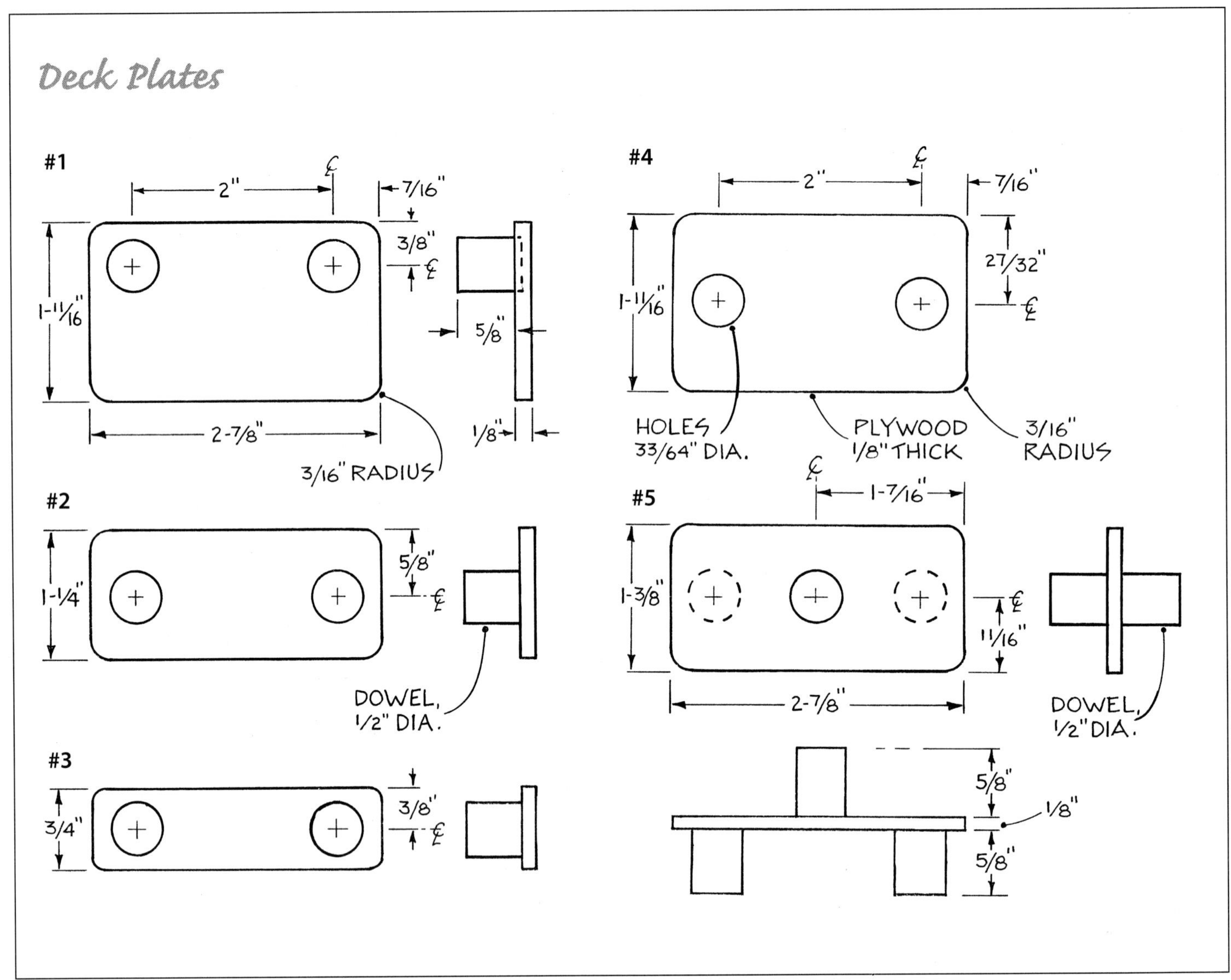

Smokestacks

All the generic smokestacks are cut from lengths of dowel in three diameters, as specified in the parts list and on the plan drawing. All drilling is done on the lathe. The top cavities of all smokestacks are drilled with a Forstner bit. They should be ¼ in. less in diameter than the dowel itself, leaving a ⅛-in.-thick ridge, and ¼ in. deep.

Stacks #1 and #3 are both mounted in place with removable 1½-in.-long lugs in the usual ½-in. diameter, which seat into the stacks' ⅞-in.-deep receiving holes.

Stacks #2 and #7 have lugs glued into their receiving holes.

Stacks #4, #6, and the dual stacks (#5) are all mounted on ⅛-in. plywood plates, which have lugs glued into their undersides in the usual fashion.

After cutting all pieces to size, complete all drilling, glue the stacks to their bases, and glue the lugs in place as the final step. Refer to the plan drawing for placement of components.

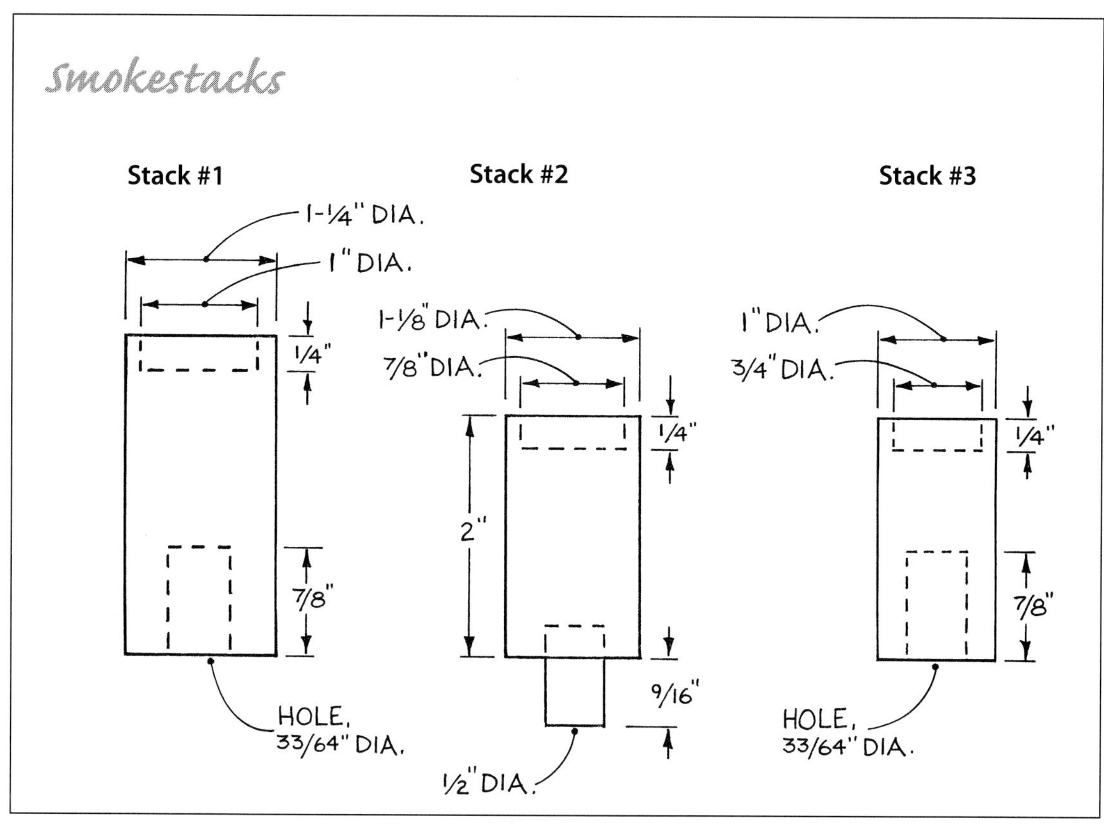
Smokestacks
Stack #1
Stack #2
Stack #3
1-1/4" DIA.
1" DIA.
1/4"
7/8"
HOLE, 33/64" DIA.
1-1/8" DIA.
7/8" DIA.
1/4"
2"
9/16"
1/2" DIA.
1" DIA.
3/4" DIA.
1/4"
7/8"
HOLE, 33/64" DIA.

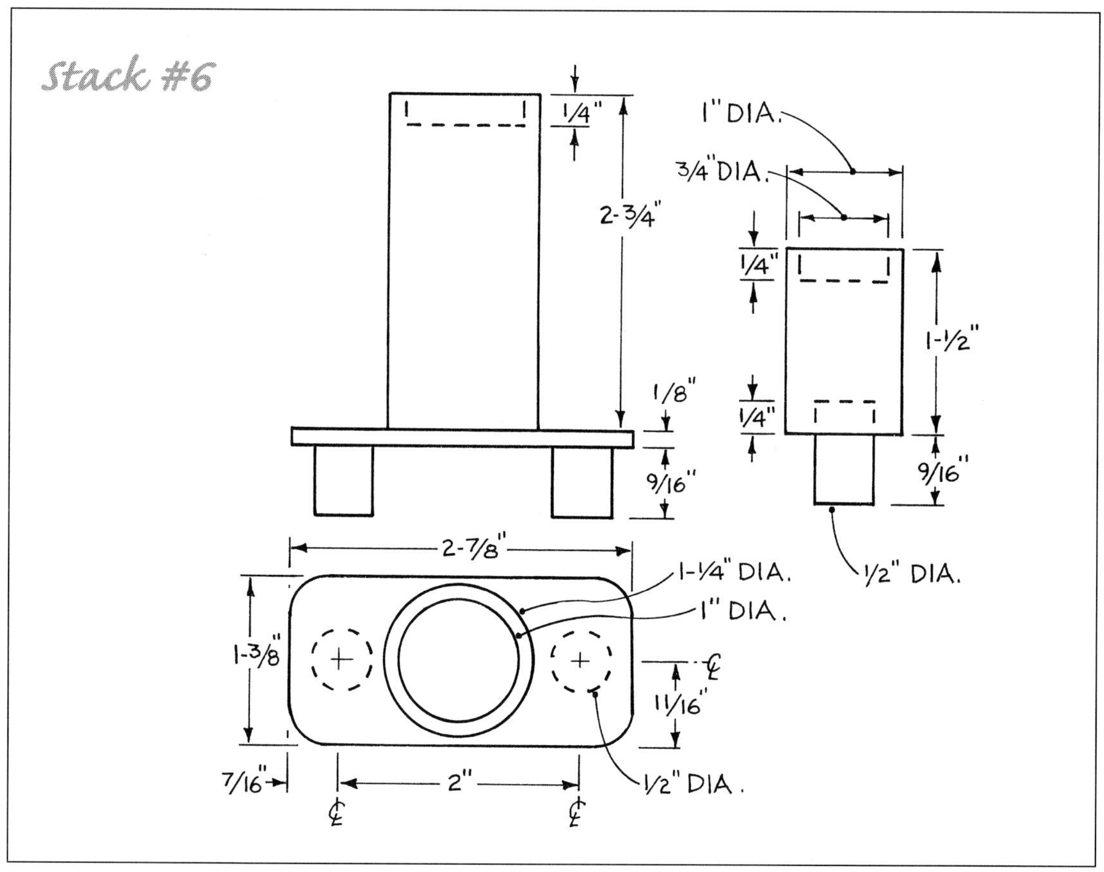
Stack #6
1/4"
2-3/4"
1/8"
9/16"
1" DIA.
3/4" DIA.
1/4"
1-1/2"
1/4"
9/16"
1/2" DIA.
2-7/8"
1-1/4" DIA.
1" DIA.
1-3/8"
11/16"
7/16"
2"
1/2" DIA.

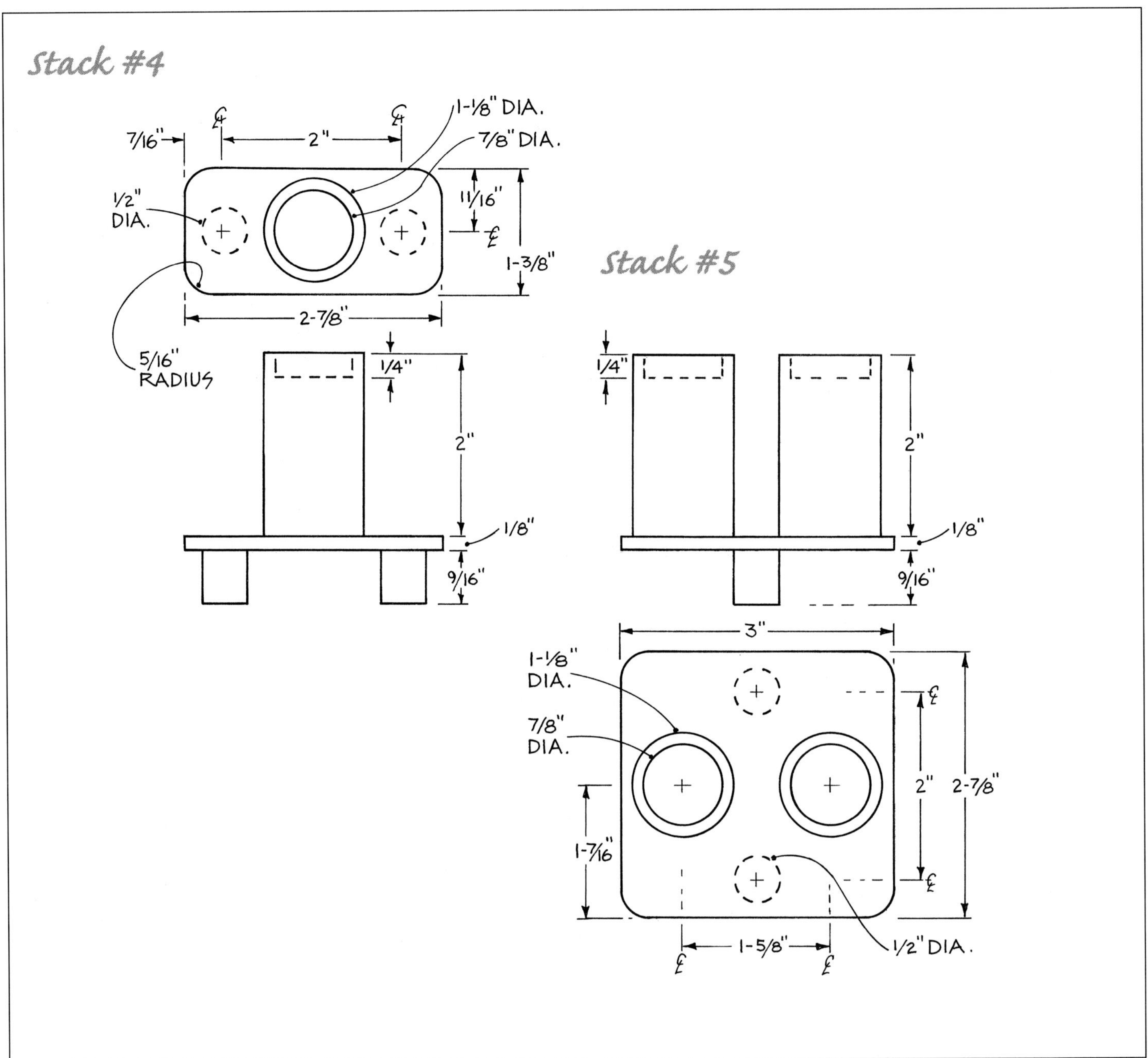

Towers

1. Cut the A-shaped blocks for the two towers to their correct overall size as indicated in the parts list.
2. Locate and drill the hole to receive the 2-in.-long by 3/16-in.-diameter dowel cross arm in each.
3. On the table saw, cut the tapers on the four sides of the A blocks using a simple jig like that used for the hoods in Vehicles (see photo H). If you're not a jig enthusiast, these cuts can also be made freehand on the bandsaw.

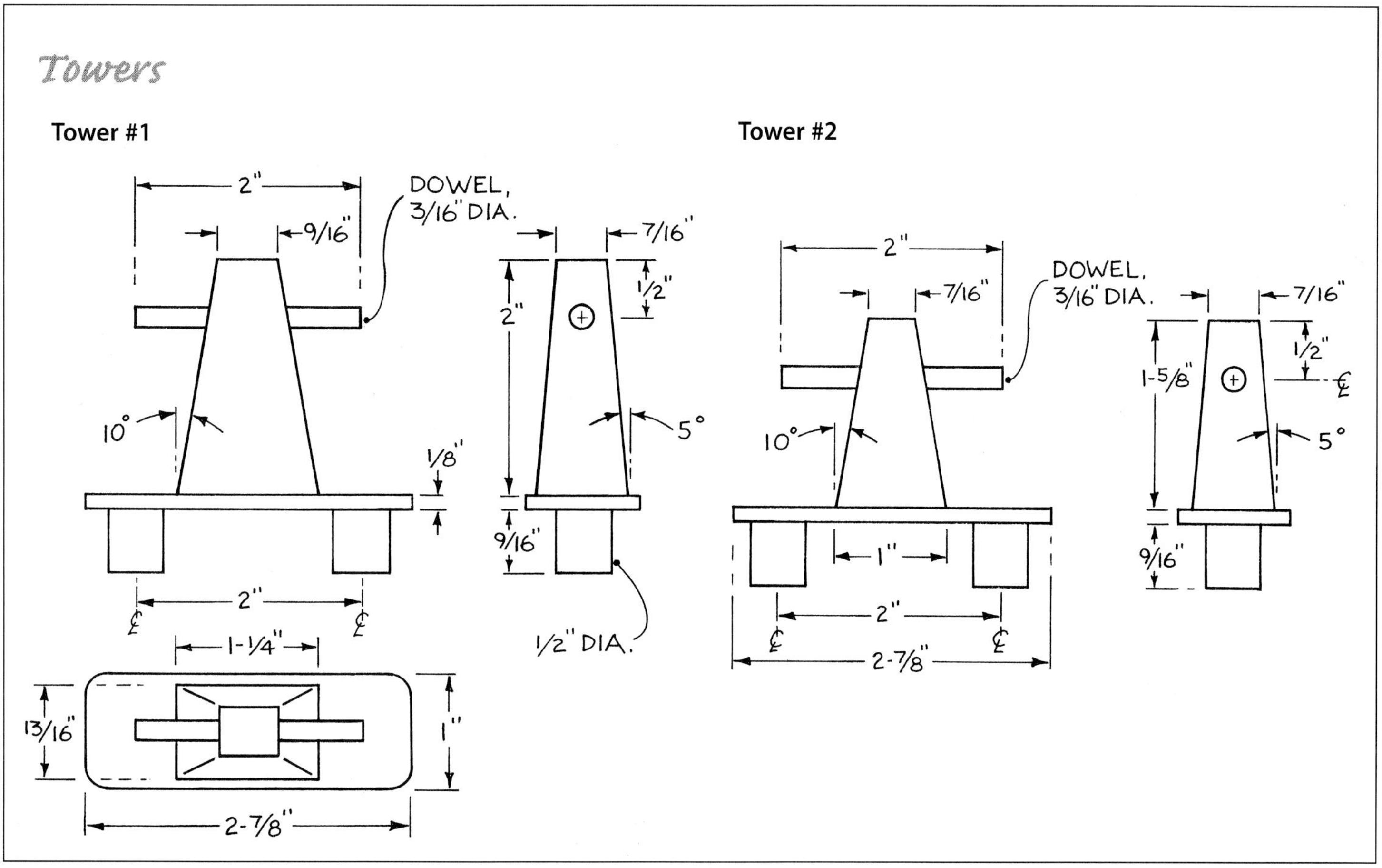

Towers

Tower #1

Tower #2

Photo H • *A simple jig gives the four side tapers of the tower A blocks. The scrap piece cut from one side helps position the piece for cutting the opposite one.*

4. Cut the base plates to size and drill the two lug cavities, with the usual 2-in. spacing centered on the width and length.

5. Glue the A-shaped blocks to the bases, centered in both dimensions. Glue the two cross arms in place.

Funnels and pegs

The funnels are simply lengths of ½-in. dowel with a 45-degree cut at one end, trimmed to correct size and glued together. The simple jig pictured in photo I on p. 160 uses a rubber band to hold the pieces together while the glue sets.

Commercial pegs (see Resources on p. 217) give the look of flagstaffs, masts, and cable ties. Their dimension is not critical; simply drill the appropriate receiving holes where indicated for the selected pegs.

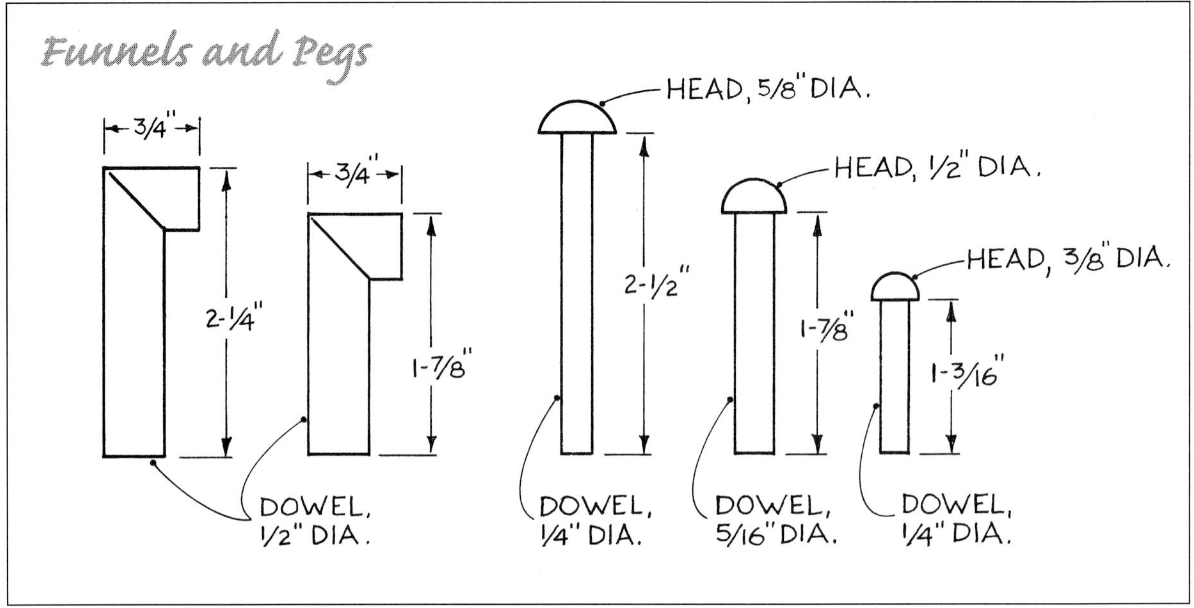

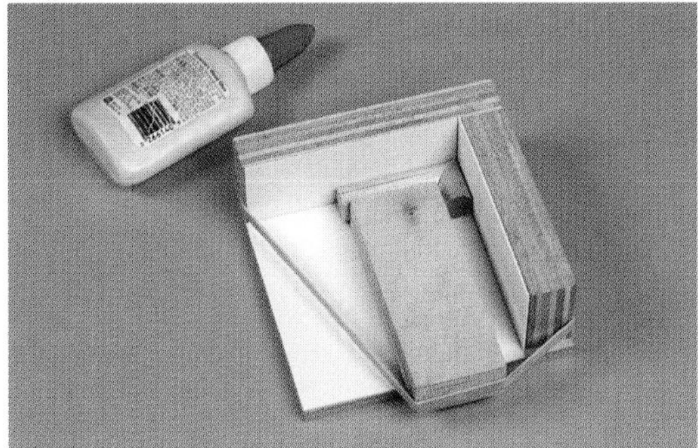

Photo I • *A gluing jig for the dowel funnels has plastic strips to prevent the workpiece from adhering to the jig and a rubber band to hold the piece in place at 90 degrees.*

DUAL-USE FREIGHTER/OIL TANKER COMPONENTS

Since freighters and oil tankers are cargo ships with some similar loading and unloading functions, several components can do double duty here.

Freighter/tanker tower

1. Cut the A-shaped block to its overall size.
2. Locate and drill the hole to receive the 4½-in.-long by ¼-in.-diameter dowel cross arm in each.
3. Drill the lug cavity, centered on the bottom of the A-shaped block.
4. Cut the four side angles with a single jig, as for the towers.
5. Cut the cross arm to length and drill a hole about ½ in. in from each end to receive a length of braided nylon string. Photo L on p. 163 shows the same operation on the crane post. Insert the cross arm into the A-shaped block. This piece is not glued in place, but left free to slide.
6. Cut two ⅜-in. lengths of ½-in. dowel and drill a hole centered through the diameter of each, to receive the nylon string.
7. Drill a 3/16-in.-diameter hole 3/16 in. deep into one end of each dowel section, also centered on the diameter.
8. Slide a length of nylon string through each one and fuse the ends that will be in the 3/16-in. cavities.
9. Glue the magnets in place with epoxy.
10. Thread the free ends of the nylon string through the cross-arm holes and fuse them at a final length of about 4½ in.

■ SHARED FREIGHTER/OIL TANKER PARTS

PART	SIZE (IN.)	QUANTITY	MATERIAL
FREIGHTER/TANKER TOWER:			
A block	$1\frac{1}{8}$ x 1 x $3\frac{3}{8}$	1	Maple
Cross arm (boom)	$\frac{1}{4}$ dia. x $4\frac{1}{2}$	1	$\frac{1}{4}$ dowel
Magnet holders	$\frac{1}{2}$ dia. x $\frac{3}{8}$	2	$\frac{1}{2}$ dowel
Magnets	$\frac{1}{2}$ dia. x $\frac{1}{4}$	2	Commercial
Tower base	$1\frac{1}{2}$ x $\frac{3}{4}$ x 3	1	Maple
Braided nylon string	approx. 12-in. length		—
FREIGHTER/TANKER CRANE POST AND ARM:			
Posts	$\frac{1}{2}$ dia. x 5	4	$\frac{1}{2}$ dowel
Arms	$\frac{1}{4}$ dia. x $4\frac{1}{2}$	4	$\frac{1}{4}$ dowel
Magnet holders	$\frac{1}{2}$ dia. x $\frac{3}{8}$	4	$\frac{1}{2}$ dowel
Magnets	$\frac{1}{2}$ dia. x $\frac{1}{4}$	4	Commercial
Braided nylon string	approx. 30-in. length		—
Drum holder	$3\frac{1}{4}$ x $\frac{3}{8}$ x $3\frac{1}{4}$	1	Maple
Oil drums	$1\frac{1}{8}$ dia. x $2\frac{5}{8}$	4	Commercial
Barrel holder	$2\frac{7}{8}$ x $\frac{1}{4}$ x $2\frac{7}{8}$	1	Maple plywood
Barrels	$\frac{7}{8}$ dia. x $1\frac{1}{4}$	4	Commercial
Cargo boxes	$1\frac{3}{8}$ x $\frac{3}{4}$ x $1\frac{3}{8}$	2	Maple
Washers	$\frac{1}{4}$	10	—

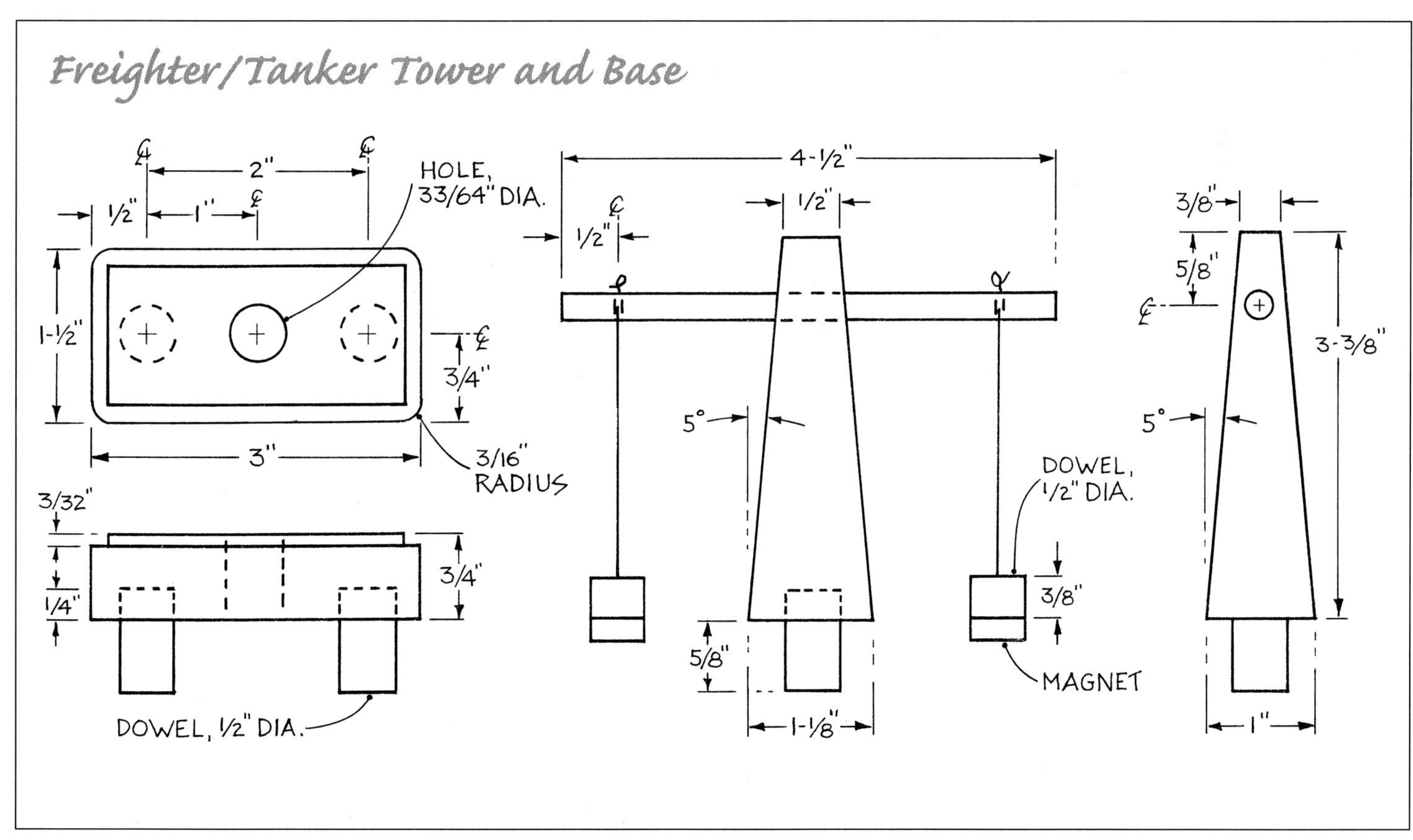

Tower base

This tower has a removable base. I like the look of a 1/16-in. by 3/16-in. rabbet around its top perimeter (which I cut after the drilling operation but before sanding the corner radii), but it's optional. To make the base:

1. Cut the block to overall size and drill a 33/64-in. through hole, centered on both dimensions.
2. Drill the 2-in. spaced lug cavities, centered on the width and length.
3. Sand the corner radii.

Freighter/tanker crane post and arm with pivot base

1. Cut the 1/2-in. dowel post to the indicated length.
2. On the lathe, drill a 9/64-in.-diameter hole 1 in. deep into one end of the post.
3. Make the crane-post drilling jig (see the sidebar).
4. Use the jig to drill a hole that passes through the center of the post at a 45-degree angle, to receive the 1/4-in. dowel arm (see photo K). Be sure to hold the dowel securely to prevent its rotation during this operation.
5. Cut the arm to length and drill the hole for the braided plastic string 1/2 in. from one end, as in photo L.
6. Drill a centered hole for the string through the post, 3/16 in. down from the top end.
7. Make a magnet assembly identical to those on the freighter/tanker tower. Total string length after assembly should be about 5 1/2 in.

Photo J • *Magnets give the crane post and arm a nice touch of lifting action.*

The pivot base is made of 1/4-in. plywood, shaped in the same manner as the deck filler plates. A centered hole about 3/16 in. deep receives a 1/4-in. dowel that protrudes 7/8 in. to support the crane post, and the opposite side of the plate incorporates a pair of lugs with the usual 2-in. spacing centered on both dimensions.

• CRANE-POST ANGLE-DRILLING JIG

This jig is useful to drill holes at angles in dowel stock for the crane post.

To make the jig:

1. Cut a 2 1/8-in. by 1 1/8-in. by 4 1/8-in. hardwood block.
2. Drill a centered vertical hole 3 3/4 in. deep into the block. The hole diameter should be 33/64 in. to easily accommodate a 1/2-in. dowel.
3. Make the two indicated 45-degree angle cuts.
4. Lay the block on its side, as in the second view in the drawing, and drill the second hole as indicated, centered on the block's thickness.
5. Use an H (0.266 in.) or I (0.272 in.) drill bit to provide clearance for the 1/4-in. dowel arm. Check for actual dowel diameter.

Freighter/Tanker Crane Post and Base

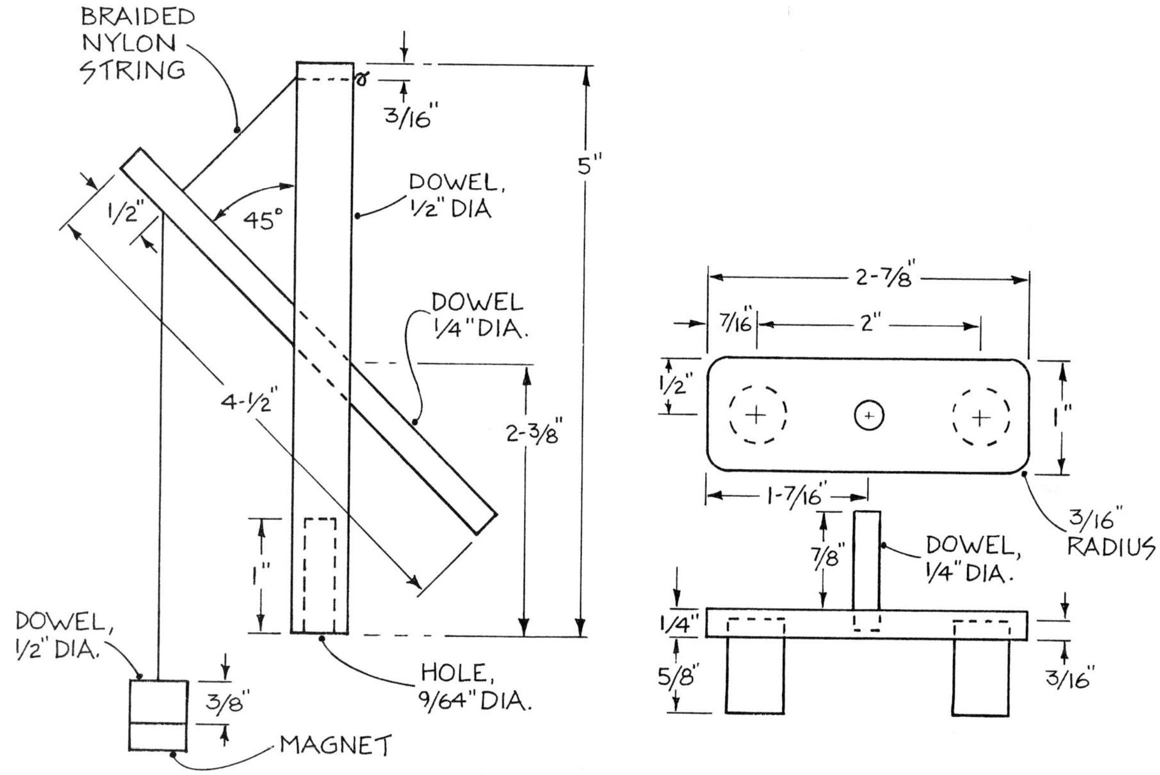

Photo K • *Notoriously difficult to do, drilling angled holes in dowels is made easy with this jig. Here the crane post gets an accurately centered 45-degree angle hole to receive the arm.*

Photo L • *A special block holds the crane post in place for drilling the holes to receive lengths of braided nylon string.*

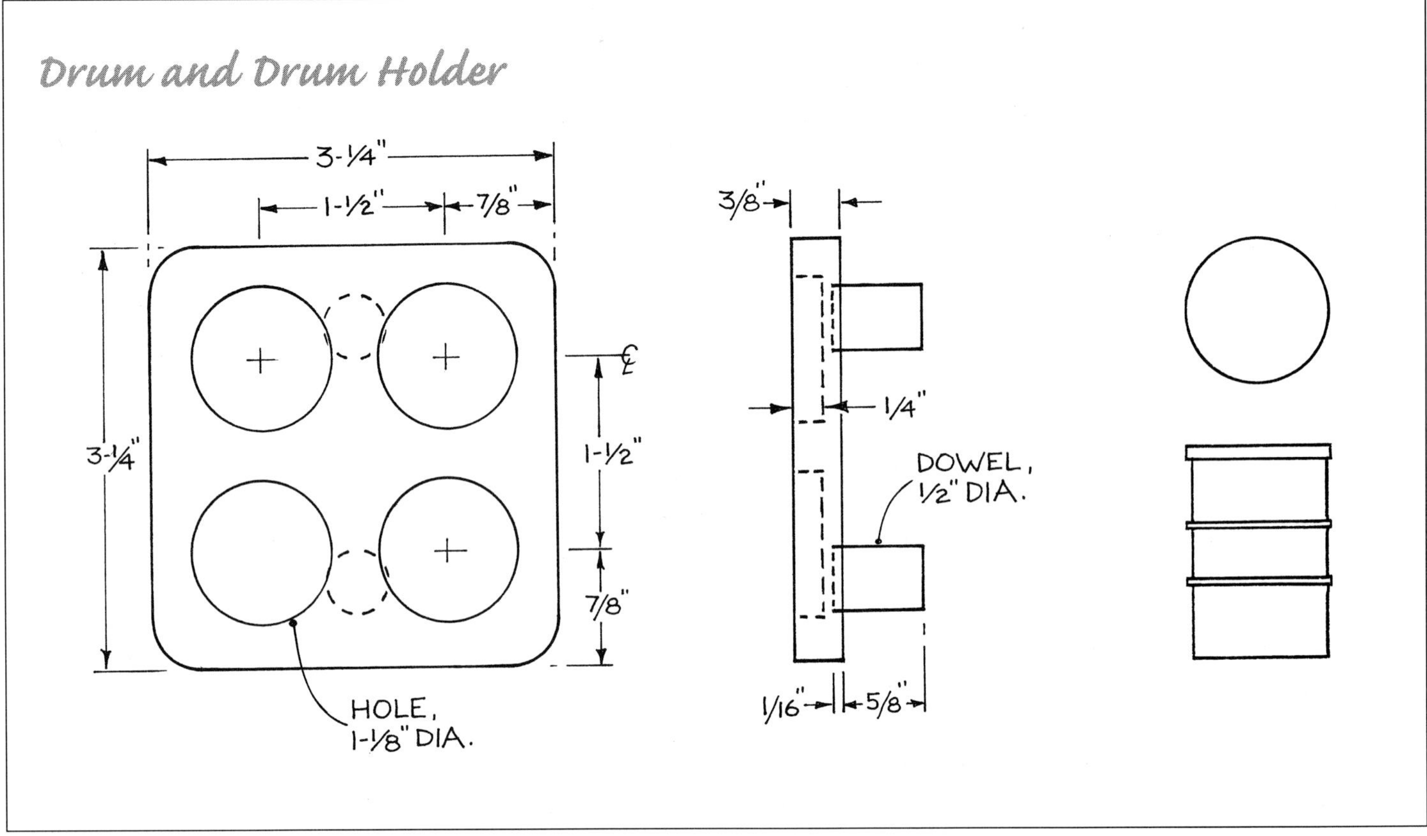

Drum holder

1. Cut the 3/8-in. plywood blank to size and lay out the four 1 1/8-in.-diameter partial depth cavities that will hold the drums.
2. Sand the corner radii.
3. Drill the cavities to a depth of 1/4 in. with a Forstner bit.
4. Drill the two lug cavities on the opposite side, with the usual 2-in. spacing centered on both dimensions. The depth should be only 1/16 in., to stay clear of the drum cavities.

Barrel holder

1. Cut the plywood blank to size and lay out the centerlines of the four 7/8-in.-diameter through holes.
2. Sand the corner radii.
3. Drill the four through holes.
4. Drill the two lug cavities on the opposite side, with the usual 2-in. spacing centered on both dimensions.

Drums and barrels

The oil drums and barrels are commercially available (see Resources on p. 217). I glue a ¼-in. washer onto one end of each piece with epoxy to provide purchase for the tower and crane magnets. Countersunk screws will fulfill this function, too.

Cargo boxes

1. Cut the blanks to overall size.
2. Set the table saw up with a thin kerf blade adjusted for a 1/16-in.-deep cut. Set the fence for a cut through the center of the 1 3/8-in. dimension of the box blanks.

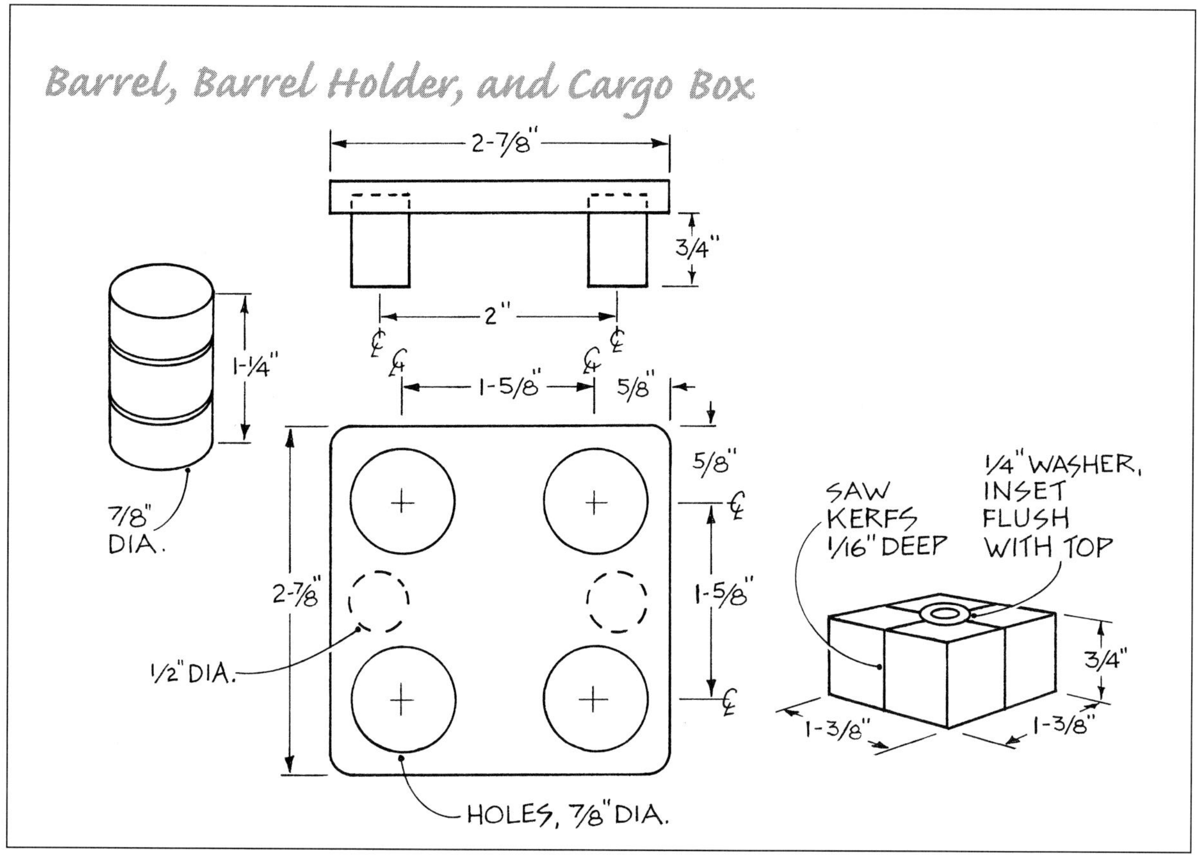

3. Make two cuts to form a cross on both faces of each blank. Make four cuts on each to join the crosses over the 3/4-in. dimension.
4. Drill a centered hole on one face of each blank to receive a 1/4-in. washer that is glued in place with epoxy, seated flush with the surface.

Deck cabin

1. Cut the deck cabin blank to its overall size.
2. Locate and drill the single porthole on each side, as indicated in the plan drawing on p. 167.
3. Locate and rout out the recessed side doorway.

FABRICATION OF FREIGHTER COMPONENTS

For an authentic look, the freighter should be assembled with deck risers. I recommend smokestack #2 here.

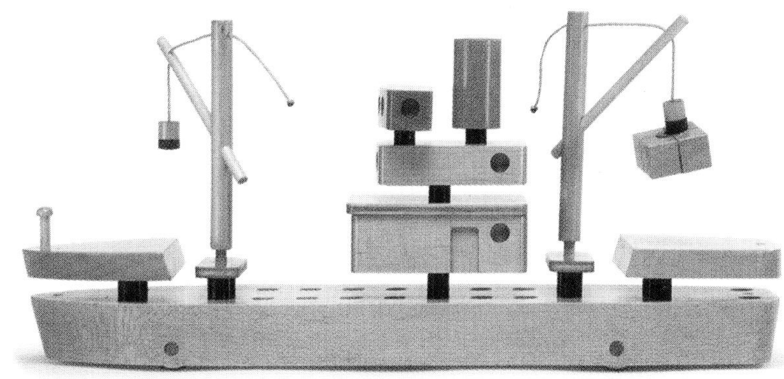

Photo M • *Freighter components in alignment.*

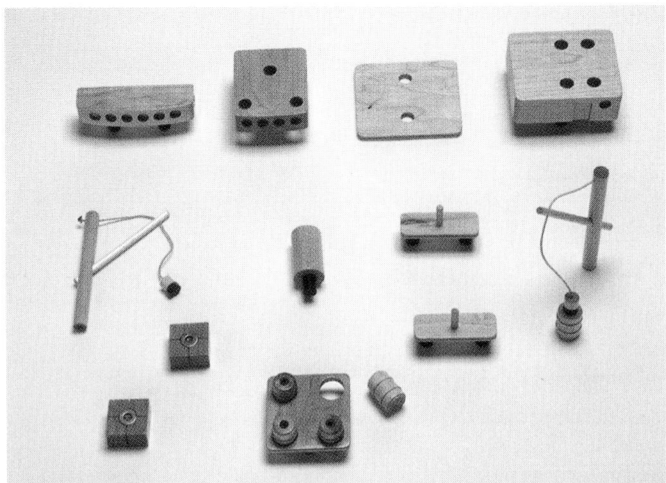

Photo N • *Freighter components, including crane post and arms, decks, cabins, and drum holder.*

■ FREIGHTER

PART	SIZE (IN.)	QUANTITY	MATERIAL
Bridge	$1^1/_4$ x $^7/_8$ x $4^1/_2$	1	Maple
Captain's cabin	$2^7/_8$ x $^7/_8$ x $3^1/_2$	1	Maple
Upper deck	$3^3/_4$ x $^1/_4$ x $4^1/_8$	1	$^1/_4$ maple plywood
Deck cabin	$3^1/_2$ x $1^1/_4$ x 4	1	Maple

4. Locate and drill the lug cavities. Using the alignment jig, drill the pair of receiving holes directly above the lug cavities.

5. Locate and drill the two remaining receiving holes.

6. Sand the corner radii.

Upper deck

1. Cut the blank to size.

2. Locate and drill the two through holes with the usual 2-in. spacing centered in both dimensions.

3. Sand the corner radii.

Captain's cabin

1. Cut the blank to its overall size. Lay out the front $8^3/_4$-in.-radius curve.

2. Locate and drill the three through receiving holes as indicated on the plan drawing on p. 168.

3. Locate and drill the two lug cavities, with the usual 2-in. spacing centered 2 in. from the back edge.

4. Lay out and drill the four evenly spaced $^7/_{16}$-in.-diameter front portholes, $^1/_4$ in. deep.

5. Sand the front radius curve and the corner radii on a stationary sander.

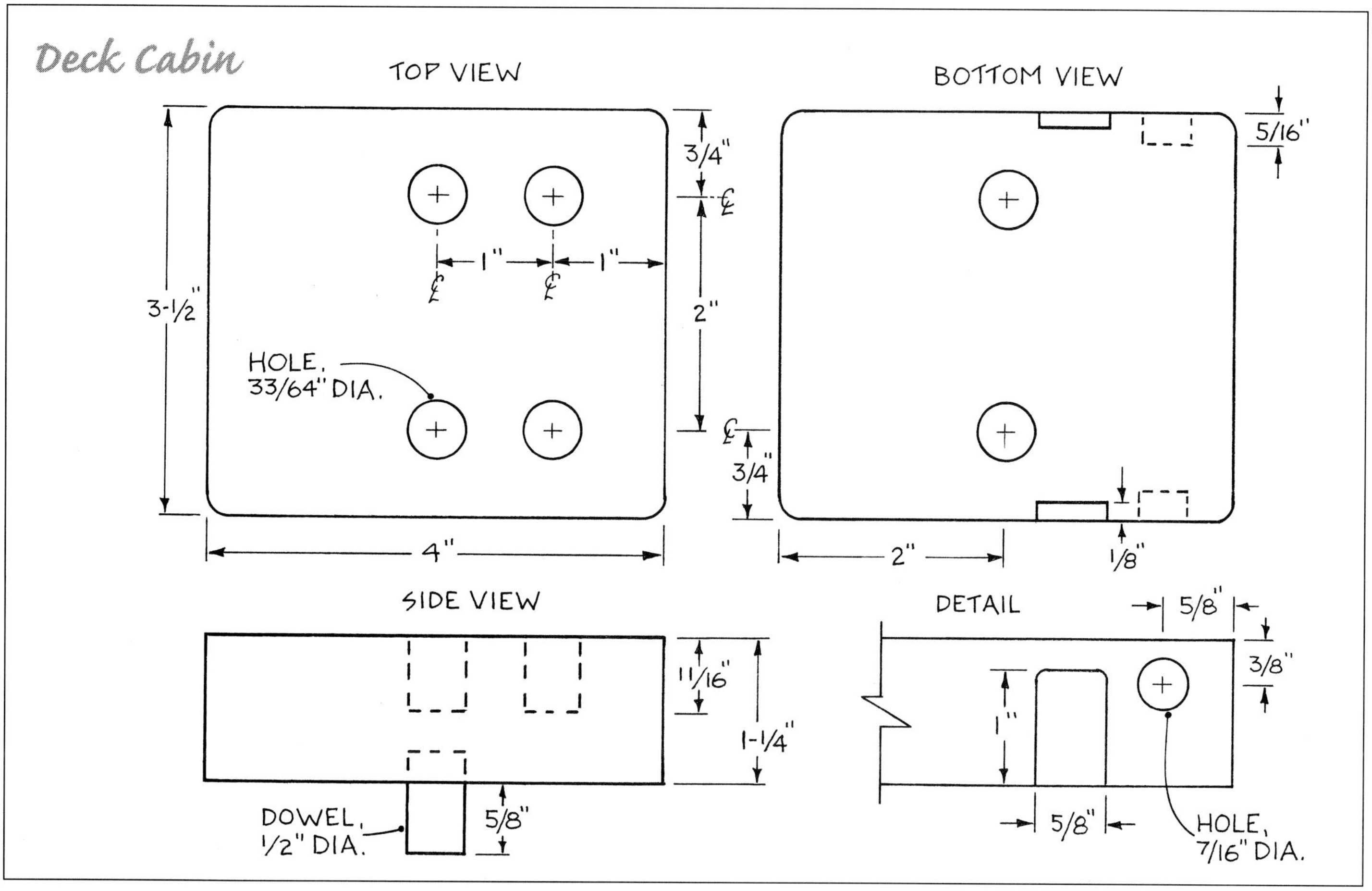

Deck Cabin

TOP VIEW
3-1/2"
4"
3/4"
2"
3/4"
1"
1"
HOLE, 33/64" DIA.

BOTTOM VIEW
5/16"
2"
1/8"

SIDE VIEW
11/16"
1-1/4"
5/8"
DOWEL, 1/2" DIA.

DETAIL
5/8"
3/8"
1"
5/8"
HOLE, 7/16" DIA.

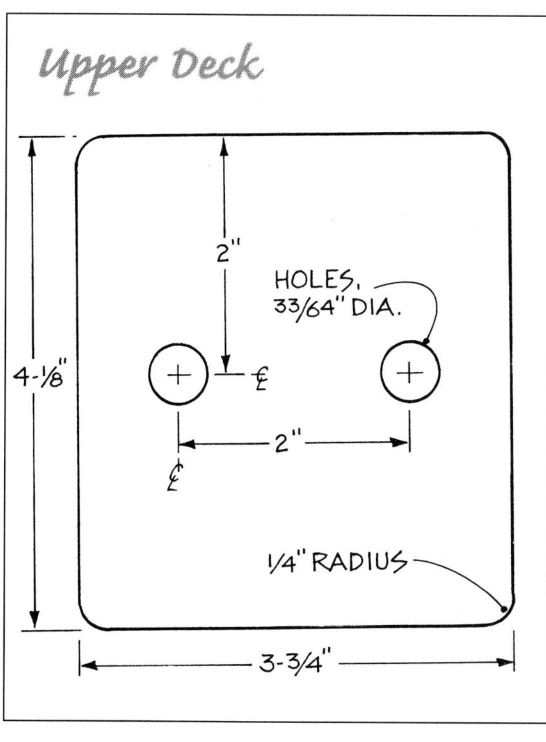

Bridge

1. Cut the blank to its correct length and thickness, leaving it 1/16 in. oversize in width to accommodate laying out the 8 3/4-in.-radius curve, as indicated in the plan drawing on p. 169.

2. Lay out the radius curve on the top view and the portholes on the front view.

3. Drill the 7/16-in.-diameter portholes to the following depths: 1/2 in. for the left and right outer ones, 7/16 in. for the next in on each side, and 3/8 in. for the two in the middle. This will result in equal depths after cutting the front curve.

4. Drill the two side portholes (one on each side) 3/8 in. deep. Note that they lie along the same horizontal centerline as those in front.

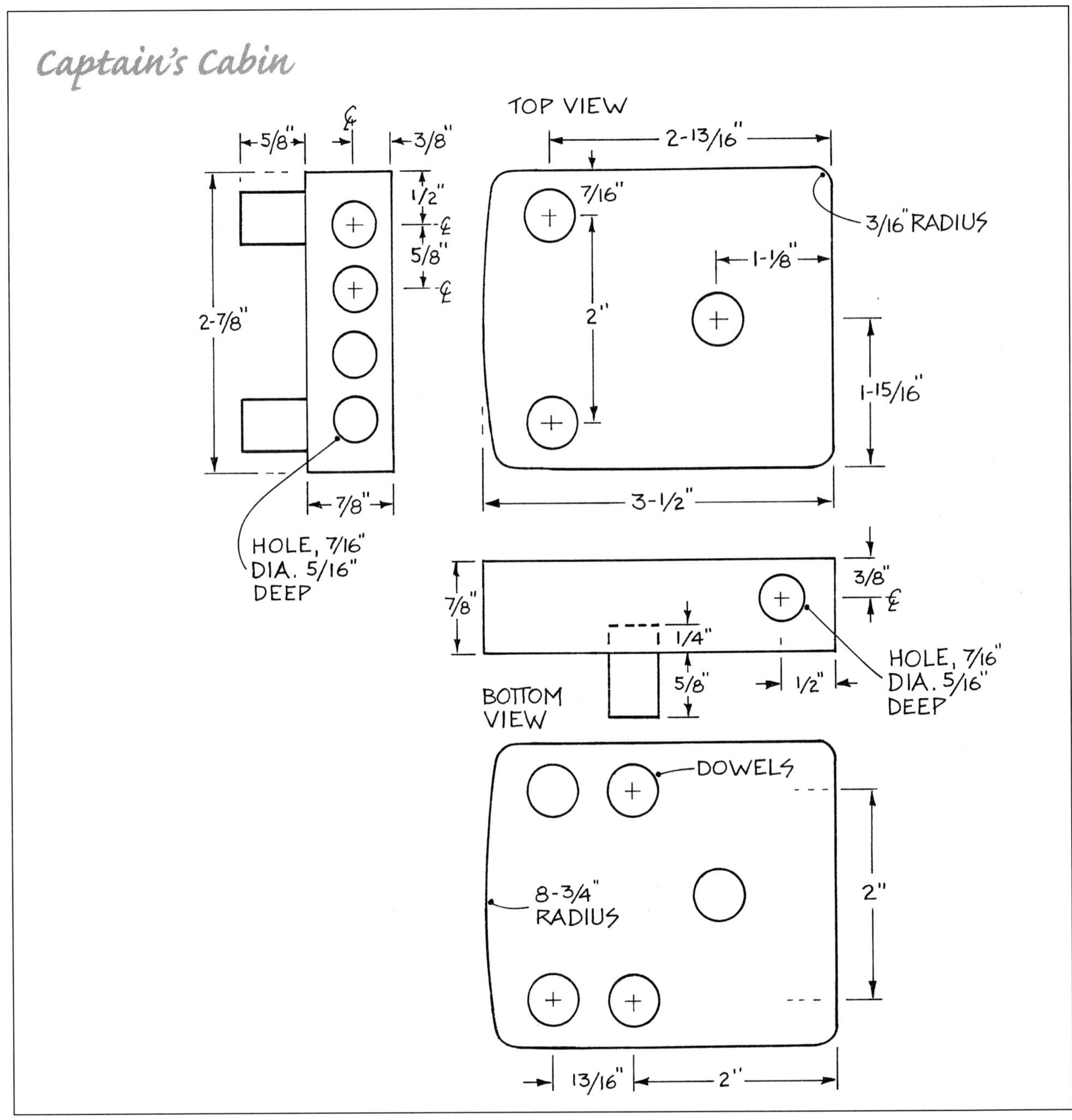

5 Locate and drill the two lug cavities.

6 Cut the front curve on either the scrollsaw or bandsaw and sand it smooth. The curve should match that of the captain's cabin.

7 Sand the corner radii.

FABRICATION OF OIL TANKER COMPONENTS

The oil tanker uses tower #1 and smokestack #1.

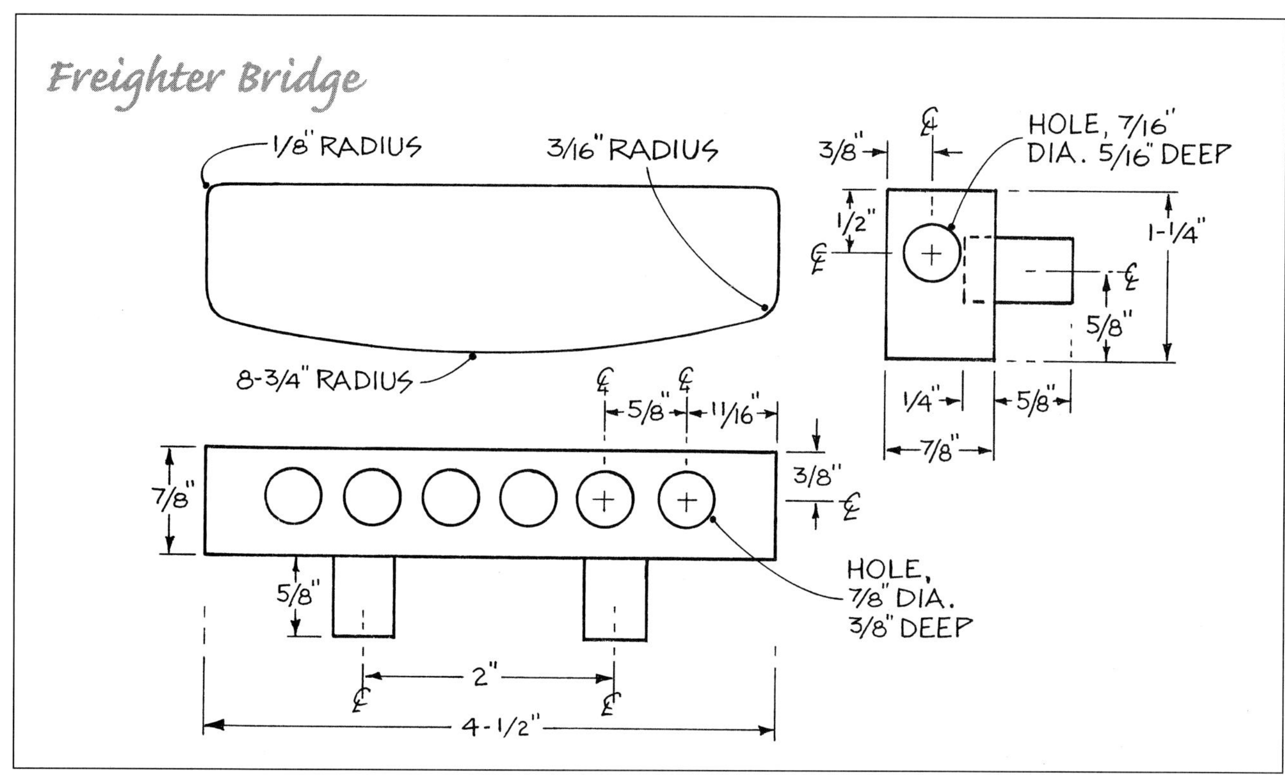

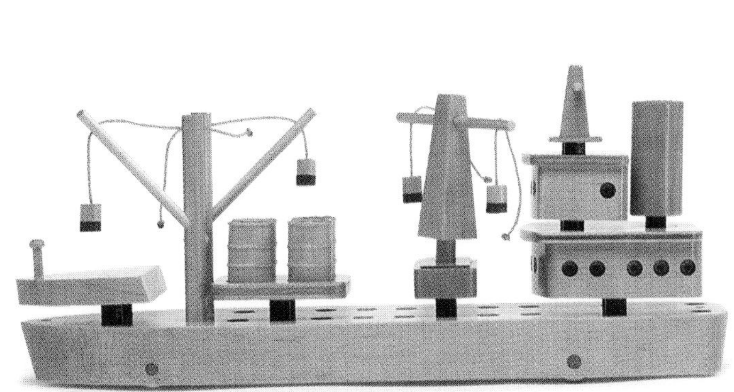

Photo Oa • *Oil tanker components in alignment.*

Photo Ob • *Detail.*

■ OIL TANKER

PART	SIZE (IN.)	QUANTITY	MATERIAL
Bridge	2¼ x 1¼ x 2⅞	1	Maple
Bridge roof	2½ x ¼ x 3⅛	1	¼ maple plywood
Upper deck	4⅜ x ¼ x 4¼	1	¼ maple plywood
Deck cabin	4 x 1¼ x 4	1	Maple

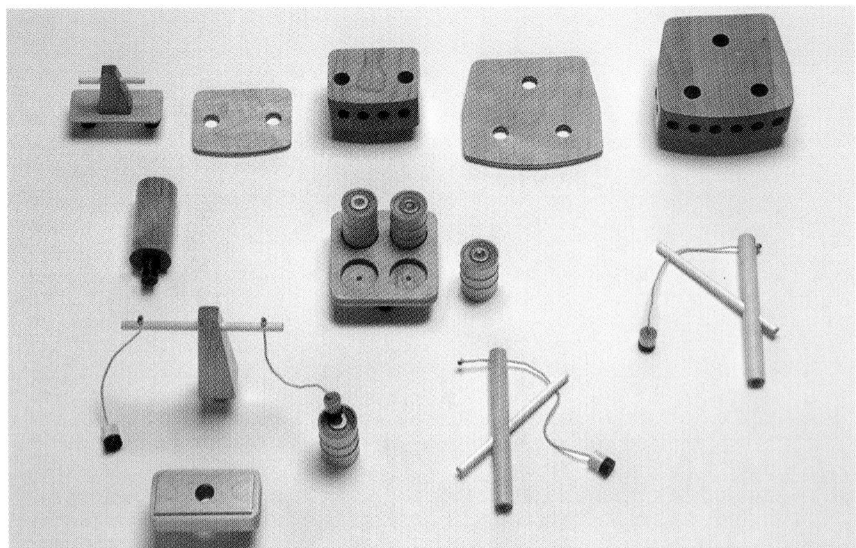

Photo P • *Oil tanker components, including deck cabin, upper deck, bridge, bridge roof, barrels, and barrel holders.*

Deck cabin

1. Cut the blank to overall size, leaving it about $^1/_{16}$ in. oversize in length to accommodate cutting the front curve.
2. Draw the top view layout on the workpiece, including the 10-degree angles at the back and the radii.
3. Locate and drill the two lug cavities, with the usual spacing centered 2 in. from the back edge.
4. Locate and drill the three receiving holes. Note that this is an exception to the paired arrangements found on most pieces.
5. Locate and drill the $^3/_8$-in.-diameter portholes on the front of the workpiece to the following depths: $^5/_8$ in. for the left and right outer ones, $^1/_2$ in. for the next in on each side, and $^3/_8$ in. for the two in the middle. Again, this will result in approximately equal depths after cutting the front curve.
6. Lay out and drill the side portholes to the following depths: $^3/_8$ in. for the front two, $^1/_2$ in. for the next two, and $^5/_8$ in. for the rear two.
7. Cut the indicated 10-degree angles on the table saw set up with an auxiliary fence on the miter gauge and a stop block. Both cuts are made with the workpiece front against the fence; flip it over for the second cut. Alternately, this cut can be made on the bandsaw.
8. Cut the front radius on the bandsaw. Round the edges by hand with a sanding block or on the stationary sander.

Upper deck

1. Cut the plywood blank to size, leaving it $^1/_{16}$ in. oversize in length. Lay out the top view.
2. Drill the three through holes as indicated.
3. Cut the 10-degree angles on the table saw to match those on the deck cabin.
4. Cut the front radius on a bandsaw or scrollsaw. Sand the rear radius curves.

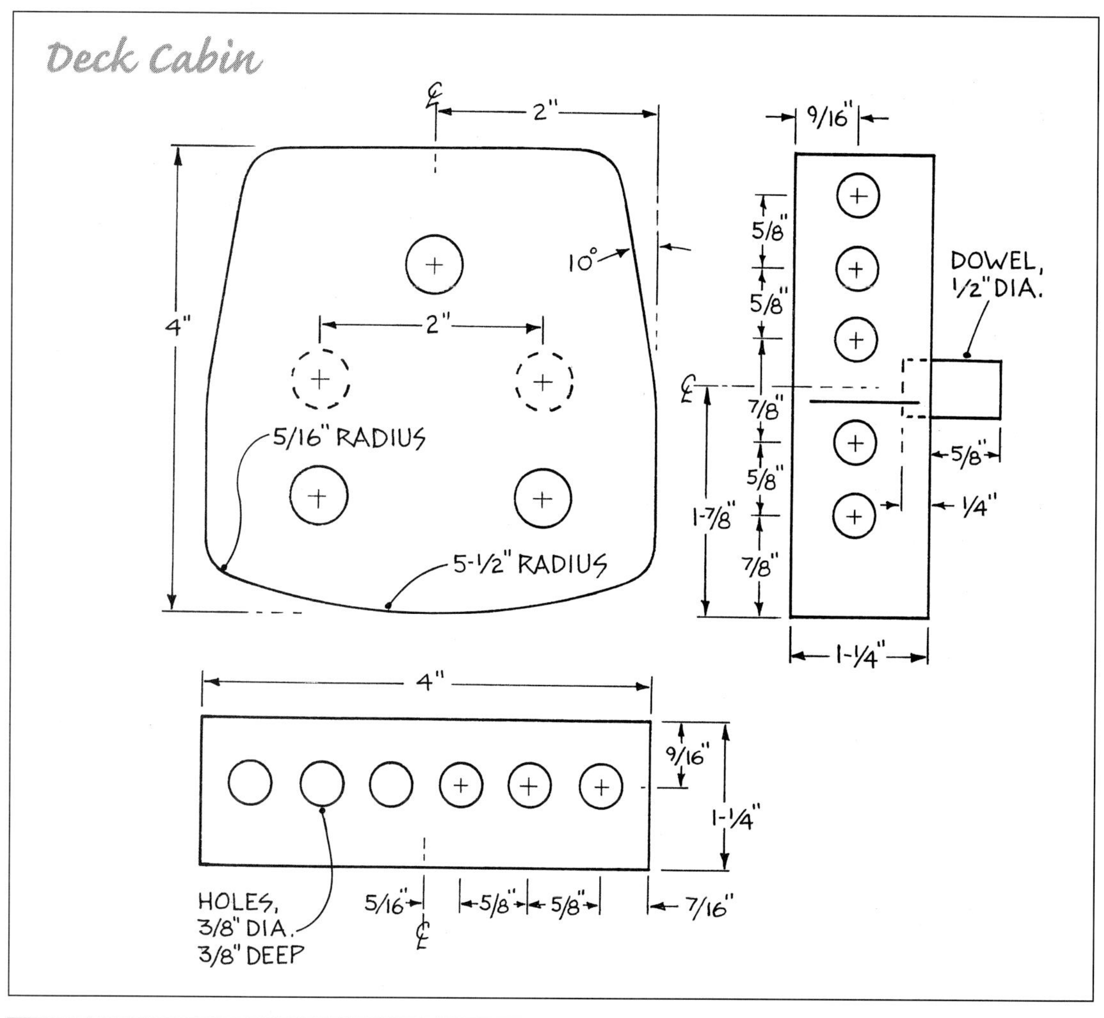
Deck Cabin
2"
9/16"
10°
4"
2"
5/8"
5/8"
DOWEL,
1/2" DIA.
7/8"
5/16" RADIUS
5/8"
5/8"
1/4"
1-7/8"
7/8"
5-1/2" RADIUS
1-1/4"
4"
9/16"
1-1/4"
HOLES,
3/8" DIA.
3/8" DEEP
5/16"
5/8"
5/8"
7/16"

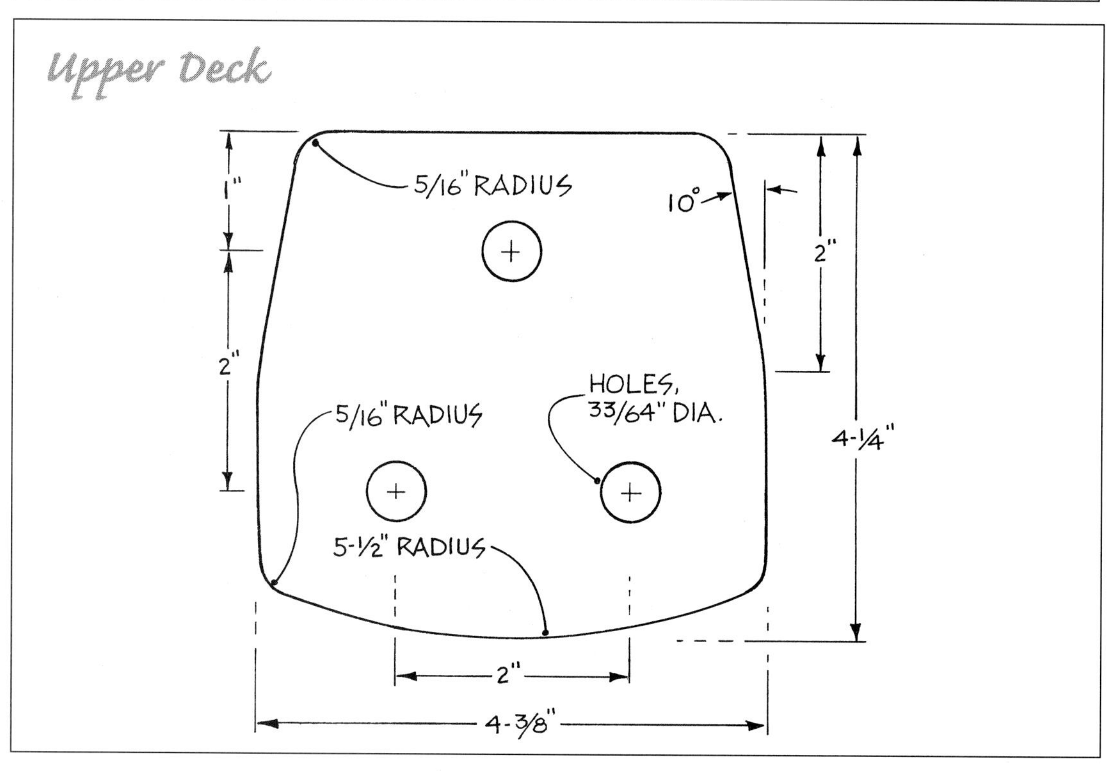
Upper Deck
1"
5/16" RADIUS
10°
2"
2"
5/16" RADIUS
HOLES,
33/64" DIA.
4-1/4"
5-1/2" RADIUS
2"
4-3/8"

Bridge

1. Cut the blank to size, leaving it 1⁄16 in. oversize in length. Lay out the top view.
2. Locate and drill the bottom lug cavities.
3. Using the aligning jig, drill the receiving holes in the workpiece's top.
4. Locate and drill the front, rear, and side portholes, all 3⁄8 in. in diameter and 3⁄8 in. deep.

Bridge roof

1. Cut the blank to size, leaving it 1⁄16 in. oversize in length.
2. Locate and drill the two through holes, centered on both dimensions.
3. Cut the front curve on the scrollsaw. Sand the rear radii.

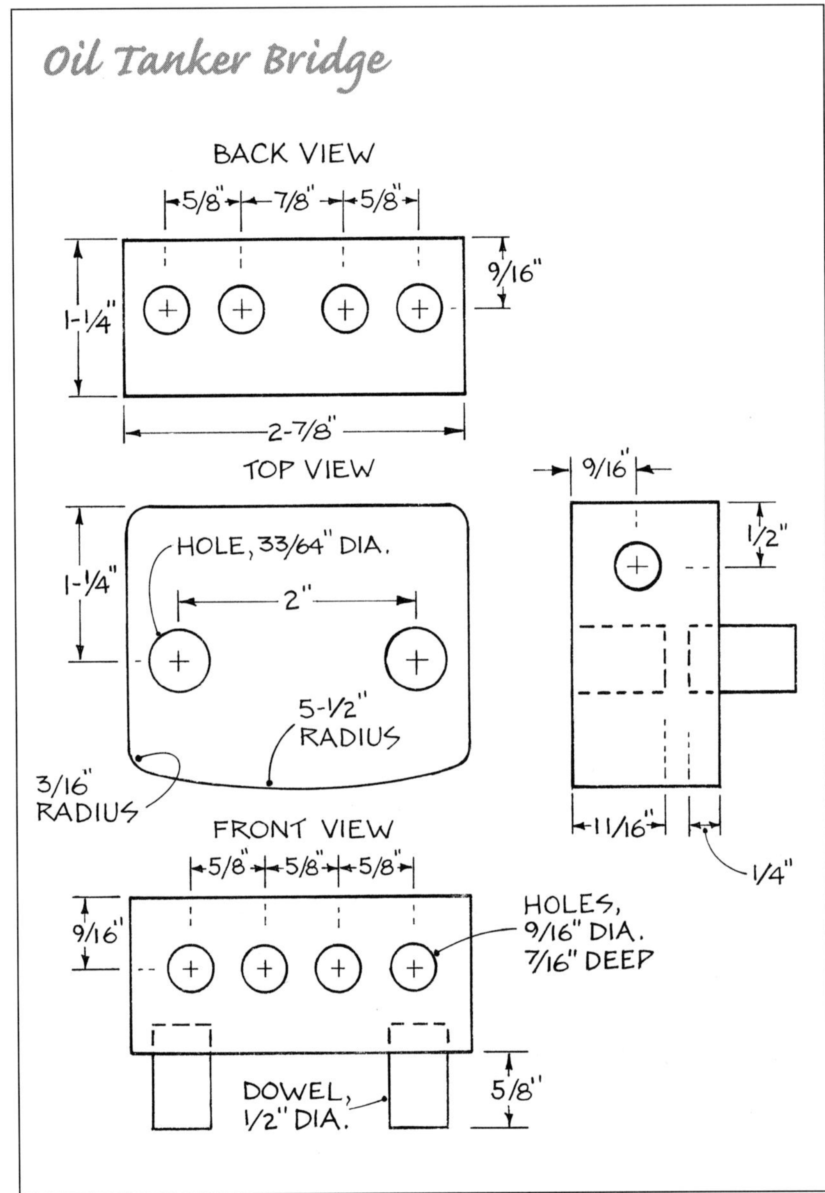

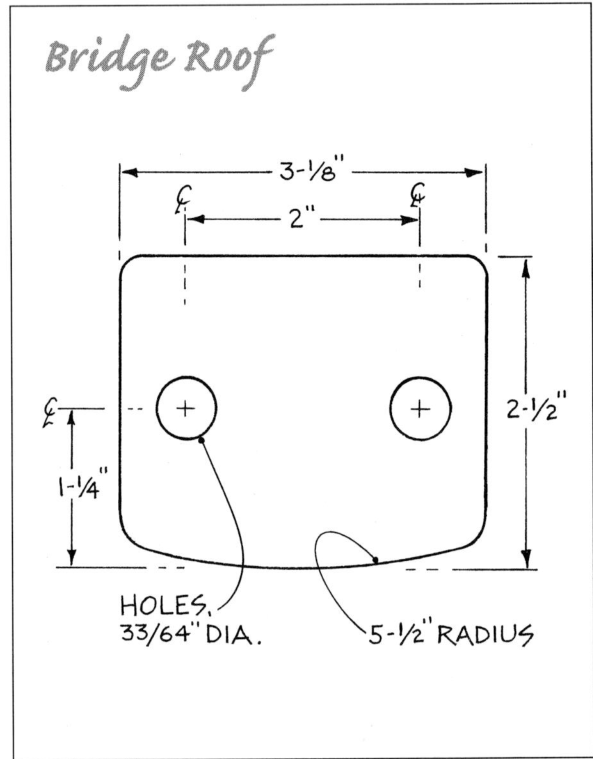

FABRICATION OF TUGBOAT COMPONENTS

Smokestack #6 is a good one for the tugboat, and I also like to match the walnut deck and roof cap with walnut funnels.

Forward deck/bridge cabins

These two pieces are identical.

1. Cut the blanks to size, leaving them 1/16 in. oversize in length. Lay out the top radius on each, as indicated on the plan drawing on p. 174.
2. Locate and drill the pair of lug cavities in each. The alignment jig can be used to drill the receiving holes.
3. Locate and drill the four 1/2-in.-diameter front portholes on each workpiece. The depth should account for the radius cut line in the next step.
4. Cut the front radii on the bandsaw.

Photo Q • *Tugboat components aligned.*

Photo R • *Tugboat components, including forward deck, bridge cabin, aft deck cabin, roof cap, mid deck, and lamp assembly.*

TUGBOAT

PART	SIZE (IN.)	QUANTITY	MATERIAL
LAMP ASSEMBLY:			
Flagstaff	1/4 w/5/8 head x 2 1/4	1	Commercial peg
Lamp housing	1 1/4 x 9/16 x 1 9/16	1	Maple
Lamp	3/4 dia. x 3/4	1	Dowel
Lens (pearl button)	11/16 dia.	1	Commercial
Base	2 7/16 x 3/16 x 2 7/8	1	Walnut
CABINS:			
Bridge	2 7/8 x 1 1/4 x 4	1	Maple
Forward deck cabin	2 7/8 x 1 1/4 x 4	1	Maple
Aft deck cabin	2 7/8 x 1 1/4 x 4	1	Maple
Roof cap	3 1/8 x 1/4 x 4 1/8	1	Walnut
Mid deck	3 1/8 x 1/4 x 8 1/8	1	Walnut

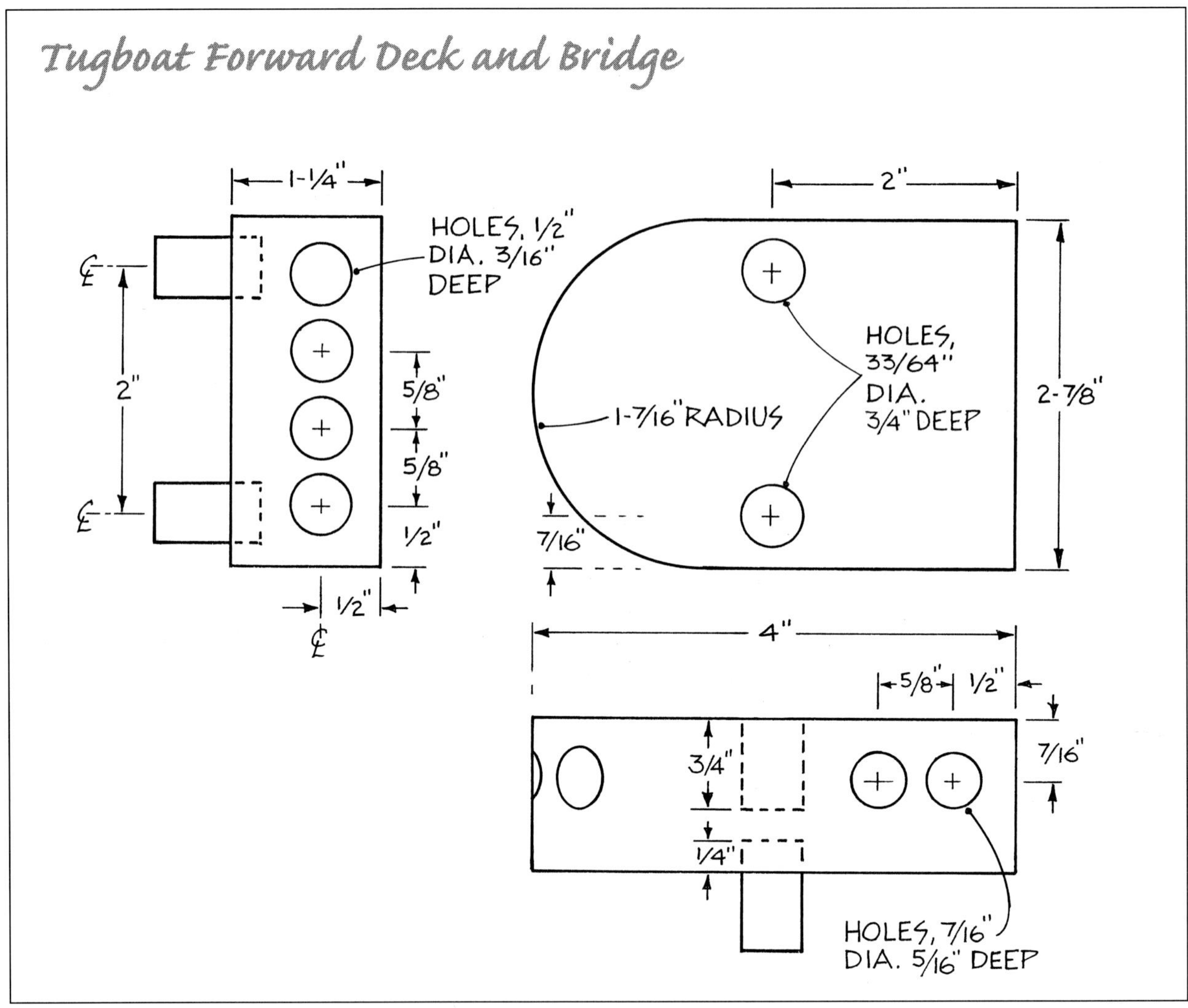

Aft deck cabin

1. Cut the blank to overall size.
2. Locate and drill the lug cavities.
3. Use the jig to drill the two aligned receiving holes and refer to the plan drawing to locate and drill the other two.
4. Locate and drill the side portholes 7/16 in. diameter and 5/16 in. deep.
5. Locate and rout out the side doors, using a 1/4-in. bit. Note that doors are at the back of the cabin's sides.

Roof cap and mid deck

1. Cut the two blanks to size, leaving them 1/16 in. oversize in length. Lay out the front curve on each, as indicated in the plan drawing on p. 176.
2. Locate and drill all through holes—six in the deck and two in the roof cap.
3. Cut the front curves on the scrollsaw.

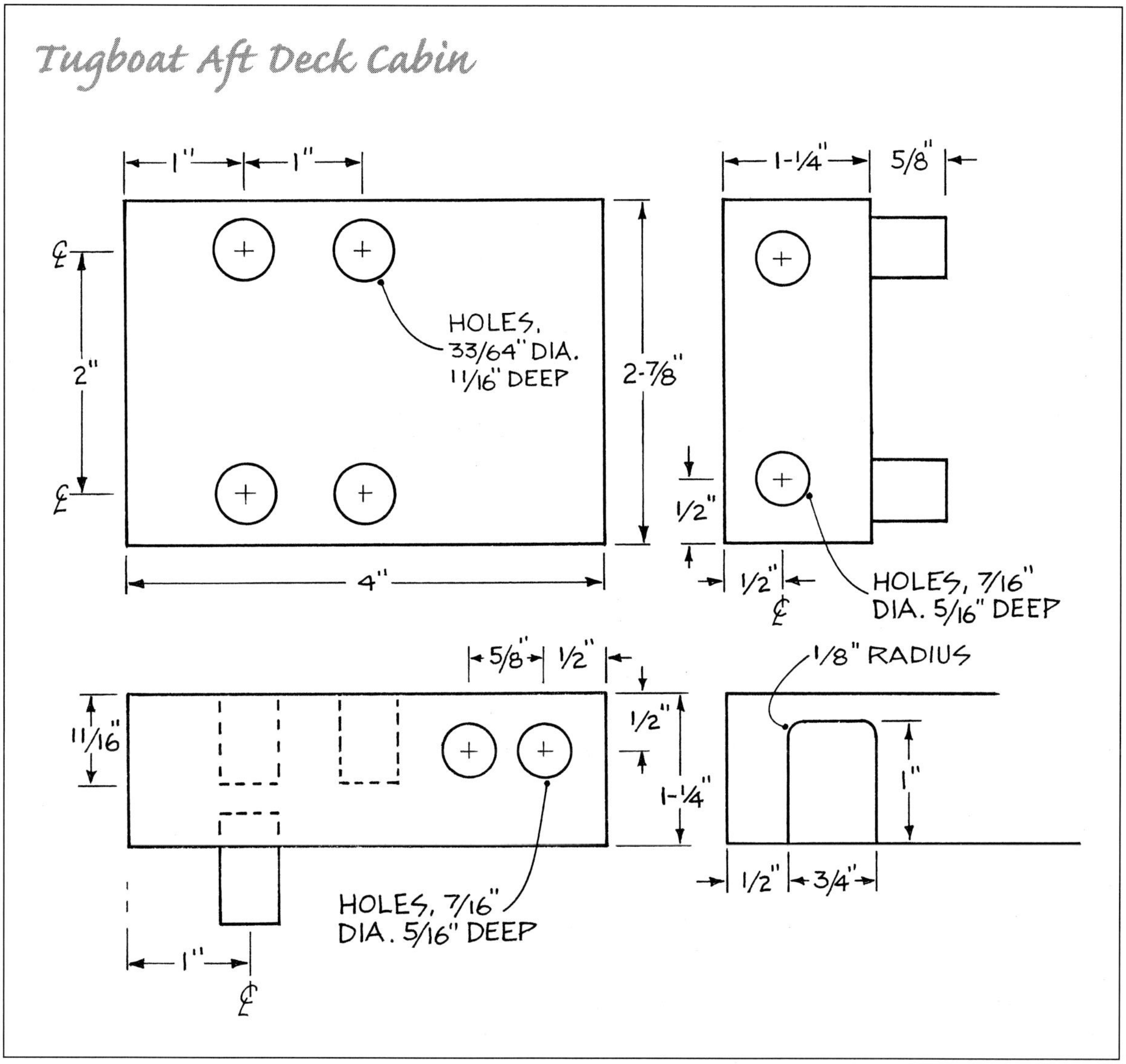

Tugboat Aft Deck Cabin

1" 1"
2"
HOLES, 33/64" DIA. 11/16" DEEP
2-7/8"
4"
1-1/4" 5/8"
1/2"
1/2"
HOLES, 7/16" DIA. 5/16" DEEP
5/8" 1/2"
11/16"
1/2"
1-1/4"
HOLES, 7/16" DIA. 5/16" DEEP
1"
1/8" RADIUS
1"
1/2" 3/4"

Lamp assembly

To make the base:

1. Cut the blank to size, leaving it 1/16 in. oversize in the front-to-back dimension. Lay out the top view.
2. Locate and drill the two lug cavities, 1/8 in. deep.
3. Cut the front curve on the scrollsaw.

To make the lamp housing:

1. Cut the blank to size, leaving it 1/16 in. oversize in length. Lay out the top view.

Photo S • *The shimmer of a pearl button suggests the beam of the tugboat's searchlight. A hand-cut rabbet fits the lamp to its housing.*

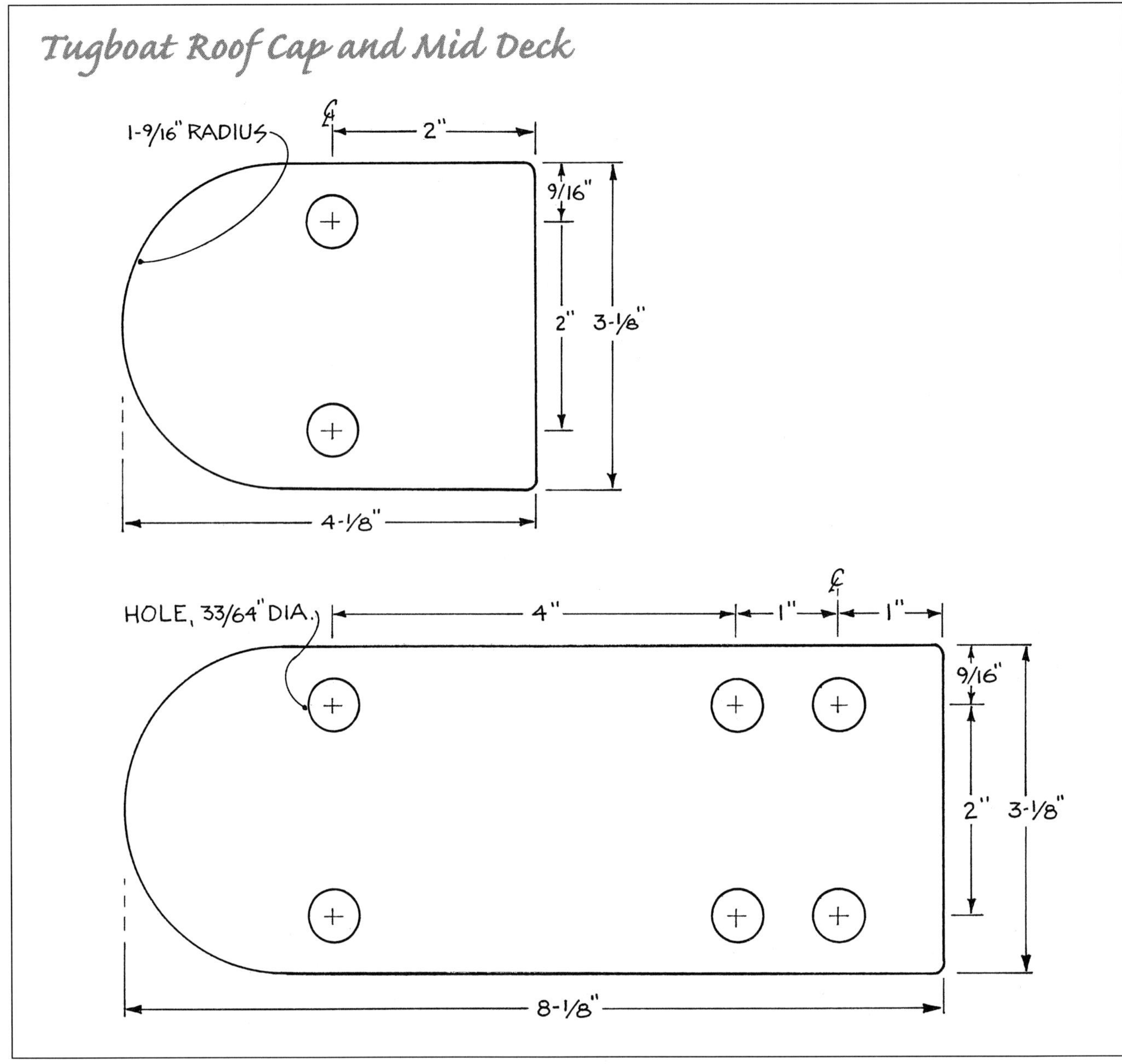

2. Measure in ½ in. from the back and drill a left-to-right centered hole ¼ in. deep, to receive a ¼-in.-diameter commercial peg as a mast.
3. Sand the front radius on the stationary sander.
4. Raise the table-saw blade to a height of ⅜ in. With the workpiece top down and its rear surface against a stop block clamped to an auxiliary fence on the miter gauge, make a cut across the front curve such that the resulting flat area is 1¾ in. from the back edge. This will receive the lamp.

To make the lamp:

1. Cut the indicated rabbet into the end of a length of ¾-in. dowel, using a razor saw.
2. Cut the workpiece to its final ¾-in. length.

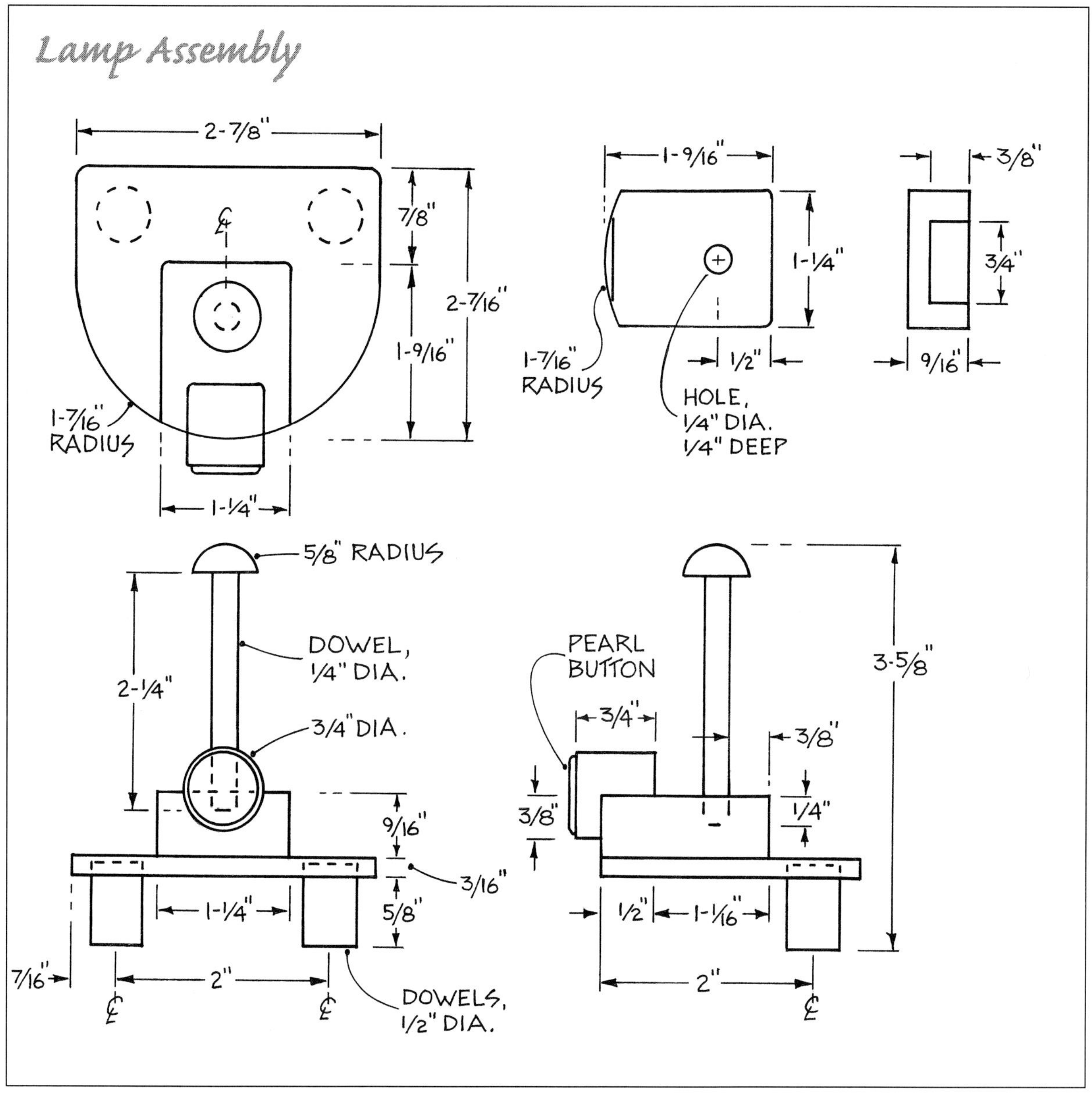

3. File off the rear post on an $^{11}/_{16}$-in. pearl button and glue it to the lamp face with epoxy.
4. Glue all components together, including the $2^{1}/_{8}$-in.-long commercial peg mast.

FABRICATION OF RIVERBOAT COMPONENTS

The riverboat is the most complicated ship in the book, with its own turned smokestacks and its detailed paddle wheel.

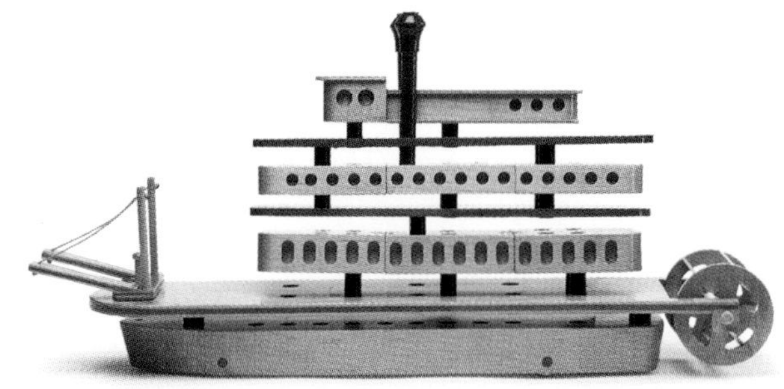

Photo T • *Riverboat components aligned.*

Photo U • *Riverboat components, including main deck and upper deck cabins, captain's cabin, bridge, decks, ramp assembly, smokestacks, and paddle wheel.*

Main deck and upper deck cabins

The forward and aft main deck cabins are identical except for their lug positions. Making the elongated portholes on these cabins requires a multi-cutout routing template like that shown in photo W. The exact dimensions of the template will be dictated by the specific bit and collar size used.

If this operation presents a problem, an alternate route is to drill 7/16-in.-diameter round portholes, which will contrast visually with the 3/8-in.-diameter ones on the upper deck cabins.

1. Cut the three main deck cabin blanks to size as indicated.
2. Locate and drill all receiving holes.
3. Drill all lug cavities, using the alignment jig. Note that on the forward and mid cabins, the lug cavities are under the pair of receiving holes centered on the 4-in. dimension, and on the aft cabin, under the pair centered 1 in. from the cabin end.

Photo V • *Walnut decks. Note that the two-piece top deck can also be made as a single unit.*

Photo W • *Template and workpiece are clamped together on a woodworking bench vise for routing out the elongated portholes on the main deck cabins.*

■ RIVERBOAT

PART	SIZE (IN.)	QUANTITY	MATERIAL
Bridge	2 x $1\frac{1}{4}$ x $2\frac{7}{8}$	1	Maple
Bridge roof cap	$2\frac{1}{4}$ x $\frac{1}{8}$ x $3\frac{1}{8}$	1	$\frac{1}{8}$ maple plywood
CAPTAIN'S CABIN:			
Compartment	2 x $\frac{3}{4}$ x 6	1	Maple
Floor panel	$2\frac{7}{8}$ x $\frac{1}{8}$ x 6	1	$\frac{1}{8}$ maple plywood
Roof cap	$2\frac{1}{4}$ x $\frac{1}{8}$ x $6\frac{1}{8}$	1	$\frac{1}{8}$ maple plywood
UPPER DECK CABINS:			
Forward cabin	$3\frac{1}{2}$ x $\frac{7}{8}$ x 4	1	Maple
Mid cabin	$3\frac{1}{2}$ x $\frac{7}{8}$ x 4	1	Maple
Aft Cabin	$3\frac{1}{2}$ x $\frac{7}{8}$ x 4	1	Maple
MAIN DECK CABINS:			
Forward cabin	$3\frac{1}{2}$ x $1\frac{1}{8}$ x 4	1	Maple
Mid cabin	$3\frac{1}{2}$ x $1\frac{1}{8}$ x 4	1	Maple
Aft cabin	$3\frac{1}{2}$ x $1\frac{1}{8}$ x 4	1	Maple
DECKS:			
Main deck	$4\frac{3}{4}$ x $\frac{3}{8}$ x 20	1	$\frac{3}{8}$ maple plywood
Paddle wheel blocks	$\frac{5}{8}$ x $\frac{13}{16}$ x $\frac{1}{2}$	2	Maple
Top forward deck	$3\frac{3}{4}$ x $\frac{1}{4}$ x $4\frac{1}{4}$	1	$\frac{1}{4}$ maple plywood
Top aft deck	$3\frac{3}{4}$ x $\frac{1}{4}$ x $8\frac{1}{4}$	1	$\frac{1}{4}$ maple plywood
Upper deck	$3\frac{3}{4}$ x $\frac{1}{4}$ x $12\frac{1}{2}$	1	$\frac{1}{4}$ maple plywood
Smokestack tops	1 dia. at top x $1\frac{1}{8}$	2	Walnut dowel
Smokestack barrels	$\frac{1}{2}$ dia. x $4\frac{5}{8}$	2	Walnut dowel
RAMP ASSEMBLY:			
Ramp base	$1\frac{1}{4}$ x $\frac{1}{4}$ x $3\frac{1}{4}$	1	$\frac{1}{4}$ maple plywood
Ramps	$\frac{5}{8}$ x $\frac{1}{4}$ x $3\frac{3}{8}$	2	$\frac{1}{4}$ maple plywood
Posts	$\frac{1}{4}$ x $3\frac{3}{16}$	2	$\frac{1}{4}$ dowel
Swivel peg	$\frac{1}{4}$ peg	1	Commercial
PADDLE WHEEL:			
Paddles	$\frac{7}{16}$ x $\frac{1}{8}$ x $3\frac{1}{8}$	8	Maple
Wheels	3 dia. x $\frac{1}{4}$	2	$\frac{1}{4}$ maple plywood
Axle	$\frac{3}{8}$ dia. x $3\frac{1}{2}$	1	$\frac{3}{8}$ plastic tube
Axle pegs	$\frac{1}{4}$ dia.	2	Commercial pegs

4. Lay out all the elongated portholes, including those on the ends of the forward and aft cabin blanks, for reference in visually aligning the routing template.
5. Rout out all portholes to a depth of $\frac{1}{4}$ in.
6. Cut the forward and aft radii on the bandsaw and hand-sand them smooth.

The sequence of steps for the upper deck cabins is exactly the same. The differences are in the dimensions and in the lug cavity positions. Also, the portholes here are round, and the mid cabin has an additional pair of receiving holes, spaced $2\frac{5}{8}$ in. apart on center, for the smokestacks. The diameter of these two holes is $\frac{17}{32}$ in., to provide a little leeway for alignment in assembly.

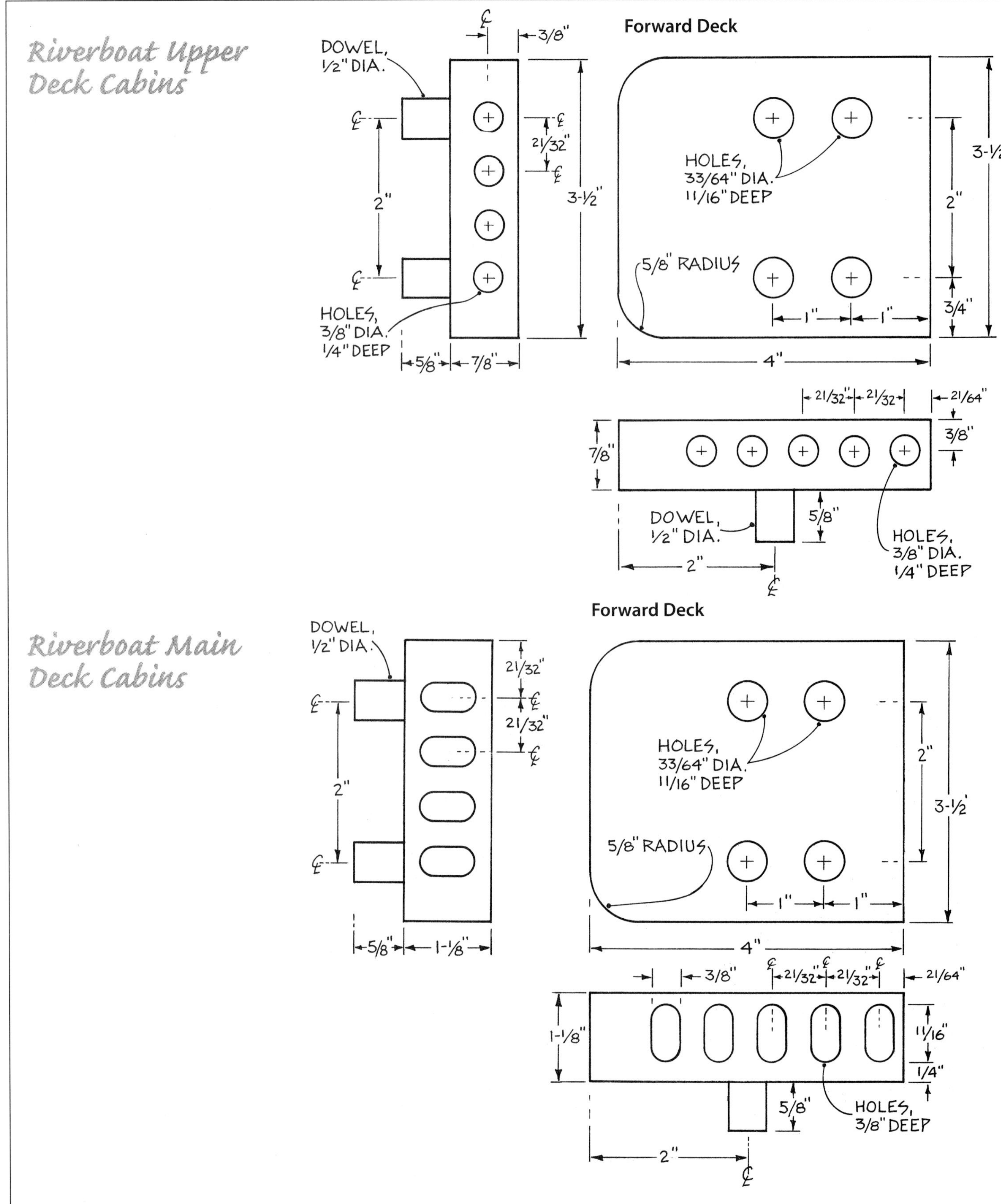

Riverboat Upper Deck Cabins
DOWEL, 1/2" DIA.
3/8"
21/32"
2"
3-1/2"
HOLES, 3/8" DIA. 1/4" DEEP
5/8"
7/8"
Forward Deck
HOLES, 33/64" DIA. 11/16" DEEP
5/8" RADIUS
3-1/2"
2"
3/4"
1"
1"
4"
21/32"
21/32"
21/64"
3/8"
7/8"
DOWEL, 1/2" DIA.
5/8"
HOLES, 3/8" DIA. 1/4" DEEP
2"
Riverboat Main Deck Cabins
DOWEL, 1/2" DIA.
21/32"
21/32"
2"
5/8"
1-1/8"
Forward Deck
HOLES, 33/64" DIA. 11/16" DEEP
5/8" RADIUS
2"
3-1/2'
1"
1"
4"
3/8"
21/32"
21/32"
21/64"
1-1/8"
11/16"
1/4"
5/8"
HOLES, 3/8" DEEP
2"

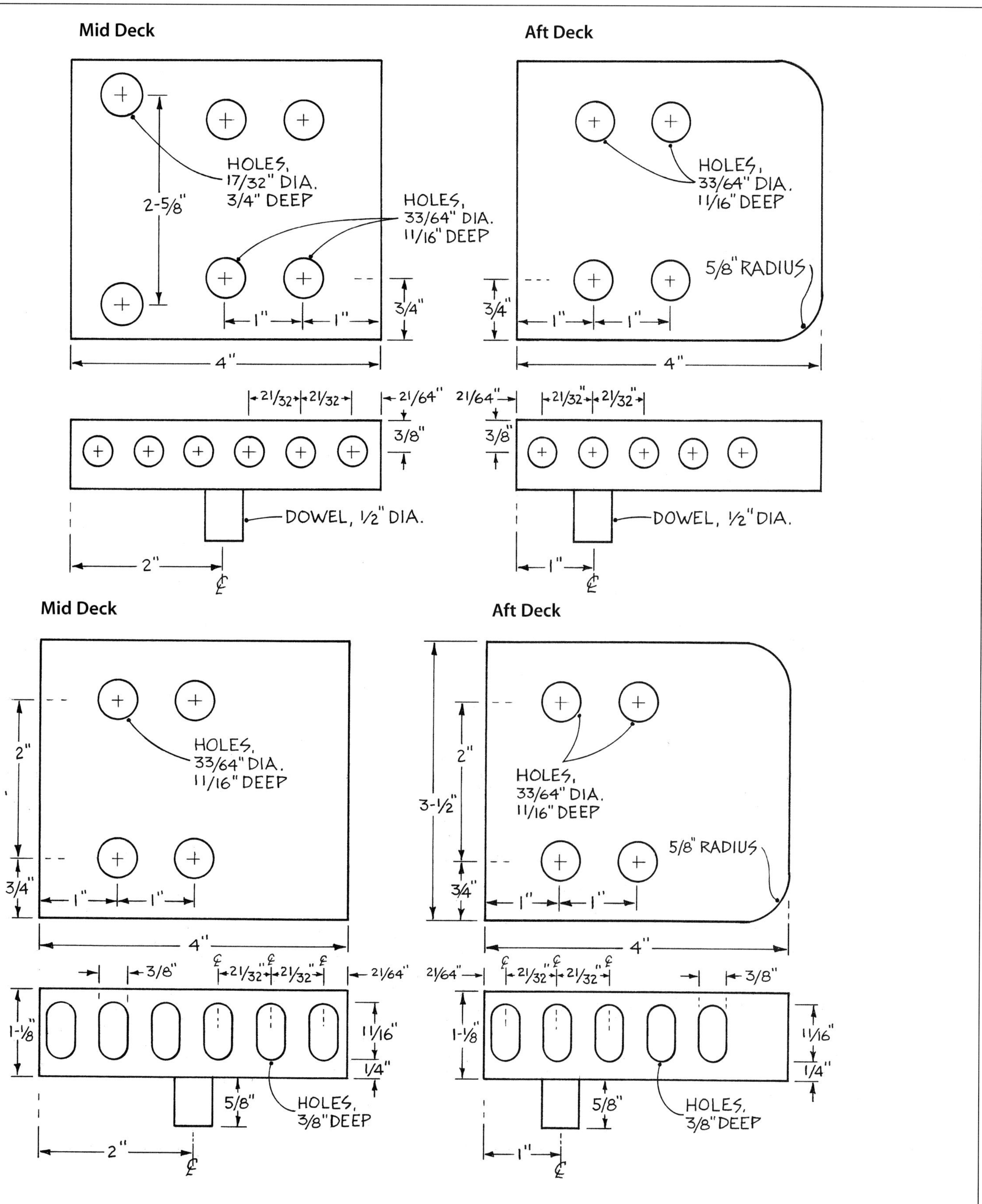
Mid Deck
HOLES, 17/32" DIA. 3/4" DEEP
2-5/8"
HOLES, 33/64" DIA. 11/16" DEEP
3/4"
1"
1"
4"
21/32
21/32
21/64"
3/8"
DOWEL, 1/2" DIA.
2"
Aft Deck
HOLES, 33/64" DIA. 11/16" DEEP
5/8" RADIUS
3/4"
1"
1"
4"
21/64"
21/32"
21/32"
3/8"
DOWEL, 1/2" DIA.
1"
Mid Deck
2"
HOLES, 33/64" DIA. 11/16" DEEP
3/4"
1"
1"
4"
3/8"
21/32"
21/32"
21/64"
1-1/8"
11/16"
1/4"
5/8"
HOLES, 3/8" DEEP
2"
Aft Deck
3-1/2"
2"
HOLES, 33/64" DIA. 11/16" DEEP
5/8" RADIUS
3/4"
1"
1"
4"
21/64"
21/32"
21/32"
3/8"
1-1/8"
11/16"
1/4"
5/8"
HOLES, 3/8" DEEP
1"

Captain's cabin

1. Cut the compartment blank to size.
2. Locate and drill the portholes and then cut and sand the rear-corner radii.
3. Cut the floor panel to size.
4. Locate and drill the two 17⁄32-in. through holes for the smokestacks. Note that these holes break the side lines of the workpiece. To prevent splitting, drill first with a 1⁄2-in. Forstner bit and then redrill with a regular 17⁄32-in. bit.
5. Drill the floor panel lug cavities, 1⁄16 in. deep. As for all very shallow holes, the use of an end mill is desirable.
6. Form the rear radii, either by hand-sanding or on the scrollsaw. Glue the floor panel to the compartment in the indicated position.
7. Cut the roof cap to size. Using a half-round file, form the two partial radii to align with the smokestack receiving holes in the floor panel.
8. Glue the roof cap to the top of the compartment.

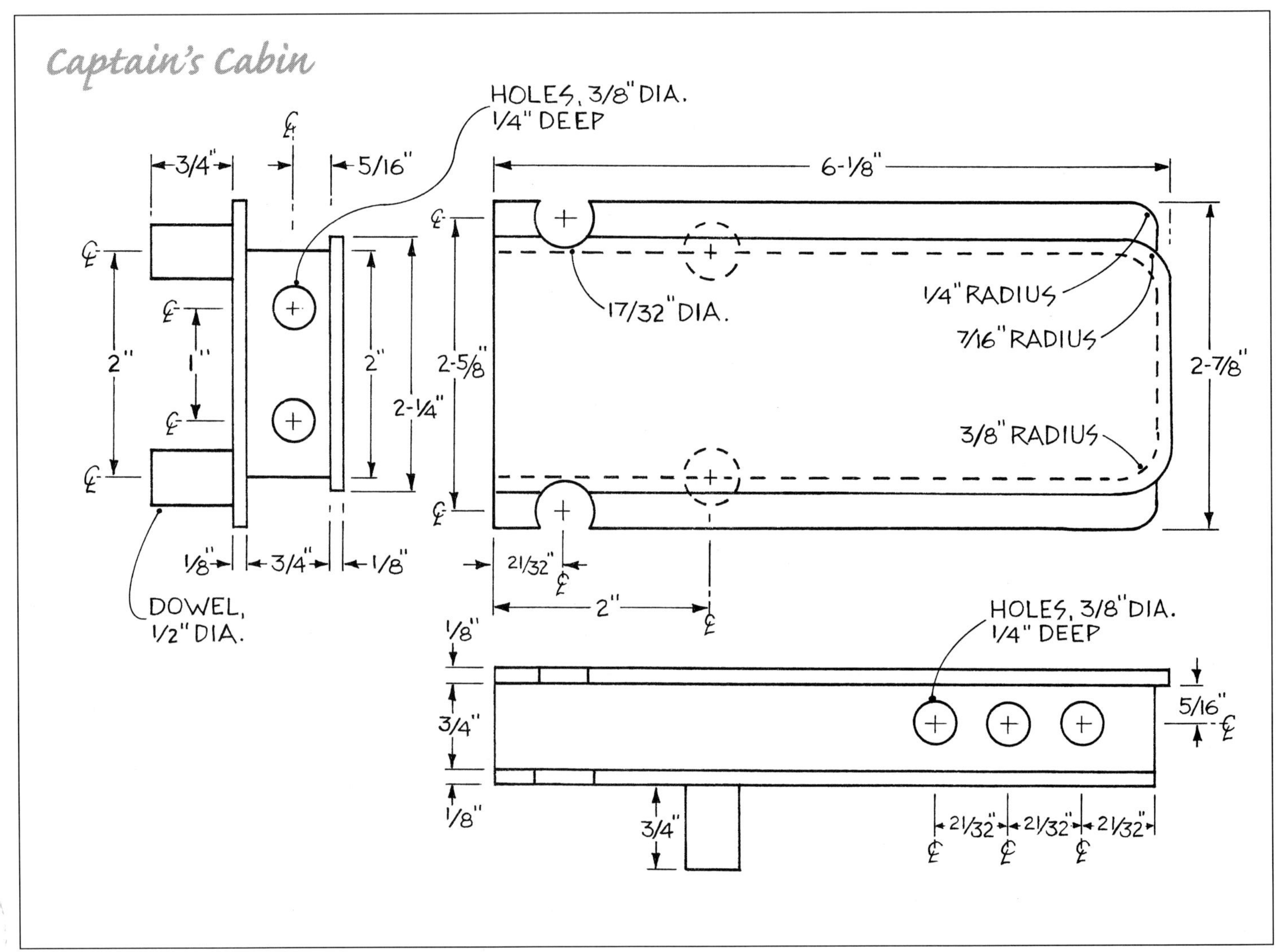

Bridge

1. Cut the blank to size. Locate and drill all portholes.
2. Locate and drill the two lug cavities. Cut and sand the front radii.
3. Cut the roof cap to size and form the front radius curves on the scrollsaw or by hand-sanding.
4. Glue the roof cap onto the bridge, flush rear and centered left to right.

Decks

Although I've specified maple plywood for all decks, the use of walnut for the upper and top decks can give a nice contrast. The main deck, which incorporates the paddle wheel at the rear and the ramp at the front, sits on the generic hull to receive all other components.

1. Cut the main deck blank to its overall size.
2. Locate and drill all receiving holes and lug cavities.

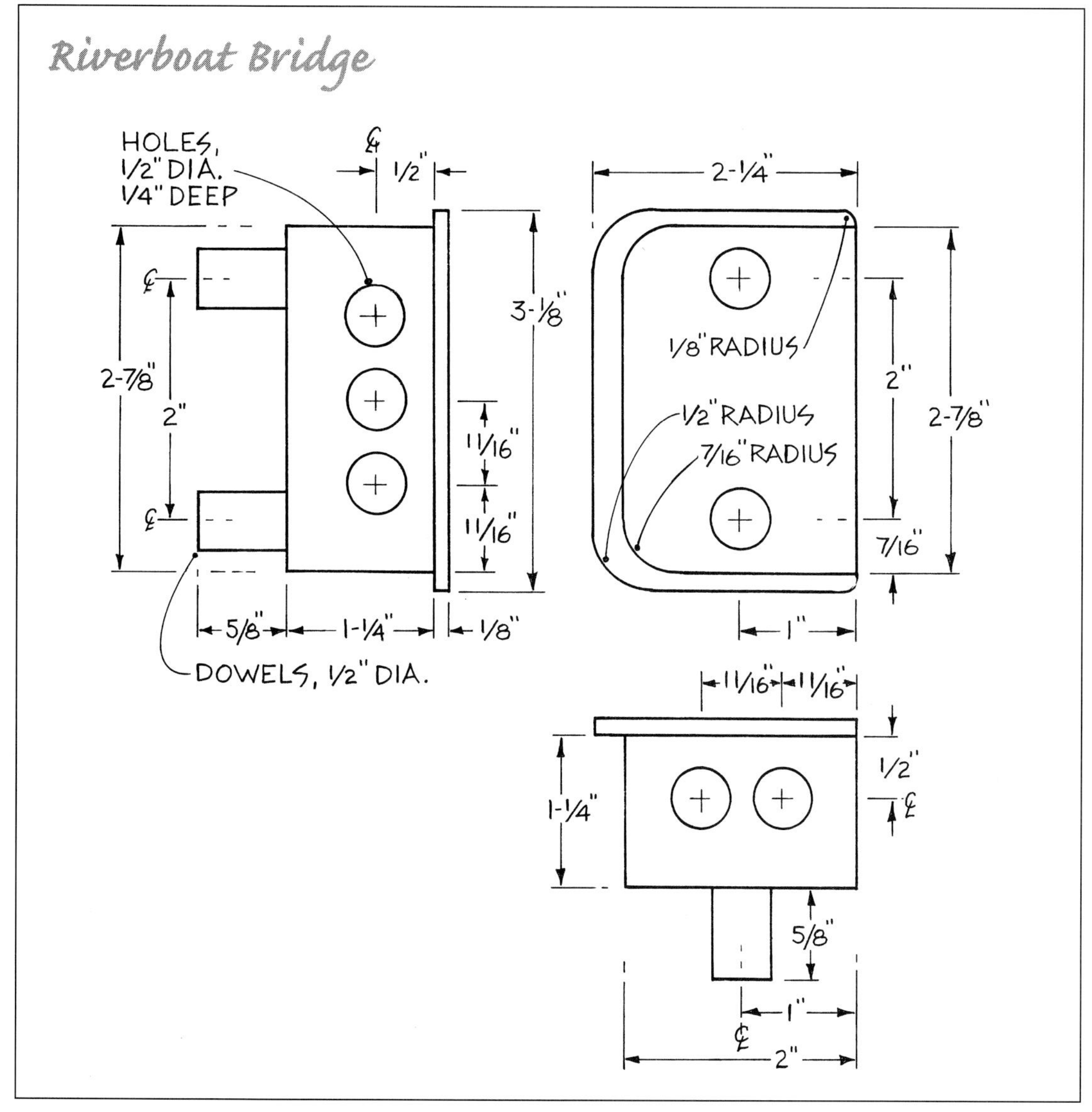

Riverboat Main Deck

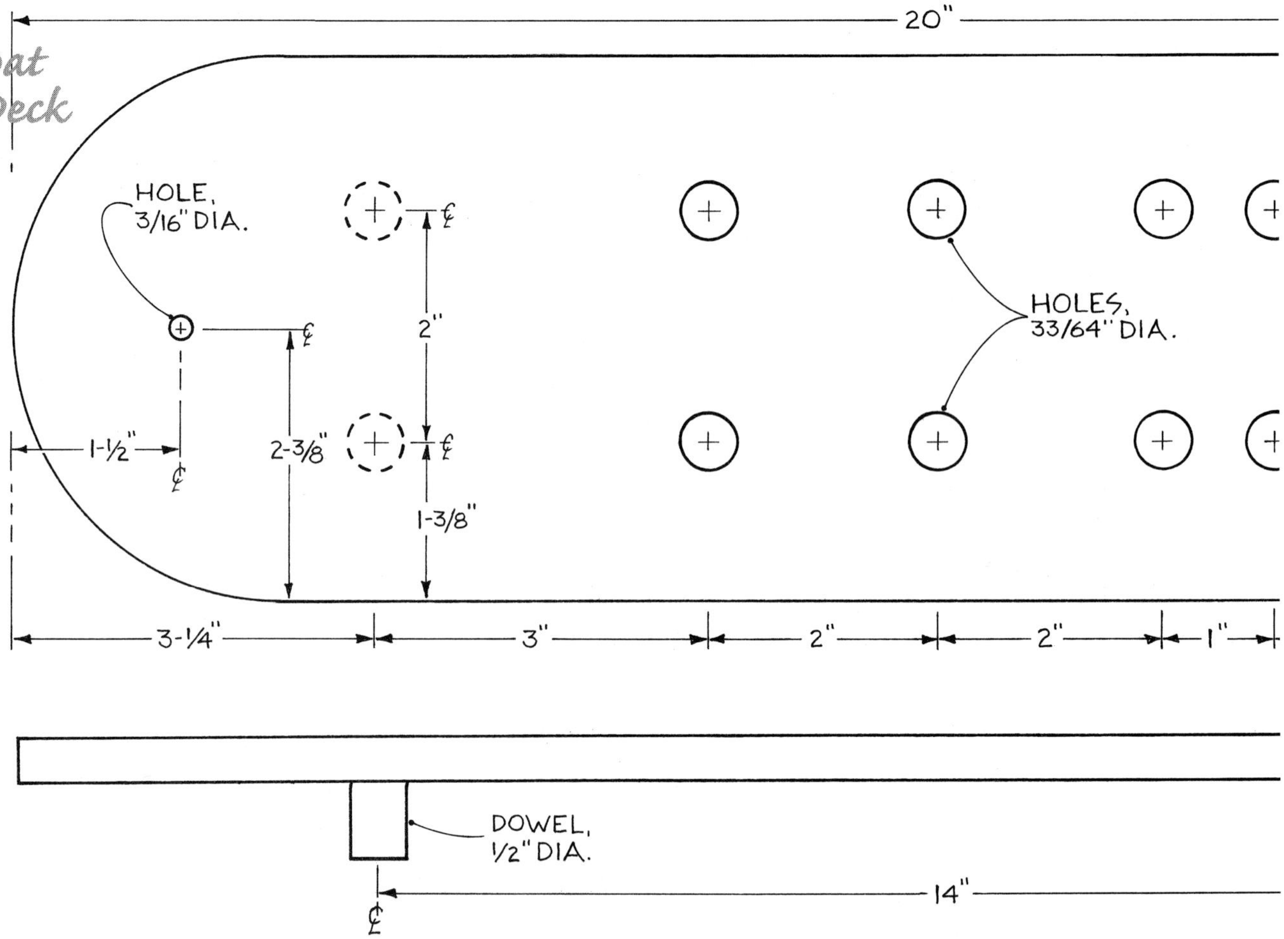

20"
HOLE, 3/16" DIA.
HOLES, 33/64" DIA.
2"
2-3/8"
1-1/2"
1-3/8"
3-1/4"
3"
2"
2"
1"
DOWEL, 1/2" DIA.
14"

Upper Deck

HOLES, 33/64" DIA.
2"
3-3/4"
11/16" RADIUS
3"
1"
3"
3-1/4"
12-1/2"
3/8"
DOWEL, 1/2" DIA.
5/8"
5-1/4"

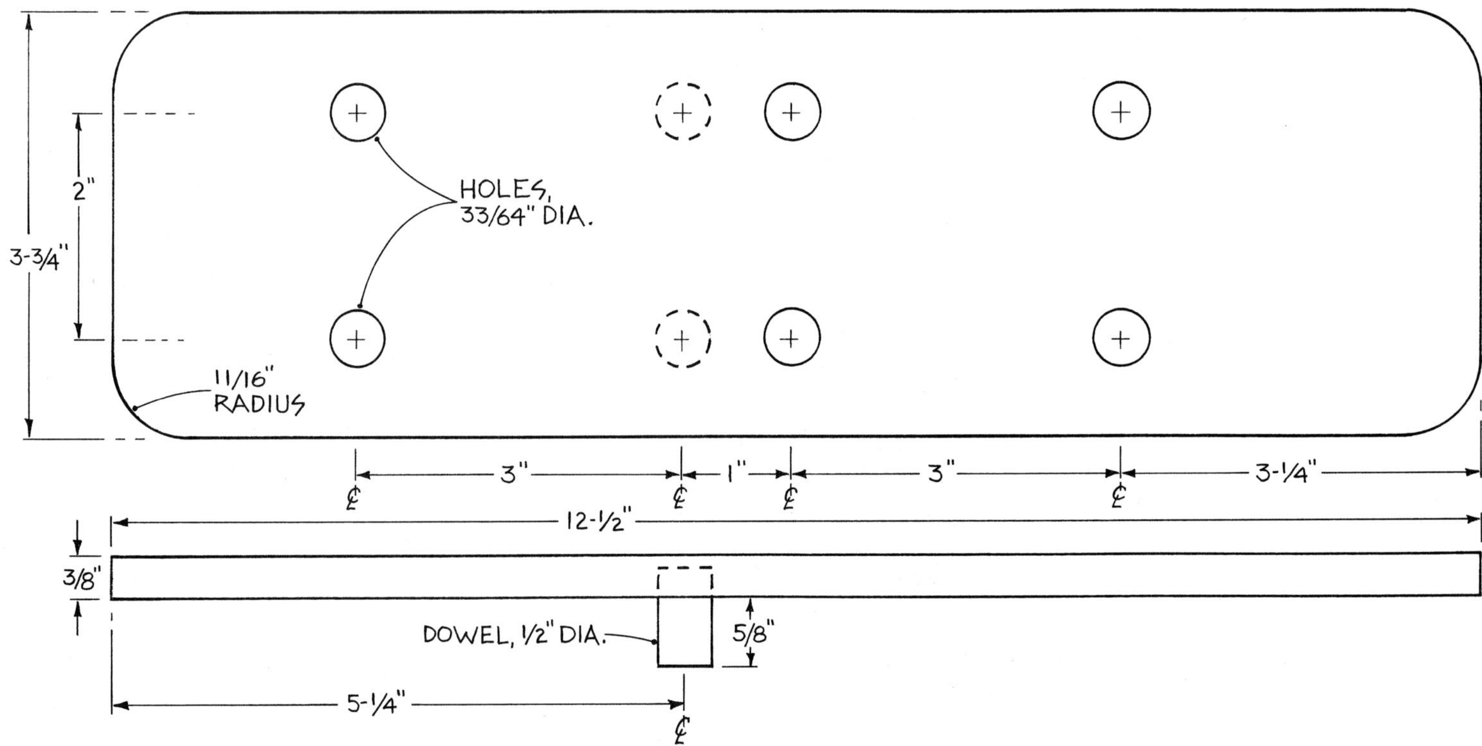

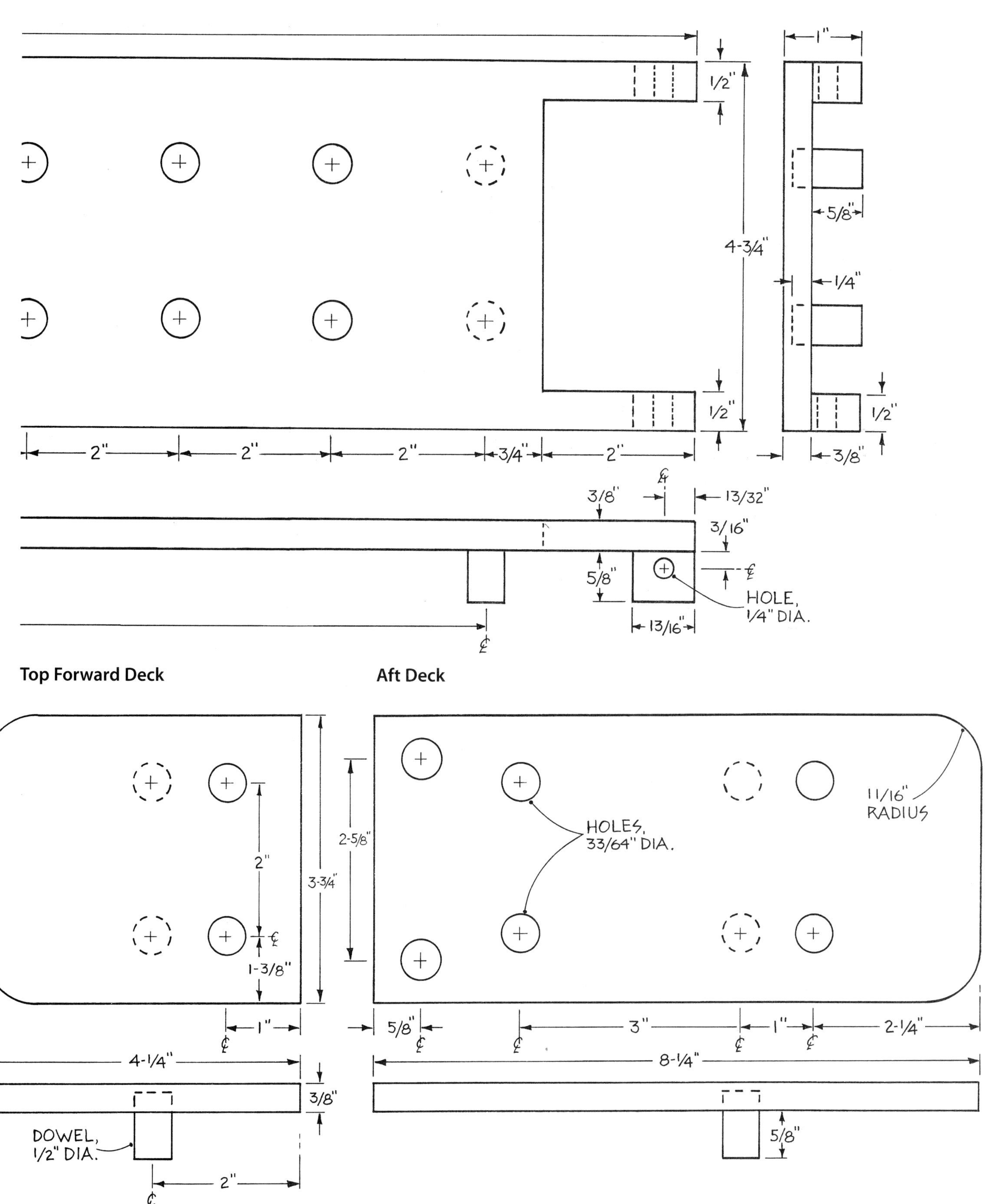

Top Forward Deck

Aft Deck

3. Cut the front radius. Drill the hole to receive the ¼-in. peg that will secure the ramp assembly.
4. Lay out the paddle-wheel cutout at the rear and make the cut on the scrollsaw.
5. Cut the two paddle-wheel blocks to size and locate and drill the hole in each to receive the ¼-in. pegs that will support the paddle wheel.
6. Glue the blocks to the underside of the deck as indicated in the plan drawing.

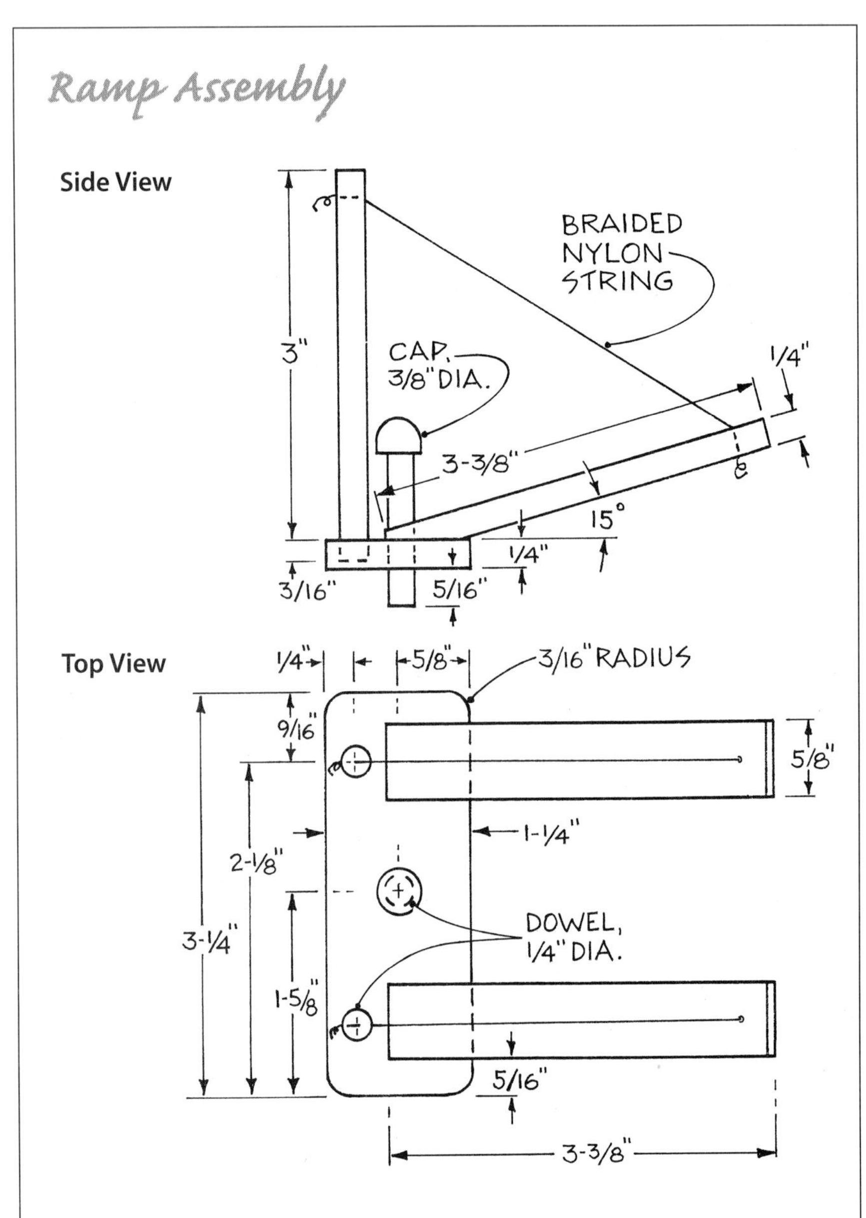

The upper deck sits atop the main deck cabins and supports the upper deck cabins.

1. Cut the upper deck blank to size.
2. Locate and drill the six through receiving holes.
3. Locate and drill the two lug cavities. Radius the corners.

I've made the top deck in two pieces, forward and aft, to allow greater flexibility in shifting the cabins around.

1. Cut the forward and aft top deck blanks to size.
2. Locate and drill all through receiving holes. Note that the aft deck also has two $^{17}/_{32}$-in.-diameter smokestack receiving holes, spaced 2⅝ in. apart center to center.
3. Locate and drill all lug cavities. Radius all corners.

Ramp assembly

1. Since riverboats ride low in the water, their decks are often below dock level, and ramps are essential for passenger access.
2. Cut a single ¼-in. maple plywood blank for the two ramps to the indicated length and to a width of 1½ in., to allow for the saw cut that will separate them.
3. Fasten the blank to an auxiliary block in a vertical position and, using the rip fence as a guide, make the indicated 15-degree cut on the table saw (see the drawing on p. 187).
4. Split the blank and trim the ramps to their final ⅝-in. width.
5. Locate and drill the hole in each ramp to receive the braided nylon string.
6. Cut the base to size. Locate and drill the centered hole to receive the ¼-in.-diameter peg.

7. Locate and drill the two 3/16-in.-deep holes to receive the 1/4-in. dowel posts.
8. Cut the posts to length. Locate and drill the holes to receive the nylon string.
9. Glue the ramps and posts in place on the base.
10. Knot and fuse one end of each of the two pieces of nylon string. Thread one piece of string through a ramp hole (with the knot at the hole's underside) and through the corresponding posthole. Tie a loose knot in the free end of the string near the post and insert a pin through the knot, advancing it toward the hole as you pull the string and knot tight. Finally, trim and fuse the string's end. Repeat for the other ramp and post.
11. The swivel peg is friction-fit into its receiving hole.

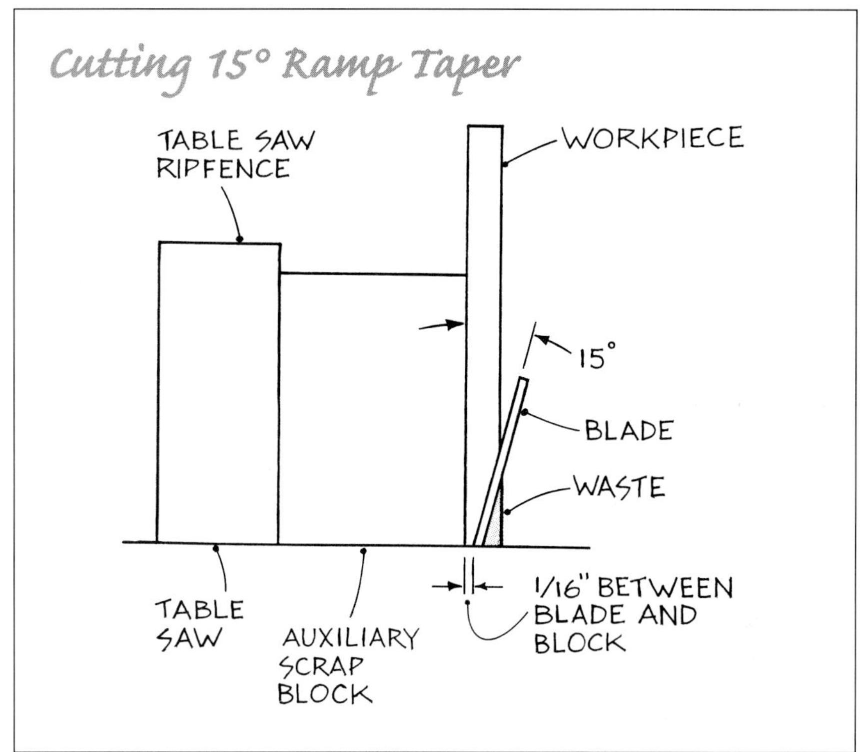

Smokestacks

1. Cut the 1/2-in.-diameter walnut dowel barrels to length.
2. Cut the 1-in.-diameter walnut dowel tops to length. On the lathe, drill a 1/2-in. through hole in each top.
3. Crimp the barrel ends at least 1/8 in. below the top with a pair of pliers to provide a greater gluing surface and glue them into the tops. They will protrude 1/8 in.
4. For the flat area, chuck each barrel into the lathe and turn the top to the indicated shape with a gouge and a skew (see photo Y on p. 188).

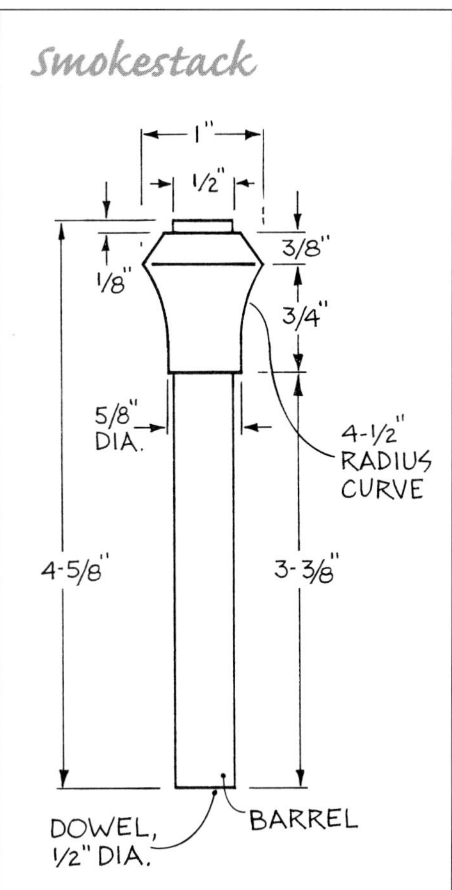

Photo X • *The smokestacks pass through three separate components. The receiving holes are 17/32 in. in diameter to provide a little extra leeway for alignment.*

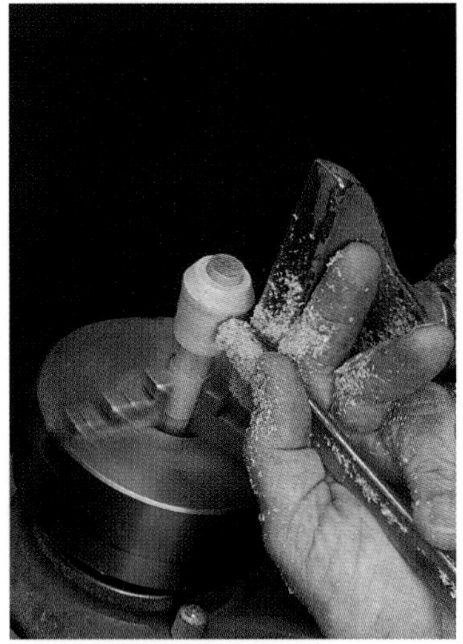

Photo Y • *A gouge and skew are used to shape the smokestack tops on the lathe.*

Paddle wheel

Though time-consuming to make, the paddle wheel really adds to the riverboat's characteristic look. For the axle, I like to use a ⅜-in.-diameter plastic tube because of its dimensional accuracy. But if you have any trouble locating this item, you can also use a length of ⅜-in.-diameter dowel, drilling out the ends to receive the ¼-in.-diameter pegs, which are friction-fitted through the blocks on the rear underside of the main deck. The dowel must rotate freely on the pegs.

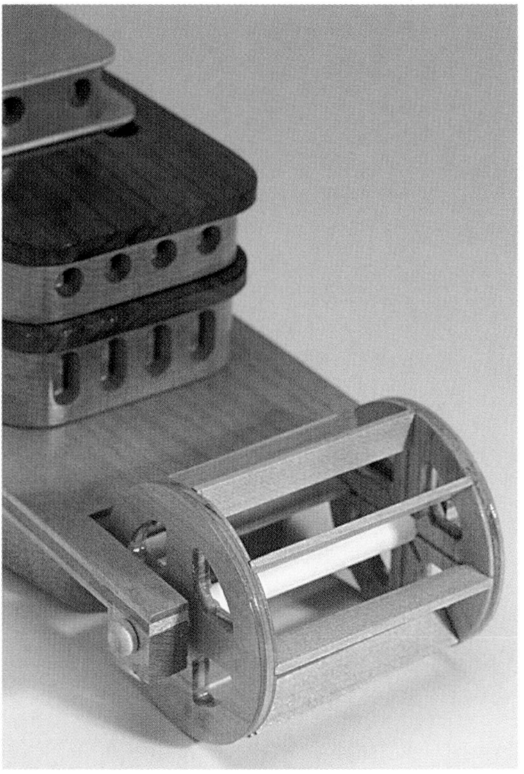

Photo Z • *The patience required to make the paddle wheel is rewarded by its appealingly detailed symmetry.*

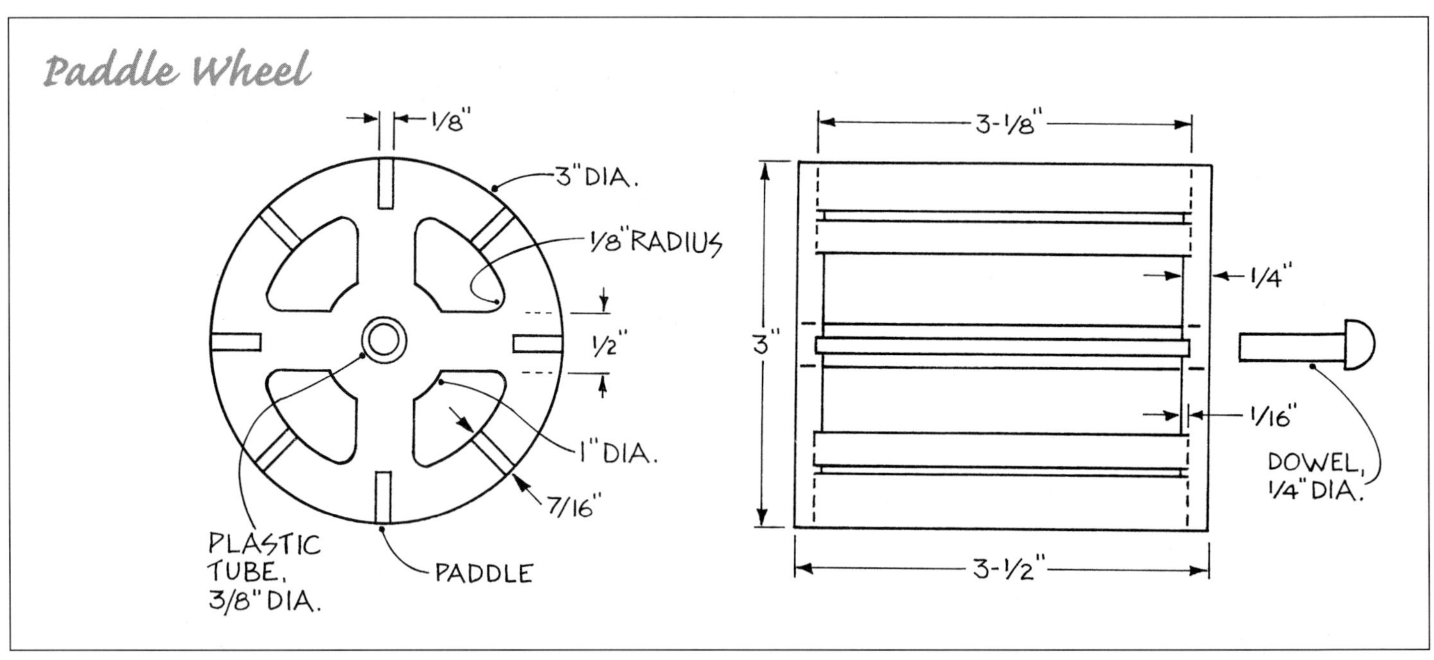

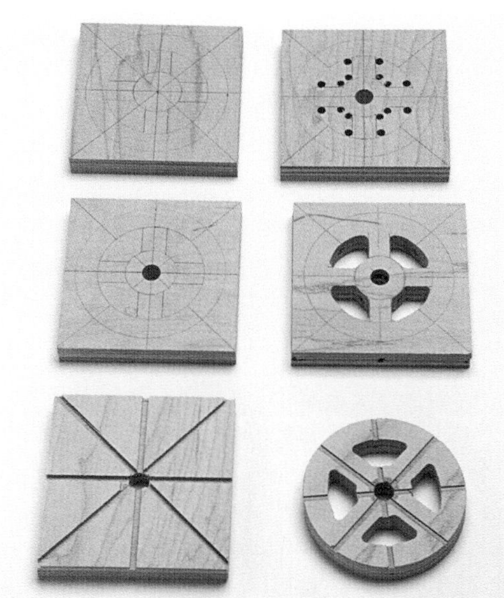

Photo AA • *Construction sequence for the paddle-wheel wheels. Two blanks are fastened together for all procedures except the cutting of the paddle receiving slots. Blanks are "sandwiched," and crosscuts must be made on both sides of the sandwich.*

1. Cut two 3 1/8-in. squares of 1/4-in. maple plywood. Lay out the top view on one and fasten the two together with double-sided tape.
2. Drill the 3/8-in.-diameter axle hole. Separate the blanks.
3. Cut the paddle receiving slots on the table saw, using the rip fence for the crisscross cuts centered on the 3 1/8-in. dimension, and the jig pictured in photo BB for the 45-degree angle cuts. Do not cut slots on the face with the layout drawn on it.
4. Spot-glue the blanks together at the corners with the slots facing inward. Insert the plastic tube axle to check alignment.
5. Drill the indicated 5/32-in. holes to define the four cutout areas. The workpiece is rotated on a 3/8-in. plastic pin protruding from a plate clamped to the drill-press table to visually locate the holes (see photo CC).

Photo BB • *A simple jig provides the corner-to-corner slots in the wheel blanks.*

Photo CC • *To drill the holes that define the cutout areas, the sandwiched wheel blanks are rotated on a plate with a protruding pin that is clamped to the drill-press table. The plate is set in one position for the outer ring of holes, another position for the inner one.*

6. Thread the scrollsaw blade through the holes to make the four internal cutouts, blending the cuts into the holes (see photo DD on p. 190).
7. Cut the outer perimeter of the blanks. The two are now separate since only the corners were glued.
8. Chuck the two wheel blanks into the lathe, using an arbor made from a 3/8-in. bolt and a wing nut to clamp them in place. True the wheels as shown in photo EE on p. 190.
9. Cut the paddle blanks to the indicated length and width, and to a thickness to match the kerf of the blade used to cut the receiving slots.

Photo DD • *The scrollsaw blade is threaded through the holes to make the internal cutouts in the blanks.*

Photo EE • *The two wheel blanks are trued together on the lathe.*

Photo FF • *This jig enables accurate visual alignment of the paddles when gluing up the paddle wheel.*

10. Preassemble the paddle wheel, including the axle, to check its fit into the main deck rear cutout. Adjust the paddle length if necessary, and trim the axle to final length.
11. To guarantee proper paddle alignment when gluing up the paddle wheel, use the jig shown in photo FF. To make it, cut a 3½-in.-square block of hardwood or hardwood plywood ½ in. to ¾ in. thick, and drill a centered ⅜-in. hole in it to the maximum depth possible without breakthrough. Cut a length of ⅜-in.-diameter plastic tube to protrude about 3¾ in. Lay the tube flat on a table and draw a straight line along its length with a pen or pencil that is also held flat against the table surface.
12. To glue up the paddle wheel, mount a wheel on the jig and line up any slot with the line on the tube.
13. Spot-glue two paddles into any pair of slots 180 degrees opposite each other.
14. Slide the second wheel, slot side down, onto the tube, aligning its cutouts with those of the bottom wheel and aligning its corresponding slot with the line on the tube. Lower the wheel to hold the paddles in place while the glue dries on the bottom wheel.
15. Repeat this process with other opposed pairs of paddles until all eight are glued in position on the lower wheel.
16. Spot-glue the tops of the paddles to the top wheel's slots. If you find it awkward to do all eight, just gluing four (every other one) will provide adequate strength.
17. Glue the axle in place with epoxy.

■ CRUISE SHIP

PART	SIZE (IN.)	QUANTITY	MATERIAL
ROOF AND DECKS:			
Top cabin roof	$3^{1}/_{8}$ x $^{1}/_{4}$ x $4^{3}/_{16}$	1	$^{1}/_{4}$ maple plywood
Aft top deck	$3^{1}/_{8}$ x $^{1}/_{4}$ x $4^{3}/_{16}$	1	$^{1}/_{4}$ maple plywood
Forward top deck	$3^{1}/_{8}$ x $^{1}/_{4}$ x $8^{3}/_{16}$	1	$^{1}/_{4}$ maple plywood
Partial aft top deck	$3^{1}/_{8}$ x $^{1}/_{4}$ x $2^{3}/_{16}$	1	$^{1}/_{4}$ maple plywood
Mid deck	$3^{3}/_{4}$ x $^{1}/_{4}$ x $12^{3}/_{8}$	1	$^{1}/_{4}$ maple plywood
Top cabin	$2^{7}/_{8}$ x $^{3}/_{4}$ x 4	1	Maple
MID CABINS:			
Forward mid cabin	$2^{7}/_{8}$ x $^{3}/_{4}$ x 4	1	Maple
Center mid cabin	$2^{7}/_{8}$ x $^{3}/_{4}$ x 4	1	Maple
Aft mid cabin	$2^{7}/_{8}$ x $^{3}/_{4}$ x 4	1	Maple
Half aft mid cabin	$2^{7}/_{8}$ x $^{3}/_{4}$ x 2	1	Maple
DECK CABINS:			
Forward deck cabin	$3^{1}/_{2}$ x $^{3}/_{4}$ x 4	1	Maple
Center deck cabin	$3^{1}/_{2}$ x $^{3}/_{4}$ x 4	1	Maple
Aft deck cabin	$3^{1}/_{2}$ x $^{3}/_{4}$ x 4	1	Maple
Half deck cabin	$3^{1}/_{2}$ x $^{3}/_{4}$ x 2	1	Maple
Smokestack base	$2^{7}/_{8}$ x $^{1}/_{8}$ x $4^{7}/_{8}$	1	$^{1}/_{8}$ maple plywood

■ FABRICATION OF CRUISE SHIP COMPONENTS

The cruise ship uses a front riser, tower #2, and three #3 smokestacks (see the parts list in p. 149) mounted on a special bottom- and top-lugged base. Note that all of the cruise ship portholes are $^{5}/_{16}$ in. in diameter.

Deck cabins

The forward and aft deck cabins are identical except for the lug cavity locations. To make them:

1. Cut the blanks to size, leaving them $^{1}/_{8}$ in. oversize in length.
2. Lay out the top view of the radius curve.
3. Locate and drill all receiving holes and lug cavities.

Photo GG • *Cruise ship components aligned.*

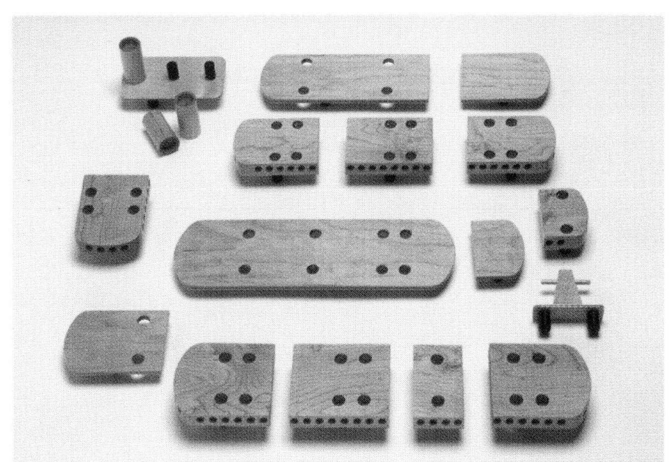

Photo HH • *Cruise ship components, including deck cabins, mid cabins, decks, and smokestack base.*

Cruise Ship Deck Cabins

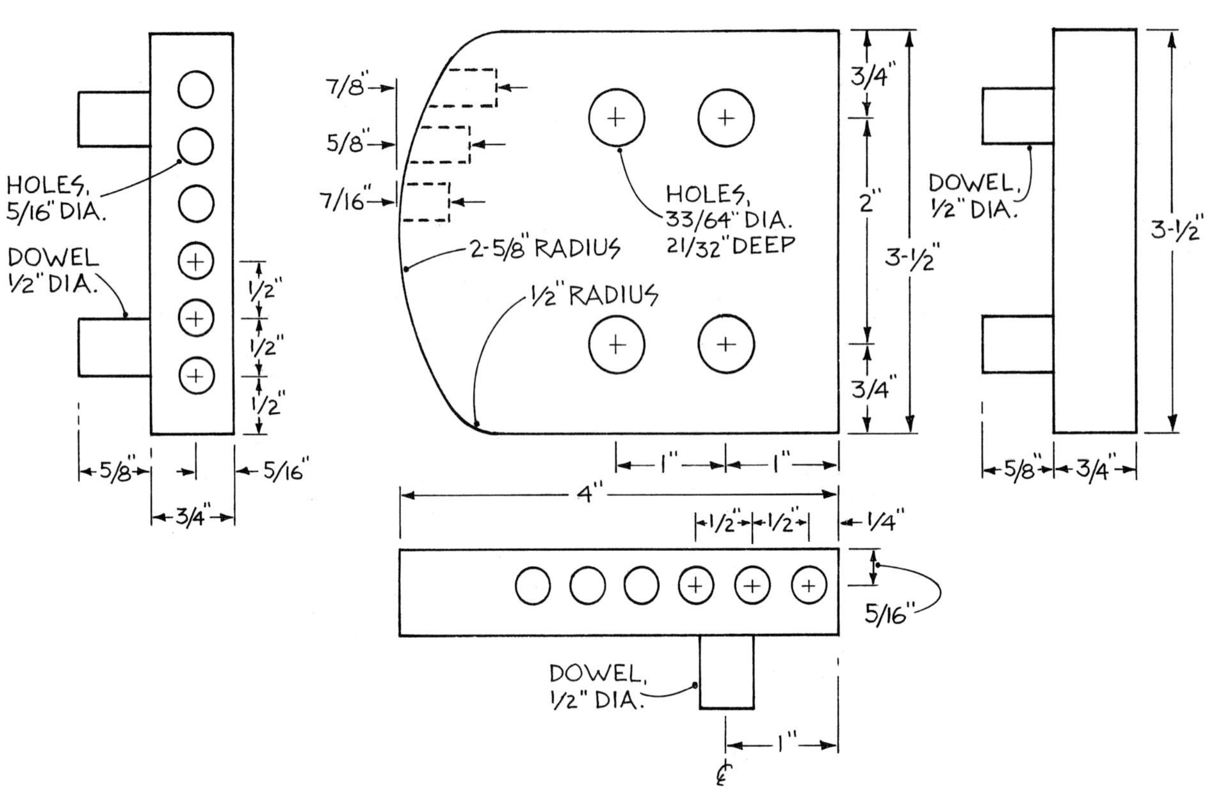

4. Locate and drill all portholes. Side portholes are 3⁄16 in. deep. For the portholes on the ends that will be radiused, the depths should be 7⁄8 in. for the left and right outer ones, 5⁄8 in. for the next in on each side, and 7⁄16 in. for the two in the middle.

5. Cut the radius on each blank on the bandsaw and sand smooth.

The center and half-deck cabins are simply cut to size and then drilled in the same sequence as above. All portholes on these pieces are 3⁄16 in. deep. The half cabin can be used either with or instead of the center cabin, providing either a longer or a shorter cabin arrangement.

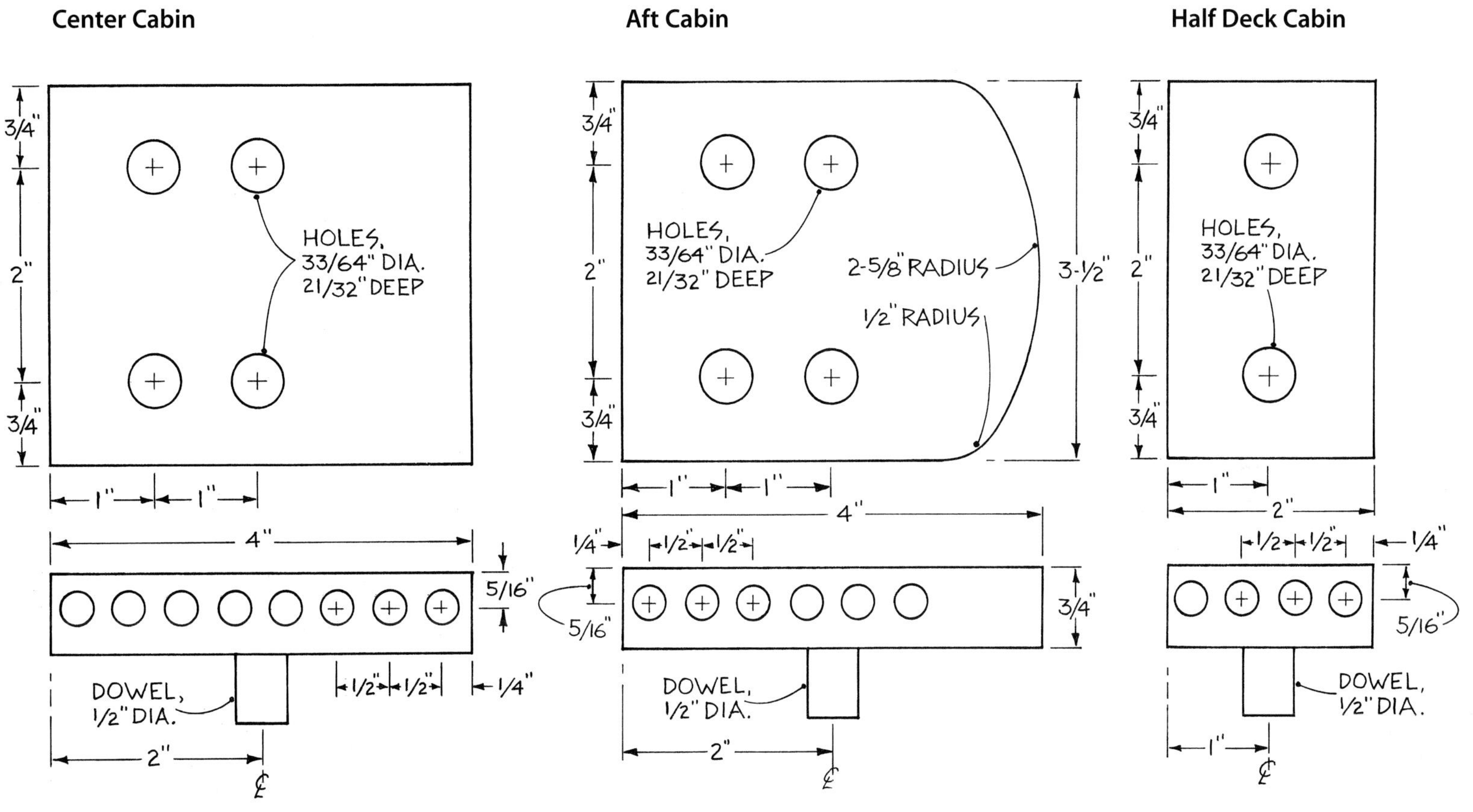

Mid cabins

The fabrication of the mid cabins follows the same sequence as for the deck cabins, utilizing the indicated dimensions. Again, the forward and aft cabins are identical except for lug location. The porthole depths for the ends of these two cabins should be the same as the central four on the ends of the corresponding deck cabins. The half aft mid cabin can be used to give the ship a stepped aft profile.

The top cabin is identical to the forward mid cabin.

Cruise Ship Mid Cabins

Forward Cabin

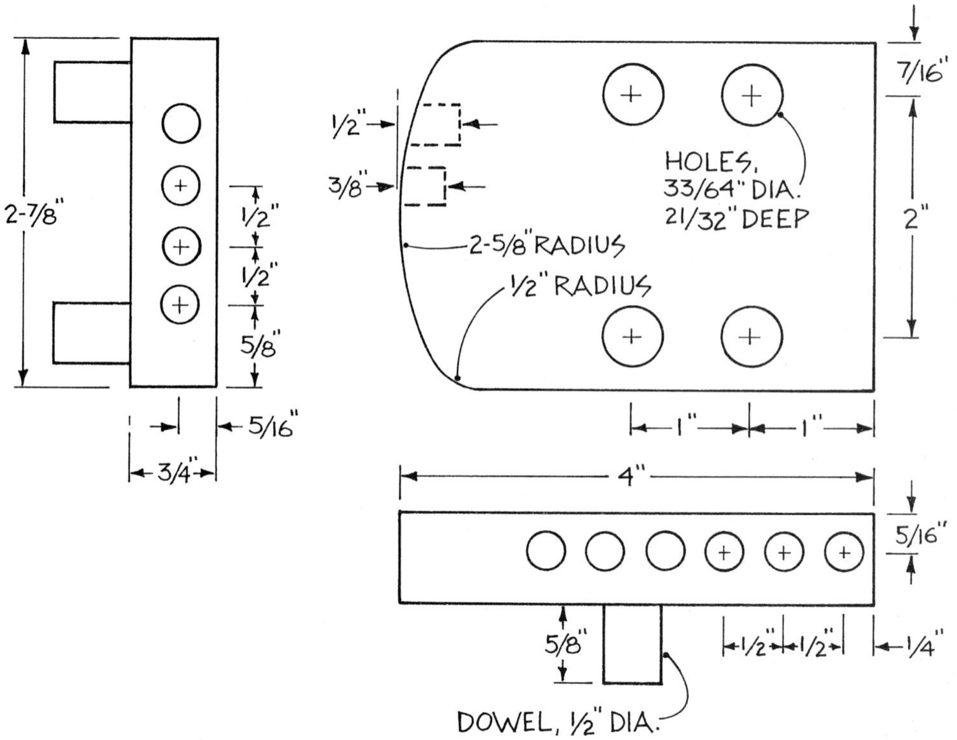

Center Cabin

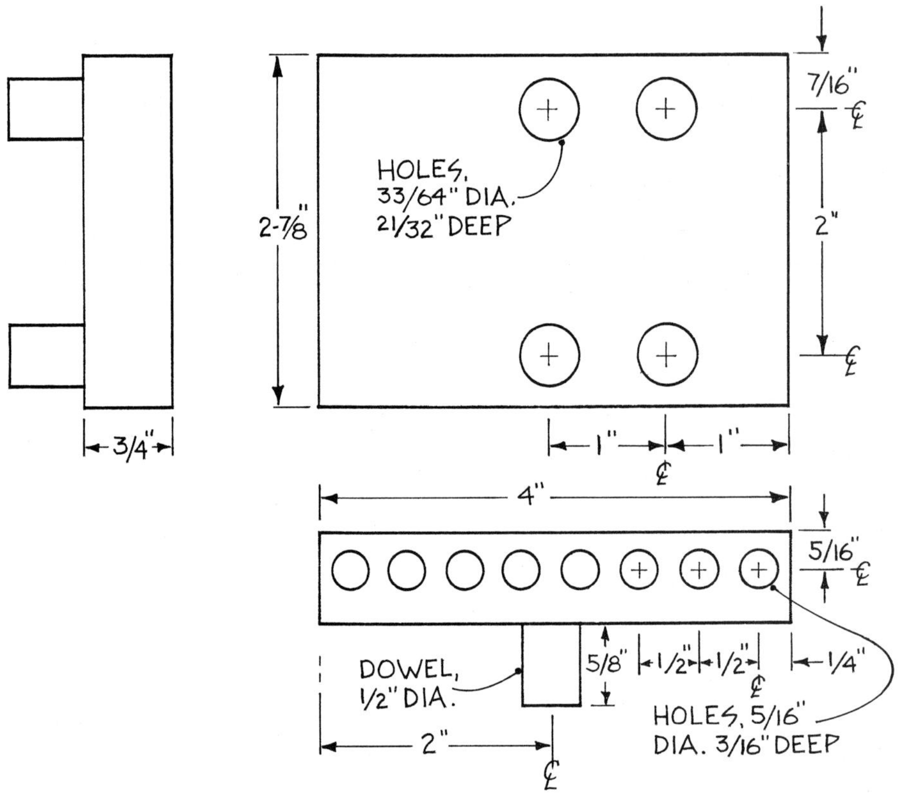

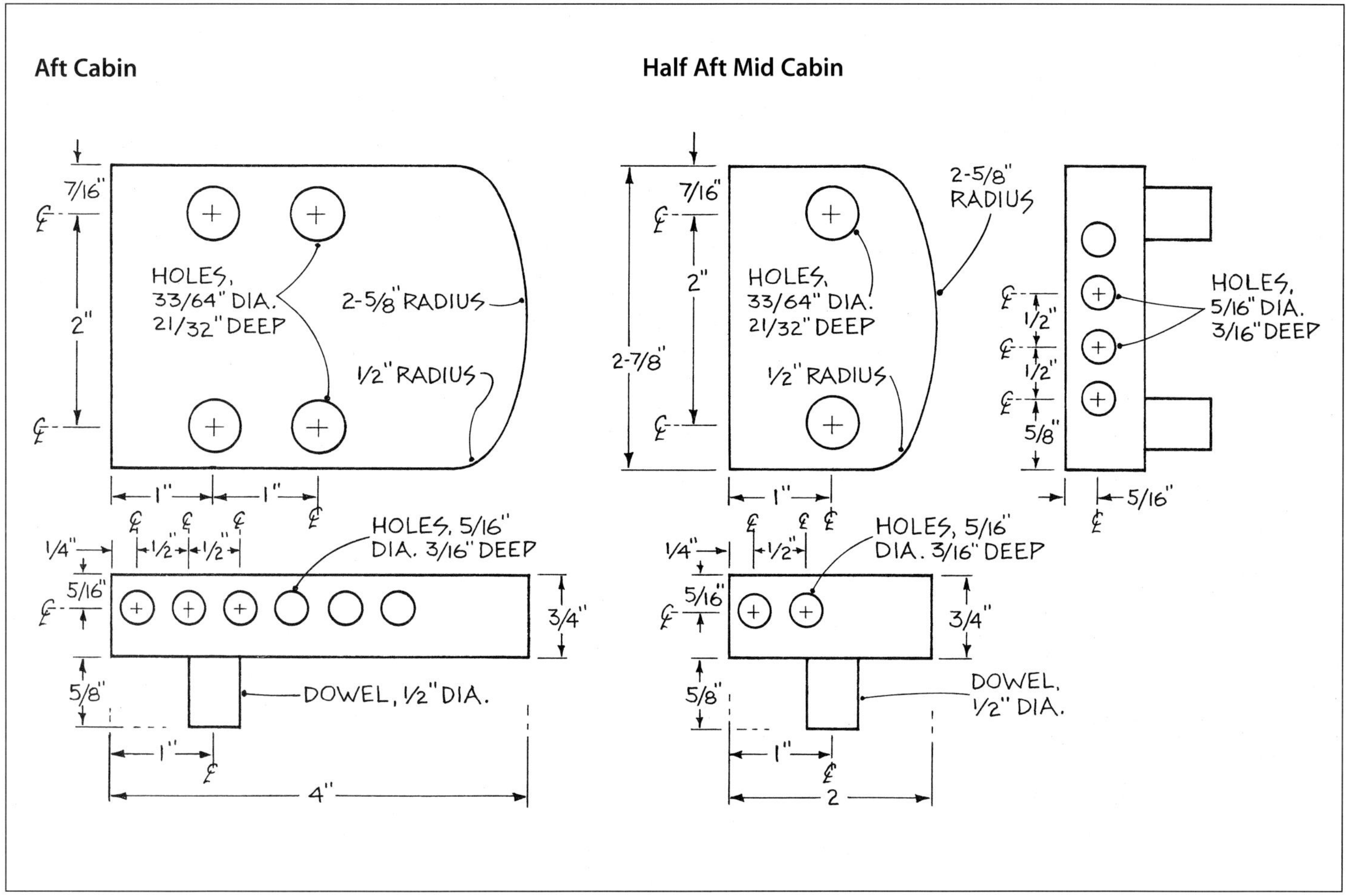

Decks

1. For the mid deck, cut the 1/4-in. maple plywood blank to size, leaving it 1/8 in. oversize in length. Lay out the end curves.
2. Locate and drill the eight receiving through holes and the two lug cavities.
3. Cut the radius curves on the scrollsaw and sand them smooth.
4. The forward, aft, and partial aft decks are made in the same fashion, from blanks that are slightly oversize in length to allow for cutting the radius curves. Note that the aft and partial aft decks have no receiving holes.
5. The top cabin roof is the same as the aft top deck but with the addition of the two indicated receiving holes.

Smokestack base

The smokestack base has three lugs on top to receive the smokestacks, and two on the underside to seat into deck and cabin components, as indicated on the plan drawing on p. 198.

1. Cut the 1/8-in. plywood blank to its overall size.
2. Locate and drill the indicated lug cavities, three spaced evenly on the workpiece's lengthwise centerline on one side, and a pair with the usual 2-in. center-to-center spacing in the indicated position on the other side.

Cruise Ship Decks

Forward Top Deck

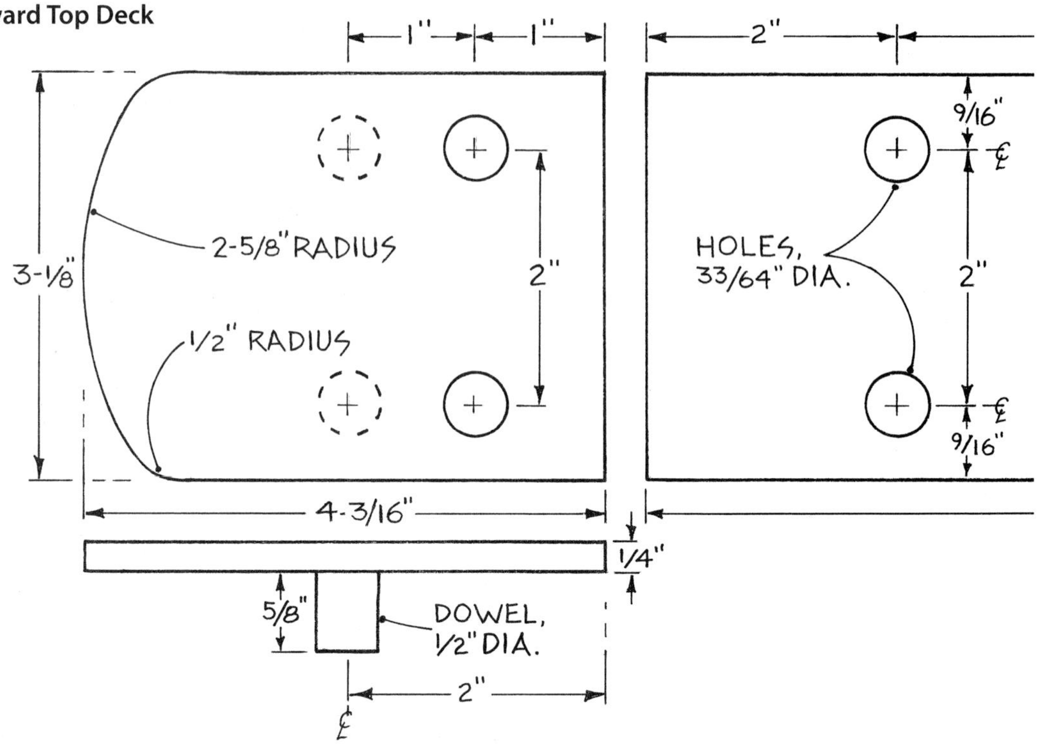

1" 1" 2"

2-5/8" RADIUS

3-1/8"

1/2" RADIUS

2"

HOLES, 33/64" DIA.

9/16"

2"

9/16"

4-3/16"

1/4"

5/8"

DOWEL, 1/2" DIA.

2"

Mid Deck

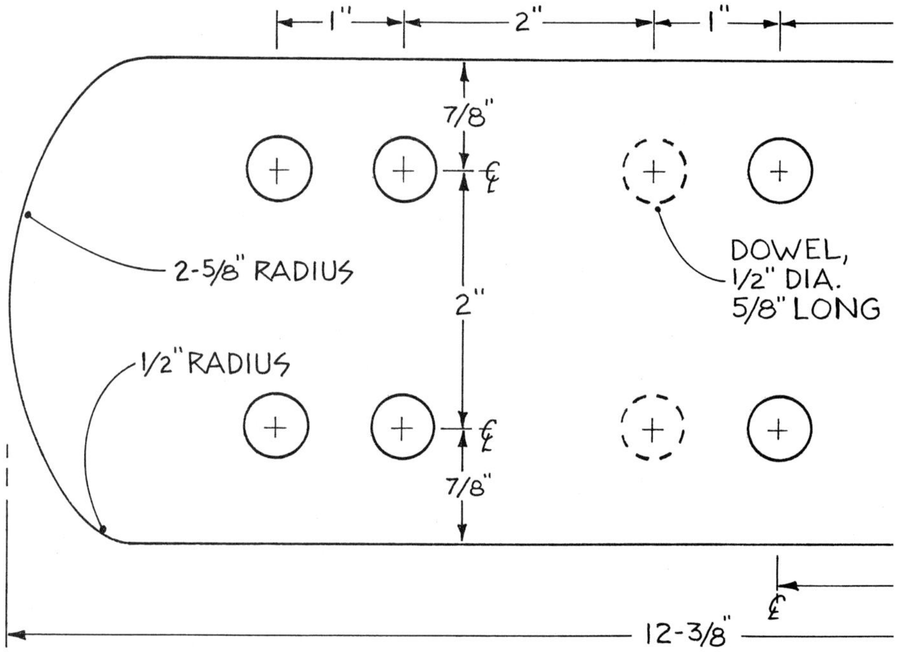

1" 2" 1"

7/8"

2-5/8" RADIUS

2"

DOWEL, 1/2" DIA. 5/8" LONG

1/2" RADIUS

7/8"

12-3/8"

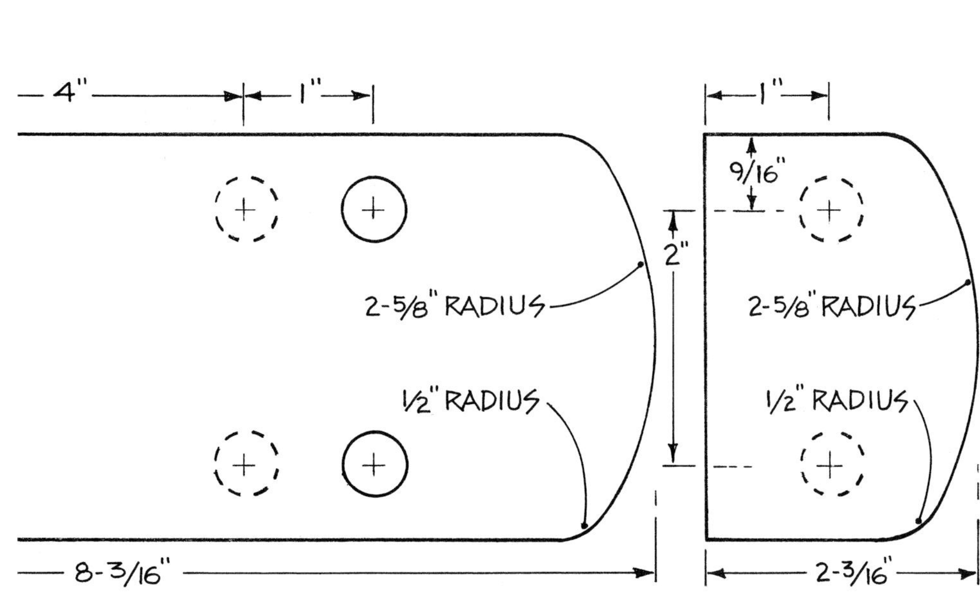
4"
1"
1"
9/16"
2"
2-5/8" RADIUS
2-5/8" RADIUS
1/2" RADIUS
1/2" RADIUS
8-3/16"
2-3/16"

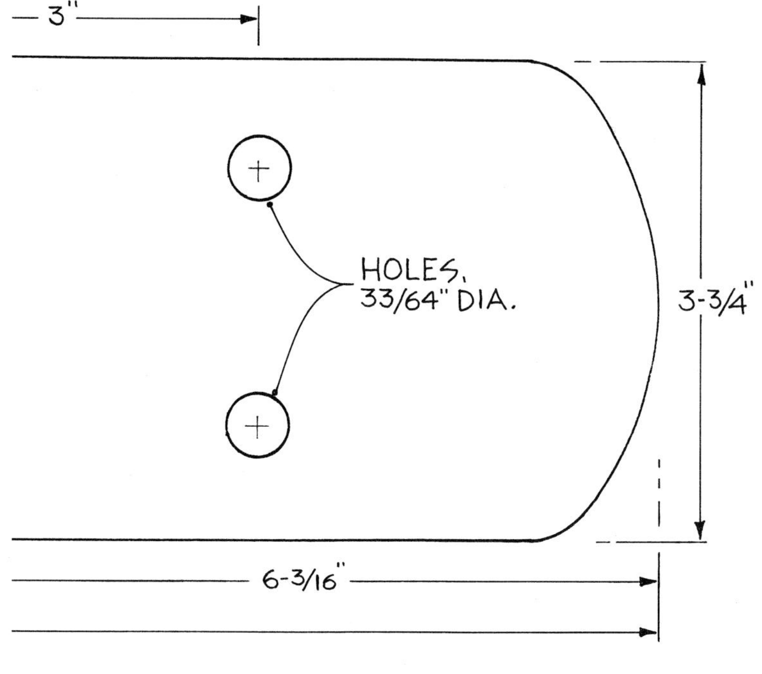
3"
HOLES,
33/64" DIA.
3-3/4"
6-3/16"

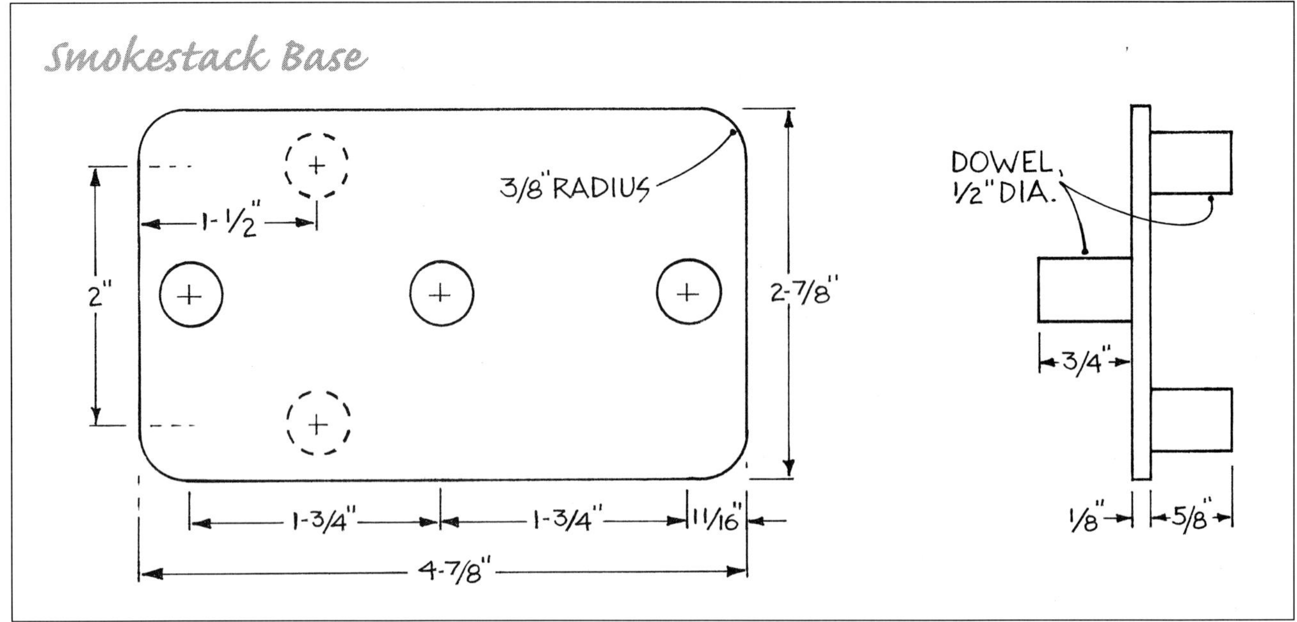

FABRICATION OF FERRYBOAT COMPONENTS

You might notice that this is a particularly long ferryboat—that's because its inspiration was the big Staten Island ferry, the first one I ever rode. Since that initial experience was, as they say, "a while back," I've chosen to give the vehicle a vintage look. Smokestacks #2 and #3 will both give the right look here (see the parts list on p. 149).

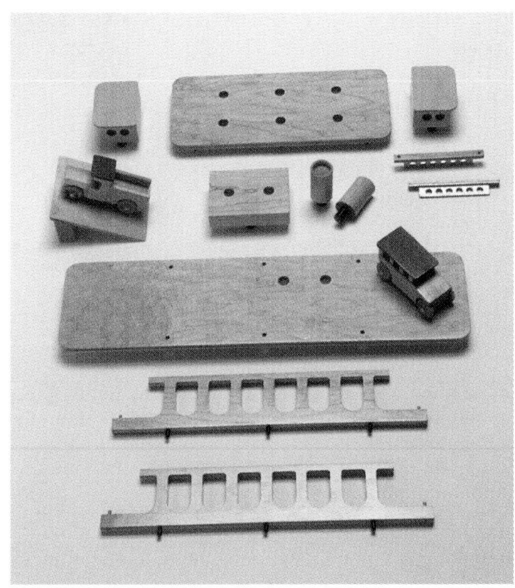

Photo JJ • *Ferryboat components, including main deck, upper deck, sidewalls, center cabin, bridges, ramp assembly, pickup truck, and sedan.*

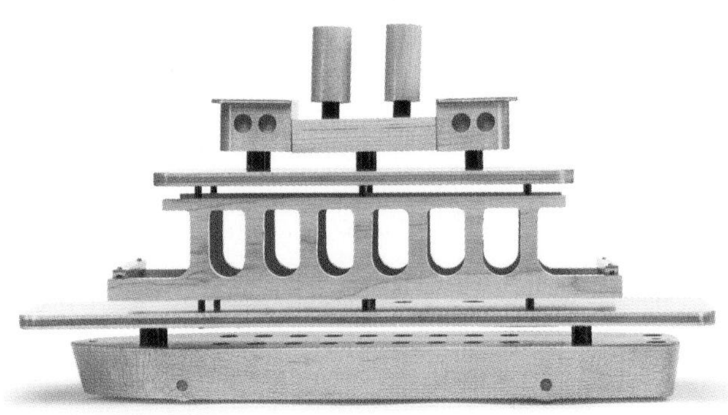

Photo II • *Ferry boat components aligned.*

■ FERRYBOAT

PART	SIZE (IN.)	QUANTITY	MATERIAL
Main deck	$4\frac{7}{8}$ x $\frac{3}{8}$ x 19	1	$\frac{3}{8}$ maple plywood
Upper deck	$4\frac{7}{8}$ x $\frac{3}{8}$ x $11\frac{1}{2}$	1	$\frac{3}{8}$ maple plywood
Sidewalls	$2\frac{5}{8}$ x $\frac{1}{2}$ x 14	2	$\frac{1}{2}$ maple plywood
Center cabin	$2\frac{7}{8}$ x $\frac{7}{8}$ x 4	1	Maple
Bridge cabins	$2\frac{7}{8}$ x $1\frac{1}{4}$ x 2	2	Maple
Bridge cap roofs	$2\frac{1}{4}$ x $\frac{1}{8}$ x $3\frac{1}{8}$	2	$\frac{1}{8}$ maple plywood
RAMP ASSEMBLY:			
Ramp	4 x $\frac{1}{4}$ x $4\frac{13}{16}$	1	$\frac{1}{4}$ maple plywood
Ramp support block	$1\frac{5}{8}$ x $\frac{3}{4}$ x 4	1	Maple
Gate rails	$\frac{3}{8}$ x $\frac{1}{4}$ x $4\frac{1}{2}$	2	$\frac{1}{4}$ maple plywood
Ported gate panels	$\frac{5}{8}$ x $\frac{1}{8}$ x $3\frac{1}{2}$	2	$\frac{1}{8}$ maple plywood
Plastic pins	$\frac{3}{16}$ dia. x $\frac{5}{8}$	12	Plastic rod
Aluminum pins	$\frac{1}{8}$ dia. x $\frac{5}{8}$	4	Aluminum rod
PICK UP TRUCK:			
Hood	$1\frac{1}{4}$ x $\frac{3}{4}$ x $1\frac{1}{4}$	1	Maple
Cab	$1\frac{3}{8}$ x $\frac{7}{8}$ x $1\frac{9}{16}$	1	Maple
Roof	$1\frac{1}{8}$ x $\frac{5}{32}$ x $1\frac{3}{8}$	1	Walnut
Cargo bed	$1\frac{1}{4}$ x $1\frac{1}{8}$ x 2	1	Maple
Undercarriage	$\frac{3}{4}$ x $\frac{1}{4}$ x $3\frac{7}{8}$	1	Maple
Wheels	$\frac{15}{16}$ dia. x $\frac{1}{4}$	4	Commercial
Aluminum pins	$\frac{1}{8}$ dia. x 1	4	Commercial
SEDAN:			
Body	$1\frac{9}{16}$ x $1\frac{1}{2}$ x $3\frac{9}{16}$	1	Maple
Roof	$1\frac{1}{2}$ x $\frac{1}{4}$ x $2\frac{5}{8}$	1	Walnut
Wheels	$\frac{15}{16}$ dia. x $\frac{1}{4}$	4	Commercial
Aluminum pins	$\frac{1}{8}$ dia. x 1	4	Commercial

Main deck

This deck is also used for the aircraft carrier.

1. Cut the blank to overall size. Lay out and drill the six $\frac{3}{16}$-in.-diameter through holes, three to a side. Then redrill the holes to 0.193 or $\frac{13}{64}$ in. to give a little leeway for alignment in assembly.
2. Locate and drill the two receiving holes and the four lug cavities.
3. Cut and sand the four corner radii.

Upper deck

1. Cut the blank to size. Locate and drill the six through receiving holes, as indicated on the plan drawing on p. 202.
2. Locate and drill the six $\frac{3}{16}$-in.-diameter holes about $\frac{1}{4}$ in. deep, three to a side, to receive six plastic pins, which should protrude $\frac{1}{2}$ in. Chuck the pins into the drill press and round the tips slightly with a file before gluing them in place. This will facilitate seating them in place during assembly.

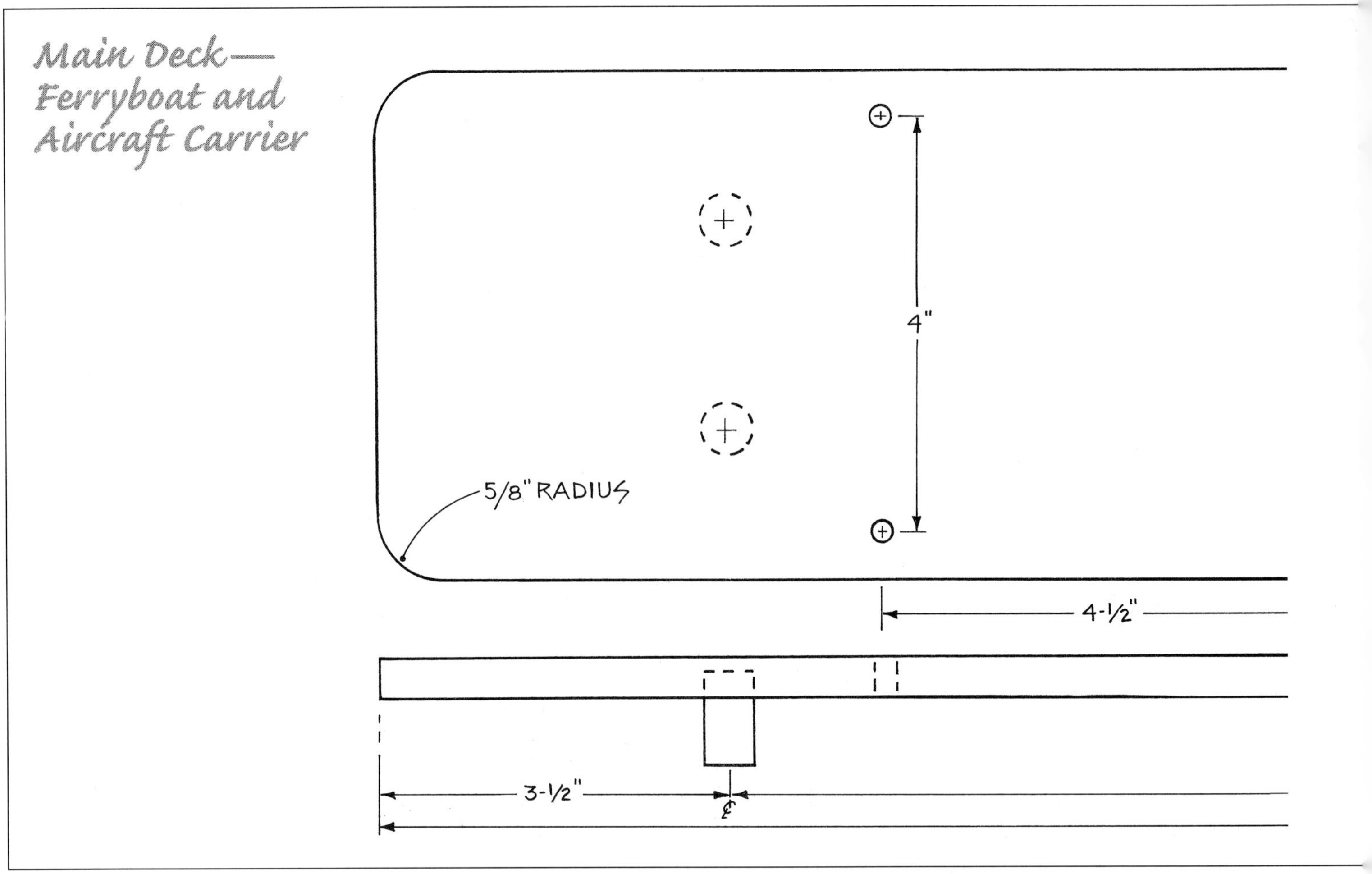

Main Deck—Ferryboat and Aircraft Carrier

4"

5/8" RADIUS

4-1/2"

3-1/2"

Sidewalls

If you're a router enthusiast, you may wish to make a template like the one shown in photo KK to rout out the sidewall apertures. If not, here's the sequence of steps to follow.

1. Cut the two blanks to overall size. Lay out the apertures and the end profiles.
2. Drill the bottom aperture radii with a 1-in. Forstner bit. Create the top corner radii with a 1/4-in. bit (a regular bit is fine for this step).
3. Complete the aperture cutouts on the scrollsaw. Cut the end profiles on the scrollsaw as well.

Photo KK • *Routing the sidewall apertures is an alternative to the drill and scrollsaw method described in the text.*

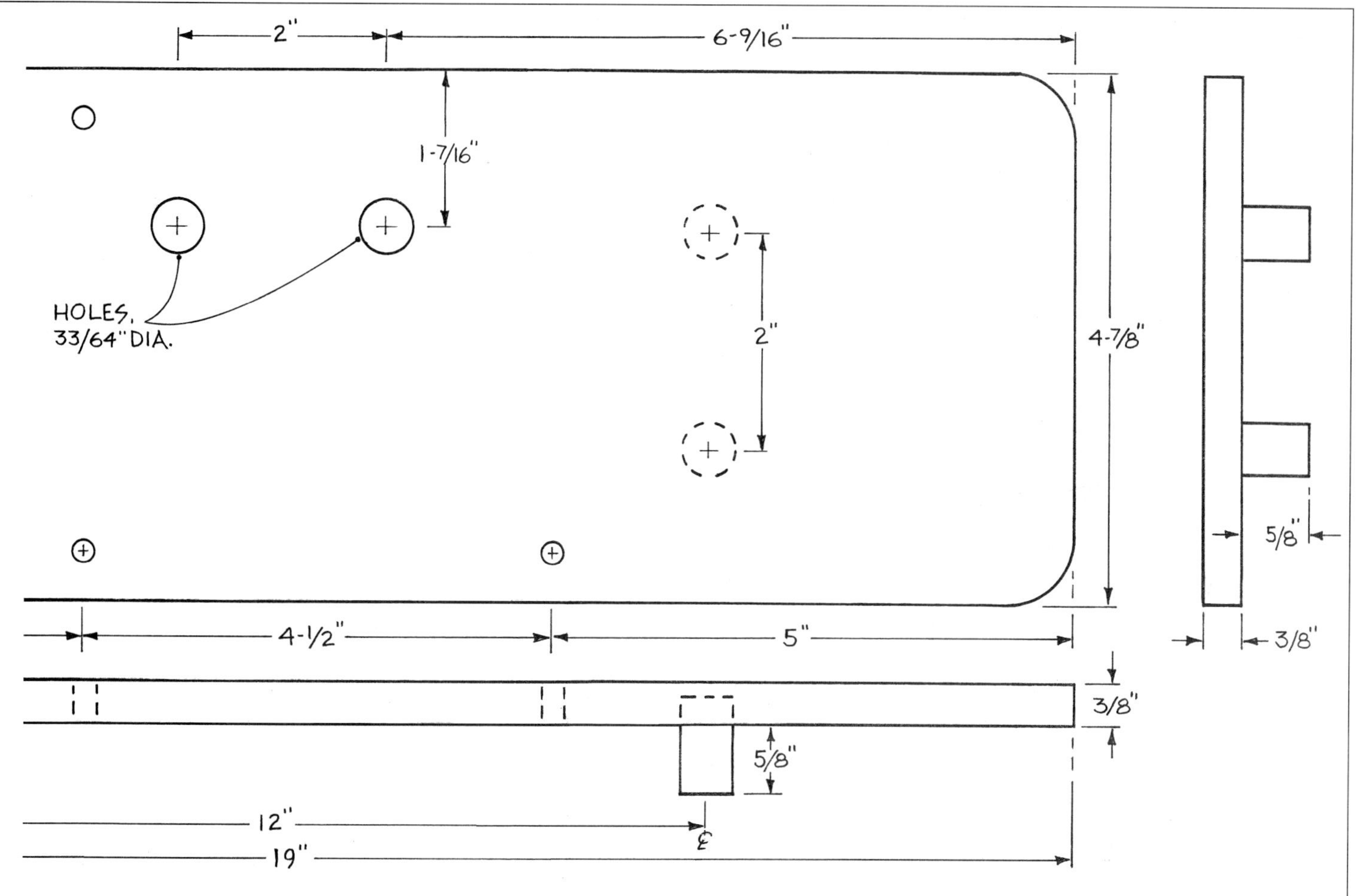

4. On the top edges of the sidewalls, locate and drill the indicated pinholes, three on each, about ½ in. deep. Redrill them as you did the corresponding holes on the main deck.

5. Locate and drill the holes to receive the ⅛-in. aluminum pins, which are glued in place with epoxy to receive the gate. Pin tips should be rounded in the same fashion as for the plastic pins.

6. On the bottom edges, locate and drill the indicated holes to receive the plastic pins, which should protrude no more than 5/16 in.

Gate

The gate consists of a ported panel glued into a channeled rail.

1. Cut the rail blank to size. Locate and drill the through hole at each end; either 9/64 in. or 5/32 in. will work here.

2. Cut a centered channel ⅛ in. deep to receive the ported panel.

3. Cut the ⅛-in. panel blank to size. Locate and drill the six evenly spaced 5/16-in.-diameter holes.

4. Hand-sand the panel's bottom corners' radii curves.

5. Glue the panel into the rail channel, centered left to right.

Ferryboat Upper Deck

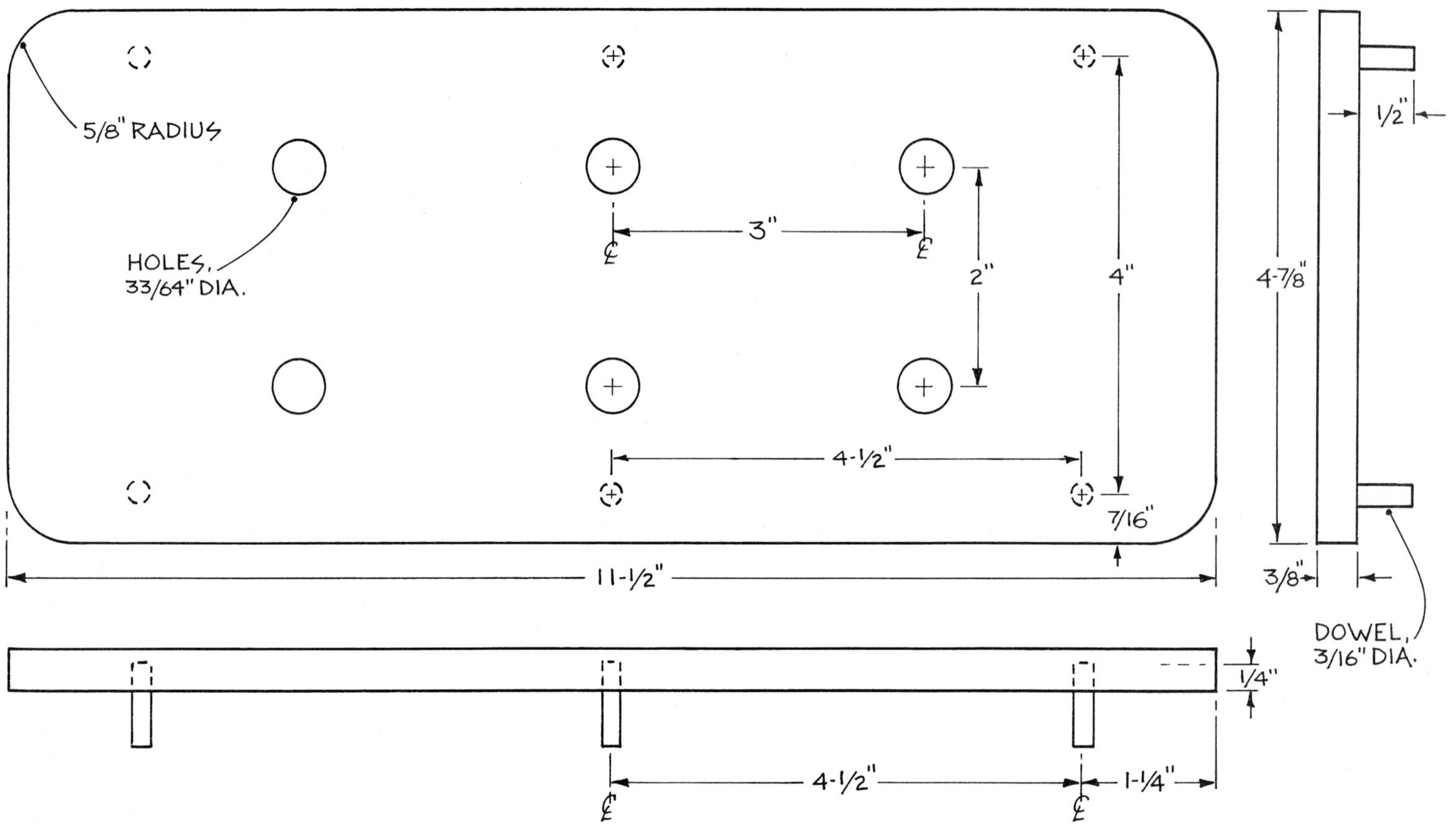

5/8" RADIUS
HOLES, 33/64" DIA.
3"
2"
4"
4-7/8"
1/2"
4-1/2"
7/16"
11-1/2"
3/8"
DOWEL, 3/16" DIA.
1/4"
4-1/2"
1-1/4"

Sidewalls

11"
DOWEL, 1/8" DIA.
1/2"
1"
5/16"
1/2" RADIUS
3/8"
2-1/2"
4-1/2"
14"

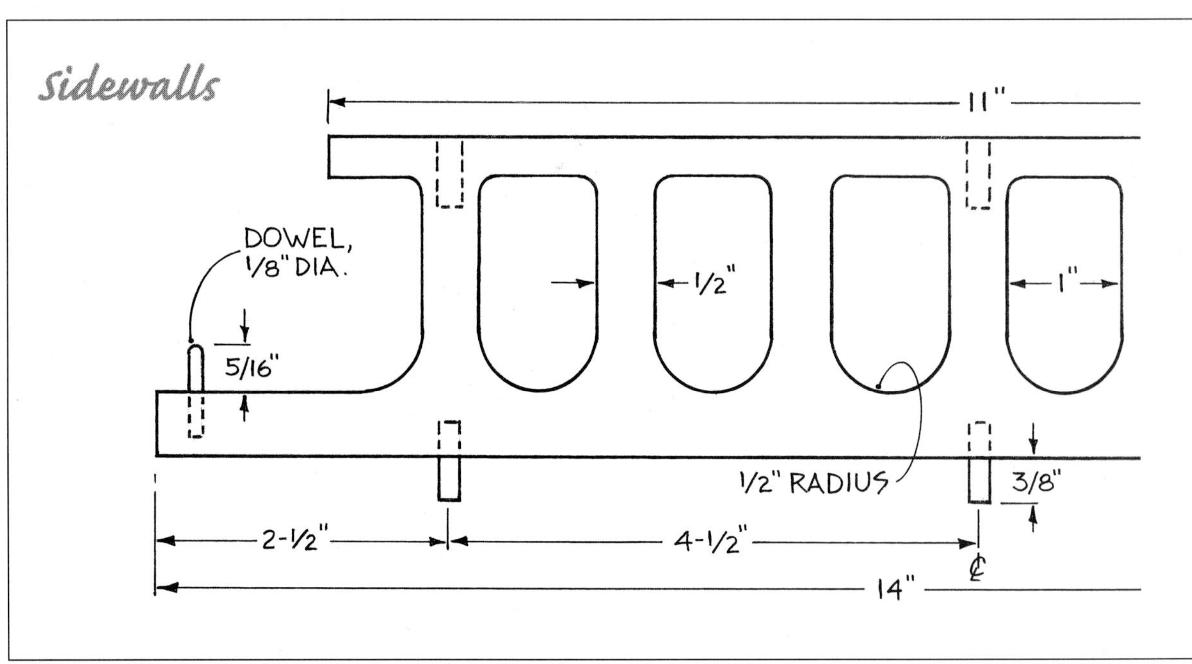

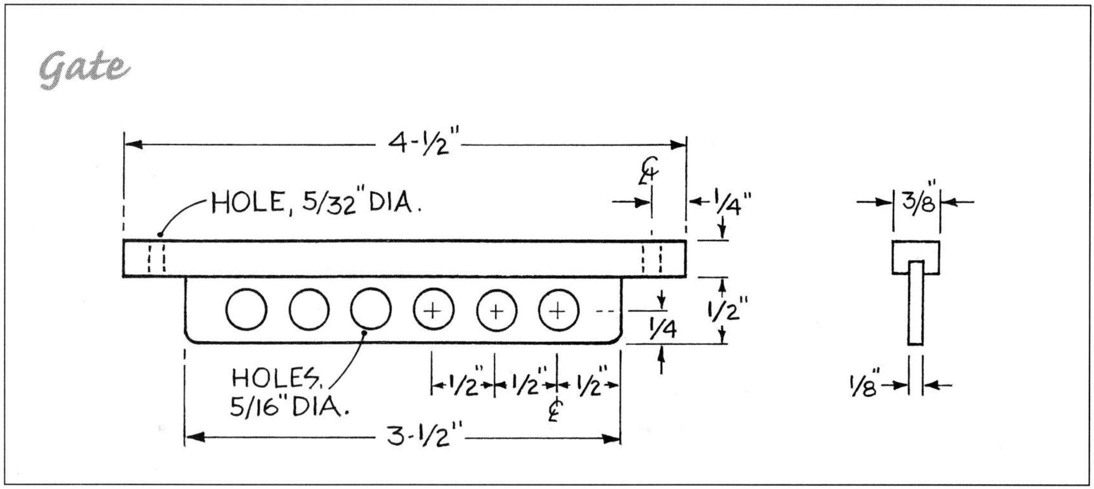

Center cabin

1. Cut the blank to size.
2. Locate and drill the two lug cavities and the two smokestack receiving holes. Note that the smokestack holes are aligned front to back and not side to side.

Bridges

The two bridges are identical, mounted in a back-to-back position.

1. Cut the blanks to size. Locate and drill the ½-in.-diameter portholes, ¼ in. deep, two on each side and three in front. Note that all portholes have the same horizontal centerlines.
2. Locate and drill the two lug cavities in each blank, with the usual spacing centered on both dimensions.
3. Cut the front radius on each blank on the table saw. Sand smooth.

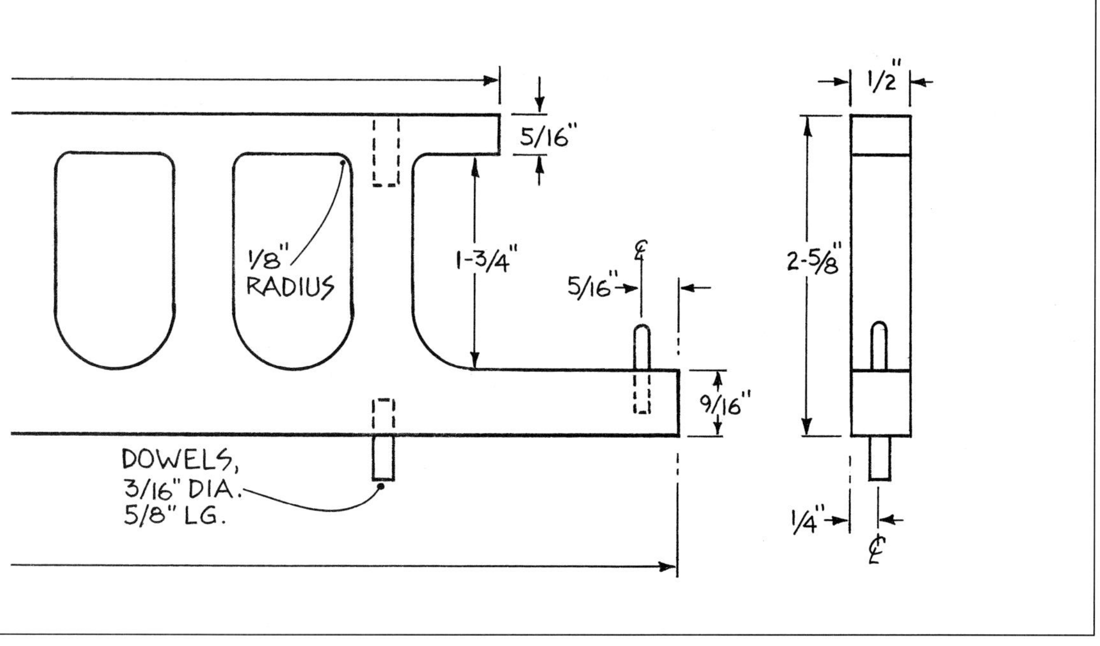

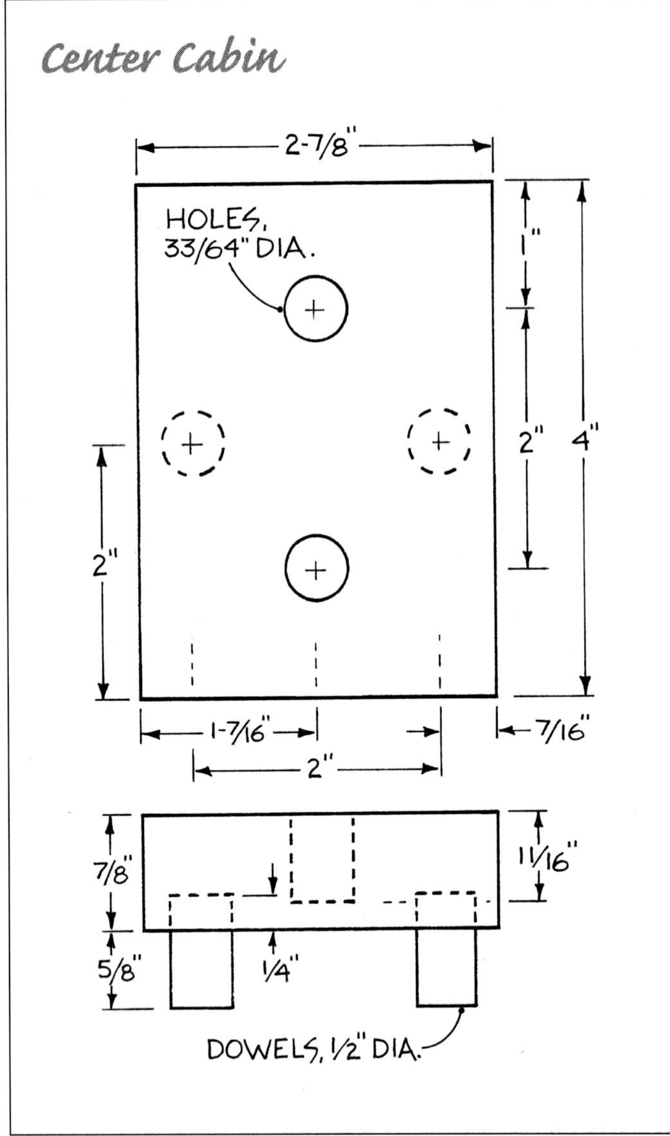

4. Cut the 1/8-in. plywood roof cap blanks to size. Cut and sand the radii.

5. Glue the roof caps to the cabin blanks, back flush and centered left to right.

Ramp assembly

1. Cut the support block to size. On the table saw, make a ripcut along one side at a 23-degree angle.

2. Cut the ramp to size. Using the same technique as for the riverboat ramps (see the drawing on pp. 180–181), cut a 23-degree angle across the 4-in. dimension at one end, as shown in the plan drawing on p. 206.

3. With the sawblade in the same position and working on its right side, cut the indicated angle on the opposite end of the workpiece.

4. Glue the ramp to the support block. Before the glue has set, check the position of the block to make sure the ramp height matches the height of the main deck mounted on the generic hull.

Pickup truck

1. Cut the cargo bed blank to size. With double-sided tape, fasten an auxiliary block, 1 1/4 in. by 2 in. by 5/8 in. (only the 1 1/4-in.-diameter is critical), to the bottom of the workpiece.

2. Using a Forstner bit, locate and drill the 1 1/8-in.-diameter wheel-well hole 1/4 in. deep.

3. Cut the top channel 7/8 in. wide by 7/16 in. deep. Use a series of cuts on the table saw with a regular blade, reversing the workpiece for a second cut at each fence position. For this operation I don't recommend a dado set, which can be dangerous when working with a piece this small.

Photo LL • *Vehicles for the ferryboat, driving off the ramp.*

Bridges

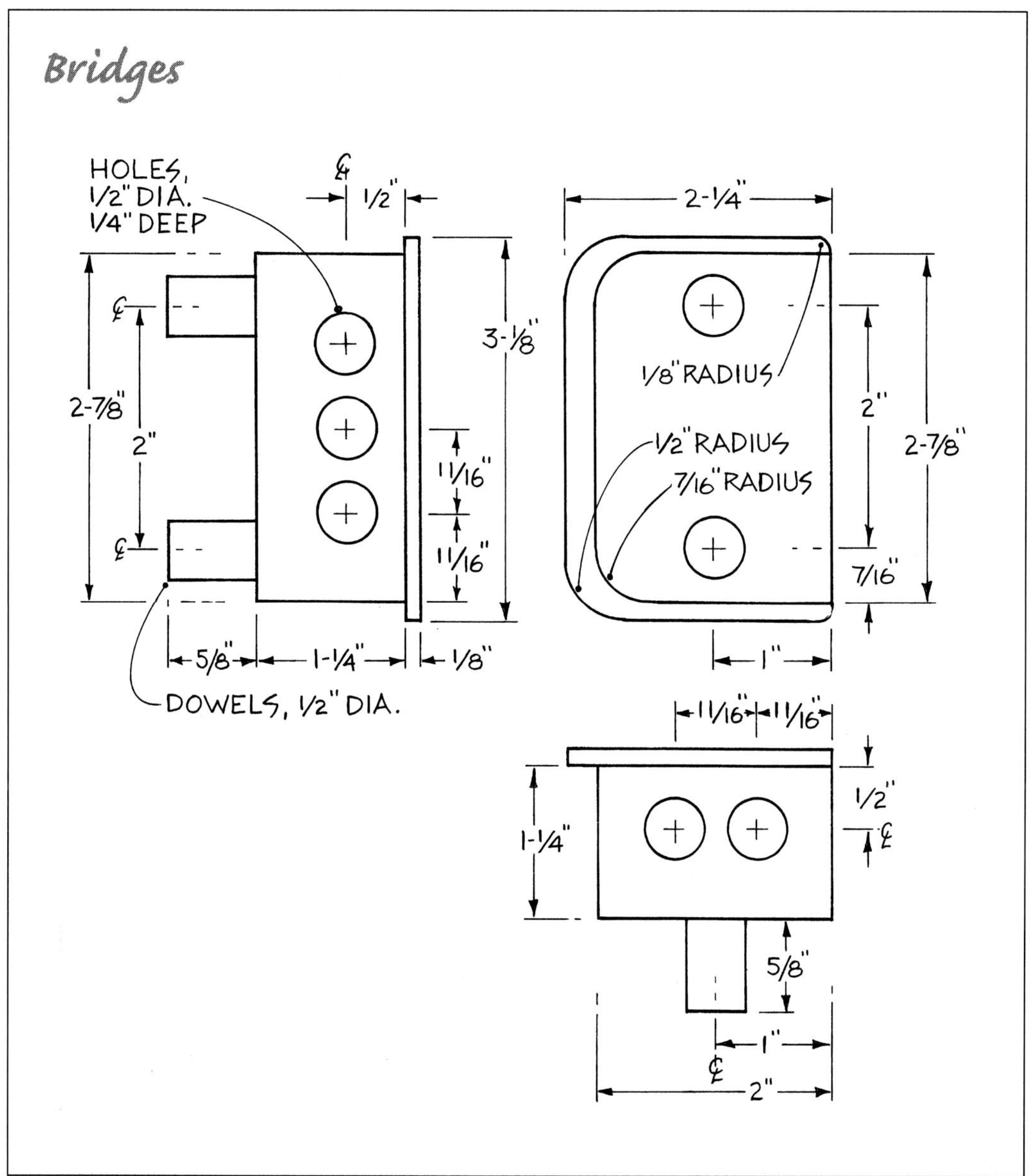

4. Cut the cabin blank to size. With a 3⁄8-in. bit, drill to form the two 3⁄16-in. radii of the front cutout area. Complete the cutout on the bandsaw, with a narrow blade.

5. Cut the hood blank to size. Make an auxiliary block as for the cargo bed to locate and drill the wheel-well holes. Hand-chisel out the front wheel-well cutout areas, as indicated in the plan drawing on p. 207.

6. On the table saw, make the indicated 45-degree angle ripcuts along the top sides of the hood.

7. Cut the undercarriage to size, with the indicated 30-degree angle cut at each end.

8. Glue the three top components to the undercarriage, with the undercarriage centered left to right and set back 1⁄8 in. from the front.

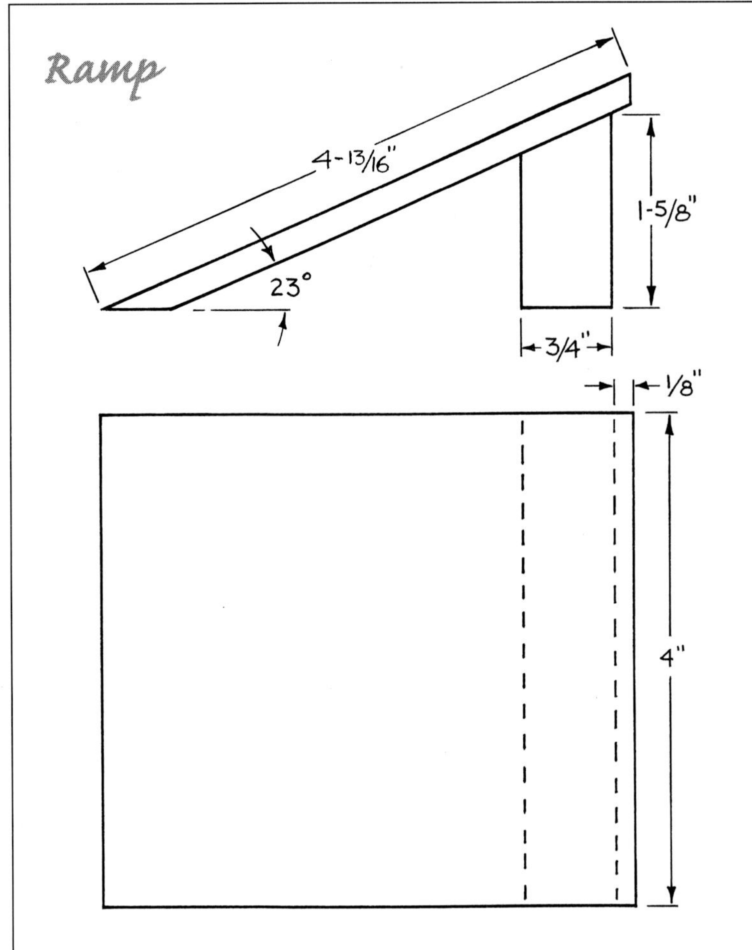

9. Using the Forstner bit center marks in the wheel wells as a guide, drill the four holes to receive the 1/8-in. aluminum pins, which are inserted through the commercial wheels and glued in place with epoxy.

10. Cut the roof cap blank to size. Tape the blank to an auxiliary blank to make a vertical table-saw cut (with the rip fence) that creates a taper of 5/32 in. at the rear edge to 1/16 in. at the front edge.

11. Glue the roof cap in place with a 1/16-in. rear overhang.

Sedan

1. Cut the body blank to overall size. With the table-saw blade set at a height of 1 7/32 in. and using the rip fence, make the indicated 9-degree angle cut, starting 7/8 in. up from the bottom edge, as indicated in the plan drawing on p. 208.

2. Lay out the interior window cutouts for visual reference purposes, as in photo MM. Make the cutouts in a series of table-saw crosscuts with the blade set to a 1/2-in. height. Make the cut to form the windshield.

3. As for the pickup truck, fasten an auxiliary block to the workpiece to locate and drill the wheel wells.

4. Cut the indicated 5-degree rear angle.

5. Make the indicated 1/16-in. by 1/2-in. rabbet cut along each side of the windows.

6. As before, use the Forstner bit center marks to drill for the pin axles and mount the wheels.

7. Cut the roof blank to size. Mount it on an auxiliary block to cut a rear to front taper of 1/4 in. to 3/32 in.

8. Glue the roof in place with a 1/16-in. rear overhang.

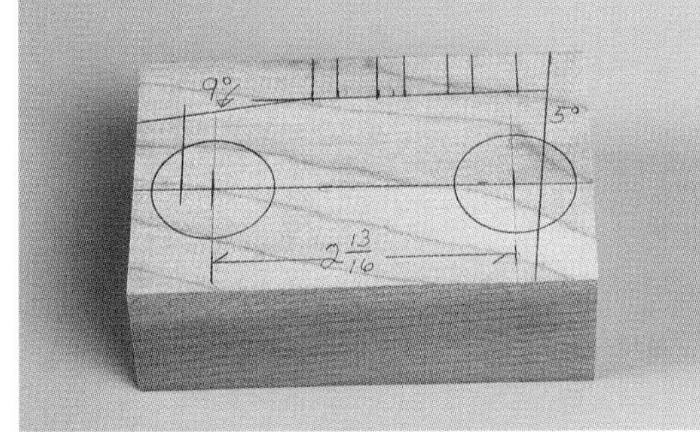

Photo MM • *An accurate layout allows freehand sedan-window cutouts on the table saw.*

Pickup Truck

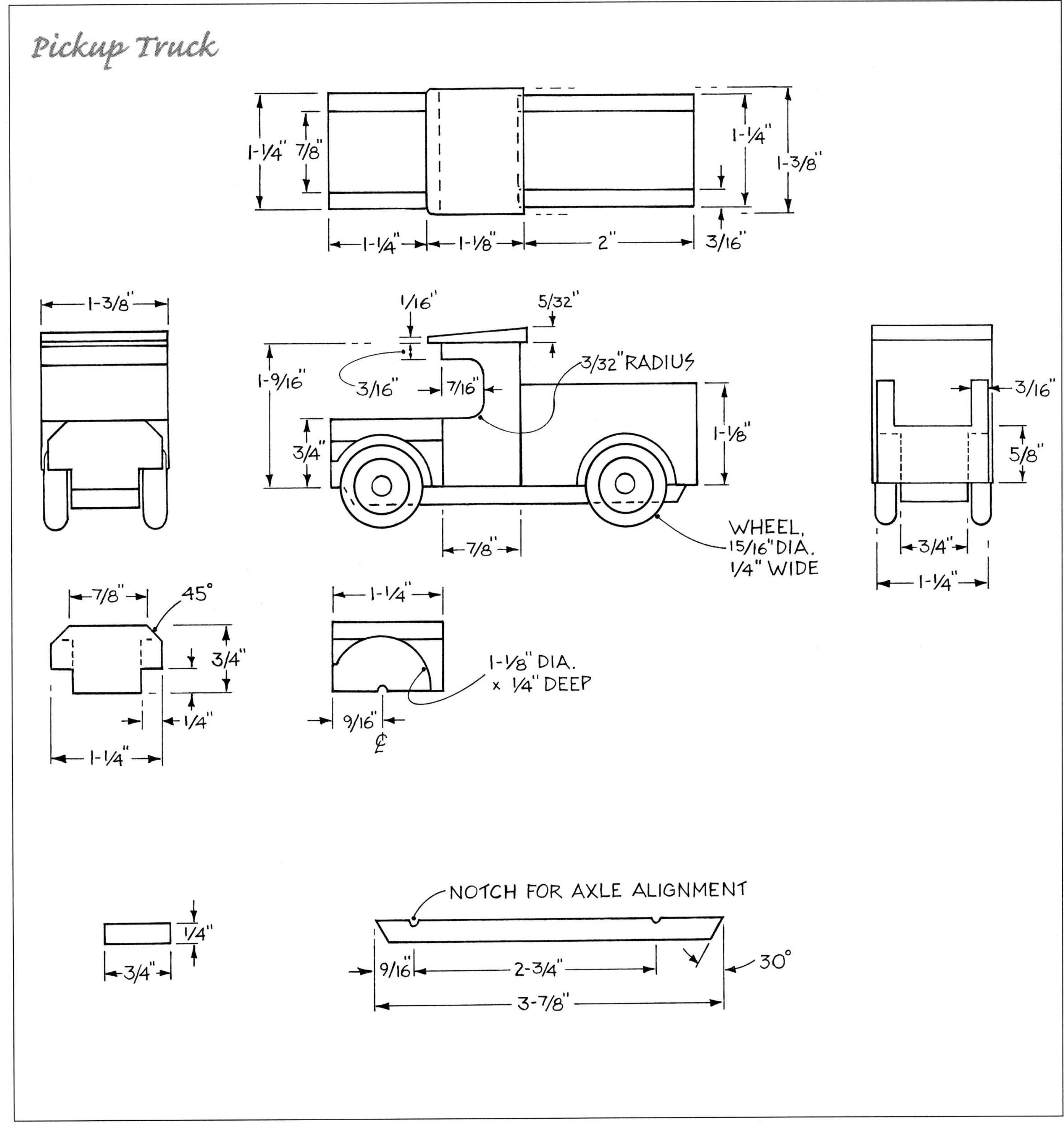

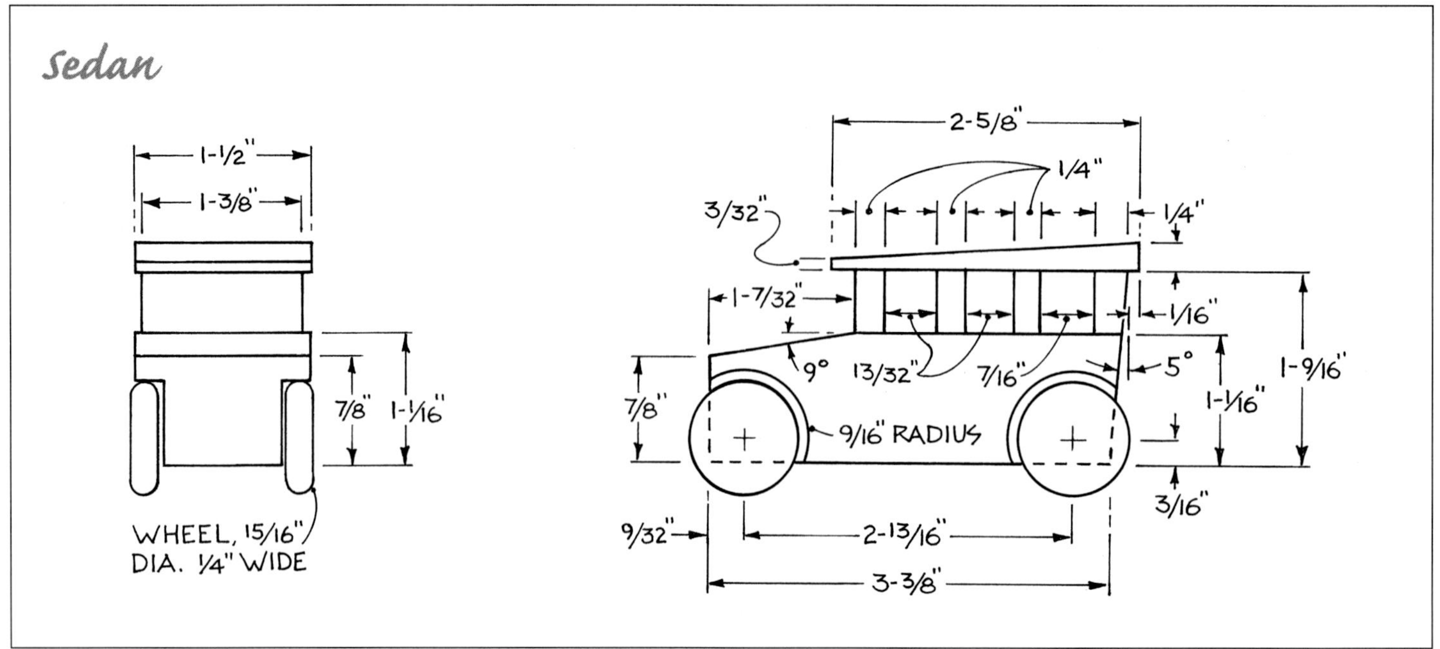

FABRICATION OF AIRCRAFT CARRIER COMPONENTS

The aircraft carrier uses the same main deck as the ferryboat (see the parts list on p. 199). Its smokestack is an integral part of its bridge and tower unit.

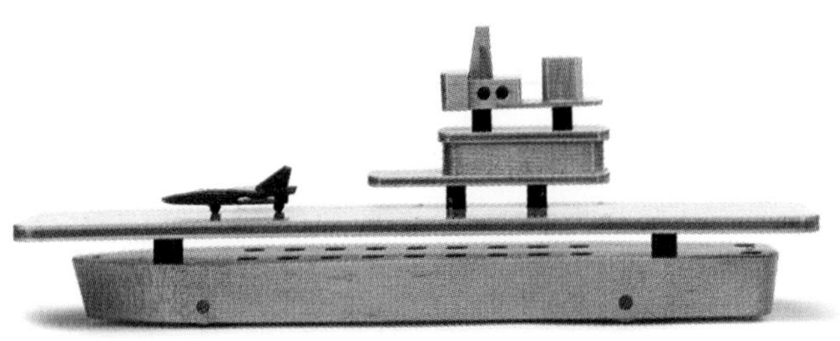

Photo NN • *Aircraft carrier components aligned.*

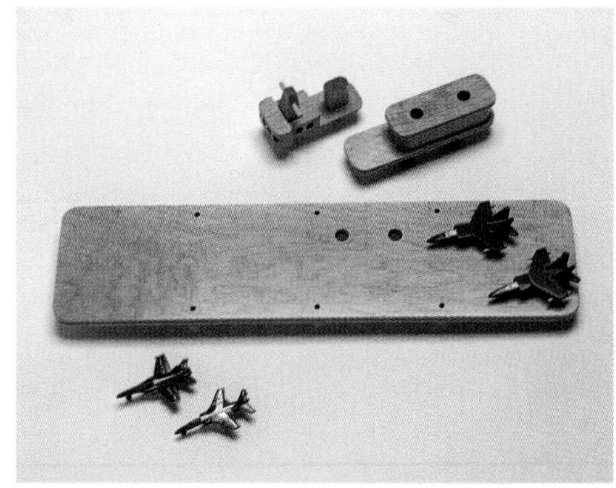

Photo OO • *Aircraft carrier components, including the superstructure, the bridge and tower unit, and jets. Note that commercial planes are an option.*

Superstructure

1. Cut the superstructure block to size, cut and sand its radii, and set it aside.
2. Cut the ¼-in. plywood upper deck blank to size. Cut and sand the radii.
3. Glue the upper deck to the block, centered in all directions.

■ AIRCRAFT CARRIER

PART	SIZE (IN.)	QUANTITY	MATERIAL
BRIDGE AND TOWER UNIT:			
Bridge	1 13/16 x 3/4 x 2	1	Maple
Bridge floor panel	1 3/16 x 1/8 x 4	1	1/8 maple plywood
Tower A block	7/8 x 5/8 x 1 1/4	1	Maple
Tower cross arm	3/16 dia. x 1 3/16	1	3/16 dowel
Smokestack	1 x 5/8 x 1	1	Maple
Superstructure block	1 1/2 x 3/4 x 4	1	Maple
Superstructure floor panel	1 3/4 x 1/4 x 6	1	1/4 maple plywood
Superstructure upper deck	1 5/8 x 1/4 x 4 1/4	1	1/4 maple plywood
JET PLANES (NUMBER OF PARTS GIVEN IS FOR ONE PLANE):			
Fuselage	5/16 x 3/8 x 3 1/8	1	Pine
Jet engines	3/8 x 3/16 x 1 15/16	2	Pine
Wings and stabilizer	1 13/16 x 1/8 x 2 1/8	1	1/8 maple plywood
Rudders	1/2 x 1/8 x 7/8	2	1/8 maple plywood
Rockets	1/8 dia. x 7/8	2	1/8 dowel
Front landing gear	1/4 dia. x 7/16	1	1/4 dowel
Rear landing gear	1/4 dia. x 1/8	1	1/4 dowel

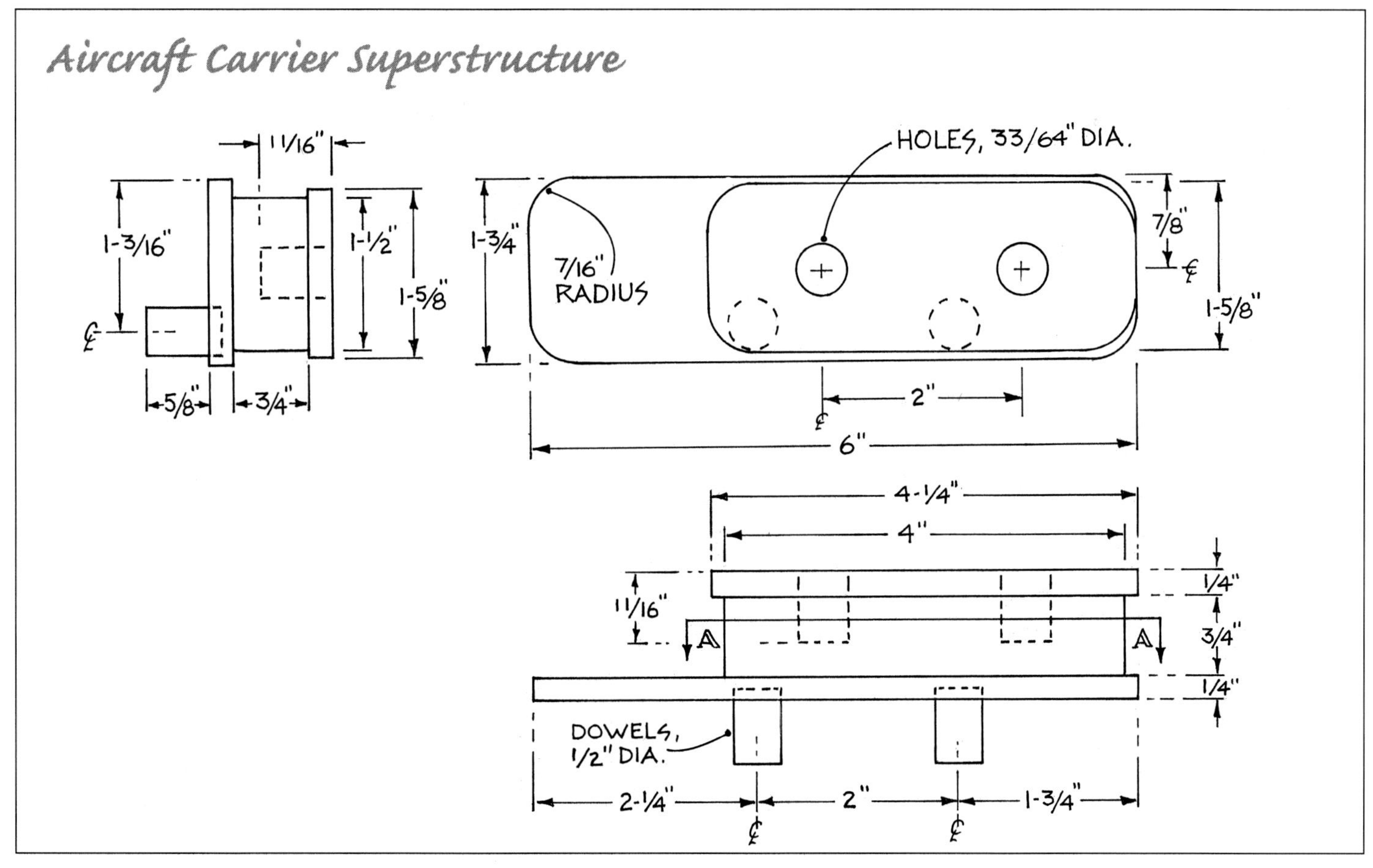

4. Locate and drill the two receiving holes.
5. Cut the floor-panel blank to size. Locate and drill the two lug cavities.
6. Cut and sand the four corner radii to match the deck radii.
7. Glue the floor panel to the bottom of the blank, centered left to right and with the rear edge flush with the rear edge of the upper deck.

Bridge and tower unit

1. Cut the bridge blank to size.
2. Locate and drill the four front portholes, 1/4 in. deep, and the two portholes on each side, 7/16 in. deep. All portholes are 5/16 in. in diameter; note that the horizontal center lines of the front and side portholes are different.

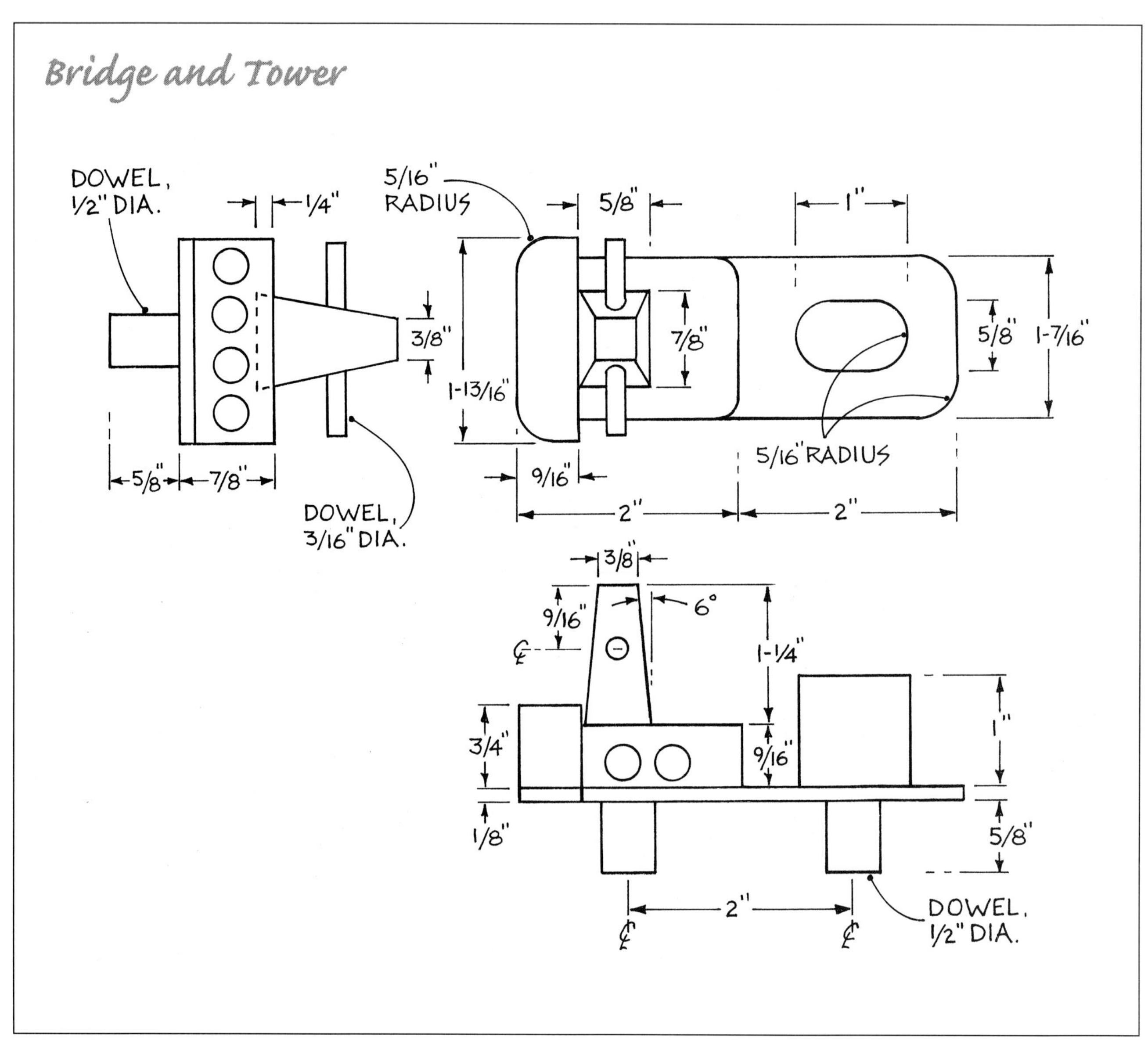

3. Viewing the top of the workpiece, measure back $^5/_8$ in. from the front edge and draw a line across it. Continue this line down each side of the workpiece. On the table saw, make a crosscut $^3/_{16}$ in. deep along this line, leaving the $^5/_8$-in.-wide area on the top and sides.

4. Make a cut along each side and along the top to meet the crosscuts and complete the rear side and top rabbets.

5. Cut the floor panel to overall size. Make a ripcut along each side from the rear edge to $^5/_8$ in. behind the front edge, to bring the centered rear width to $1^7/_{16}$ in. Make two side cuts to join the ripcuts $^5/_8$ in. back from the front edge.

6. Locate and drill the two lug cavities.

7. Glue the floor panel to the underside of the bridge. Sand to match the perimeters.

8. Cut the smokestack to size. Form the front and rear $^5/_8$-in. radius on the stationary sander and glue it in place.

9. Cut the tower A block in place. Locate and drill the hole to receive the $^3/_{16}$-in.-diameter dowel cross arm.

10. Cut the four tapers, either with a jig or on the bandsaw. Note that the back tapers are 6 degrees, and the side tapers 10 degrees.

11. Glue the cross arm in place and glue the tower in place against the rear of the bridge's front section.

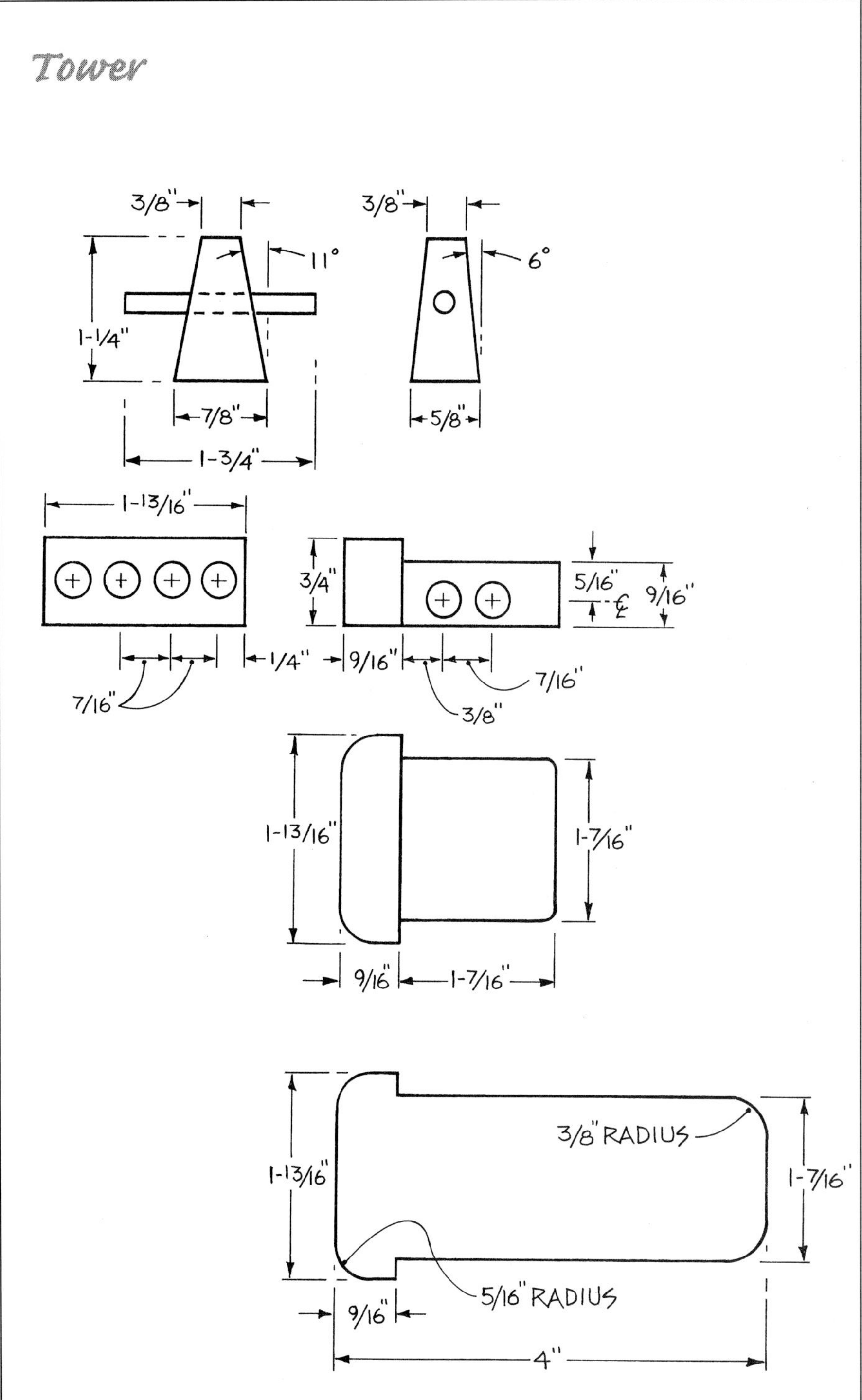

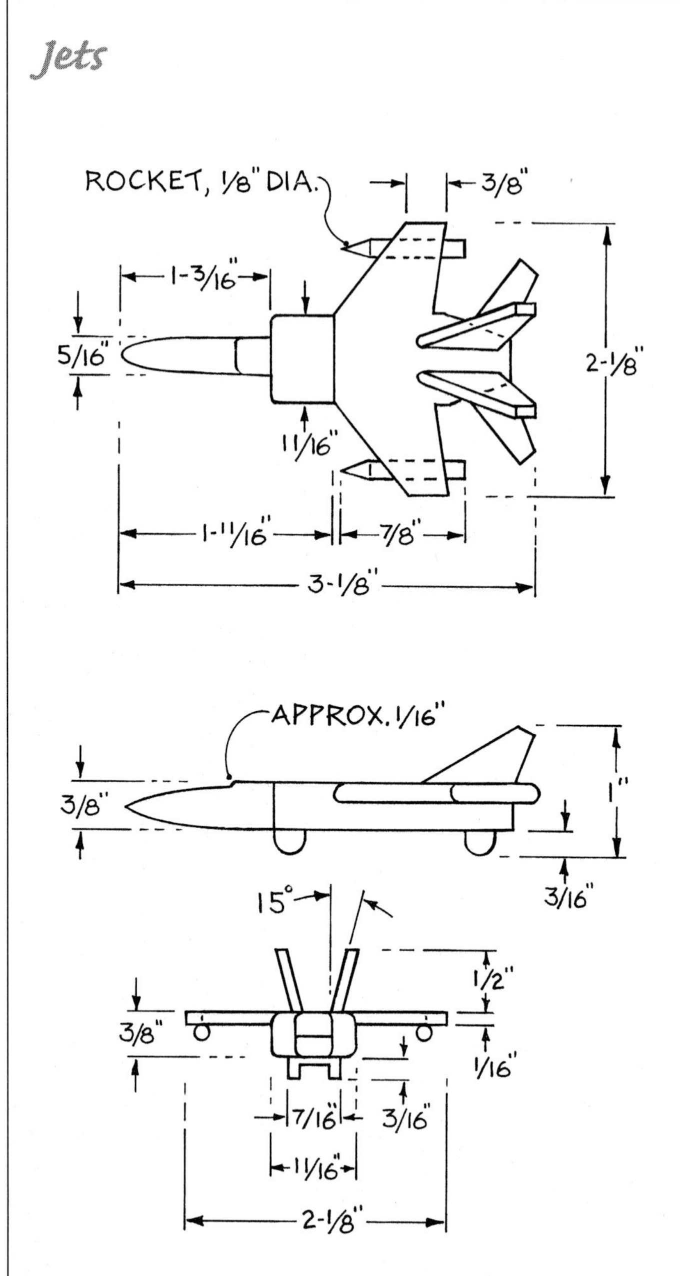

Jets

You can either buy metal die-cast jets for the aircraft carrier or make them. For all the jet plane parts not made of plywood, I prefer using pine because there's a fair amount of hand-shaping involved, which is easier with the softer wood.

***Photo PP •** Jet planes on the aircraft carrier are a sure bet to engage active imaginations.*

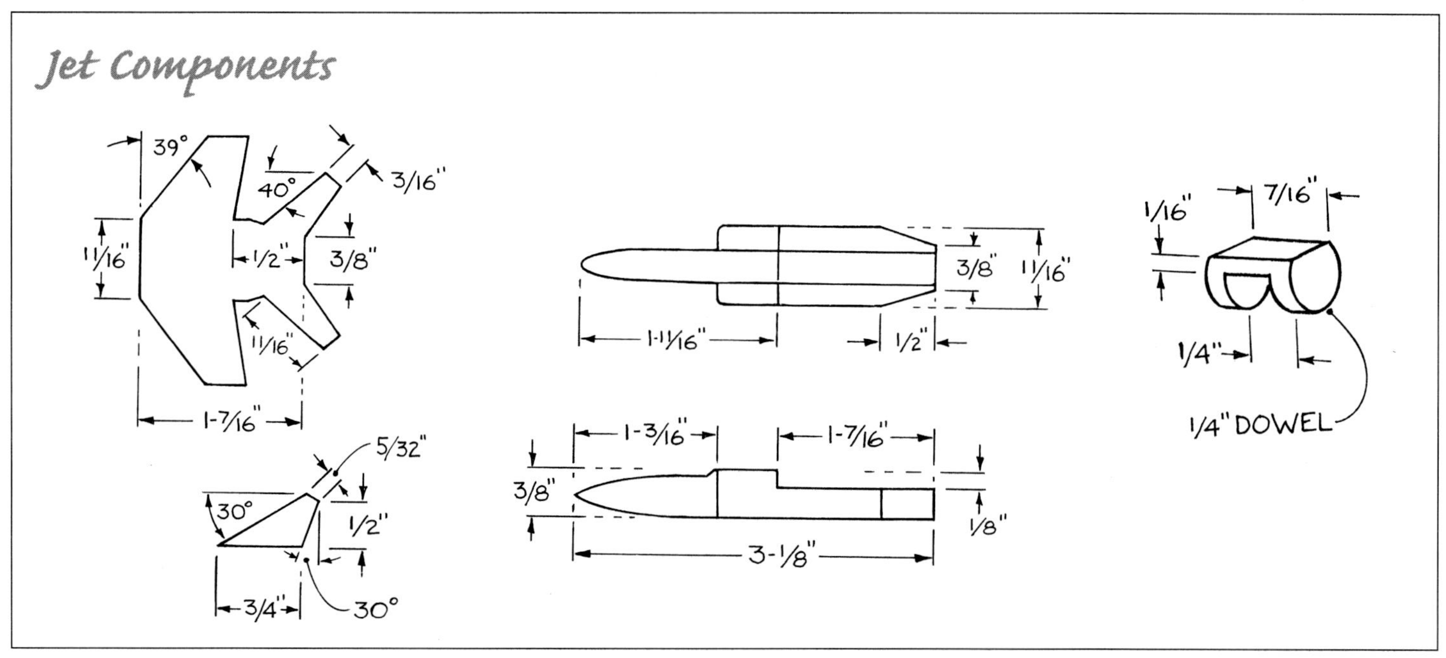

Photo QQ • *Commercially made die-cast jets are an alternative to making them yourself.*

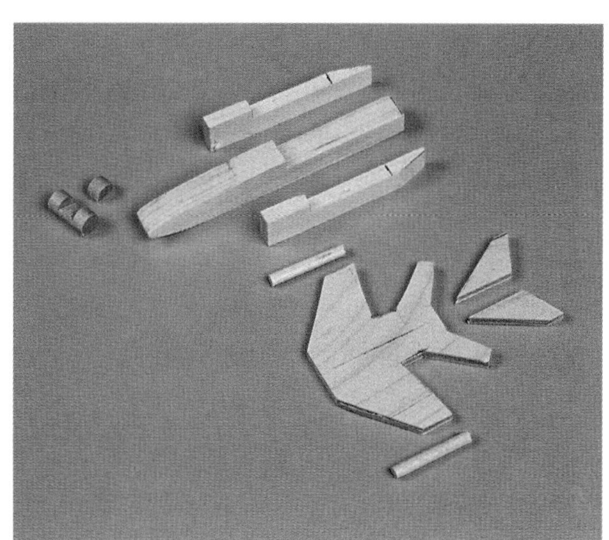

Photo RR • *Jet plane components.*

1. Transfer the wing and stabilizer pattern to a plywood blank and cut it to shape on the scrollsaw (see photo SS).
2. Cut the fuselage blank to size. Draw the side profile on the blank and cut to shape on the scrollsaw.

Photo SS • *Jet plane wings and stabilizers are cut from a single plywood blank on the scrollsaw.*

Photo TT • *The front landing gear is cut free from an oversize length of dowel spot-glued at its ends to a scrap block for cutting the center channel on the table saw.*

3. Cut the jet engine blanks to size. Draw the rear fuselage profile onto their sides and cut them on the scrollsaw.
4. Glue the engine blanks to the sides of the fuselage, flush rear.
5. Sand to true the rear flat area. Sand the side-to-side nose taper.
6. Sand the rear side-to-side taper and sand to radius all side edges.
7. Spot-glue the ends of an approximately 4-in. length of 1/4-in. dowel to a piece of scrap to cut the front landing gear channel on the table saw, as in photo TT.
8. Cut the workpiece to its correct length (it will fall free), and chip off about 1/16 in. to create a flat area opposite the bottom of the channel.
9. Cut a section of 1/4-in.-diameter dowel to length for the rear landing gear and chip off a flat area like that on the front landing gear.
10. Cut the rockets to length. Chuck each one into the drill press and sand to a point at one end.
11. Glue all pieces together.
12. The planes look great with a nice detailed paint job. I've chosen blue as the overall color, silver for the cockpit area and the rockets, black for the landing gear, and bright yellow for the warheads (the rocket tips).

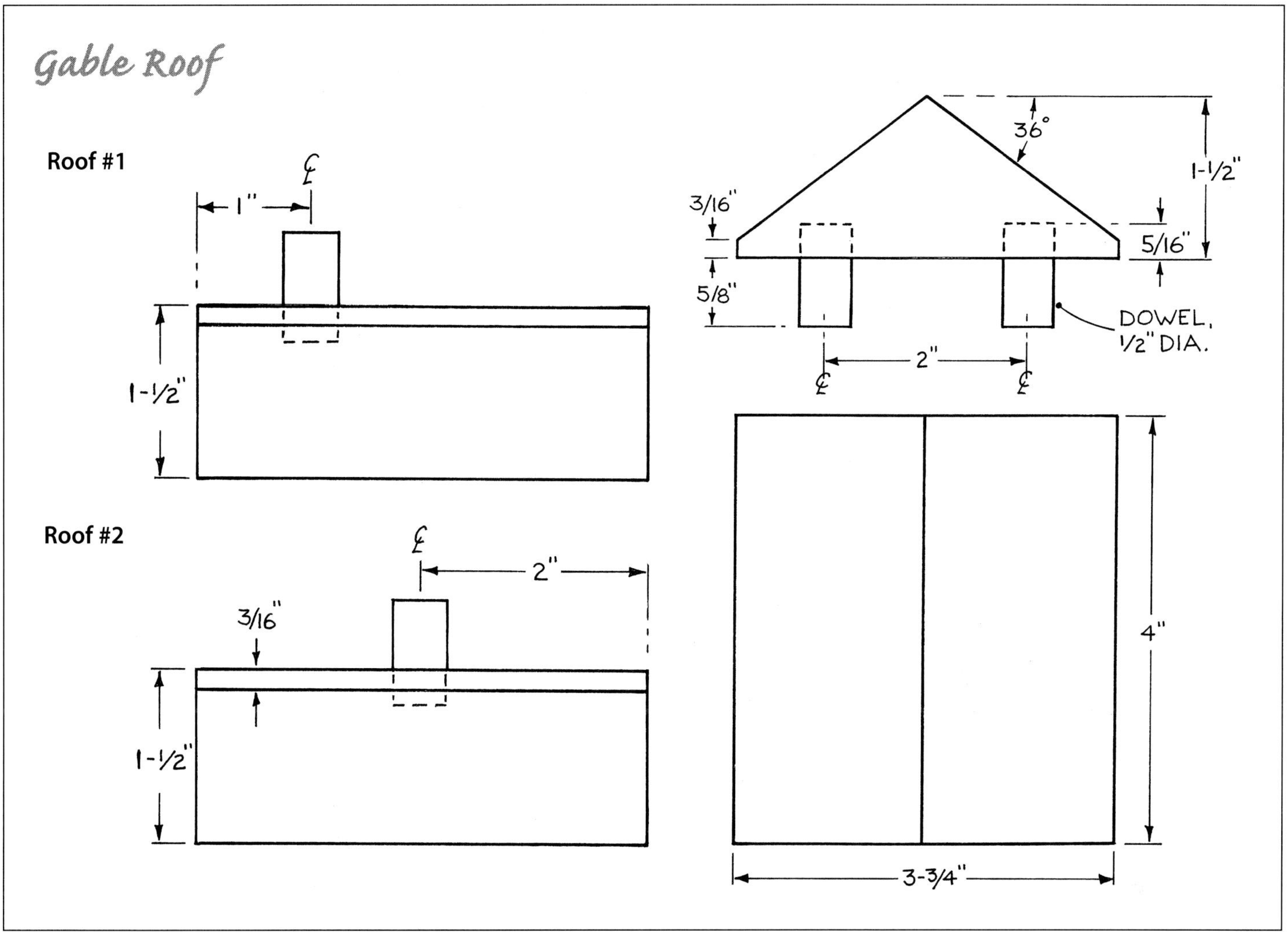

Gable Roof

Roof #1

1" 1-1/2"

Roof #2

2" 3/16" 1-1/2"

36° 1-1/2" 3/16" 5/16" 5/8" DOWEL, 1/2" DIA. 2" 4" 3-3/4"

FABRICATION OF HOUSEBOAT COMPONENTS

The only specific houseboat components are three gable roofs, which I make of walnut for contrast. They can be used with any of the square or rectangular cabins, like the main freighter cabin and the main deck riverboat cabins. Different cabin heights will give different roof levels for variety in profiles.

Photo UU • *Houseboat components aligned.*

HOUSEBOAT

PART	SIZE (IN.)	QUANTITY	MATERIAL
Gable roof #1	3¾ x 1½ x 4	2	Walnut
Gable roof #2	3¾ x 1½ x 4	1	Walnut

Photo VV • *Houseboat components, including roofs from the riverboat main deck cabins and the main freighter cabin.*

1. Cut the roof blanks to size. Locate and drill the pair of lug cavities in each. Note that for one pattern the pair is centered back to front, and for the other, 1 in. in from one end.
2. On the table saw, cut the roof angles to leave a $^3/_{16}$-in. shoulder and taper up to full height at the centerline; this will be about a 35-degree angle.

RESOURCES

Toy Parts

Casey's Wood Products
P.O. Box 365
Woolwich, ME 04579
(800) 452-2739
All-wood products such as wheels, pegs, dowels, cargo drums, and novelty shapes

Cherry Tree
P.O. Box 369
Belmont, OH 43718
(800) 848-4363
All-wood products, as above, including threaded dowels and toy plans

Woodworks
4521 Anderson Blvd.
Fort Worth, TX 76117
(800) 722-0311
Dowels, wheels, and other project supplies

General Woodworking Supplies

Albert Constantine & Son, Inc.
2050 Eastchester Rd.
Bronx, NY 10461
(800) 223-8087
www.constantines.com
Exotic and domestic woods, veneers, finishing supplies, drums, pegs, wheels

Garrett Wade Co.
161 Ave. of the Americas
New York, NY 10013
(800) 221-2942
www.garrettwade.com
Tools, Behlen's finishes, shellac flakes, alcohol, and brushes

Woodcraft Supply Corp.
P.O. Box 1686
Parkersburg, WV 26101
(800) 225-1153
www.woodcraft.com
Tools, project supplies, finishes, wood, and veneers

Woodworker's Supply, Inc.
1108 N. Glen Rd.
Casper, WY 82601
(800) 645-9292
Tools, hardware, dowels, and miscellaneous wood parts

Rockler Woodworking & Hardware
(formerly The Woodworker's Store)
4365 Willow Dr.
Medina, MN 55340
(800) 279-4441
Tools, hardware, dowels, domestic hardwoods, and exotic woods

Woodworkers Warehouse
(chain of stores in the Northeast)
(888) 234-8665
www.woodworkerswarehouse.com
Tools, hardware, miscellaneous supplies

Finishes

The Natural Choice
1365 Rufina Circle
Santa Fe, NM 87505
(800) 621-2591
Citrus-based, nontoxic finishes

Torginol, Inc.
(formerly Peterson Chemical Corp.)
710 Forest Ave.
P.O. Box 102
Sheboygan Falls, WI 53085
(800) 558-7596
#100 clear gloss epoxy

Woodfinishing Enterprises
1729 N. 68th St.
Milwaukee, WI 53213
(414) 774-1724
Nontoxic finishes

Other books from The Taunton Press

Frid, Tage. *Tage Frid Teaches Woodworking*. Two volumes in one. Book 1: Joinery. Book 2: Shaping, Veneering, Finishing. A step-by-step guide to essential woodworking techniques. Paperback. $29.95

Hack, Garrett. *The Handplane Book*. Explores the technique, tuning, history, and mechanics of the hand plane. Paperback. $24.95

Hoadley, R. Bruce. *Understanding Wood 2nd edition.* A craftsman's guide to wood technology. Hardcover. $39.95

Landis, Scott. *The Workbench Book*. A craftsman's guide. Paperback. $22.95

Landis, Scott. *The Workshop Book*. A craftsman's guided tour. Paperback. $22.95

Lee, Leonard. *The Complete Guide to Sharpening*. Paperback. $22.95

Tolpin, Jim. *The Toolbox Book*. A craftsman's guide to tool chests, cabinets, and storage systems. Paperback. $22.95

Also by Jim Makowicki:

Making Heirloom Toys. 22 classic toy projects. Paperback. $19.95

For more information about these books or to request a catalog, contact
Taunton Direct, Inc.
63 South Main St., P.O. Box 5507
Newtown, CT 06470-5507
(800) 888-8286
www.taunton.com